U.S. International Exhibitions during the Cold War

U.S. International Exhibitions during the Cold War

Winning Hearts and Minds through Cultural Diplomacy

Andrew James Wulf

ROWMAN & LITTLEFIELD
Lanham • Boulder • New York • London

Published by Rowman & Littlefield
A wholly owned subsidiary of The Rowman & Littlefield Publishing Group, Inc.
4501 Forbes Boulevard, Suite 200, Lanham, Maryland 20706
www.rowman.com

Unit A, Whitacre Mews, 26-34 Stannary Street, London SE11 4AB

British Library Cataloguing in Publication Information Available

Library of Congress Cataloging-in-Publication Data
Library of Congress Cataloging-in-Publication Data Available
ISBN 978-1-4422-4642-3 (cloth : alk. paper) – ISBN 978-1-4422-4643-0 (electronic)

∞™ The paper used in this publication meets the minimum requirements of
American National Standard for Information Sciences—Permanence of Paper
for Printed Library Materials, ANSI/NISO Z39.48-1992.

Printed in the United States of America

Contents

Acknowledgments

This study came to fruition through the generous assistance of many people. First and foremost I must thank Professor Simon J. Knell, School of Museum Studies, University of Leicester. As my doctoral supervisor, Simon provided rich intellectual inspiration throughout the thesis process. His insights into the history of collecting and display for nationalistic goals led me time and again to new material and ideas I would not have otherwise considered. His creative analysis of my chapters was a revelation as was his moral support and good cheer over these last six years. Also from my thesis committee, I wish to thank Dr. Suzanne MacLeod, Director and Head of the School of Museum Studies at the University of Leicester, for sharing her expertise on exhibition design and her constructive reading of my manuscript in the last stages. Lastly, Professor Scott Lucas of the University of Birmingham, an outstanding scholar of U.S. foreign policy, provided many creative and useful observations during my thesis defense.

This work would not have been written without the assistance of Dr. Nicholas J. Cull, Professor of Public Diplomacy at the University of Southern California, who suggested the idea of conducting an archival and interview-based study of American cultural exhibitions sent overseas during the Cold War. His research in this area has vastly enriched this field and his tireless support has pushed me to road test my ideas through scholarly conferences, book reviews, working papers, and his sponsorship of my role as a research fellow and blog contributor at the Center on Public Diplomacy at USC.

I benefited immensely from my discussions with Mr. Martin Manning, State Department historian, who shepherded me through the rich
USIA Historical Collection of which he is the steward. His generosity will be
remembered always. Special thanks go to the staff at the National Archives
in College Park, Maryland, who facilitated the research into the OITF,
USIA and Bicentennial archives. The staff at the Library of Congress made
my visit with the Charles and Ray Eames Papers a great pleasure. I am thank-
ful both to Vera Ekechukwu and Geoffrey Stark in the Special Collections
of the University of Arkansas, Fayetteville, who enabled me to explore the
archives of the Bureau of Educational and Cultural Affairs.

Dick Arndt and Mark Smith, former Foreign Service Officers, provided
support through emails and face-to-face interviews. As veterans from the
front line of America's battle to win hearts and minds, I look up to them and
their vast experience. Maurice Tuchman, former director of the Los Angeles
County Museum of Art, graciously agreed to an interview to discuss his cu-
ratorship of the *Art and Technology* exhibition which premiered at the U.S.
pavilion at the Osaka Expo in 1970.

It is impossible to quantify the thrill and awe in knowing Jack Masey,
who played a central role in many of the exhibitions I explore in this study.
I learned much during our two full days of interviews at his design offices
in New York City. In addition to his status as a former government cultural
diplomat, he is a curator's curator who has also influenced me tremendously
as a museum professional. Beverly Payeff-Masey has also been a gift to my
understanding of the sometimes-byzantine history of modern design as it influenced public diplomacy and vice versa. I was fortunate to cross paths, with
the help of Jack and Beverly, with Ivan Chermayeff and Peter Chermayeff,
two of the original Cambridge Seven, one of the preeminent design teams of
the twentieth century.

Heartfelt thanks go to Tyson Gaskill, dear friend and polymath, who
serves as the Executive Director of Programming and Events at the University of Southern California. I count my six years working for him and our
countless curatorial collaborations the most interesting in my career as a
cultural historian. Museum mentors Dr. Selma Holo and Dr. Grace Cohen
Grossman continue to inspire both as colleagues and friends. Lifelong friends
Dr. Phil Stephens and Drs. Edgar and Mary Williams provided encouragement throughout this process. This study is also dedicated to the memory of
my dear friend Dr. Levi Meier who passed away during the writing of this
study. He taught me so much, including, ". . . be patient toward all that is
unsolved...and try to love the questions themselves," one of Rilke's lessons
from *Letters to a Young Poet*.

Lastly, special recognition goes to my family. My parents, Robert and Dr. Kathleen Wulf, my brother Thomas Wulf and his family, offered love and support at every turn. My daughter, Margo Belén, entered this world just about the same day my research began on this project. Her transition during this time, from baby to toddler to little girl has been a blessing and joy to experience. The honor of being her daddy makes my life nothing short of beautiful each and every day. Above all, I thank my wonderful wife Amparo Valenzuela Wulf. Her friendship, generous good spirit, intellectual curiosity, spectacular sense of humor, and loving support is the fuel that keeps me going. This work is dedicated to her from the bottom of my heart. *Tuyo para siempre.*

Introduction

> Without pitting one Soviet soldier against one American soldier, the Soviet has won a staggering series of victories. In the few years since World War II, Russia has added 700,000,000 people to the multitude already under direct rule. Its land empire has been swollen by about 5,000,000 square miles. In Asia alone, Communist arms have won wars in China, Indochina, and Tibet, and gained prestige and a restless stalemate in Korea. In Italy, Egypt, Indonesia, Cambodia, Laos, to name a few, Communist parties have become strong contenders for power. In a recent poll taken in India, Chou En-Lai, the Chinese Communist leader, was a three-to-one favorite over President Eisenhower. In the Middle East our prestige has rapidly diminished while that of Russia has increased. In South America our Vice President has been spat upon and assaulted in a shameful demonstration of antagonism toward our country.[1]

The above epigraph cogently describes the global zeitgeist in which the United States introduced in the early years of the Cold War a new weapon specifically designed to contain and ultimately, in the words of President Dwight D. Eisenhower, "rollback"[2] the Soviet communist threat. For forty years, the United States enticed foreign publics around the world—from NATO allies to Warsaw Pact countries to nonaligned nations—with promises of the rightness and availability of the American Dream through a variety of endeavors, including Voice of America (VOA) radio broadcasts, jazz artist tours, people-to-people educational exchanges, and cultural exhibitions. On October 1, 1999, the United States Information Agency (USIA), the government department that had since its establishment in 1953 been the dominant public diplomacy instrument "to tell America's story to the world" in order "to win hearts and minds" was abolished by the Clinton administration, and its functions were integrated into the U.S. Department of State. This landmark action quietly brought an end to the organization created by President Eisenhower to counter peacefully the threat of global communist expansion. Recognized by some policy makers as an agency that found its *raison d'être* in the forty-year face-off with the Soviet Union, the USIA seemed to have lost its purpose, including its remit for developing international cultural exhibitions. Now more than a decade after the tragedy of September 11, it is clear that many questions remain as to how to revitalize a U.S. cultural diplomacy generally and international cultural exhibitions specifically.[3] New media advocates, for example, question whether the ubiquity of Web 2.0 technologies and cell phones plugged into networks foreshadows the irrelevance and shorter life span of international exhibitions. While some believe the golden age of these events is now over, a number of governments maintain cultural relations agencies (for example, the British Council, the Alliance-Française, the Goethe Institute, and Confucius Institute) to make their domestic issues known to the rest of the world, sometimes through international exhibitions. As long as nations find the need to enhance their reputations to as broad an audience as possible, it is arguable whether Internet-based, collective participation platforms can in any way replace the cultural understanding that is a primary goal of international exhibitions. The current trend of tens of millions of visitors who attend international exhibitions predicts longevity to the life span of these unique phenomena.

The purpose of this study is to investigate the flourishing of U.S. cultural exhibitions at various venues throughout the world from the mid-1950s through the mid-1970s and to determine the problems they raise in relation to understanding this period in the history of collecting and display for national prestige. The ultimate aim of this is to clarify the significance of this singular aspect of cultural diplomacy[4]—the intercultural communication of national values and foreign policy intentions to international audiences—in what became a dominant weapon in Cold War America's arsenal of soft-power alternatives against the ubiquitous risk of nuclear cataclysm.

This time period witnessed the zenith of U.S. cultural exhibitions in the four primary categories of international trade fairs, official exchange exhibitions with the Soviet Union, world's fair pavilions, and, lastly, museum exhibitions. Spurred by Soviet success in international trade fairs in the early 1950s, President Eisenhower addressed the uncertain global political climate by promulgating official U.S. participation in these events beginning in 1954. Though the United States had exercised its cultural muscle through exhibitions overseas since the early days of the American republic, it was only in this crucial span of time—roughly 1955 through 1975—the United States excelled in producing an array of exhibitions on creative themes that centered on the primacy of the individual. These exhibitions were developed to demonstrate to all visitors—regardless of geographic locale, ethnic identity, or religious affiliation—the attractiveness and superiority of the American way of life. They also aggressively conveyed to foreign publics the risks of not buying into the national ethos: the American Dream. In this either-or scenario of West versus East, capitalism versus communism, or America versus the Evil Empire, the United States was selling more than just department-store-like windows onto a graspable national utopia, a guarantee of material, spiritual, and political prosperity. This was also, arguably, a form of cultural Manifest Destiny, the colonizing of other cultures through the manipulation of images of what "America" is. The paradox of how cultural exchanges turned into symbolically powerful monologues touting the merits of one culture over another serves as a running theme throughout this investigation of a variety of U.S. cultural exhibitions during this chapter of the Cold War.[5]

This study attempts to demonstrate conclusively the process of how these exhibitions came to fruition, from drawing-board concept to reality. In the discussion of scholarly research later in the introduction, it becomes evident that the important practical principles of exhibition development have not been firmly explored, particularly surrounding the question of which individuals were responsible for the ultimate message and appearance of these exhibitions. Likewise, the major research questions that are considered throughout this study are: What was America showing of itself at these exhibitions? How did the United States represent its real or apparent changing world status to other states and actors in the international system?[6] How did these efforts to use images in order to represent a type of utopian "America" challenge believability? In what ways do these exhibitions reveal U.S. declarations or aspirations of power? And, moreover, who was responsible for making the decisions that yielded the final message and appearance of these exhibitions? How much has perceived anti-Americanism, particularly as witnessed in anti-American propaganda published by the Soviet Union after World War II, pushed the nation to engage foreign publics with cultural diplomacy tactics like exhibitions? And, in this sense, can American cultural diplomacy efforts through international exhibitions be construed not only as offensive measures to win hearts and minds but also as reactive safeguards against losing influence among foreign publics?

The central hypotheses that drove this analysis, based on the research questions above, were subjected to investigation by study through the careful synthesizing of archival evidence, personal interviews of individuals who were on-hand participants in each of these exhibitions during the main timeframe of this study, and theoretical considerations from the fields of American history, international relations, and museum studies. These hypotheses are as follows:

1. For each exhibition, America found actively or reactively specific reasons to project a version of its realities and values to foreign publics.
2. America at times succeeded and at times failed to represent effectively its real status to other actors in the international system.
3. Through these exhibitions America gave object lessons of power that distorted knowledge and believability in order to establish a hegemonic position.
4. America actively sought to share the best of U.S. cultural entrepreneurialism based on the aims not of government agencies but of the private world of museum professionals, industrial designers, and architects for whom the U.S. government was a client.

Because I have delimited my subject to this specific time frame, 1955–1975, I have further delimited it to the literature that has been available to me on selected exhibitions sponsored by the U.S. government in Europe, Asia, North America, and South America. While this study is not exhaustive in addressing every individual exhibition in these parts of the world in this time frame, nevertheless the study focuses on important exhibitions that yield snapshots of American cultural diplomacy efforts during these particular twenty years as well as the specific actors involved in the process.

In addition to the books and articles that give broad historical background to the phenomena under scrutiny, this research achieved considerable focus through the exploration of various key archives. Over the past three years, I have made extensive visits to the USIA archives at the Department of State in Washington, D.C., which, with the assistance of Martin Manning, librarian and scholar of U.S. international exhibitions, proved enormously fruitful to my understanding the sheer breadth of my research topic as well as recommendations of limiting my original scope of 1938 to 2003 to a manageable 1955 to 1975, to what I argue is the heyday of U.S. international exhibitions. Visits to the National Archives housed in College Park, Maryland, supplied my research with substantive discoveries within the process and personalities that made these exhibitions possible. Research trips to the Library of

Congress produced a more thorough understanding of the role of industrial designers, including Charles and Ray Eames, and how these individuals were given extraordinary creative freedoms to execute a certain image of America at various trade fairs, world's fair pavilions, and museum exhibitions. Visits to the Bureau of Educational and Cultural Affairs (CU) holdings at the University of Arkansas, Fayetteville, clarified much of the data gathered at the aforementioned archives and gave a particular point of view, from within the U.S. Department of State, that helped triangulate the information gathered from the other archives, secondary sources, and interviews with those involved in these exhibitions. Immersion in these government and design archives have proved extraordinarily valuable in this study to understand better the flourishing of these exhibitions during this twenty-year period.

Importantly, much understanding of these exhibitions is owed to the extensive personal interviews that yielded unique information that has yet to be found in publications that address these cultural events. Specifically, Jack Masey, Beverly Payeff-Masey, and Ivan Chermayeff offered vital insights into their work with the USIA exhibitions from the 1950s through the 1970s. Maurice Tuchman, former curator of the Los Angeles Museum of Art and collaborator on the U.S. pavilion at Osaka in 1970, shared particularly fruitful insights into that event. Dick Arndt, cultural diplomacy veteran from the Bureau for Educational and Cultural Affairs, and Mark Smith, a former colleague from the University of Southern California and active Foreign Service officer, patiently provided me with ample understanding of why government exhibition programs sank into disrepair by the late 1970s. These interviews concluded the fieldwork for this work.

Research Design and Organization of This Study

This study uses a mixed-methods design of collecting and analyzing archival material, personal interviews, and scholarly works in order to understand the intentions of the U.S. government and those designers, historians, and advertising professionals who were enlisted to propagate a type of aspiration to cultural hegemony, to prove at the very least to foreign publics the superior quality of life in America. As is discussed in this chapter's section on the historiography of the target period of this study, much intellectual inquiry into international exhibitions has evolved over the recent decades. For Cold War scholars, these exhibitions themselves are, in a way, cultural objects that facilitate new understandings of cultural history. Historians and social scientists have interrogated these events from a range of theoretical perspectives, including media studies, sociology (impression management), art history, museology, and international relations. Akira Iriye explores a particularly useful term, "cultural internationalism," in understanding the role of culture in international affairs. His cultural-historical approach suggests that the "world order can and should be defined through interactions at the cultural level across national boundaries,"[7] a scenario to which international exhibitions can ideally contribute.

What scholars often overlook, however, is the U.S. government's collaboration with the private sector of museums, curators, designers, artists, and the exhibitions they created throughout the Cold War. These events provide much rich data from the perspective of architectural and industrial design evolution as well as design as a political force within this public diplomacy framework.[8] Yet other scholars deride the effectiveness of international exhibitions, condemning these events as idealized portraits of nations or groups that blinker the true economic, political, and social realities of these participants. Marxist discourse, for instance, indicts these exhibitions simply as instruments that recklessly enable the cupidity in human nature. Undeniably, on one level the materialist spirit of the nineteenth century was triumphed at these world's fairs, forums in which commodities were fetishized at the expense of any real improvement of understanding between peoples of different class and culture.[9] As these exhibitions are temporary conveyors of cultural politics and national values, an additional challenge of studying these historical moments is that they no longer exist.

Further, citing what has become a generative concept in discussions of state-sponsored displays for national prestige, Tony Bennett's "exhibitionary complex" usefully frames an approach to understanding the significance of U.S. cultural exhibitions and their role in influencing audiences that were aligned neither with Western values nor Soviet communism. Bennett's thesis, linked to Michel Foucault's concept of "power/knowledge," declares that modern international exhibitions, beginning with the Great Exhibition of 1851, reveal

the tendency for society itself—in its constituent parts and as a whole—to be rendered as spectacle. . . . This ambition towards a specular dominance over a totality was even more evident in the conception of international exhibitions which, in their heyday, sought to make the whole world, past and present, metonymically available in assemblages of objects and peoples they brought together and, from their towers, to lay it before a controlling vision.[10]

Exhibitions, in this sense, can also be construed as instruments that generate through their display of images and artifacts certain types of knowledge that reveal among other insights the will to power of the exhibitor.[11] Historians Robert Rydell, John Findling, and Kimberley Pelle engage Bennett's argument that international exhibitions reflect their organizers' "need to be understood as vehicles intended to win popular support for national imperial policies."[12]

U.S. efforts at cultural diplomacy through exhibitions in the early to mid-1950s were focused predominantly on displaying material prosperity through the exhibition of the best of industrial design, which had originated by and large from émigré European designers who had escaped the horrors of Nazi fascism before and during the Second World War. This study goes further chronologically to analyze the multidecade evolution of American display methods and persuasion through these methods at the 1959 *American National Exhibition* in Moscow, the result of an official exchange with the Soviet Union; the U.S. participation at the Montreal Expo in 1967 and the Osaka Expo in 1970; and finally the *World of Franklin and Jefferson* exhibition that traveled as one of the official events of the American Bicentennial celebrations from 1974 to 1977. By the late 1970s, U.S. cultural exhibitions began to deteriorate both in quality and in creative vision as a result of mismanaged mandates for the USIA and the rise of détente with the U.S.S.R. This heyday of the U.S. cultural exhibitions abroad, addressed for the first time in this study across exhibition genres over this twenty-year period, was punctuated by the efforts of brilliant, and brilliantly unorthodox, exhibition "teams," which included Madison Avenue advertising execs, Museum of Modern Art (MoMA) curators, industrial designers as noteworthy as Herbert Bayer, Charles Eames, George Nelson, Peter Blake, R. Buckminster Fuller, and the Cambridge Seven, and national agencies such as the National Aeronautics and Space Administration, and the Smithsonian Institution. Unnumbered individuals, some from the unlikeliest of professional domains, had succeeded in representing America at literally hundreds of shows that communicated an image of American prestige through symbolic displays.

Historiographical Context

Certainly, a number of scholars have brought into question the manifest and latent intentions of U.S. foreign policy surrounding these sites of cultural production.

In the winter of 1960, for instance, historian Daniel Boorstin visited the American pavilion at the Indian Agricultural Fair in New Delhi, one of hundreds of appearances the United States would make at international trade fairs starting in 1954, through a program President Eisenhower adopted and which was established with joint cooperation between the Department of Commerce and the United States Information Agency. As Boorstin has described this event:

> The American Pavilion, a light and graceful structure, dances in the sun. Inside, it was neat and uncluttered. One of the sights most impressive to all comers was an American farm kitchen—a dazzling porcelain-and-chrome spectacle, complete with refrigerator, disposal, deep-freeze, automatic washer and dryer, and electric stove. Before it walked a procession of Indian peasant women. Long pendant earrings, bangles on arms and ankles, objects piercing their noses—these pieces of gold were their savings which they dared not put in the hands of banks. In their arms they carried bare-bottomed infants. They stopped and stood in bewilderment. What was this? It was the image of America.[13]

In his analysis of American culture, Boorstin predicted a society dominated by the images and sounds of mass media and popular culture. He argued that Americans were "the most illusioned people on Earth," and lamented that it is "all the more fitting that the images which we make wittingly or unwittingly to sell America to the world should come back to haunt and curse us."[14] These quotations symbolize the motivation for this study, which is an investigation of what Boorstin might call "pseudo-events" that promoted images of an idealized American lifestyle. The various types of cultural diplomacy exhibitions under discussion in this study—trade fairs, official exhibition exchanges with the U.S.S.R., pavilions at world's fairs, and museum exhibitions—also, at times, signaled a return to the display of founding American values and conform to this operational definition of an international exhibition: a public event staged by participants to showcase the industrial, technological, and artistic achievements of nations, private business interests, and selected nongovernmental organizations (NGOs). The most common of these events is known variously as a world's fair, an *exposition universelle*, and an expo. An important by-product of these temporal events is their globalizing effect by fostering intercultural relations. These events are organized to (1) increase tourist activity, (2) promote trade, and (3) propagate symbolically the ideas and values of their participants.

A number of scholars from various fields have demonstrated a similar skepticism of U.S. efforts to use images to represent an "America" that may challenge plausibility. Social theorist Thorstein Veblen, who coined the terms "conspicuous consumption" and "conspicuous leisure" as a "keeping up with the Joneses" syndrome in which the desire for emulation supplants rational utility in consumer culture, observed that this suspension of the utilitarian in addressing one's actual needs requires an embrace of the "make-believe."[15]

Semiotician Umberto Eco is also openly critical of trade fairs and world's fair pavilions as examples of modern-day *wunderkammern* in which the visitor is subject to a "prestige function" that celebrates "a dynasty or a town as a commercial, cultural, or religious center." Eco's new term "hyperreality" includes fairs and expos, which he deems adult Disneylands, where "concern for the Space Age is combined with nostalgia for a fairytale past."[16] Furthermore, sociologist George Ritzer maintains a parallel approach in his critical analysis of consumer settings, which he dubs "cathedrals of consumption," where "these places do more than simply permit us to consume things; they are structured to lead and even coerce us into consumption."[17] In his list of commercial settings that transcend the basic functions of fair trade, Ritzer includes country fairs, the Parisian arcade, the department store, and the "world exhibition" as examples of the growing rationalization of the "unreal." He writes:

> If in the modern world everything seemed pretty clear-cut, on the cusp of the postmodern world many things seem quite nebulous. This is especially true of the realm of consumption. The implosion of the real and the unreal leaves us with an unclear sense of the distinction between them. Virtually every means of consumption is a simulated setting, or has simulated elements, simulated people, or simulated products. . . . As a result, it is no longer so clear what is real and what is unreal.[18]

While a discussion of simulated settings is broadened in chapter 2 in an exploration of how industrial designers themselves approached the creation of what I call *propaganda scenography* in international exhibitions, a thorough historiography of design as a tool to boost consumer activity is outside the scope of this study. However, the design techniques employed in the exhibitions to be analyzed later will address aspects of design as a persuasive force in these instances of "America" on display. The primacy of appearances and impression management in a large sense subverted the reality of the image of America the U.S. government was attempting to project to foreign audiences. I aim to unpack the complexities of how these diplomatic events evolved from basic concept to finished product—set against the backdrop of world events—and how they illustrate the intentions of those involved in transmitting their ideas to foreign publics. This study is a call to boost consideration of the ways in which the U.S. cultural diplomacy apparatus of exhibitions has fulfilled its mandate in the past and, ultimately, how these events can offer lessons for American cultural diplomacy in the future.

This chapter (1955–1975) of U.S. history coincides with the time period characterized by magazine editor Henry Luce, who in 1941 described this era as "the American Century."[19] This vision of U.S. global ascendancy, embraced by conservatives and spurned by liberals, invoked an aggressive unilateral approach to foreign affairs, but with a twist. No longer would the United States spread its influence only through political, economic, or military means. Rather, culture itself would become a formidable weapon in the arsenal to shape an American vision of individualism, democratic principles, and free enterprise abroad.[20] Since the late 1970s and 1980s, scholarly research on cultural globalization has exploded, at times taking the ethical position on the potential pitfalls of cultural diplomacy transforming into cultural imperialism, particularly during the Cold War.[21] More recent discussions from both sides of the Atlantic have addressed American cultural hegemony as a phenomenon that began with Marshall Plan aid following World War II, though few of these works refer to exhibitions as part of the arsenal of diplomatic weapons the United States employed in spreading American ideas and ideals abroad.[22] Robert Keohane and Joseph Nye define hegemony as a scenario in which "one state is powerful enough to maintain the essential rules governing interstate relations, and willing to do so."[23] A scholarly methodology that has gained recent prominence bridging the fields of globalization theory and public diplomacy is the study of nation branding. Selected literature from this mode of inquiry has proved valuable in the appraisal of U.S. image management through cultural endeavors such as international exhibitions. As Ying Fan defines this concept:

> A nation brand is the total sum of all perceptions of a nation in the mind of international stakeholders which may contain some of the following elements: people, place, culture/language, history, food, fashion, famous faces (celebrities), global brands. . . . A nation's "brand" exists, with or without any conscious efforts in nation branding, as each country has a current image to its international audience, be it strong or weak, clear or vague.[24]

This study gives particular focus to how U.S. culture manipulates its image through the project of international exhibitions, which from this singular perspective makes its impact on America's nation branding.

The field of cultural diplomacy as a subgenre of public diplomacy has exploded in the past decade. Since 9/11, in particular, the field has witnessed a prodigious flow of books, journals, articles, and websites[25] devoted to certain aspects of American cultural diplomacy and the media it used to shape public opinion overseas. These government-driven apparatuses include Voice of America radio, traveling music tours, the dissemination of films, and person-to-person educational exchanges. Significant work has been done recently in the study of American public diplomacy from a cultural standpoint. Scholars

Nicholas Cull and Richard Arndt offer the most exhaustively sweeping studies of the history of American public diplomacy.[26] They differ immensely in their scope, whereas Cull takes on an archive-based approach to produce a broad, seamless view of the forty-plus-year public diplomacy face-off between the United States, via the United States Information Agency (USIA), and the Soviet Union. Arndt's study investigates the historical minutiae of names, dates, and rationales surrounding the activities of Foreign Service personnel devoted to America's cultural outreach during this period. While both studies, one by an academic and the other by a twenty-five-year veteran of American cultural diplomacy, brilliantly outline the sheer breadth of American cultural diplomacy during the Cold War, both historians provide scant insights into the rich, yet all too historically clandestine, story of U.S. cultural exhibitions during the Cold War. In addition, Cull posits that the heads of the USIA consistently named the Voice of America radio program (VOA) as their most important tool of cultural diplomacy. Perhaps this is the main drawback of these studies, though also a signal to historians to take up the subject of international exhibitions as a focus of study. Refreshingly, Cull's critical interpretation avoids certain of the authorial pitfalls of other studies that take on U.S. cultural diplomacy during the Cold War, whereas Arndt and fellow USIA former field officers Wilson Dizard and Fitzhugh Green[27] share a sometimes emotional position on the successes and failures of the USIA. Cull, a leading scholar on American public diplomacy, approaches his subject with an objectivity that relies more on exhaustive research than on personal recollection.[28] It is with a similar approach that I undertake an investigation of these events.

More nuanced analyses of these specific aspects of cultural diplomacy have emerged beyond the general background on the use of culture (film, art, music) as a diplomacy instrument from a U.S. governmental point of view. Historian Kenneth Osgood studies the concurrent rise of communications technologies and public relations tactics from the early twentieth century through the Cold War, beginning with Woodrow Wilson, who was the first American commander in chief to speak directly to foreign publics, in essence bypassing foreign governments and influencing public opinion abroad for American aims. By exploring the U.S. implementation of cultural exchange as a new apparatus of American statehood, Osgood theorizes, based on Harold Lasswell's discussion of the rise of "public relations experts, psychological warfare specialists, image consultants, and spin doctors," that as important as it was for America to direct psychological warfare at the enemy, it was of equal importance to maintain ties with allies and keep nonaligned actors from siding with the enemy.[29] Osgood's research includes a crucial understanding of the proximity

U.S. presidents, in this case Eisenhower, were to the implementation of their public diplomacy: "Another thing I expected to find was that the presidents were only marginally involved in creating propaganda strategy . . . but I found instead that President Eisenhower in particular was remarkably influential and involved in shaping U.S. propaganda strategy."[30]

Scholars such as Greg Castillo and Laura Belmonte study early Cold War propaganda asserting that not only were these displays of "America" used as cultural diplomacy instruments, they were also vehicles that enabled industrial design and the consumer items they produced to grow as a discipline.[31] By radically increasing the role of everyday domestic items, these exhibitions recast these objects into exhibition themes—such as "Industry in the Service of Man"—that would find their way to the farthest reaches of the globe, most conspicuously through international trade fairs. Both Castillo and Belmonte offer through their studies of 1950s exhibitionary culture an understanding through exhibitions during the early Cold War, leading up to the time frame of my study. Chapter 2 will revisit and take on new scholarly sources that address, in the words of Grant McCracken, "the symbolic character of consumer goods and activities."[32]

Though a number of these exhibitions have been acknowledged in various studies of American cultural diplomacy, these scholarly works have positioned these events either in isolation of one another,[33] as products of a single decade,[34] or as a theme surrounding a singular artifact,[35] while others are told from the perspective of Foreign Service officers in the field.[36] Historian Emily Rosenberg offers an analysis that gives ample discussion of the geopolitical conditions in which American foreign policy officially adopted an office for cultural relations.[37] This scholar presents valuable insights into the formation of an official American foreign policy that included a significant cultural dimension, beginning with the 1890 Columbian Exposition, where a young Frederick Jackson Turner introduced his "frontier thesis." This would be followed by U.S. efforts to shape world public opinion after World War I and the communist takeover of Russia to American attempts in stanching the feared ideological infiltration of Nazism in Latin America in the years leading up to and during World War II and after.

Remarkably absent from studies of Cold War propaganda and its dissemination through international exhibitions is an art historical and museological approach that takes into account the history of the display of collections in the name of national prestige. As these two fields have produced ample literature to serve as models for intellectual engagement with artifacts, collectors, and the politics of display, only recently has art historical scholarship converged with museum practice, which, for the purposes of this study, I am calling the history of collecting and display, to produce new interpretations of temporary exhibitions that have come and gone. As the field of museum studies is extremely holistic and transdisciplinary, it has effectively combined the academic field of art history with the history of collecting and display.[38]

As there are many ways to develop an interpretive approach to a history of artifacts and their display, studying exhibitions can be a process fraught with pitfalls. The problem with "reading" exhibitions in general is that they may not say what their makers intended. They may not be read as intended. Or the intentions may be intellectually weak.[39] Perhaps a leading question as to an art historical and museological approach could be: What might an art historical and museological approach to diplomatic history look like? As the study of temporary collections on display is the focus of this research, how does one manage an approach to a collection that no longer exists? This is a perennial issue that frustrates scholars of the history of collections and their display, who must reconstruct these bygone events while upholding the intentions of their makers, based on various primary and secondary sources.

Museum consultant Elaine Heumann Gurian frames a method for seeing the exhibition as a unified whole that takes into account the motives of the producer, the contents of the collection on display, and the viewer:

> In analyzing exhibitions, the roles played in the creation process by the producer of the exhibition, the content, and the audience need to be considered. An exhibition is a cultural artifact that articulates a producer's visions, biases, concerns. It also allows the contemplation of the exhibition content. In addition to the producer and the content, a silent participant—the audience—influences the creation of the exhibition.[40]

While discussion of an exhibition can devolve into a study of the exhibition's contents, the effort to make objects speak from the grave can frustrate what art historian Thomas Crow would call the "intelligibility" of the event. The very act of describing the history and meaning of a singular object on display poses literal and conceptual challenges. Perhaps, as Eco generalizes, an exhibition of objects should be treated instead as a collection, a whole in which these questions may find greater traction. The contents of a world's fair pavilion, for example,

> assume the form of an inventory, an enormous gathering of evidence from Stone to Space Age, an accumulation of objects useless and precious, an immense catalogue of things produced by man in all countries over the past ten

thousand years, displayed so that humanity will not forget them. They seem to be a final recapitulation in the face of a hypothetical end of the world.[41]

Yet if one sets aside the concept of an exhibition as a story of artifacts, what other approach does a researcher have to convey the meaning of an exhibition? Cal Tech scholar John Brewer asks: "Do we write the history of collecting as a history of spaces? Are catalogues, photos, and diaries representative of spaces? Are collections, then, from this point of view, static realities?"[42] Further, are the archives consulted and interviews conducted in the service of understanding the story of exhibitions epistemological structures that are representative of spaces? Or do they emphasize instead the shifting in meaning of exhibitions over time? Perhaps a way into teasing out a workable methodology for understanding the meaning of exhibitions can be found looking in unlikely art histories.

The art historiographies of Susan Sontag and Thomas Crow have retrained my sensibilities in taking on the interpretive work of Cold War cultural exhibitions. Heeding Susan Sontag's argument that "the contemporary zeal for the project of interpretation is often prompted not by piety towards the troublesome text . . . but by an aggressiveness, an overt contempt for appearances,"[43] it behooves me to adopt an alternative interpretive methodology of these cultural exhibitions. Until now, these events have, for the most part, been treated by political historians merely as instruments of government policy with particular focus given to various periods and themes and objects (kitchens as ideological battlegrounds, for instance, or as soft-power alternatives to militarism and economic methods that coerce rather than influence foreign publics).

These examples of cultural production arguably carry a considerable freight of their makers' intentions as evidenced through interviews and archival research. Thus, a careful reappraisal, even a distrust of the rhetorical devices used by historians of diplomatic history to approach this subject matter, is not out of order. For this, I recruit what will seem on the surface an audacious and wholly unorthodox referent: Meyer Schapiro's 1939 essay on the Romanesque stone tympanum at Souillac, which Crow celebrates the unlikely choice of an incomplete—"dis-coordinate," in Shapiro's opinion—medieval church sculpture series in his attempts to understand the social history surrounding it. Crow advises: "One should look away from the obvious center of any highly developed artistic complex and instead concentrate on more marginal, seemingly incomplete examples, where stable orders seem to come unstuck. There the processes of artistic thought are more likely to attain a certain visibility."[44] This study, in a sense, follows the model by Schapiro and offers a robust formal analysis of lesser-known examples of cultural diplomacy exhibitions based on what evidence remains of them—archival resources (memos, letters, photos, floor layouts), personal interviews, and scant published scholarly interpretations. The aim of this study, then, is to shed light not only on the sociopolitical circumstances surrounding these individual case-studies events but also on the history of American cultural diplomacy exhibitions as a whole. Crow insists, in surveying Schapiro's choice of the obscure Souillac sculpture system: "Both in its dis-coordinate internal arrangements of motifs and in its eccentric relation to the larger body of related objects: these traits become the condition for maximum intelligibility in a work of art."[45]

Importantly, Crow takes his cues from Schapiro when pronouncing the dangers of isomorphism as a tool for art historians, as the researcher of the Souillac tympanum demonstrates that an attempt to make simple connections between an artifact (in my case, an exhibition) and meaning can deny the particular essence of the artifact. A potential rationale for Schapiro's enterprise is to teach the reader/observer to see beyond the tendency to isomorphize historical phenomena—of simplifying the object's meaning by equating it with the artist or specific historical causes. The same can be argued for how a historiographical approach to exhibition planners and their displays has been treated at times too generally by historians of diplomatic history.

While it is not possible to do every kind of interpretive work based on archival investigations and interviews with designers, the intention of this study is to use archives and personal interviews more than just as primary sources. Arguably, these types of evidence should be conceived as holding their distinctive place in the history of collecting and display. In this way, they can be used as a screen for reading shifts in how these sites of cultural production are presented.[46] Certainly, it is worth asking: Does one, in the end, receive a false impression of an exhibition based on a representation (archives, interviews) if one has never seen the event? By juxtaposing archival findings and interviews with scholarly research, these types of sources can work synergistically and allow multiple meanings to surface around this chapter of American cultural diplomacy history.

Art historian Stephen Bann calls the exercise of interpretation of singular artifacts a process by which we "measure its participation in the multiple codes which govern the collective consciousness."[47] Simon Knell has likewise proposed an alternative—or perhaps better phrased as a corrective—to focusing solely on the "exhibition as artifact" and its composition: "So rather than reading the order, which has survived in museums to the present day . . . we need to uncover the 'looking' (the interpretive frame) of the founders."[48] These exhibitions are ultimately complex ideological symbols in which concepts of national identity and global cultural influence both coincided and clashed. The investigation of these exhibitions enhances a better understanding of a significant chapter of U.S. cultural diplomacy at the height of the Cold War and how America constantly reimagined itself.[49]

Overview of Chapters

The chapters of this study take the reader chronologically through exhibitionary examples of specific instances of American cultural diplomacy, each raising their own questions as to what America was trying to show of itself through these efforts at soft-power foreign policy. Chapter 1 offers a historical perspective on American attempts at display for national prestige in the nineteenth century and investigates the historical specificity of these events. These address the seemingly unrelated efforts of Thomas Jefferson's display of the American mastodon in Europe for the sole purpose of dispelling European prejudices of a "degenerate" America, as well as America's representation at the Great Exhibition of 1851, in which the U.S. effort was cosponsored by the fledgling Smithsonian Institution, and the creation of a cultural Monroe Doctrine during World War II through art exhibitions aimed to thwart Nazi encroachment in South America. These illustrations will formulate the contention that the American government, since its inception, has not only had an eye cocked to outside perceptions and used exhibitions to shape them, but has revealed a zealousness to prove at all costs a certain image of America through these public ventures. However, though the United States had actively employed the medium of museum exhibitions to project American values to international audiences 150 years prior to the onset of the Cold War, it was not until the 1950s that any formal instrument, such as the USIA, was formed to execute these exhibitions abroad.

Chapter 2 addresses trade fairs. These events, established between the USIA and the Office of International Trade Fairs of the Department of Commerce in 1954, have provided me with a sound understanding of the evolution of industrial design and how design itself served as a political force within this specific type of international exhibitions. A mass of primary source material has been investigated at the National Archives in College Park, Maryland, and undergirds a rich discussion of how the government and the private sector allied to create what on the surface can be construed as industrial design spectacles at trade fairs around the world for a concentrated period during the mid-1950s. This chapter investigates the American pavilions at key international trade fairs during the mid-1950s.

Chapter 3 investigates the *American National Exhibition* in Moscow (ANEM) in 1959, the first of many international exhibitions sent to the Soviet Union to fight Soviet disinformation about America while winning the hearts and minds of the Russian citizenry. This cultural exhibition—modulated through the participation of the U.S. government and a crack team of industrial designers (including George Nelson, R. Buckminster Fuller, Charles and Ray Eames, and Peter Blake)—served as a foreign-policy tool to raise awareness of America and its values among a Soviet audience of nearly three million people. These cultural exchanges continued on a lesser scale until the collapse of the Soviet Union in 1991.

Chapter 4 looks specifically at the American pavilions at the Montreal Expo in 1967 and at the Osaka Expo in 1970. Since the Great Exhibition of 1851, world's fair country pavilions have been preoccupied with taking on not only international markets with new designs that were aesthetic, utilitarian, and commercially available to the rank-and-file visitors but also international attitudes, biases, and critiques of these pavilion hosts. They would also offer to more powerful nations and NGOs a certain hegemonic function in which their individual pavilions (and their contents) would serve symbolically to remind visitors of the balance or imbalance of power among the various participants.

Chapter 5 is a case study of *The World of Franklin and Jefferson*, an exhibition that traveled to Paris, Warsaw, London, and Mexico City. As the Bicentennial of the Declaration of Independence approached, an unwieldy government apparatus—the American Revolution Bicentennial Administration (ARBA)—was created to develop programming to celebrate this milestone event in U.S. history. The dominant cultural diplomacy instrument that was chosen by the USIA to represent America abroad was the Charles and Ray Eames designed *Franklin and Jefferson* exhibition.

The final chapter offers conclusive interpretations of the preceding chapters and revisits the initial research questions and hypotheses posed in the introduction.

Notes

1. William J. Lederer and Eugene Burdick, *The Ugly American* (New York: Norton, 1958), 283. For an appraisal of this book's effect on shaping the behavior of U.S. Foreign Service officers, see Michael Meyer, "Still 'Ugly' after All These Years," *New York Times*, July 10, 2009, BR23.

2. See NSC 20/4, "U.S. Objectives with Respect to the USSR to Counter Soviet Threats to U.S. Security," in *Foreign Relations of the United States, Vol. 1* (Washington, DC: Government Printing Office, Department of State, 1948), 663–69.

3. See Hans N. Tuch, *Communicating with the World: U.S. Public Diplomacy Overseas* (New York: St. Martin's, 1990), and Richard T. Arndt, *The First Resort of Kings: American Cultural Diplomacy in the Twentieth Century* (Washington, DC: Potomac, 2006). These former practitioners of cultural diplomacy enunciate the crucial years of U.S. cultural diplomacy activities—including international exhibitions—as the mid-1950s through the mid-1970s. Tuch, for example, states: "Exhibitions used to constitute a major public diplomacy medium. In 1955 a two-year project to develop *Atoms for Peace* exhibits all over the world resulted from President Eisenhower's 1953 United Nations General Assembly speech promoting the peaceful uses of nuclear energy as a major U.S. foreign policy objective. . . . During the sixties and early seventies, USIA was the principal organizer or coordinator of overseas U.S. government exhibitions at world's fairs, at international trade fairs, at theme exhibitions, and art shows. At the end of the 1970s, however, large-scale exhibits lost their popularity as public diplomacy media. They required long lead time—for planning, preparation, and building—but made a relatively fleeting impact in most places," *Communicating with the World*, 62–65. Likewise, Arndt states: "The golden years of cultural diplomacy began to fade four decades ago. . . . Meanwhile, the sharp rise in foreign non-understanding has become a national nightmare. Yet few have suggested that a crippled cultural diplomacy might have anything to do with either cause or cure. Cultural diplomacy's decline has thus passed unnoticed, leaving a nation baffled by its apparent defenselessness against the cultural onslaught of an enraged Islamic fragment," *First Resort of Kings*, xxi.

4. Public diplomacy, of which cultural diplomacy is an important aspect, was defined in 1965 by Edmund Gullion, dean of the Fletcher School of Law at Tufts University, who founded the Edward R. Murrow Center on Public Diplomacy, as "the influence of public attitudes on the formation and execution of foreign publics. It encompasses dimensions of international relations beyond traditional diplomacy; the cultivation by governments of public opinion in other countries; the interaction of private groups and interests in one country with another; the reporting of foreign affairs and its impact on policy; communication between those whose job is communication, as diplomats and foreign correspondents; and the process of intercultural communications." For further insight into the term "public diplomacy," see Nicholas J. Cull, "'Public Diplomacy' before Gullion: The Evolution of a Phrase" (Los Angeles: USC Center on Public Diplomacy, 2006). Joseph Nye, coiner of the term "soft power," has theorized extensively on the growing role of cultural relations on the government level and its effectiveness over the age-old carrot-and-stick politics that focus more on hard-power tactics of militarism and economic leveraging. See Joseph S. Nye Jr., *Soft Power: The Means to Success in World Politics* (New York: Public Affairs, 2004). For an expanded scholarly discussion that addresses the theory and methods of public diplomacy, see Nancy Snow and Philip M. Taylor, eds., *Routledge Handbook of Public Diplomacy* (New York: Routledge, 2009).

5. Geoffrey Cowan and Amelia Arsenault at USC's Center on Public Diplomacy theorize the various types of communication adopted by public diplomacy practitioners

in "Moving from Monologue to Dialogue to Collaboration: The Three Layers of Public Diplomacy," *Annals of the American Academy of Political and Social Science* 616, 1 (March 2008): 10–30.

6. I owe the development of this question to a conversation with Geoffrey Wiseman, director of the University of Southern California's Center on Public Diplomacy, and Dr. Shashi Tharoor, on March 10, 2009, USC Annenberg School for Communication, Los Angeles.

7. See Akira Iriye, *Cultural Internationalism and World Order* (Baltimore: Johns Hopkins University Press, 1997), x.

8. For a personal take on the interchange of ideas between government organizers (whether they be representatives from the USIA, the Office of International Trade Fairs [OITF], or the American Revolution Bicentennial Administration, for example) and members of the design and advertising worlds, see Jack Masey and Conway Lloyd Morgan, *Cold War Confrontations: U.S. Exhibitions and Their Role in the Cultural Cold War* (Baden, Switzerland: Lars Müller, 2008). See also, for an introduction to Cold War–era industrial design as it interfaced with international exhibitions—to be addressed in chapter 2 in greater depth—Misha Black, ed., *Exhibition Design* (London: Architectural Press, 1950) and George Nelson, ed., *Display* (New York: Whitney, 1953).

9. For an excellent survey of world's fairs in which America participated from the last decades of the nineteenth century to World War I, see Robert W. Rydell, *All the World's a Fair: Visions of Empire at American International Expositions, 1876–1916* (Chicago: University of Chicago Press, 1984).

10. Tony Bennett, "The Exhibitionary Complex," *New Formations* 4 (Spring 1988): 78–79. See also Michel Foucault's "Governmentality," in *The Foucault Effect: Studies in Governmentality*, ed. Graham Burchell, Colin Gordon, and Peter Miller (London: Harvester Wheatsheaf, 1996), 87–104.

11. See Jonathan Xavier Inda, "Governmentality," in *The Wiley-Blackwell Encyclopedia of Globalization*, ed. George Ritzer (Oxford: Blackwell Publishing, 2012). According to Inda, Foucault's work on governmentality present three main points: "First, the term 'government' . . . refers essentially to the conduct of conduct . . . to any rational effort to influence or guide the comportment of others—whether these be workers, children, communities, families, or the sick—through acting upon their hopes, desires, or milieu. Second . . . what counts in thinking about governmental power is thus not simply the state but also all these other actors, organizations, and agencies concerned with exercising authority over the conduct of human beings. And third, Foucault argues that the principal target of government is population."

12. Robert Rydell, John E. Findling, and Kimberley D. Pelle, *Fair America: World's Fairs in the United States* (Washington, DC: Smithsonian Institution, 2000), 5.

13. Daniel Boorstin, *The Image: Or What Happened to the American Dream* (New York: Atheneum, 1961), 243.

14. Ibid., 245–246.

15. See Thorstein Veblen, *The Theory of the Leisure Class: An Economic Study of Institutions* (New York: Macmillan, 1899). For a thorough explication of Veblen's theories that include mention of Jean Baudrillard's concept of the "age of simulation," in which "images generated by consumer culture . . . assume a life of their own," see Clare Virginia Eby, *Dreiser and Veblen: Saboteurs of the Status Quo* (Columbia: University of Missouri Press, 1998). Eby asserts: "According to Veblen, ritualistic constructs such as status and 'make believe' events such as sports and military parades function as ceremonial surrogates for reality," 13. See also Richard Handler, "Is 'Identity' a Useful Cross-Cultural Concept," in *Commemorations: The Politics of National Identity*, ed. John R. Gillis (Princeton, NJ: Princeton University Press, 1994), 27. Handler addresses the "'invention' of cultures and traditions, particularly as this process is associated with nationalist and ethnic politics."

16. Umberto Eco, "A Theory of Expositions," in *Travels in Hyperreality: Essays*, trans. William Weaver (San Diego: Harcourt, 1986), 293. See also Jean Baudrillard, *Simulations* (New York: Semiotext[e], 1983); Siegfried Kracauer, *The Mass Ornament: The Weimar Essays* (Cambridge, MA: Harvard University Press, 1995); and Paul A. Taylor, "Hyperreality," in *The Wiley-Blackwell Encyclopedia of Globalization*, ed. George Ritzer (Oxford: Blackwell, 2012). According to Taylor, "For Baudrillard, the hyperreal's status as that which is more real than life itself, is marked by the absence or increasing irrelevance of any original model upon which the imitation is based."

17. See George Ritzer, *Enchanting a Disenchanted World: Revolutionizing the Means of Consumption*, 2nd ed. (Thousand Oaks, CA: Pine Forge, 2005), x, 177–80.

18. Ibid., 180.

19. Originally published in *Life* magazine, February 7, 1941. For the discussion of the "American Century," see Alan Brinkley, *The Publisher: Henry Luce and His American Century* (New York: Knopf, 2010), 266–72; Frank A. Ninkovich, *The Wilsonian Century: U.S. Foreign Policy since 1900* (Chicago: University of Chicago Press, 1999); Roberto Rabel, ed., *The American Century? In Retrospect and Prospect* (Westport, CT: Praeger, 2002).

20. Some critics of Luce's theory of American dominance in global affairs argue over the nature and longevity of American hegemony and exceptionalism. Robert Keohane, for instance, claims that "one of the most important features of American hegemony was its brevity," in Robert O. Keohane, *After Hegemony: Cooperation and Discord in the World Political Economy* (Princeton, NJ: Princeton University Press, 1984), 139. Keohane loosely frames the era of American hegemony by the introduction of the Truman Doctrine and the Marshall Plan in the late 1940s and America's dismissal of the gold standard in 1971. After this, Keohane argues, the United States had lost influence in the three critical areas essential to hegemony: "1) A stable international monetary system, 2) Provision of open markets for goods, 3) Access to oil at stable prices," ibid.

21. See John Tomlinson, *Cultural Imperialism: A Critical Introduction* (Baltimore, MD: Johns Hopkins University Press, 1991); David Rothkopf, "In Praise of Cultural Imperialism," *Foreign Policy* 107 (Summer 1997): 44; Bernd Hamm and Russell

Smandych, *Cultural Imperialism: Essays on the Political Economy of Cultural Domination* (Peterborough, ON: Broadview, 2005); Harvey B. Feigenbaum, "Globalization and Cultural Diplomacy" (Washington, DC: Center for Arts and Culture, 2001), available at http://xa.yimg.com/kq/groups/22587837/659966199/name/global+6.pdf; Tyler Cowen, *Creative Destruction: How Globalization Is Changing the World's Cultures* (Princeton, NJ: Princeton University Press, 2003).

22. For an early Cold War example of European anxiety toward Americanization, see "Foreign News: The Pause That Arouses," *Time*, March 13, 1950: "France's Communist press bristled with warnings against U.S. 'Coca-Colonization.'" For scholarly literature on American cultural globalization, see Richard H. Pells, *Not Like Us: How Europeans Have Loved, Hated, and Transformed American Culture since World War II* (New York: Basic, 1997); Alexander Stephan, *The Americanization of Europe: Culture, Diplomacy, and Anti-Americanism after 1945* (New York: Berghahn, 2006); Reinhold Wagnleitner, *Coca-Colonization and the Cold War: The Cultural Mission of the United States in Austria after the Second World War* (Chapel Hill: University of North Carolina Press, 1994); Reinhold Wagnleitner and Elaine Tyler May, eds., *Here, There, and Everywhere: The Foreign Politics of American Popular Culture* (Hanover, NH: University Press of New England, 2000); Jessica C. E. Gienow-Hecht and Frank Schumacher, eds., *Culture and International History* (New York: Berghahn, 2003); Rob Kroes, *If You've Seen One, You've Seen the Mall: Europeans and American Mass Culture* (Urbana: University of Illinois Press, 1996); David W. Ellwood, Rob Kroes, and Gian Piero Brunetta, eds., *Hollywood in Europe: Experiences of a Cultural Hegemony* (Amsterdam: VU University Press, 1994). Popular culture has acknowledged the global infiltration of American culture among foreign populations, such as in Wim Wenders's film *Kings of the Road* (1976), in which one character quips, "The Yanks have colonized our subconscious."

23. Robert O. Keohane and Joseph S. Nye Jr., eds., *Power and Interdependence: World Politics in Transition* (New York: Little, Brown, 1977), 44.

24. See Ying Fan, "Branding the Nation: Towards a Better Understanding," *Brunel Business School Research Papers* (2009): 3, available at http://bura.brunel.ac.uk/handle/ 2438/3496. For critical perspectives, see Nadia Kaneva, "Nation Branding: Toward an Agenda for Critical Research," *International Journal of Communication* 5, (2011): 117–41; Melissa Aronczyk and Devon Powers, eds., *Blowing Up the Brand: Critical Perspectives on Promotional Culture* (New York: Peter Lang, 2010); Keith Dinnie, ed., *Nation Branding: Concepts, Issues, Practice* (Oxford: Butterworth-Heinemann, 2008), 22–23; Manuel Castells, *The Power of Identity* (Malden, MA: Blackwell, 1997). For studies of American nation branding, see Simon Anholt and Jeremy Hildreth, *Brand America: The Mother of All Brands* (London: Cyan, 2004); Jian Wang, "Telling the American Story to the World: The Purpose of U.S. Public Diplomacy in Historical Perspective," *Public Relations Review* 33, no. 1 (2007): 21–30.

25. Three studies that illustrate the conditions in which cultural diplomacy became a formal instrument of American foreign policy are the pioneering Ruth McMurry and Muna Lee, *The Cultural Approach: Another Way in International Relations* (Chapel Hill:

North Carolina University Press, 1947); J. Manuel Espinosa, *Inter-American Beginnings of U.S. Cultural Diplomacy, 1936–1948* (Washington, DC: Bureau of Educational and Cultural Affairs, U.S. Dept. of State, 1976); and Frank A. Ninkovich, *The Diplomacy of Ideas: U.S. Foreign Policy and Cultural Relations, 1938–1950* (Cambridge: Cambridge University Press, 1981). More recent general studies since September 11, 2001, come in the form of recommendations for how the U.S. government should revamp its cultural diplomacy activities. For this, see Cynthia P. Schneider, "Culture Communicates: US Diplomacy that Works," Discussion Papers in Diplomacy 94 (The Hague: Netherlands Institute of International Relations, 2004), 1–22; Helena K. Finn, "The Case for Cultural Diplomacy: Engaging Foreign Audiences," *Foreign Affairs* 82, no. 6 (Nov./Dec. 2003): 15–20; and U.S. Advisory Committee on Cultural Diplomacy, *Cultural Diplomacy: The Lynchpin of Public Diplomacy* (Washington, DC: U.S. Department of State, September 2005).

26. For a thorough overview of U.S. public diplomacy during the Cold War, see Nicholas J. Cull, *The Cold War and the United States Information Agency: US propaganda and Public Diplomacy, 1945–1989* (Cambridge: Cambridge University Press, 2008) and Arndt, *The First Resort of Kings.* Arndt's survey, similarly to Cull's, gives brief accounts of international exhibitions, including the Arts in Embassies Program (AIEP) and Edward Steichen's *Family of Man* exhibition in 1955. See also Yale Richmond, *Cultural Exchange and the Cold War: Raising the Iron Curtain* (University Park: Pennsylvania State University Press, 2003) and Walter L. Hixson, *Parting the Curtain: Propaganda, Culture, and the Cold War, 1945–1961* (New York: St. Martin's, 1997).

27. See Wilson P. Dizard, *Inventing Public Diplomacy: The Story of the U.S. Information Agency* (Boulder, CO: Lynne Rienner, 2004) and Fitzhugh Green, *American Propaganda Abroad: From Benjamin Franklin to Ronald Reagan* (New York: Hippocrene, 1988).

28. A pronounced strength of Cull's study that helps my own is the author's attention to the interstitial relationships between branches of the U.S. government and the sometimes byzantine process of bringing cultural diplomacy initiatives to fruition. It is this inclusion of White House, National Security Council (NSC), and congressional involvement with the USIA's work that demystifies, to a certain extent, the domestic machinations of a cultural foreign policy. Last but not least, the author offers an in-depth concluding discussion of the possible and recommended trajectories that U.S. cultural diplomacy shall take in the future.

29. Kenneth Osgood, *Total Cold War: Eisenhower's Secret Propaganda Battle at Home and Abroad* (Lawrence: University of Kansas Press, 2006), 27. Curiously, Osgood defends his decision not to "attempt to assess systematically the effectiveness of Ike's psychological operations because the global and chronological sweep of the book would have made such an effort nearly impossible." He adds: "Any arguments I might have made to that end would have stretched the available evidence beyond credulity. In addition there were also intrinsic problems with some of the sources that were available. The USIA's records, for example, are filled with documents

titled 'Evidence of Effectiveness,' but these were compiled for the express purpose of selling the information program to Congress. They were anything but proof of effectiveness." H-Diplo, "*Total Cold War* Roundtable Review," *H-Net: Humanities & Social Sciences Online* (February 26, 2007): 21, accessed April 4, 2010, http://h-diplo .org/roundtables/PDF/TotalColdWar-complete.pdf. For a discussion of a variety of cultural diplomacy efforts in one volume, including the *American National Exhibition* in Moscow in 1959, see David Caute, *The Dancer Defects: The Struggle for Cultural Supremacy during the Cold War* (Oxford: Oxford University Press, 2003). Arndt, similarly, points out, "Cultural diplomacy is ill-understood because it is complex, proliferant, and multi-tasked. It is also reticent—its successes are most often invisible," *First Resort of Kings*, xii.

30. Kenneth Osgood, from March 10, 2008, lecture at the Miller Center for Public Affairs, YouTube video, 5:09, posted by MaAmericanpresident, March 10, 2008, http://www.youtube.com/watch?v=0rBdjBZooas.

31. See Greg Castillo, *Cold War on the Home Front: The Soft Power of Midcentury Design* (Minneapolis: University of Minnesota Press, 2010), and Laura Belmonte, *Selling the American Way: U.S. Propaganda and the Cold War* (Philadelphia: University of Pennsylvania Press, 2008).

32. While not central to this study, a discussion of important academic writing on the intertwining of culture and consumption, especially in relation to the promotion of national prestige, will be acknowledged more fully in the chapter of this study that looks into international trade fairs as sites of "consumer" cultural production.

33. For an understanding of the trajectory of the use of art in U.S. Cold War cultural diplomacy, see Michael, L. Krenn, *Fall-Out Shelters for the Human Spirit: American Art and the Cold War* (Chapel Hill: University of North Carolina Press, 2005). For the troubled *Advancing American Art* exhibition that briefly traveled in the Soviet bloc, see Taylor D. Littleton and Maltby Sykes, *Advancing American Art: Painting, Politics and Cultural Confrontation at Mid-Century* (Tuscaloosa: University of Alabama Press, 1989) and Serge Guilbaut, *How New York Stole the Idea of Modern Art: Abstract Expressionism, Freedom and the Cold War* (Chicago: University of Chicago Press, 1983).

34. See Robert H. Haddow, *Pavilions of Plenty: Exhibiting American Culture Abroad in the 1950s* (Washington DC, Smithsonian Institution, 1997) and Tomas Tolvaisas, "Cold War 'Bridge-Building' U.S. Exchange Exhibits and Their Reception in the Soviet Union, 1959–1967," *Journal of Cold War Studies* 12, no. 4 (Fall 2010): 3–31.

35. For a discussion of the modern Western kitchen as a cultural diplomacy tool, see Ruth Oldenziel and Karin Zachmann, *Cold War Kitchen: Americanization, Technology, and European Users* (Cambridge, MA: MIT Press, 2009).

36. See, for example, Tuch, *Communicating with the World*; Cynthia P. Schneider, "Diplomacy That Works: 'Best Practices' in Cultural Diplomacy" (Cultural Diplomacy Research Series, Center for Arts and Culture, Washington, DC, 2003), among others.

37. See Emily S. Rosenberg, *Spreading the American Dream: American Economic and Cultural Expansion, 1890–1945* (New York: Hill and Wang, 1982).

38. For an investigation into how art historical theory has collided and converged with the history of collecting and display, see, for example, Christopher Whitehead, "Establishing the Manifesto: Art Histories in the Nineteenth-Century Museum," in *Museum Revolutions: How Museums Change and Are Changed*, ed. Simon J. Knell, Suzanne MacLeod, and Sheila Watson (New York: Routledge, 2007), 48–60.

39. These conceptual problems with understanding exhibitions were clarified for me by Simon Knell, email, March 2009.

40. Elaine Heumann Gurian, "Noodling Around with Exhibition Opportunities," in *Exhibiting Cultures: The Poetics and Politics of Museum Display*, ed. Ivan Karp and Steven D. Lavine (Washington, DC: Smithsonian Institution, 1991), 178.

41. Eco, "A Theory of Expositions," 292.

42. John Brewer, from discussion at a one-day conference on "The History of Collecting and Display," cosponsored by the University of Southern California and the Getty Research Institute, Los Angeles, April 2, 2004.

43. Susan Sontag, "Against Interpretation," in *Art History and its Methods: A Critical Anthology*, ed. Eric Fernie (London: Phaidon, 1995), 218.

44. See Thomas Crow, *The Intelligence of Art* (Chapel Hill: University of North Carolina Press, 1999), 35; Meyer Schapiro, *Romanesque Art: Selected Papers* (New York: George Braziller, 1977), 102–30.

45. Crow, *The Intelligence of Art*, 23.

46. I would like to acknowledge Malcolm Baker, whose course on the history of collecting and display at USC in the spring of 2005 provided me with various creative conceptual methods for understanding exhibitions that have come and gone.

47. Stephen Bann, "Meaning/Interpretation," in *Critical Terms for Art History*, 2nd ed., ed. Robert S. Nelson and Richard Shiff (Chicago: University of Chicago Press), 128.

48. See Simon J. Knell, "Museums, Fossils and the Cultural Revolution of Science: Mapping Change in the Politics of Knowledge in Early Nineteenth-Century Britain," in *Museum Revolutions: How Museums Change and Are Changed*, ed. Simon J. Knell, Suzanne MacLeod, and Sheila Watson (London: Routledge, 2007), 30.

49. See, for instance, Iwona Blazwick, "Temple/White Cube/Laboratory," in *What Makes A Great Exhibition?*, ed. Paula Marincola (Philadelphia: Philadelphia Exhibitions Initiative, 2006). Blazwick supports the idea that any exhibition space is a biased cultural landscape: "The exhibition space, be it museum or laboratory, can no longer be understood as neutral, natural, or universal but rather as thoroughly prescribed by the psychodynamics of politics, economics, geography, and subjectivity," ibid, 118.

Abbreviations

AIEP	Arts in Embassies Program
ANEM	*American National Exhibition* in Moscow
ARBA	American Revolution Bicentennial Administration
Archives II	National Archives (College Park, Maryland)
CIAA (OIAA)	Office of the Coordinator of Inter-American Affairs
CPI	Committee on Public Information (in World War I)
CU	Bureau of Educational and Cultural Affairs
FRUS	Foreign Relations of the United States
LACMA	Los Angeles County Museum of Art
LBJL	Lyndon B. Johnson Library
MoMA	Museum of Modern Art
NA	National Archives
NATO	North Atlantic Treaty Organization
NSC	National Security Council
OCB	Operations Coordinating Board (in Eisenhower era)
OITF	Office of International Trade Fairs
OWI	Office of War Information (World War II)
PPF	President's Personal File (Truman Library Archives)
PPP	Public Papers of the Presidents
RG	Research Group
USIA	United States Information Agency
USICA	United States International Communication Agency
USIS	United States Information Service (term for USIA overseas)
VOA	Voice of America
WAC	War Advertising Council

CHAPTER ONE

From Megafauna to Megashows to MoMA

A Historical Overview of U.S. Cultural Exhibitions Abroad

What then is the American, this new man? . . . He is an American, who, leaving behind him all his ancient prejudices and manners, receives new ones from the new mode of life he has embraced, the new government he obeys, and the new rank he holds. He has become an American by being received in the broad lap of our great Alma Mater. Here individuals of all races are melted into a new race of man, whose labors and posterity will one day cause great changes in the world. Americans are the western pilgrims.[1]

In order to understand better the exhibitions that fall within the main timeline of this study (1955–1975) and the nationalistic elements they reveal, this chapter offers a historical perspective on American attempts at display for national prestige from the early years of the nineteenth century through World War II. This discussion takes on three important historical episodes that bring into high relief the argument that since its inception, the U.S. government has not only had an eye trained on outside perceptions and used exhibitions to shape them but has revealed a zealousness to prove a certain image of America through these cultural ventures. These examples will also demarcate various methods the U.S. government used to influence foreign audiences. Ranging from scientific displays to popular entertainment to fine art, they represent exhibitionary practices that would be mimicked throughout the nineteenth century, the early decades of the twentieth century, and later, during the main timeframe of this study. The additional questions this chapter takes on are: How does a national government shape a message

1

through the content of an exhibition to be sent overseas? In what ways do private partners, such as commercial interests and learned societies as well as museums, shape these decisions?

Each of the exhibitions to be addressed in this chapter was developed at a crucial juncture in American history and was supported directly and indirectly by the U.S. government to teach the world about America. These are: (1) Rembrandt Peale's voyage to London to show the exhumed remains of the American mastodon, a display that was encouraged by President Thomas Jefferson; (2) the American pavilion at the Great Exhibition of 1851, organized by the fledgling Smithsonian Institution; and (3) the United Hemisphere Poster Competition, one of many competitions-turned-exhibitions that toured Latin America through the Office of the Coordinator of Inter-American Affairs (CIAA) in the early 1940s, made possible by the Museum of Modern Art in New York. It will be shown that these exhibitions carried nationalistic intentions, born of a uniquely American attitude based on insecurity and pretensions to a distinctly American indomitability.

Moreover, these events constituted an effort that far transcended the mere sharing of culture. These exhibitions were also ideological weaponry deployed to counter misinformation about America. In this sense, this chapter will address how the United States decided to represent itself through exhibitions overseas as its status as a nation was a new and ever-changing phenomenon to a global political community that continued to be shaped by the influence of European powers. A guiding consideration at the outset is:

> How do sovereign states represent their real or apparent changing world status to other states and actors in the international system? Public diplomacy cannot be seen as a static model. It's simply changing all the time. Dynamic models in how a country represents itself to the world are necessary since conditions of power, both hard and soft, can change, wax and wane, and so forth.[2]

The Genesis of Projecting Nationhood through Cultural Exhibitions

Since before the days of the American republic, the founders of what would become the United States expressed concern of how the new nation, based on democratic principles forged in the Revolutionary War, would be viewed on the world political stage. George Washington stated, "We are a young nation and have a character to establish. It behooves us therefore to set out right, for first impressions will be lasting, indeed are all in all."[3] The Founding Fathers had already declared on July 4, 1776, to "let Facts be submitted to the candid world" thereby to maintain a "decent respect to the opinion of mankind." This call for a nascent public diplomacy, that is, a transparent foreign-policy-making process, was symbolic in the building of what historian Strobe Talbott calls "not a nation-state so much as an idea-state—a new light unto the other nations of the world."[4] While young America and its newly minted citizens certainly expressed notions that they were exceptional people in extraordinarily auspicious circumstances, these feelings of moral superiority would be tempered by a unique inferiority complex to prove to other countries that America should be acknowledged "the first new nation."[5] The observation that America was exceptional is linked to Alexis de Tocqueville, the first writer to describe the United States as such in 1831.[6] Historian Gordon Wood adds, "Our beliefs in liberty, equality, constitutionalism, and the well-being of ordinary people came out of the Revolutionary era. So too did our idea that we Americans are a special people with a special destiny to lead the world toward liberty and democracy."[7]

However, the message of "submitting Facts to the candid world" carried a second meaning during the American Revolution. In a way, this phrase primed the pump for several attempts by the colonials to provide the enemy with their own version of the "Facts," what Nicholas Cull terms "international disinformation," "ideological projection," or, more plainly, propaganda. This reframing of the truth for political ends served as analogue to American military efforts, which together represented the reaction to George III and what were considered Great Britain's intolerable policies toward the American colonies. Cull writes: "New and radical governments have always needed to explain their politics to the world, and hence America's Declaration of Independence was crafted with an international audience in mind, and introduced its catalog of grievances against the British crown."[8]

This depiction of the U.S. government suggests that the American republic, by virtue of its newness and innate sense that it was in many ways exceptional, became aware of the obligation to take the pulse of world public opinion and used soft-power diplomacy, in this case persuasive information, to explain its policies and values. The project of international exhibitions, however, would turn these explanatory efforts into cultural outreach for national prestige, which quite often heralded an idealized image of America.

The nation was, in a way, inventing itself, and, as Talbott insists, "its self-invention required a distinctive myth of nationhood, based not on purity of blood but on purity of ideals."[9] The exploration, then, of historical episodes in which America invented (and reinvented) itself through cultural exhibitions that were sent abroad to shape the attitudes of foreign audiences serves to locate historically the origin and evolution of a nationalist exhibitionary impulse. Starting in the early nineteenth century, the United States became, in the words of Edward Bernays, "a creator of events,"[10] and deployed cultural exhibitions that often challenged verisimilitude. These events, or "pseudo-events," as has been noted by Boorstin, trod a fine line between reality, myth, and make-believe, often in order to counter jingoistic attitudes toward America but also to forge an as yet unachieved identity.

Certainly the founding leaders of the United States were not the first to question America's self-image. As historian David Kennedy maintains, European powers had interpreted and reinterpreted the meaning of what would eventually become the United States, *bien avant la lettre*:

> All commentators on America . . . had drawn from a conceptual inventory that was abundantly stocked even before 1492, and substantially enriched immediately thereafter. That inventory contained countless possible images—America as the land of promise or delusion, a natural Eden or a howling wilderness, home to Fortune's favorites or fools, Nature's noblemen or ignoble savages, the enlightened or the duped, just to name a few.[11]

America was essentially an image and a myth before it became a concrete reality, much less a sovereign identity. No one really knew or could agree on what America was, and this vagueness, this lack of scientific method in gaining a conceptual foothold, would ultimately serve as less of a blessed *tabula rasa* upon which America could form itself than a curse wrought by centuries of conjecture, most of which was negative.[12] Antonello Gerbi's *The Dispute of the New World: The History of a Polemic, 1750–1900* tackles the heterogeneity of the European argument about America, whose fundamental concern was not truth but rather "a search for synthesis, a need to account for all parts of the world, both behind and beyond Europe, to bring within reach of man's mind and understanding the entire world, and within that world to find Europe the most complete and richest part."[13] With the discovery of the New World came the discussion of its character, from its human inhabitants to its flora and fauna. Kennedy emphasizes: "What is at issue here is the emergence in the immediate aftermath of Columbus's discovery of a dialogue about the American character that has recognizably endured with only slight modifications for more than five centuries."[14] While extreme theories abounded as to whether the New World would evolve into nothing short of a biblical paradise or Dante-like hell, one of the common beliefs that gained traction was the assertion that the quality of all things American was weaker than what could be found on the European continent. Furthermore, it would be this theory of American degeneracy that would preoccupy the Founding

Fathers well into the first two decades of America's nationhood. While the broad theme of anti-Americanism is outside the purview of this research, it is important to acknowledge that the European imagining of America was conjectural and sorely uninformed. In a way, these early years of identity and soul searching witnessed, in Kennedy's words,

> America's transition from a tabula rasa, or at least an unformed youth—a historyless object onto which various representations, hopes, and fears could be projected—to a mature subject whose own actions increasingly defined its identity, and which, not merely incidentally, at the same time began seeking ways of asserting itself in the world as never before.[15]

America needed first to "represent itself to itself," according to Christopher Looby, who describes a postcolonial America whose leaders feared social disintegration as a result of cultural heterogeneity. The nation was fragmented by its conflicting "racial, ethnic, religious, linguistic, sectional, local, and ideological categories of self-definition and social loyalty."[16] Based on this idea, it was incumbent on American leaders to represent itself to the world. As Looby engages, it was by way of the "universal language" of scientific inquiry, fostered by philosophical societies in America and Europe, that Thomas Jefferson found a method to communicate with the Comte de Buffon, the leading naturalist of his day who was the foremost champion of the spurious claim of American degeneracy. For this reason, the Linnaen system of classification of the natural world provided the impression of an explanation for the totality of nature as well as the appearance of social unanimity.[17]

The first of the three historical episodes that follow in this chapter substantiates the origin of American cultural diplomacy through international exhibitions.

I. An American Mastodon in London

In early America, the founding fathers combined patriotism and prehistoric nature to create an American monster—a symbol of overwhelming power in a psychologically insecure society. The doctrine that gave birth to this ferocious prehistoric creature was the common belief in the savagery of the natural world, including the human inhabitants of the lands that the European settlers termed an uninhabited wilderness. In many respects, the master metaphor of early American culture was this idea of the wilderness, or what might be more appropriately called the myth of wild nature.[18]

Legends abounded surrounding the mysterious animal, from stirring Indian portrayals of a rampaging quadruped that gorged itself on elk and deer whole to the religious fervor endowed by Puritan religious reformer Cotton Mather, based upon the first partial remains unearthed in 1705.[19] For centuries, Europeans had exhumed bones and fossils of large terrestrial animals that became "highly prized items in early 'cabinets of curiosities.'"[20] In 1739, a French military party found at Big Bone Lick, Kentucky, on the Ohio River, a potter's field of an array of bones and tusks. These were sent to Paris and remained largely unnoticed in the royal Jardin du roi, King Louis XV's private *wunderkammer*. In 1741 the Royal Society in London published a report on mammoth bones discovered in Siberia that "made its identification as an elephant convincing to naturalists and well-known throughout the Republic of Letters."[21] Why the reception of the mammoth bones in Siberia yielded a subtler reaction from Europeans than the discovery of the American "mammoth" is as follows:

> The close parallel between the Russian and American sides of this issue has been obscured by the assumption of "exceptionalism" among United States historians of the colonial and early republican periods. For naturalists, there was no practical difference between a fossil bone collected by a servant of the absolutist Russian empire and one acquired from a citizen of the newly independent and relatively democratic United States; the sharply contrasted political cultures of the respective territories were totally irrelevant to the interpretation of the fossil specimens.[22]

By 1762, Buffon, keeper of the Jardin, theorized in his *Histoire naturelle* "the mammoth as one of the animals common to both Old and New Worlds."[23] However, Buffon and anatomist Louis-Jean-Marie Daubenton would wrestle for decades with the true identity of the American *incognitum*, or "unknown." Important questions lingered as late as the early nineteenth century as to the animal's status as an herbivore or carnivore (a result of the American animal's curiously pointed molars versus the flat grinders of the Siberian mammoth) and whether or not it was a living mammal or an extinct antediluvian monster. These mysterious bones exhumed from Big Bone Lick and the Upper Hudson River Valley in Orange County, New York, during the second half of the eighteenth century fulfilled a need for Jefferson: they would leave no doubt as to a grand prehistory to what would become the United States. He was keenly aware that although the United States had gained political freedom from Great Britain and France, it just as vitally needed both to measure up to and separate itself symbolically from the

Old World. This included making itself distinct from Eurocentric notions of culture.

A Deist, like many of his generation, Jefferson held an unpalatable view on extinction, and this idea extended to the discovery of the mastodon fossils that he would collect, study, and promote for most of his life and which would, in his mind, silence the promoters of the American degeneracy claim.[24] Further, the Founding Fathers believed in the "Great Chain of Being," as explored by authors John Locke and Alexander Pope, that the hierarchy of nature, the *scala naturae*, was established by God's will alone and therefore immutable.[25] Jefferson and his peers adhered to Enlightenment values that centered on the idealization of human reason through science and the perfection of human life through the rational application of laws, education, and moral instruction. In a sense, they were millenarians both in the Christian and also arguably in the romantic sense of the word: they believed in the arrival of an age of peace and prosperity, based on reason and justice.[26]

While the story of Charles Willson Peale's "mammoth" and its display to Europeans is well documented by a number of scholars,[27] it serves an altogether different purpose when this tale is considered as the start of a much longer historical trajectory of American attempts at cultural diplomacy through international exhibitions. This first historical episode of the three addressed in this chapter ably conforms to Bennett's theory of the exhibitionary complex. These displays, in other words, should perhaps be seen as examples of the young American republic's declaration of sovereignty through exhibitions or, in Bennett's terms, the "public dramaturgy of power" for foreign audiences, whom he reads as "witnesses whose presence was just as essential to a display of power."[28]

It should not be forgotten that Jefferson was anti-British and pro-French, the French who saw the Revolutionary War as a fight by colonists against the tyranny of George III. War of Independence historians acknowledge the patriots versus tyrants point of view, while others see the events surrounding the struggle for independence as America's first foray into self-management and political resolve. A comment from a French officer to an English politician in 1782 promotes the idea of a unique American identity based on self-reliance and self-defense to the point of isolationism: "No opinion was clearer than that though the people of America might be conquered by well-disciplined European troops, the country of America was unconquerable."[29]

It would be the year before, in 1781, that Jefferson began drafting his *Notes on the State of Virginia*. In part conceived as a statement outlining the political structure, geographical features, and the flora and fauna of the region, it served principally as a rebuke to the assessment of American culture

by Abbé Raynal, who readily spread the degeneracy theory to American society: "One must be astonished that America has not yet produced one good
poet, one able mathematician, one man of genius in a single art or a single
science."[30] Jefferson responded in his *Notes*: "As in philosophy and war, so in
government, in oratory, in painting, in the plastic art, we might shew that
America, though but a child of yesterday, has already given hopeful proofs
of genius. . . . We therefore suppose, that this reproach is as unjust as it is
unkind; and that, of the geniuses which adorn the present age, America
contributes its full share."[31] Written during the final years of the Revolutionary War, Jefferson methodically defended what was tantamount to a young
America's global reputation. This intellectual battle continued with Buffon,
who perpetuated the theme of American degeneracy: "In America, therefore,
animated Nature is weaker, less active, and more circumscribed in the variety
of her productions; for we perceive, from the enumeration of the American
animals, that the numbers of species is not only fewer, but that, in general,
all the animals are much smaller than those of the Old Continent."[32]

Jefferson's rejoinder contained his point of view on the American "mammoth," eschewing what was at the time pseudoscientific speculation on the
American mastodon's true nature and embracing indigenous mythology fueled by patriotic drive.[33] At a time when America knew it could not boast
of great traditions in the visual or literary arts, science would become the
catalyst toward the creation of learned societies such as the American Philosophical Society and the American Academy of Arts and Sciences.[34] The
practice of employing ancient myth and the bones that inspire it is not new.
Scholar Don Fowler conducts archaeological case studies on specific cultures that commandeered indigenous myths and archaeological remains to
legitimize and persuade others to meet nationalistic goals: "Nation states, or
partisans thereof, control and allocate symbolic resources as one means of legitimizing power and authority, and in pursuit of their perceived nationalistic
goals and ideologies. A major symbolic resource is the past."[35] Jefferson and
Charles Willson Peale embraced the Indian legends that conveniently fit
into this proto-paleontology, creating ultimately an era marked by the geomythology or cryptozoology of fossils turned political instruments. As scholar
Manfredo Tafuri confirms: "Throughout the greater part of the eighteenth
century, principles of scientific classification testified to a mixture of theo-
cratic, rationalist, and protoevolutionist systems of thought."[36] In 1789, Jefferson was apprised of the discovery of unidentifiable fossils in Virginia, what
Gerbi describes as a "prehistoric anteater" that Jefferson later "invented" or
transformed wishfully into an "American super-lion or super-tiger." In what
would become known in scientific circles as the Megalonyx, or "the Great

Claw," Jefferson found another opportunity to prove to European naysayers the physical vibrancy of the New World.[37]

Exhuming the Mastodon and Its Display in London

In 1799, Vice President Jefferson had learned of significant fossil remains in upstate New York. It would be two years later that Charles Willson Peale,[38] Jefferson's longtime colleague from the American Philosophical Society, would make the journey and acquire the bones for two hundred dollars. Exhuming the mastodon bones from the marl pit was no easy task. The swampy conditions and physical distance from a major city made preparations all the more challenging.[39] Peale's son Rembrandt, after helping his father assemble mastodon skeletons in his Philadelphia museum, decided to take the second, mostly complete skeleton on a European tour in 1802. For the London audience, Rembrandt published two separate pamphlets with the singular focus of declaring that the mastodon was indeed a carnivore, based on the structure of its molars and the downward turned tusks (figure 1.1).[40] The following year, armed with President Thomas Jefferson's personal endorsement,[41] Rembrandt Peale set out to London with a nearly complete skeleton of an American mastodon. Conveyed to Europe during the Peace of

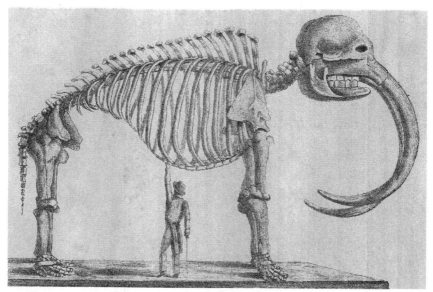

Figure 1.1.   Lithographed illustration showing the "Skeleton of the Young Mammoth in the Philadelphia Museum."
From Édouard de Montulé, *Voyage en Amérique, en Italie, en Sicile, et en Egypte, Pendant les Années.* London: Printed for Sir Richard Phillips and Co., 1821.

Amiens, the intention was to make a visit to France after the London showing of the skeleton.

The mastodon was ridiculed in the British press. Rembrandt Peale wrote
to his father "that the British would much prefer a dancing bear to their
scientific curiosity."[42] Yet while the intent of displaying the mastodon was
for entertainment and scientific comparative anatomy, this was Peale's nationalist gesture, spurred by Jefferson's shared fascination with the mastodon
as national symbol. As historian Joel Orosz explains, Peale's own identity as
a patriot shaped much of his practice as a museum professional:

> Many of the early museum proprietors were self-consciously patriotic in the
> realms of art, science, and history. They understood and envied Europe's cul-
> tural primacy in these fields and sought to promote American achievements
> in them. This effort to cultivate American accomplishments in intellectual
> endeavors, to the exclusion of European influences, will be referred to as cul-
> tural nationalism.[43]

Ultimately, the mastodon display in London should be viewed more as
an example of the exhibitionary complex in action, an attempt to shape
pervasive views toward America through the persuasive power of museum
display.[44] In his treatise on the mammoth that saw various editions published
in Great Britain at the time the mastodon was on display, Rembrandt Peale
satisfies both personal and nationalist agendas. The introduction, a missive
to his father and sponsor, Charles, curiously extols the latter's growing reputation in the museum trade: "The Museum, of which you are the founder,
already rivalling many in Europe," as well as invoking the mammoth itself as
the inspiration for the first national museum in America:

> The bones of the Mammoth first produced the idea of a Museum, which, after
> eighteen years of rapid approach to maturity, under the unprecedented exer-
> tions of an individual, has in its turn enabled you to place among its treasures
> nearly a perfect skeleton of the Mammoth—the first of American animals, in
> the first of American Museums.[45]

Though the question at this juncture is not which came first, the "mammoth" or the museum, it is noteworthy that Peale takes on Buffon's argument
and his charge of American degeneracy by virtue of the display of the mastodon, stating it is "a well established fact, that every country has its peculiar
inhabitants. Had the celebrated Buffon attended better to this truth, he
would have saved himself some needless observations and theoretic fancies,

with respect to the old and new world; but we should likewise have lost the able reply of Jefferson."[46]

Conclusion

The transmutation of this animal symbol into an identifier of the United States poses questions not only to the science of the times but also to contemporaneous belief systems. The appropriation of indigenous myth as well as the construction of wholly false claims based on archaeological evidence thrust Thomas Jefferson, Charles Willson Peale, and Rembrandt Peale into a world of pseudoscience, geomythology, and cryptozoology. Rudwick claims that Jefferson "may well have hoped that his country would in fact be able to boast the world's largest living terrestrial animal. But his argument was not just a piece of chauvinistic boosterism. It was also a variant of an argument long used by other naturalists to explain more humble fossils: the Ohio animal, like the sea lily, might turn out to be a living fossil."[47] Loren Eiseley comments on the unsure footing the proto-paleontological community held in assessing the real nature of prehistoric animals and the idea of change in this realm:

> It must be remembered that the eighteenth century and the beginning years of the nineteenth marked the rise of intense zoological interest among the intelligentsia of the New and Old Worlds. The great eighteenth century forerunners of Darwin—Buffon, Cuvier, and others—were beginning to approach, with much hesitancy and many misgivings, the problem of specific change. Others fought back with vigor. America, with its strange animals, its mysterious bones, and a human race unaccounted for in Biblical terms, had contributed to those uneasy stirrings.[48]

The lack of full knowledge surrounding the origins and contemporary status of the mastodon was perhaps not entirely a reckless prevarication on the part of Jefferson and Peale. As Looby illustrates, these men could have had misgivings about the "history" they were trying to sell to themselves and to Europeans.

> . . . even Peale, otherwise the least likely individual to entertain nominalistic doubts, wondered, perhaps unconsciously, whether his assured, static view of the world wasn't, in fact, an illusion. . . . And this again raises the question of whether all these attempts to present something as reconciled that actually is not, whether it be the heterogeneous elements of nature, or the social diversity and conflict that natural disorder represented . . . isn't one of the standard ideological reflexes of the period.[49]

Though Charles Willson Peale saw his role as a collector of natural animal specimens and educator of the people and showman who offered "rational amusement" to the public, he also followed what was arguably a doctrinal focus to make a museum that would not only educate Americans but eventually rival his European counterparts. Joel Barlow, one of the Hartford Wits, a group of Connecticut intellectuals, rallied against the European theory of American degeneracy in a work entitled "The Anarchiad," in which he supported his friend in "the idea of seeing ourselves vindicated from those despicable aspirations which have long been thrown upon us and echoed from one ignorant scribbler to another in all languages of Europe."[50]

There is a final point to consider in the context of Jefferson's concerns to make clear to the European superpowers of Great Britain and France the worthiness of America's character based on the prehistoric past. This was the president's sponsorship of Meriwether Lewis and William Clark's exploration of upper Louisiana and the Missouri River Valley, starting in 1803. As historian George Herring avers, this "scientific expedition" was truly a ruse for Jefferson to ascertain the limits of Spanish military power in the region. But it also lends credibility to Jefferson's expansionist bent toward creating a nation that would one day span from the Atlantic to the Pacific.[51] It was Jefferson who said in 1801: "[Our success] furnishes a new proof of the falsehood of Montesquieu's doctrine, that a republic can be preserved only in a small territory. The reverse is the truth."[52] He had also stated earlier in 1785 to John Jay: "Our people are decided in the opinion that it is necessary for us to take a share in the occupation of the ocean . . . and that line of policy be pursued which will render the use of that element as great as possible to them. . . . But what will be the consequence? Frequent wars without a doubt. . . . Our commerce on the ocean and in other countries must be paid for by frequent war."[53] There, also, in Jefferson's "empire of liberty," was where the natural history of America's past and future strength resided. According to Andrew Isenberg, Jefferson was convinced that all large animal species had fled the Atlantic coast due to Euro-American settlement and that there had to exist in the West "not only 'elephants and lions' but 'mammoths and megalonyxes.'"[54]

Jefferson eventually gathered his fair share of detractors on both sides of the Atlantic concerning the popularity of the mastodon. John Adams condemned Jefferson's overemphasis on what the fossils indicated for the identity of the American republic. In a letter to the mystic philosopher Francis Adrian van der Kamp during Jefferson's first term as president, Adams ridicules Jefferson's evangelical belief in the "mammoth." In short, this righteous symbol of a young America had run out of steam, and Jefferson's political opponents knew this well, while in London the exhibition fizzled without making any notable cultural, much less political, impression.[55]

One of the main foreign-policy objectives of the United States in its early years was to endeavor to project the right image of this young, insecure, but seemingly privileged nation that would serve as an example to the world. The interstitial relationship between Jefferson, Charles Willson Peale's American Museum, and the scientific nature of the mastodon, reveal the complex origins of a nation seeking to define itself, an effort bordering at times on the sensational. Political conditions in early America, shaped by the Revolution, indicated the exceptional position the United States held domestically and globally. Exactly how the young nation would fulfill John Winthrop's inference of America as an example of freedom and democracy to the world, as "a city upon a hill," had yet to be thoroughly explored.[56]

As the following two sections of this chapter will further demonstrate, the leaders of the United States would continue through its displays, in the words of Phillip K. Dick, to "build universes which . . . fall apart."[57] It is worthwhile, then, to treat the mammoth story as a parable for all later attempts of the United States to represent itself through cultural exhibitions overseas.

II. American Slavery at the Great Exhibition of 1851

After Jefferson made his case, and for the next seventy years, other Americans . . . such as Washington Irving, Henry David Thoreau, and Ralph Waldo Emerson—would not only denounce the insidious idea of degeneracy, but would use it in ways that would have made Buffon, Raynal, and de Pauw cringe. For what happened was this: in countering the idea of New World inferiority, these writers and poets created a novel self-image for the United States and its inhabitants—America as a beautiful, vast, resource-rich region, and its inhabitants as healthy, hardworking people in tune with nature.[58]

We are so young a people that we feel the want of nationality, and delight in whatever asserts our national "American" existence. We have not, like England and France, centuries of achievements and calamities to look back on; we have no *record* of Americanism and we feel its want.[59]

In 1850, America was an independent, creative, entrepreneurial nation, with an explosion of new inventions and unlimited potential for what would become its own Industrial Revolution in the second half of the nineteenth century. Politically, the United States witnessed the fracturing of the po-litical system with the Whig Party disappearing and the emergence of the

Republican and Know-Nothing Parties. Though several issues of national importance were debated, such as immigration, temperance, and tariffs, the central political discussion in the United States in the 1850s was over slavery. During this time, the nation began aligning itself regionally between slave versus free states, based on agreements in the Compromise of 1850. In addition, the ideologically split United States, growing more distant from Old World influences, enjoyed what Frederick Jackson Turner asserts the country has identified with all along, something no other nation in the world had: Manifest Destiny.

> American social development has been continually beginning over again on the frontier. This perennial rebirth, this fluidity of American life, this expansion westward with its new opportunities, its continuous touch with the simplicity of primitive society, furnish the forces dominating American character. The true point of view in the history of this nation is not the Atlantic coast, it is the Great West.[60]

For a country whose citizens St. John de Crèvecoeur deemed "western pilgrims," the frontier held unlimited notions for thousands of Americans who sought a new beginning for themselves. Wagon trains headed west from St. Joseph, Missouri, the leaping-off point to the "Wild West," Sutter's Mill, and the California Gold Rush. Immigration as a result of the Irish potato famine spurred romantic notions of land ownership as settlers sought to stake their claim on the ever-receding frontier. From Europe alone, between 1836 and 1914, there exceeded thirty million immigrants, people who came to America in search of opportunity, escape, and new starts.[61] According to historian Robert Dalzell, democracy in America during this period meant not only entrepreneurial equality of opportunity and *laissez-faire*, but Manifest Destiny and the desire to see American ideas and institutions spread throughout the world as well.[62]

However, despite all the advances of westward expansion and achievements in the industrial arts, the national psyche of the United States in the 1850s suffered "a disturbing sense of remoteness from the heroic age of the Revolution."[63] Looby hints at the fragility of the young republic:

> Operating after 1776 under a bad constitution that was not even adopted until 1781, and then replaced by 1789, the viability of the republic was very much in question for several decades following independence. The threat of monarchical counter-revolution or military putsch, local insurrections like Shays' Rebellion and the Whiskey Rebellion, several secessionist movements, a series of treasonous plots against the state, and regular eruptions of mob violence were the conspicuous features of political life in the early republic.[64]

The nation needed visible, steadfast proof that it stood on a firm conceptual ground. As historian Robert Byer asserts, it would be the production of public symbols in the form of grand monuments, such as that devoted to George Washington, begun on the Federal Mall in 1848, that would, ". . . it was hoped, 'rebuild continuity with the past,' in particular with its heroisms of republican civic virtue that to many seemed to have given way to a pervasive, selfish materialism, and with the idea of a national community and the passion of a unifying patriotism that sectional conflict was making more remote."[65] The nation had much to show of itself to symbolize its success, and the opportunity to present America on a grand scale at the first world's fair, devoted to "the Industry of All Nations," would prove auspicious.[66]

While there had already been on the European continent a long history of trade fairs and fine art exhibitions, including among them shows that addressed industrial progress, France still held the monopoly on success in this medium.[67] This inspired the Lord Consort Prince Albert, husband to Queen Victoria, to predict while at Mansion House in London on March 21, 1850, that the Great Exhibition of 1851 would serve as "a true test and a living picture of the point of development at which the whole of mankind has arrived . . . and a new starting point from which all nations will be able to direct their further exertions."[68] Henry Cole, co-organizer of the exhibition, and his committee would support the prince to press for the 1851 exhibition to be international, with emphasis on British design, its superiority, and its potential to improve taste. The *Official Descriptive and Illustrated Catalogue of the Great Exhibition* would later celebrate the vision of these men in rhetorical pomp, concretizing the aesthetic and commodified nature of the Exhibition itself, "the most varied and wonderful collection of objects ever beheld."[69] Wornum's award-winning essay, "The Exhibition as a Lesson in Taste," addressed the underpinning philosophy of the Great Exhibition: "The great object of attainment is Taste, which is not a mere impulse of the fancy, but dependent upon the operations of reason as completely as any other conclusion respecting good or bad, or right or wrong, to which we attain by the mind's experience."[70] In short, the philosophy behind the event was informed by the Enlightenment value of education, lessons of democracy, and liberalism as promoted by the French Revolution, national healing in Britain from the Napoleonic wars, and the advent of free trade. These factors fostered an aura of cosmopolitan vigor in the minds of British manufacturers and designers and played a significant role in Henry Cole's thinking about the goals of the Great Exhibition. Cole's mandate, to improve life through social reforms for all people, in Great Britain and elsewhere, reflected, as historian Davis suggests, the "'Victorian cult of progress,' for which the Great Exhibition was talismanic."[71]

The United States government jumped at the news surrounding the planning for the Great Exhibition. On February 22, 1850, the American minister to London, Abbott Lawrence, took "an early interest in the matter, writing to the Secretary of the American Institute in New York . . . asking that he would pass on the information to other such organizations."[72] One of the hallmarks of the Great Exhibition that greatly appealed to Lawrence, which has become the norm for all world's fairs, *expositions universelles*, and world expos since, was its attempt to include all nations. While Great Britain would commandeer the largest physical presence in relation to floor space occupied, the spokesman for American foreign policy toward Great Britain saw a promising opportunity for his country to make a strong impression at the exhibition. The theme of Manifest Destiny is potently registered in his letter to the secretary: "I entertain an abiding confidence that we possess the material to present at the proposed exhibition such a combination of Science and Art, as will gratify the highest anticipation of that class of men who have been and will continue to be the creators of wealth, and through their inventions and labors the civilisers of mankind throughout the world."[73]

Meanwhile, Joseph Henry, the first secretary of the Smithsonian Institution and member of the organizing committee of the National Institute for the Promotion of Science and the Arts, began the byzantine task of garnering federal support for America's role in the exhibition, an opportunity he sensed would clearly be of benefit to the United States. Though the National Institute had been tapped by the State Department to serve as the central authority in coordinating the American effort at the exhibition, there was little interest in funding what was then mostly a push by the scientific community and its achievements to be represented at the Crystal Palace.[74] But Henry pressed on, nevertheless: "By means of this exhibition not only will our reputation be enhanced and our national credit increased—objects of greater importance at this time than perhaps ever before—but we shall be able to derive much valuable information from the various devices and products which will be exhibited."[75] While letters were sent to the governors of each of the United States, planning lagged. Aside from President Millard Fillmore's recommendation for the government to offer the services of a cargo ship to haul some of the exhibits to Britain, this singular instance of federal support became bogged down in congressional debate in December 1850. As Henry complained to the American botanist Asa Gray: "After much trouble the Executive Department of the Government . . . was induced to grant the use of a ship to convey the goods to England but declared its inability to appropriate a single dollar towards employing an agent to attend to the business abroad."[76] Congress could not agree on which ship would perform the duty. Ultimately, no other congressional appropriations were anticipated, and "expenses involved in representing the country were to be left to interested citizens."[77] In other words, the U.S. government, aside from lip service given from state governors and congressmen, did not have a conscious intention and little, if any, prescriptive advice in how the American section would look at the Great Exhibition. As Dalzell concludes, "In retrospect, this pattern of organization seems to have been most appropriate in the America of 1850—an America, as we have noted, thoroughly imbued with the doctrines of *laissez faire*."[78] If the United States were to have a rhetorical strategy in what America would show of itself at the Crystal Palace, this would derive entirely from individual effort and ingenuity.

During the preceding autumn, the popular press showed much interest and a measure of bravado in how America would present itself to the world:

> The Industrial Exhibition of 1851, to come off in London . . . will be a great test, full of glorious meaning in truth, and inevitable in the development of facts instructive in the morals, systems of religion, modes of government, and intellectual progress of every nation which it may represent. . . . If we mistake not, the English will learn some important lessons from their western child, whom they still associate with savage life and whom many among them regard with dignified superciliousness.[79]

While there were other examples in the press for and against the nature of the American displays at Hyde Park, the actual number of U.S. contributions was fewer than five hundred exhibits, which would not fill the space adequately. The *New York Herald* of March 26, 1851, was perhaps fearful, according to Dalzell, that the United States would take "a serious beating at the hands of the rest of the world." The popular press openly criticized the Great Exhibition itself, declaring it "a humbug" for England to raise its prosperity at the expense of the rest of the world. However, as cited above, most of the printed commentary listed the opportunity of the Great Exhibition as a chance for America to show the best it had to offer. This latter view won out, according to Dalzell.[80]

While William Makepeace Thackeray's poetic description of the Crystal Palace as a "blazing arch of lucid glass/leaps like a fountain from the grass/ to meet the sun"[81] celebrated the architectural derring-do and whimsy of the building itself, the floor plan was demarcated soberly into three broad divisions with numerous classifications for what would be displayed there. Half of the exhibition space was devoted to British goods and those of its colonies, the other half for foreign exhibitions. The main avenue would showcase objects that could be used as didactic material and designs that could positively influence the tastes of the visitors (figure 1.2, figure 1.3). Davis suggests,

Figure 1.2.   "Waiting for the Queen."
From *Dickinson's Comprehensive Pictures of The Great Exhibition of 1851*. London: Dickinson, Brothers, Her Majesty's Publishers, 1854.

"The attempt was made not only to use the space to attract the visitor, but also to emphasize the Exhibition's system of priorities. Where the transept had focused on art, however, the main avenue betrayed the wider discussion that had gone on between the Exhibition's supporters. Here, science, commerce, education, art were all honored and their union promoted."[82] The

Figure 1.3. "Waiting for the Queen" (2).
From *Dickinson's Comprehensive Pictures of The Great Exhibition of 1851*. London: Dickinson, Brothers, Her Majesty's Publishers, 1854.

exhibition contained four main categories of exhibits: manufactures, machinery, raw materials, and miscellaneous. In a pamphlet he authored in the middle of 1850, Cole visualized that "the exhibition will be one enormous unrivalled storehouse for the useful results of all human industry."[83]

The *Southern Quarterly Review* volunteered a prescient vision of success for the American section of the Great Exhibition: "The axis of civilization has been shaken and displaced . . . the scales of destiny are shifting their pieces—and while the scale of Europe descends, that of America must ascend."[84] But the U.S. effort suffered early on from poor decision making, well before the first wares arrived from the United States. The problem was this: on an enormous parcel of gallery floor space requested by the American committee that included Associate Justice Levi Woodbury of the Supreme Court, Senator Jefferson Davis, who was on the board of regents of the fledgling Smithsonian Institution, and oceanographer Matthew Maury, the U.S. exhibition commissioners displayed a curious array of products. On view were Cyrus McCormick's Virginia grain reaper, Matthew Brady's daguerreotypes, Indian rubber goods by Charles Goodyear, and Samuel Colt revolvers. Lesser items included an "air-exhausted coffin" that could hold off a corpse's physical decay, transparent soaps meant to resemble stained glass, a plaster cast of Daniel Webster, specimens of banknote printing, samples of teeth filled with gold, New Orleans moss, India-rubber shoes, specimens of alum rock and lard oil, Indian ornaments, and Cincinnati pickles (figure 1.4).

Horace Greeley, one of the American judges on hand, complained of the utilitarian aspects of the U.S. contributions, while *Punch* ridiculed the vast open space guarded by the giant cardboard American eagle.[85] Though the "pioneer simplicity and utility that dominated the American display" derived much ridicule early on from the press, in reality, the American section was moderately impressive as a result of the utility of its objects on display. On this point, however, Dalzell adds, "the British could not afford to admit it."[86] Hermione Hobhouse touches on the rich irony of the American offerings:

> The United States section was substantial, dominated by an eagle. In the centre was a full-sized model of Rider's improved Suspension Truss Bridge, surmounted by a trophy of vulcanized rubber from the Goodyear Rubber Company. . . . A large number of manufactured goods were displayed including chairs of various sorts, carriages, usually less showy and more practical than some of the European exhibits. . . . The best known of its exhibits was probably Hiram Powers' 'Greek Slave' in Parian ware, widely copied, but now somewhat of an embarrassment as it is seen as deeply politically incorrect.[87]

Figure 1.4. The United States section at the Great Exhibition of 1851.
From *Dickinson's Comprehensive Pictures of The Great Exhibition of 1851*. London: Dickinson, Brothers, Her Majesty's Publishers, 1854.

The Americans, it should be noted, were equally outspoken in their apprais-
als of European sections. The U.S. effort saw the rift between their displays
and those of the British and other European departments as "a vast contest
between the luxury, the ornamentation of absolutism on the one hand, and
republican utilitarianism on the other."[88] More severe interpretations from
the American side were also shared, calling Old World inventions "devices
which minister to the pomp of wealth and the gratification of vanity, which
feed the pride of a pampered royalty and distinguish the effeminacy of a degenerate aristocracy" and toward Russia, regarding the double-headed eagle
on their banner: "fit emblem for that two-faced incarnation of cowardice and
tyranny, which hovers to the northeast of Europe, flinging down the baleful
shadow of its power . . . on all the rising germs of freedom, love and social
intercourse." Moreover, D. Eldon Hall's appraisal of the Exhibition cited the
America section as "the one consecrated spot where freedom lives."[89]

Among the cultural capital exhibited by the United States, the most
contested American contribution was Hiram Powers's sculpture *Greek Slave*,
which *Punch* took as a cue to mock directly America's lack of humanity toward its enslaved peoples: "Why not have sent us some choice specimens of
slaves? We have the Greek Captive in dead stone—why not the Virginian
slave in living ebony?"[90] The antislavery movement at home also provided
sardonic commentary on the ideological schism between the displays of useful objects conceived as a result of American invention for the benefit of all
people with the appearance of the *Greek Slave*:

> The North American Republic will exhibit many specimens of the ingenu-
> ity and enterprises of its inhabitants. Some of them will be similar, in kind,
> to those which will be exhibited by other nations. But there is one specimen
> of human ingenuity and industry which distinguishes this Republic from all
> other nations, and that is AMERICAN SLAVERY. In this article, the United
> States stand alone and unrivalled. It is the distinctive characteristics of this
> Republic.[91]

The presentation of a thinly veiled imperial idiom like the Powers sculpture
plays to both American notions of Manifest Destiny and the racism endemic
to Victorian imperialist ideology. In both nations, Paul Young argues, the
price to be paid for the process of globalization as the exhibition defined it
was "the loss of those races unable to respond to the progressive, civilizing
climate in which they now found themselves."[92] Did then America, which
began its journey to the Great Exhibition concerned with a poor showing of
its accomplishments, reposition itself (through its displays) as superior not

only to slaves but to Europeans as well? In other words, what sort of suspension of disbelief was the American delegation expecting from European visitors? The elevation of slavery from its harsh reality into a fine art medium that harks to antiquity hints at a reactive America at the Great Exhibition and its attempt to control the inherent tension of the undeniable reality of American slavery at this time. This warring between reality versus representation and the type of knowledge imparted through the display of this aspect of America informs, moreover, what Bennett declares the intentional construction of world's fairs, based on nineteenth century classificatory schemes that bluntly represent hegemonic symptoms of participating nations. This operating assumption, or license, rather, to display examples of members of disenfranchised races or social classes, such as the slave, favored the white races and fueled Victorian notions of social, racial, and imperial superiority. This order "organized the implied public—the white citizenries of the imperialist powers—into a unity, representationally effacing divisions within the body politic in constructing a 'we' conceived as the realization, and therefore just beneficiaries, of the processes of evolution and identified as a unity in opposition to the primitive otherness of conquered peoples."[93] Paul Greenhalgh acknowledges the contradictory message between the stated goal of the exhibition of bringing people together in the name of industrial progress and the abject racism and pretensions to imperialism evident in the displays of the exhibition: "Brotherly love and understanding between nations was the single most labored aspect of exhibition diatribe, the sentiment usually being ridiculed by displays of military technology, imperial conquest and abject racism on the sites themselves."[94] In this sense, world's fairs from the beginning have expressed through nationalistic displays certain dualistic functions that satisfied on the one hand the virtues of brotherhood, education, and free trade, with the morally and physically corrupt hegemonic pretensions of the *nation displayed* on the other. It is questionable as to how the politics of memory surrounding British condemnation of American slavery eventually succumbed to extreme praise of the American showing at the exhibition.[95] Perhaps the myth of America or the myth surrounding America's evolution from a colony to a growing industrial power outshone the paradoxical nature of a display that several popular media interpreted as symbolic of the institution of slavery. Kylie Message, for instance, argues that the entertainment value of the exhibition and "its association with education" required the suspension of disbelief, which "led to a taste for otherness, so that the images of otherness became increasingly familiar due to mass production and popularity, thus constituting a recognized—and paradoxically 'authentic'—code of otherness."[96] In a way, the Great Exhibition, in its general approach to addressing improved taste through advancements in industry, represented, according to Henry Mayhew,

> the first attempt to dignify and refine toil; and, by collecting the several products of scientific and aesthetic art from every quarter of the globe into one focus, to diffuse a high standard of excellence among our operatives, and thus to raise the artistic qualities of labour, so that men, no longer working with their fingers alone, shall find that which is now mere drudgery converted into a delight, their intellects expanded, their natures softened, and their pursuits ennobled by the process.[97]

The *Illustrated Exhibitor* featured a lithograph of the *Greek Slave*, complete with explanation that smacks of travelogue instead of social statement. Without reading too much into this singular artifact, the theme of slavery was made transparent and, arguably, palatable to visitors of the American section.[98] Donald Preziosi describes the Great Exhibition as embodying the "most effective vocabulary or medium for imagining nation, empire, ethnicity, and identity in a manner that neutralized otherness while simultaneously fetishizing differences as but stylistic variations of the same."[99] This "epistemological structure" of the Crystal Palace, Preziosi notes, sets the scene for what has become a staple of world's fairs, *expositions universelles*, and expos since the beginning: nationalized pretension to power. In a sense, national pavilions at these events angle for a global prestige,[100] and this politicizing of culture through the visual harmony of display legitimized even the darkest aspects of national culture. In the case of the United States, the slavery issue would be displaced by the razzle-dazzle of commercial ingenuity and gimmickry, or "Yankee notions," which persuasively shifted the mood of the press toward the American section.

The United States would have to wait until June and July of 1851 for positive reviews of its section. American successes included the picking of the British locks by the American locksmith Hobbs, Starbuck's dray plows, reaping machines, and so forth. American daguerreotypes also won high praise, both by the popular press and the exhibition judges. The biggest American victory came, arguably, from the display of technical prowess that had no direct connection to the Great Exhibition at all. At Cowes, the U.S.-sponsored yacht *America* beat the British *Titania* at the Royal Yacht Club for the first "America's Cup" win on August 28, 1851.[101] The *Liverpool Times* delivered effusive praise to the American yachting victory and to the United States in general:

> The Yankees are no longer to be ridiculed, much less despised. The new world is bursting into greatness—walking past the old world, as the Americans did to the yachts at Cowes, "hand over hand." She dipped the Star-Spangled

Banner to the royalty of Great Britain, for superiority is ever courteous, and this grateful act indicates the direction in which our inevitable competition should proceed. America, in her own phrase, is "going ahead" and will assuredly pass us unless we accelerate our speed.[102]

For the remainder of the exhibition, the United States maintained its streak of success, receiving awards for "excellence" for Colt, Day, and Newell and overall collecting 159 medals total among its 559 exhibits, including Council and Prize medals and Honorable Mentions. According to Dalzell, "The Americans had little to complain of, to say the least. The five Council Medals awarded to Americans went to: McCormick for the reaping machine; Goodyear for his India rubber displays; a Mr. Dick for tools and presses; William Bond and Son for the invention of a new method of observing astronomical phenomena; and Gail Borden, Jr., for his 'patent meat biscuit.'"[103] In the end, while this global platform was meant to celebrate first and foremost the achievements of the British Empire, the portrayal of cultural signifiers like the *Greek Slave* and examples of American technological ingenuity served two functions: they admitted to the "candid world" that the United States was a nation fraught with troubling social institutions like slavery, and they showed that U.S. industrial ingenuity heralded America's imminent cultural ascendancy.[104]

This marked success of private contributions and individual initiative was not lost on the New York State commissioner to the fair. In his report on the Great Exhibition, Benjamin Johnson reflected on the nature of America's contribution:

> It is not by any means certain but that the influence of our exhibition has been far better upon the world, has more powerfully demonstrated the peculiar advantages of our free institutions, in the development of the energies of the people, than could have been done if the government had made a large appropriation for the purpose of preparing articles specially for the exhibition. Our exhibition was made by our citizens themselves, and showed their enterprise, their energy, their skill and ingenuity; and when this was known it was a matter of surprise to foreigners that we exhibited as much as we did.[105]

Conclusion

The Great Exhibition embodied a number of aspects of the trade fairs and world expos of the modern era in the following ways: they pioneered the peaceful bringing together of disparate peoples across all social strata. They were spectacular events in which culture was shaped, presented, and ultimately politicized through the theatrical display of commercial, industrial, and artistic items. Highlighting the entrepreneurial drive of the exhibit designers, the spatial composition and stylistic order of the exhibition pavilions themselves became part and parcel of the visitors' experience and would further contribute to the competition in cultural messages between fair participants.[106] For Americans, according to Dalzell, their reactions to it were prophetic "because while the particular ideas, attitudes, and aspirations that were brought into play by the Exhibition on this side of the Atlantic were not new, the combination of them that developed was to a considerable degree original and was to play an increasingly important role in America in the years after 1851."[107]

Taking the Great Exhibition as its cue, future international exhibitions would be preoccupied with taking on international markets with new designs that were aesthetic, utilitarian, and available to the rank-and-file visitors. They would also offer to more powerful nations a certain hegemonic function in which their individual pavilions would serve symbolically to remind visitors of the balance or imbalance of power between the various participants.[108] The United States would explore its ever-widening global influence at these events, at world's fairs at home and abroad, for the remainder of the nineteenth century, which had, according to Cull, "sharpened ideas of American exceptionalism, ethnic chauvinism, the missionary drive of the American churches, and the reformist impulse of the social campaigners. Such currents would profoundly shape American foreign policy."[109]

III. Pretenders to Hegemony: America versus Ideological Aggressors in Latin America

The fundamental purpose of a program of "Cultural Relations" in any country is to correct the image of that nation formed abroad by those who know it only through its political and military and commercial enterprise in foreign markets and in foreign places. We in this country have good reason to know how false and defamatory an image of the American people was created in the minds of the peoples of Latin America by the commercial imperialism and military interference and diplomatic condescension of the last decades of the last century and the first decades of this. We have good reason to know also what it has meant to the mutual understandings of the Western Hemisphere, to say nothing of the prestige of the United States, that the peoples of the other American Republics have been persuaded over the last twelve years that we have something more than a knowledge of investment banking, of the extraction of minerals and of the deployment of marines—that we have in fact a literature and an art and a scientific development worthy of study and respect.[110]

The idea of an "official culture" is alien to us.[111]

It would not be until the twentieth century that the first official government body would be founded devoted to the strategizing of the communication of American values abroad. The Committee on Public Information (CPI) or Creel Committee[112] would be established in April 1917 as a wartime agency to counter the propaganda of the Central Powers as the United States was drawn into World War I. Various private initiatives were also attempted throughout the interwar period to foster cultural rapprochement between the United States and the rest of the world. David Kennedy emphasizes the realpolitik of Woodrow Wilson, who "was offering a contingent internationalism for the United States, one that insisted on changing the rules and the character of the international order as a precondition for U.S. participation in it. Wilsonianism thus revealed its deep roots in notions of American exceptionalism reaching back to the time of Columbus."[113] Though the Division of Intellectual Cooperation would be established by the Pan-American Union in the 1920s, international cultural exchange remained ineffectual. American statesman Elihu Root held fast to the belief that political frictions were born from cultural differences.[114] These early attempts to forge an official cultural approach to geopolitics were not seen as frivolous tasks:

> The founders of the American cultural programs and their successors possessed a weighty anthropological sense of their task . . . beginning with an elitist fixation on the virtues of intellectual exchanges and expanding in later years to embrace the manipulation of mass education and technological diffusion. . . . By the very nature of their concerns, the cultural personnel were forced to confront, if not traditional foreign policy issues, the assumptions underlying those issues. Their consignment to the diplomatic basement, so to speak, gave them access to the foundations of U.S. foreign policy.[115]

In the early 1930s, President Herbert Hoover's administration strategized how to relieve the economic depression and other social problems at home through governmental initiatives such as the Reconstruction Finance Corporation. Meanwhile, the American Communist Party and other extreme political groups gained momentum as the Soviet Union initiated its first Five-Year Plan that featured enormous public works accomplishments like the building of dams and factories.[116] Italy saw the rise of Benito Mussolini, Nazi Germany the ascendancy of Adolf Hitler, and Portugal the installment of authoritarian ruler António de Oliveira Salazar, as these dictatorships professed answers to relieve their nations of their own dire economic dispositions. With the arrival of Franklin Delano Roosevelt, however, a new political philosophy emerged, that the government can and will help average Americans. In a 1932 speech, Roosevelt made clear what in his mind was most important for the United States: employment and security. This was the era of John Steinbeck's *Grapes of Wrath*, of Dust Bowl migration westward, and what was a bleak socioeconomic outlook for most Americans.

On March 4, 1933, on the East Portico of the United States Capitol in Washington, D.C., Roosevelt, winner of the 1932 election over incumbent Hoover, briefly enunciated his administration's foreign policy goals toward Latin America and the Caribbean. This statement marked the end of a series of military interventions by the U.S. government in the region. At a time when America was faced with intractable economic challenges, this Good Neighbor policy would favor Pan-Americanism over unpopular military coercion, diplomacy over imperialistic meddling by the "Colossus of the North." Roosevelt, in a reversal of Teddy Roosevelt's "Big Stick" diplomacy, proclaimed on his inaugural day: "In the field of world policy I would dedicate this Nation to the policy of the good neighbor—the neighbor who resolutely respects himself and, because he does so, respects the rights of others—the neighbor who respects his obligations and respects the sanctity of his agreements in and with a world of neighbors."[117]

FDR's inheritance as U.S. president and statesman transcended economic issues at home as well as dangerous political scenarios abroad. At the Montevideo conference in 1933, he successfully projected a positive image of America to a region that had grown stubbornly suspicious of the United States and its manner of involvement in the politics of South America. Roosevelt came to understand, after much persuasion by his foreign-policy advisors, that what was needed was a government agency with a special focus. The United States was aware of its negative reputation in Latin America after decades of military interventions, usually in the defense of American commercial interests.[118] In a conscious effort to reverse symbolically the ill-fated Roosevelt Corollary[119] of 1904, which modified the original official policy of American intolerance of foreign, mainly European intervention in Latin America, made clear in the Monroe Doctrine of 1823, Franklin Roosevelt also felt the growing suspicion that American hemispheric domination would transcend economic considerations. After the Montevideo conference, several committees on inter-American cultural dialogue were arranged, though with little fanfare.

Ultimately, America had no viable public information agency between the two world wars, while it practiced an isolationist foreign policy. There would be no further official developments until 1936, when Roosevelt called the Pan-American Conference for the Maintenance of Peace in Buenos Aires, Argentina, which would witness early discussions toward an agreement of educational and cultural exchanges between the United States and governments in Latin America and the Caribbean. These agreements would yield a concrete student exchange program between North and South America. As Ninkovich points out, Assistant Secretary of State Sumner Welles wanted a more conspicuous and effective private-sector presence in U.S. government-sponsored cultural endeavors. By 1937, several individuals who supported American cultural participation in Latin America, including Secretary of State Cordell Hull and preacher Dr. Samuel Guy Inman, agreed that what was needed was "a coordinated program in which the government and private organizations and individuals could cooperate without overlapping."[120] On May 23, 1938, the Division of Cultural Relations was created with a particular focus to thwart totalitarian influence in Latin America, which was, historically, the ersatz territory of the United States. Still, as was made popular in earlier discussions of cultural sharing, the conversation revolved around international educational exchanges of students and professors only at this time.[121]

Beyond this formal yet vague commitment of fair play and diplomatic openness by the new administration, it was not until a few years later that the United States would implement a specific strategic agency dedicated to the soft power side of realpolitik. The Division of Cultural Relations would be a neighborly, though strategic, plan to continue to present American values and culture to foreign audiences. Crucially, the United States feared the encroachment of Nazism and fascism in Latin America and would use throughout World War II cultural diplomatic resources as a principal weapon to stave off this ideological infiltration. South America was largely non-aligned with no particular allegiance toward any major world power.[122] According to John Brown,

> It was in direct response to this perceived threat, rather than from a tradition-defined desire to engage the government in arts promotion abroad, that the State Department's Division of Cultural Relations was established. . . . The Departmental Order of July 28 of that year establishing the division noted that among its goals was "cooperation in the field of music, art, literature and other intellectual and cultural attainments."[123]

Franklin Roosevelt's new policy focus was also a response to private-sector philanthropists[124] who believed that a softer cultural approach was necessary for the United States to adopt if it wished to avoid repeating the carnage of the Great War. In so doing, the United States became "the last major power to enter formally the field of cultural diplomacy."[125] On August 16, 1940, the Office for Coordination of Commercial and Cultural Relations between the American Republics came into being. It would not be until 1941, however, following the creation of the Office of Coordinator of Inter-American Affairs (CIAA), led by art patron and oil investor Nelson Rockefeller, that the United States would begin official wartime cultural incursions into Latin

American countries. It would be Rockefeller's "eagerness to get things done in the artistic field right away [that] contrasted with the cautious, scholarly bureaucrats in the State Department who pursued 'mutual understanding' through academic exchanges, in their view the longer term the better."[126] By December of 1941, with the bombing of Pearl Harbor, there was little choice but for the CIAA to buy into the information cause completely.

This new cultural department within the U.S. government turned once again to what has already been demonstrated as a precedent in this chapter: the reliance on private-sector partnerships. This time, a full arsenal of cultural approaches would be implemented unilaterally toward Latin America, from radio broadcasts, to film showings, to the building of libraries, and also to art exhibitions from notable American museums.[127] However, as scholar Clarissa Ceglio emphasizes, U.S. museum exhibitions, though they traveled extensively throughout Latin America, did not enjoy the same political reach as these other media. It would be Rockefeller's ties to the Museum of Modern Art, coupled with his mandate of "one-way diplomacy" that would set the tone for the U.S. government's approach to cultural rapprochement with America's southern neighbors.

The third and last example of American attempts at cultural diplomacy through international exhibitions predating the main timeframe of this study is the Museum of Modern Art's 1942 United Hemisphere Poster competition, one of many collaborative partnerships between the MoMA-driven U.S. government policy and artists from Latin America, an effort endorsed by the CIAA. As will be made clear, the choice of this exhibition for discussion is to round out the three episodes under scrutiny in this chapter.

The fall 1942 *Bulletin of the Museum of Modern Art* carried the title "The Museum and the War," and the subsection "Posters for the War" declared: "In promoting design, production and critical study of war posters the Museum has been extremely active by means of three large competitions, ten exhibitions and one publication."[128] This partnership between the MoMA and the U.S. government was struck, according to Ceglio, in the CIAA's efforts "to stimulate U.S. interest in Latin America and construct a supranational imagined community characterized by shared cultural, political, and economic interests."[129] Posters as advertisements for commercial purposes had been popular for decades. As the Second World War arrived, government and private organizations sought out this medium to transmit messages to the citizenry at large. This medium offered a seldom-used opportunity for advertising specialists, graphic designers, and artists to come to the aid of the government eager to spread wartime messages on a wide scale.[130] In 1941, the MoMA had already launched a domestic poster competition "to encourage the creation of propaganda posters in an environment free from the pressures of government or commerce."[131] The following year, the War Advertising Council (WAC) partnered with the Office of War Information (OWI) to establish the Advisory Council on Government Posters to take on the domestic concerns "to help coordinate war bonds, food conservation and labour recruitment campaigns."[132] This effort aimed to communicate far and wide President Roosevelt's Four Freedoms as enunciated in his 1941 State of the Union Address. Advertising would become a staple of government information dissemination efforts during the war and was seen "as a means of mass education and persuasion, to be deployed on behalf of American business through campaigns aimed at the public interest. In this way the industry saw itself as part of the world struggle with totalitarian tyranny."[133]

The role of a single individual can make a significant statement in matters of cultural diplomacy. The museum's former president, considered by many as shrewd a business mind as much an art aficionado, stood firmly at the helm of the CIAA, what on the surface seemed a natural alliance formed between the two organizations. Rockefeller's third identity, that of head of Creole Petroleum, the South American subsidiary of the Rockefeller family's Standard Oil, appeared only to confirm his manifold commitment to Latin America and its role in the U.S. sphere of influence. For Rockefeller and other American business interests, "Latin America transformed itself into an experimental laboratory for the world's most powerful nation. . . . Therefore, Rockefeller defended the increase in foreign investment in the region, but in the spirit of defense of the free market."[134] While the economic defense of Latin America was an obvious need to Good Neighbor policy adherents, it would be the cultural aspect of U.S. intervention that would nuance the sometimes heavy-handed approach of the very same economic intervention. After all, the U.S. frontier spirit was not used up, according to Tota. In the spirit of Frederick Turner's *Significance of the Frontier in American History*, Rockefeller took up the mantle of the American expansionist spirit as museum professional, as government figurehead, and as an oilman. For him, "the wealth of the Western Hemisphere would be achieved with the expansion to the *sertao*, the South American frontier."[135]

The stated purpose of the United Hemisphere Poster Competition was "to stimulate pictorial expression of the unified determination of the nations of the Americas to remain free."[136] With cash prizes for a projected thirty-four winners and an exhibition tour in the United States and throughout Central America and South America, the museum received 855 posters before the deadline of July 28.[137] Of these, more than half came from artists in Latin America. The jury for the competition was made up of Don Francisco, Office of the Coordinator of Inter-American Affairs; Fred Cooper, Artists Guild; John Falter, Society of Illustrators; William A. Irwin, Art Directors Club; Rene d'Harnoncourt, General Manager, Indian Arts and Crafts Board; and Alfred H. Barr Jr., Monroe Wheeler, and Captain Eliot F. Noyes of the Museum of Modern Art. The criteria for the competition were straightforward: entries were to be anonymous while decisions were made on the winners; competitors were able to submit any number of entries; and there were no color restrictions. Decisively, each poster had to contain one of the following slogans in English, Spanish, or Portuguese:

HANDS OFF THE AMERICAS	UNA SOLA AMERICA, UNA SOLA ACCION	VIVAM AS AMERICAS UNIDAS
21 REPUBLICS—1 DESTINY	AMERICA UNIDA ES LA PAZ DEL MUNDO	UMA SO AMERICA, UMA SO ACAO
UNITE AGAINST AGGRESSION	LUCHEMOS POR UNA AMERICA LIBRE	A AMERICA UNIDA E A PAZ DO MUNDO
FIGHT FOR A FREE AMERICA	UNAMONOS CONTRA LA AGRESION	CONTRA UM INIMIGO COMUN, UNIAO

The trilingual catalog for the *United Hemisphere Posters* exhibition featured all winning entries. Two thousand five hundred dollars was awarded to seventeen winners from the Latin American section and seventeen were awarded from the United States and Canada. The first-place winner from the southern region came from Mexican artist Jose Renau, employed the "Unite Against Aggression" slogan, and featured three hands driving a sharpened flagpole that flies all the national flags of the twenty-one republics into a flailing serpent. Stanley W. Crane's entry, from Woodstock, New York, the first-place winner from the United States and Canada section, shows a stark, emaciated victim of war, partially eclipsed by Nazi and Japanese flags, hovering over the message "Unite Against Aggression." Other posters ran a gamut of pictorial styles, from the primitive and naïve to Art Deco and those that used a heavy-handed totalitarian aesthetic—reminiscent of Nazi propaganda posters—as an ironic approach against the fascist and Nazi ideologies (figure 1.5). The "Museum and the War" bulletin further elucidated the rationale and lengths taken to make the competition an inclusive opportunity for all the American republics:

UNAMONOS CONTRA LA AGRESION

UNAMONOS CONTRA LA AGRESSION

Demetrio Urrúchua
Buenos Aires, Argentina

Nelson Boeira Faedrich
Rio de Janeiro, Brasil

CUARTO PREMIO • QUARTO PRÊMIO • FOURTH PRIZE
SECCIÓN LATINOAMERICANA • SEÇÃO LATINO-AMERICANA • LATIN-AMERICAN SECTION

Cristina Brull
Habana, Cuba

Rodrigo Frank (Guatemalteco. Guatemalan)
Buenos Aires, Argentina

AMERICA UNIDA

ES LA
PAZ DEL MUNDO

HANDS OFF THE AMERICAS

Figure 1.5.   Examples of the winning entries from exhibition catalogue of *Un hemisferio unido carteles. Um hemisferio unido cartazes. United hemisphere posters.*
New York: Museum of Modern Art, 1943.

To unite the republics of North and South America against our common enemy is an urgent national problem which has deeply involved the Museum. . . . But well before we or our Latin American allies declared war the Museum had carried on a manifold program of exhibitions, concerts, competitions, and publications which we believe has helped lay the foundation for mutual respect and understanding among the Americas.[138]

As was stated in the Introduction, the focus of this study concentrates on what the United States was showing of itself through these efforts. This private and public alliance between the MoMA and the U.S. government represents an inclusive gesture toward all the unaligned nations that the government feared would fall under the influence of totalitarian ideologies. In a way, this system of classification, rules, and slogans is not unlike the role of the Royal Commission of the Great Exhibition of 1851. In this case, the United States prescribed the rules by which the competition would be judged by hosting and thereby controlling the competition among the participants. As Bennett asserts, the exhibitionary complex works in favor of the hegemon. In this scenario, then, the Latin American nations suffered the pull between two irreconcilable ideologies (democracy versus fascism/ Nazism), and through their participation in the creative endeavor of poster making with slogans required by the United States, ultimately favored one worldview over another. This ability to self-regulate symbolically, through "the democratizing eye of power," reached the point that the United States no longer needed to apply overt control to the situation:

The exhibitionary complex . . . perfected a self-monitoring system . . . in which the crowd comes to commune with and regulate itself through interiorizing the ideal and ordered view of itself as seen from the controlling vision of power—a site of sight accessible to all. It was in thus democratizing the eye of power that the expositions realized . . . a model lesson in civics in which a society regulated itself through self-observation. But, of course, of self-observation from a certain perspective.[139]

The CIAA (later the OIAA) richly informed the template for the creation of the United States Information Agency, established in 1953 by President Eisenhower, and which will be explored in the next chapter. The cross-fertilization of business, art, and government in U.S. cultural diplomacy had now been tried, tested, and deemed successful.[140]

While the Good Neighbor policy is seen as a hiatus of U.S. ideological involvement in Latin America in the 1930s, there is no doubt that "hemispheric affairs assumed topmost priority in U.S. foreign policy," and while "it is only in European (or Asian) perspective that U.S. policy during this period might be construed as isolationist, in the perspective of the Americas, it most decidedly was not."[141] John Brown notes that "as the war progressed, the Division of Cultural Relations—and, to a lesser extent, the OIAA, which was more active in organizing artistic events until its arts and music programs were turned over to the Department of State in 1943—was greatly overshadowed by the Office of War Information (OWI), founded in 1942."[142]

Immediately after the war, hemispheric solidarity was no longer a priority, according to Smith: "To be sure, the 'Western Hemisphere idea' declined sharply after World War II. United States policy took on a global cast, with strong commitments to European affairs, and the postwar world witnessed new kinds of division—between communist and noncommunist, North and South. In this context the notion of hemispheric solidarity became irrelevant and obsolete."[143]

Chapter Conclusion

What is the importance of acknowledging preexisting evidence to what became a systematic method by the U.S. government to show itself through often-spectacular displays overseas? Heeding historian Jonathan Crary's criticism of Guy Debord's *Society of the Spectacle*, in which he laments "the absence of any kind of historical genealogy of the spectacle,"[144] this chapter addressed the relationship between key exhibitionary examples from the late eighteenth century through the mid-twentieth century with dominant aspects of the exhibitions that form the main subject of this study. Unlike Debord's spectacles, which, according to Crary, appeared "full-blown out of the blue," the cultural exhibitions employed by the U.S. government between 1955 and 1975 draw out direct references to earlier American attempts at cultural production through exhibitions for national prestige.

Cultural historians mostly discourage making cross-history comparisons of important events since they take place in fundamentally different contexts and the parallels that are drawn are rarely meaningful or useful. While this analysis embraces a mode of transhistoricity in its approach to understanding common ground between past exhibitionary events and those that followed a century later, it does not presume to sacrifice the historian's mandate of historical specificity, how these exhibitions came to be configured at various historical junctures. The cultural exhibitions employed by the U.S. government between 1955 and 1975 draw out direct references, be they ideological, stylistic, or at times, literal, to these earlier American attempts at cultural production through exhibitions for national prestige. The key theme shared

by the early exhibitions and those to be interrogated in the following chapters is the public/private partnership between government agencies and
institutions of high culture. This alliance, as Bennett avers, benefits policy:

> Public museums . . . provided the modern state with a deep and continuous
> ideological backdrop but one which, if it was to play this role, could not be
> adjusted to respond to shorter term ideological requirements. Exhibitions met
> this need, injecting new life into the exhibitionary complex and rendering its
> ideological configurations more pliable. . . . They made the order of things dy-
> namic, mobilizing it strategically in relation to the more immediate ideological
> and political exigencies of the particular moment.[145]

Cultural exhibitions were indeed pliable and could conceivably meet the ideological imperatives of the state at a given time. All three episodes covered
in this chapter share other important traits, which include that of national
identity as constructed through the display of decontextualized objects; the
requisite suspension of disbelief; and the production of otherness.

In a way, they all represent a will to power of a United States going
through national rites of passage. Elements of cultural chauvinism in the
animal symbols of the mastodon and the eagle at the Great Exhibition of
1851 are echoed in the cultural paternalism of the poster competition that
advocates a distinct U.S. superiority over its hemispheric neighbors. As David Kennedy theorizes, between the two world wars, America, "the nation
that the world had long bent to its own imaginative purposes now began to
dream seriously of bending the world to its image of itself" and "embraced
some of the oldest myths that others had long projected upon them, including the alluring idea that they were children of nature unencumbered by
history, whether their own or others."[146]

Moreover, the insecurity of the nation is more bluntly revealed in these
efforts. While they were indeed creative exploits that at times relied on the
sensational and the make-believe, they also indicate, from a point of view, a
national identity in flux.

Identifying a congruence between theories of impression management[147]
and the concepts within Bennett's exhibitionary complex, this and the following chapters demonstrate that these events reveal a "public dramaturgy
of power"[148] that the United States practiced in order to maintain certain
sociopolitical identities based on truthful or fantasy criteria. By nuancing
the approach to one of the guiding questions of this research, that which
addresses what America was showing of itself through these exhibitions, it
will be made clear that this is a question of national self-expression in its

perpetual cycle, as Goffman puts it, of *self-making* through exhibitionary events. The examples in this chapter should be seen invariably as forecasts, advertisements, and pretensions not only to a conclusive self-concept but more incisively as rites of passage toward a never ending "becomingness" of national identity.[149]

The goal of subsequent chapters, then, is to use synergistically and in meaningful juxtaposition the exhibitions that serve as the focus of this study and exhibitionary precedents that this chapter has explored. In a way, the 1955–1975 exhibitions represent the culmination of these U.S. efforts at cultural diplomacy that came before.

Notes

1. See Letter III from 1782 in J. Hector St. John de Crèvecoeur, *Letters from an American Farmer and Sketches of 18th-Century America*, ed. Albert E. Stone (Harmondsworth: Penguin, 1981), 68–70.

2. From a conversation between Geoffrey Wiseman, director of the University of Southern California's Center on Public Diplomacy and Dr. Shashi Tharoor, on March 10, 2009, Los Angeles.

3. George Washington to John Augustine Washington, June 15, 1783. *The Writings of George Washington from the Original Manuscript Sources*, ed. John C. Fitzpatrick, 27:8, accessed August 10, 2010, http://etext.virginia.edu/washington/fitzpatrick/. For more context, see Andrew S. Trees, *The Founding Fathers and the Politics of Character* (Princeton, NJ: Princeton University Press, 2004). Historian David Schoenbrun describes what Arndt calls the "culturalist" diplomatic approach of Thomas Jefferson and Benjamin Franklin in quoting a Foreign Ministry memo by an anonymous author: "This [the American nation] is a people already civilized by its understanding and which, having acquired its political independence, is about to choose for itself the legislation that is to establish its identity for all time. The history of the world, perhaps, shows no spectacle more interesting, and the political stage has never, perhaps, presented an event, the consequences of which are more important and widespread in the general condition of the globe," in Arndt, *The First Resort of Kings: American Cultural Diplomacy in the Twentieth Century* (Washington, DC: Potomac, 2006), 13–14; see also David Schoenbrun, *Triumph in Paris: The Exploits of Benjamin Franklin* (New York: Harper & Row, 1976).

4. Strobe Talbott, *The Great Experiment: The Story of Ancient Empires, Modern States, and the Quest for a Global Nation* (New York: Simon & Schuster, 2008), 129–30. See also John Winthrop, "A Modell of Christian Charity" (1630), in *Settlements to Society, 1584–1763*, ed. Jack P. Greene (New York: McGraw-Hill, 1966), 66–68.

5. See Seymour Martin Lipset, *American Exceptionalism: A Double-Edged Sword* (New York: Norton, 1996), 18. "America's key values—equality and achievement—stem from our revolutionary origins. The United States was the first major colony

successfully to revolt against colonial rule. In this sense, it was the first 'new nation,'" ibid., 2.

6. Alexis de Tocqueville, from *Democracy in America*, (1835), as quoted in Marie-France Toinet, "French Pique and *Piques Françaises*," *Annals of the American Academy of Political and Social Science*, May 1988, 137. De Tocqueville also observes: "The Americans, in their intercourse with strangers, appear impatient of the smallest censure and insatiable of praise. . . . They unceasingly harrass you to extort praise, and if you resist their entreaties they fall to praising themselves. It would seem as if, doubting their own merit, they wished to have it constantly exhibited before their eyes," ibid.

7. Gordon Wood, *The Idea of America* (New York: Penguin, 2011), 3.

8. Nicholas J. Cull, *The Cold War and the United States Information Agency: American Propaganda and Public Diplomacy, 1945–1989* (Cambridge: Cambridge University Press, 2008), 2.

9. Talbott, *The Great Experiment*, 129–30.

10. See Boorstin, *The Image*, 9–11, and one of the classic studies on the shaping of public opinion: Edward L. Bernays, *Crystallizing Public Opinion* (New York: Boni and Liveright, 1923).

11. David M. Kennedy, "Imagining America: The Promise and Peril of Boundlessness," in *Anti-Americanisms in World Politics*, ed. Peter J. Katzenstein and Robert O. Keohane (Ithaca, NY: Cornell University Press, 2007), 50.

12. Ibid., 41. See also Daniel Boorstin, *The Americans: The National Experience* (New York: Random House, 1965), 219.

13. Antonello Gerbi, *The Dispute of the New World: The History of a Polemic, 1750–1900*, trans. Jeremy Moyle (Pittsburgh: University of Pittsburgh Press, 1973), 158. See also Karen Ordahl Kupperman, ed., *America in European Consciousness, 1493–1750* (Chapel Hill: University of North Carolina Press, 1995); Fredi Chiappelli with Michael J. B. Allen and Robert L. Benson, eds., *First Images of America: The Impact of the New World on the Old* (Berkeley: University of California Press, 1976).

14. Kennedy, "Imagining America," 43–44.

15. Ibid., 50. See also the conclusion to Katzenstein and Keohane, where the editors aver that the symbolism generated by America is so polyvalent that it continually generates and diffuses anti-American views. Arndt describes the diplomatic impulse of sharing national culture as a phenomenon unto itself: "Americans had assumed since the early decades of their republic that sharing with others was a fundamental duty; the idea flowed from the distinctive American idea of stewardship, fed mainly by churches of all persuasions," *First Resort of Kings*, x.

16. Christopher Looby, "The Constitution of Nature: Taxonomy as Politics in Jefferson, Peale, and Bartram," in *Museum Studies: An Anthology of Contexts*, ed. Bettina Messias Carbonell (Malden, MA: Blackwell, 2004), 148–49.

17. Ibid.

18. Paul Semonin, *American Monster: How the Nation's First Prehistoric Creature Became a Symbol of National Identity* (New York: New York University Press, 2000), 392.

19. See Martin J. S. Rudwick, *Bursting the Limits of Time: The Reconstruction of Geo-history in the Age of Revolution* (Chicago: University of Chicago Press, 2005), 270. Rud-wick references Thomas Pennant's *Synopsis of Quadrupeds* (Chester, 1771). In this work, Pennant inferred that the "mammoth," as it was incorrectly labeled based on conjecture that it was the same animal as the Siberian mammoth, still roamed the American West. For related, see also Silvio A. Bedini, "Jefferson and American Vertebrate Paleontol-ogy," Virginia Division of Mineral Resources Publication 61 (Charlottesville: Common-wealth of Virginia, 1985), and Semonin, *American Monster*, chapter 9.

20. Rudwick, *Bursting the Limits of Time*, 264.

21. Ibid., 265. See also John Phil Breyne, "A Letter from John Phil. Breyne, M.D. . . . with Observations, and a Description of some Mammoth's Bones Dug Up in Siveria, Proving Them to Have Belong to Elephants." *Philosophical Transactions* 40 (1737–38): 124–38.

22. Rudwick, *Bursting the Limits of Time*, 265.

23. Ibid., 267.

24. Dumas Malone explores the motivation that lay behind Jefferson's war of ideas with French detractors Buffon and Daubenton: "The esteem of his peers was always dear to Jefferson, but what he was most anxious to do was to spread correct ideas about America." See Dumas Malone, *Jefferson and the Rights of Man* (Boston: Little, Brown, 1951), 103.

25. See Semonin, *American Monster*, 115.

26. For a museological explanation of how Enlightenment values aided the trans-formation of curiosity cabinets into the first public museums, see Tony Bennett, *Pasts beyond Memory: Evolution, Museums, Colonialism* (London: Routledge, 2004), 15–16. Bennett's insights shed understanding on Charles Willson Peale's museum agenda of showing the breadth of primary evidence from the natural world: "The programme of evolutionary museums was, in this sense, continuous with the rational programme through which the Enlightenment museum had earlier struggled to detach itself from the baroque principles of display that had characterized cabinets of curiosity." See also Joel J. Orosz, *Curators and Culture: The Museum Movement in America, 1740–1870* (Tus-caloosa: University of Alabama Press, 1990), 13; and D. H. Meyer, "The Uniqueness of the American Enlightenment," *American Quarterly* 28, no. 2 (Summer 1976): 165–86.

27. The most thorough study of the mastodon and its role in the formation of American identity is Semonin's *American Monster*. See also Keith Thomson, *The Legacy of the Mastodon: The Golden Age of Fossils in America* (New Haven, CT: Yale University Press, 2008).

28. Bennett, "The Exhibitionary Complex," *New Formations* 4 (Spring 1988): 73.

29. See Piers Mackesy, *The War for America, 1775–1783* (Cambridge, MA: Harvard University Press, 1964), 510. For a similar approach to the subject, see Alexander Deconde, "Historians, the War of American Independence, and the Persistence of the Exceptionalist Ideal," *International History Review* 5, no. 3 (Aug. 1983): 399–430.

30. As quoted in I. Bernard Cohen, *Science and the Founding Fathers: Science in the Political Thought of Thomas Jefferson, Benjamin Franklin, John Adams & James Madison*

(New York: Norton, 1995), 79; and in the original: Guillaume Thomas François Raynal, *Histoire Philosophique et Politique des Établissements et du Commerce des Européens dans les deux Indes* (Amsterdam, 1770).

31. Thomas Jefferson, *Writings* (New York: Library Classics of the United States, 1984), 191.

32. Georges Louis LeClerc Buffon, *Natural History: General and Particular*, vol. 5, 2nd ed., trans. William Smellie (London: W. Strahan and T. Cadell, 1785), 114. See also: Gerbi, *Dispute of the New World*, chapter 5, sections xvii–xx.

33. From Jefferson, *Writings*, "The bones of the Mammoth which have been found in America, are as large as those found in the old world. . . . To add to this, the traditionary testimony of the Indians, that this animal still exists in the northern and western parts of America . . . parts still remain in their aboriginal state, unexplored and undisturbed by us, or by others for us. He may as well exist there now," 176.

34. The presidential election of 1800 featured John Adams, president of the American Academy of Arts and Sciences competing against Thomas Jefferson, president of the American Philosophical Society. For more on this theme, see Heather Ewing, *The Lost World of James Smithson: Science, Revolution, and the Founding of the Smithsonian* (New York: Bloomsbury, 2007), 201–2.

35. Don D. Fowler, "Uses of the Past: Archaeology in the Service of the State," *American Antiquity* 52, no. 2 (April 1987): 229.

36. As quoted in Bennett, "The Exhibitionary Complex," 90.

37. See Gerbi, *Dispute of the New World*, 266–67.

38. For more information on Charles Willson Peale, his career as a painter and paleontologist, and his involvement with the creation of the early museum movement in America, see Lillian B. Miller and David C. Ward, eds., *New Perspectives on Charles Willson Peale: A 250th Anniversary Celebration* (Pittsburgh: University of Pittsburgh Press, 1991); Charles Coleman Sellers, *Mr. Peale's Museum: Charles Willson Peale and the First Popular Museum of Natural Science and Art* (New York: Norton, 1980), 123–58. As his painting career relates to the mastodon, see Lillian B. Miller, "C. W. Peale as History Painter: The Exhumation of the Mastodon," *American Art Journal* 13, no. 1 (Winter 1981): 47–68; Carrie Rebora Barratt, "Inventing American Stories, 1765–1830," in *American Stories: Paintings of Everyday Life, 1765–1915*, ed. H. Barbara Weinberg and Carrie Rebora Barratt (New York: Metropolitan Museum of Art, 2009), 2–27; Susan Stewart, "Death and Life, in That Order, in the Works of Charles Willson Peale," in *The Cultures of Collecting*, ed. John Elsner and Roger Cardinal (London: Reaktio, 1994), 204–23; and Mark P. Leone and Barbara J. Little, "Artifacts as Expressions of Society and Culture: Subversive Genealogy and the Value of History," in *Museum Studies: An Anthology of Contexts*, ed. Bettina Messias Carbonell (Malden, MA: Blackwell, 2004), 362–74. For an early discussion of the American mastodon story, from the first reported discovery of fossils in the early eighteenthth century through the exhumation of the mastodon in 1801 by Charles Willson Peale with additional discussion of its display in Philadelphia, see John D. Godman, *American Natural History*, Vol. 2, Part 1, *Mastology* (Philadelphia: H. C. Carey & I. Lea, 1826), 211–37.

39. For a scholarly treatment of visual culture as fulfilling certain nationalist needs, see Laura Rigal, "Peale's Mammoth," in *American Iconology: New Approaches to Nineteenth Century Art and Literature*, ed. David C. Miller (New Haven, CT: Yale University Press, 1993), 18–38. For a general discussion of nineteenth-century visual culture, see Vanessa R. Schwartz and Jeannene M. Przyblyski, eds., *The Nineteenth-Century Visual Culture Reader* (New York: Routledge, 2004).

40. *Complete Dictionary of Scientific Biography*, Vol. 15, ed. Charles C. Gillespie (Detroit: Scribner's, 1981), s.v. "Rembrandt Peale," 471–72.

41. See letter from Thomas Jefferson to Charles Willson Peale, in Horace W. Sellers, "Letters of Thomas Jefferson to Charles Willson Peale, 1796–1825," *Pennsylvania Magazine of History and Biography* 28, no. 2 (1904): 139.

42. The British press published satirical poems deriding the display of the skeleton as a metaphor for Napoleon Bonaparte. See "Mammoth and Bonaparte," *Newcastle Courant* (Newcastle-upon-Tyne, England), Saturday, July 9, 1803, issue 6613; "The Mammoth," *Hampshire Telegraph & Portsmouth Gazette* (Portsmouth, England), Monday, May 23, 1803, issue 189. See also "Rembrandt Peale to C. W. Peale, July 30, 1803," in *Rembrandt Peale, 1778–1860: A Life in the Arts*, ed. Carol Eaton Hevner and Lillian B. Miller (Philadelphia: Historical Society of Philadelphia, 1985): 97, 40. The display of the skeleton perhaps fit more neatly into the contemporaneous tradition of freak shows and animal shows in London that were popular at the time. For these, see Richard D. Altick, *The Shows of London: A Panorama History of Exhibitions, 1600–1862* (Cambridge, MA: Harvard University Press, 1978).

43. Orosz, *Curators and Culture*, 4.

44. See Rembrandt Peale, *An Historical Disquisition of the Mammoth, or, Great American Incognitum* (London: C. Mercier, 1803), iv–v. For theoretical discussion of how authors of exhibition catalogs lay status on the displayed artifact(s) by virtue of the catalog entry, see Krzysztof Pomian, *Collectors and Curiosities: Paris and Venice, 1500–1800*, trans. Elizabeth Wiles-Porter (Cambridge: Polity, 1990), 138–184, 300–312. For more on Rembrandt Peale's time in London, see Charles Coleman Sellers, "Rembrandt Peale, 'Instigator,'" *Pennsylvania Magazine of History and Biography* 79, no. 3 (July 1955): 331–42.

45. See Peale, *Historical Disquisition of the Mammoth*, iv–v.

46. Ibid., 72.

47. Rudwick, *Bursting the Limits of Time*, 270.

48. Loren Eiseley, "Myth and Mammoth in Archaeology," *American Antiquity* 11, no. 2 (Oct. 1945): 85. For elaboration on the mammoth myth, see Adrienne Mayor, *The First Fossil Hunters: Dinosaurs, Mammoths, and Myth in Greek and Roman Times* (Princeton, NJ: Princeton University Press, 2000), xiii. Here she explains geomythology, the science of recovering ancient folk traditions about complex natural processes or extraordinary events.

49. Looby, "Constitution of Nature," 155.

50. Quoted in Alan Lee Dugatkin, *Mr. Jefferson and the Giant Moose: Natural History in Early America* (Chicago: University of Chicago Press, 2009), 119. See

this work for Jefferson's initial attempt to display American megafauna to European audiences, specifically to Buffon on October 1, 1787, with the intention to dispel misinformation about America. Also by Dugatkin, see "Jefferson's Moose and the Case against American Degeneracy," *Scientific American* no. 2 (2011): 84–87.

51. See George C. Herring, *From Colony to Superpower: U.S. Foreign Relations since 1776* (Oxford: Oxford University Press, 2008), 104–5.

52. In Albert Ellery Bergh, ed., *The Writings of Thomas Jefferson*, Vol. 9 (Washington, DC: Thomas Jefferson Memorial Association, 1907), 232.

53. As quoted in Merrill D. Peterson, ed., *The Political Writings of Thomas Jefferson* (Charlottesville, VA: Thomas Jefferson Foundation, 1993), 65. An excellent resource on the idea of the American West in the nineteenth century is James P. Ronda, "Passion and Imagination in the Exploration of the American West," in *A Companion to the American West*, ed. William Deverell (Malden, MA: Blackwell, 2004), 53–76. In this chapter, Ronda explains Jefferson's long-held belief in an "American Eden," in that "the forces of change and decay, irresistible in the Atlantic world, could be held at bay in the West. The past would be forgotten and the future secured by the simple act of going into the West. This was Jefferson's greatest temptation, his most enduring illusion as a patron of exploration," ibid., 55.

54. Andrew C. Isenberg, "Environment and the Nineteenth-Century West: Or, Process Encounters Place," in Deverell, *Companion to the American West*, 81.

55. See John Adams, *Adams Papers*, September 1, 1800, Massachusetts Historical Society. See also *The Adams Centinel*, Gettysburg, Pennsylvania, November 23, 1803, which derided Rembrandt Peale's efforts to show the skeleton in Europe.

56. For discussion on this concept, see Stephen G. Calabresi, "'A Shining City upon a Hill': American Exceptionalism and the Supreme Court's Practice of Relying on Foreign Law," *Boston University Law Review* 86 (2006): 1335–1416.

57. See Philip K. Dick, "How to Build a Universe That Doesn't Fall Apart Two Days Later," in *I Hope I Shall Arrive Soon* (New York: Doubleday, 1978), 6. The author cites Disneyland as an example of a "fake" reality: "Fake realities will create fake humans. Or, fake humans will generate fake realities and then sell them to other humans, turning them, eventually, into forgeries of themselves. So we wind up with fake humans inventing fake realities and then peddling them to other fake humans. . . . You can have the Pirate Ride or the Lincoln Simulacrum or Mr. Toad's Wild Ride—you can have *all* of them, but none is true," ibid.

58. Lee Alan Dugatkin, *Mr. Jefferson and the Giant Moose*, 117.

59. George Templeton Strong, diary, November 8, 1854, as quoted in Boorstin, *The Americans: The National Experience*, 376.

60. Frederick Jackson Turner, *The Frontier in American History* (New York: Holt, 1920), 2–3. For further discussion of the frontier as an unprecedented land of opportunity, see Nelson Manfred Blake, *A History of American Life and Thought* (New York: McGraw-Hill, 1963), 313–14.

61. Nicholas J. Evans, "Indirect Passage from Europe: Transmigration via the UK, 1836–1914," *Journal for Maritime Research* 3, no. 1 (2001): 70–84.

62. Robert F. Dalzell, *American Participation in the Great Exhibition of 1851* (Amherst, MA: Amherst College Press, 1960), 17. See also Arthur M. Schlesinger Jr., *The Age of Jackson* (Boston: Little, Brown, 1945), 427–28; Marcus Cunliffe, "America at the Great Exhibition of 1851," *American Quarterly* 3, no. 2 (Summer 1951): 115–26.

63. See Robert H. Byer, "Words, Monuments, Beholders: The Visual Arts in Hawthorne's 'The Marble Faun,'" in *American Iconology: New Approaches to Nineteenth Century Art and Literature*, ed. David C. Miller (New Haven, CT: Yale University Press, 1993), 164–85.

64. Looby, "Constitution of Nature," 254–55.

65. Byer, "Words, Monuments, Beholders," 164.

66. It also gave the United States a voice to refute who was then one of the more outspoken men of British letters, Charles Dickens, who savaged America in the picaresque novel *Martin Chuzzlewit*. His opinion on slavery upheld a strict indictment of American character: "Thus the stars wink upon the bloody stripes; and Liberty pulls down her cap upon her eyes, and owns oppression in its vilest aspect for her sister." See Charles Dickens, *The Life and Adventures of Martin Chuzzlewit* (London: Chapman and Hall, 1844), 257.

67. For a discussion of the planning for public art galleries and museums in late eighteenth-century France, see Andrew McClellan, *Inventing the Louvre: Art, Politics, and the Origins of the Modern Museum in Eighteenth-Century Paris* (Berkeley: University of California Press, 1994).

68. As quoted in Elizabeth Bonython and Anthony Burton, *The Great Exhibitor: The Life and Work of Henry Cole* (London: V&A Publications, 2003), 130.

69. *Official Descriptive and Illustrated Catalogue of the Great Exhibtion of 1851* (London: Spicer, 1851–52), advertisement.

70. Ralph N. Wornum, "The Exhibition as a Lesson in Taste," in *The Crystal Palace Exhibition Illustrated Catalogue, London, 1851, The Art-Journal: Special Issue* (New York: Dover, 1970), I. See also John Gloag, in his introduction to the reissue of the *Art-Journal* catalogue of the Great Exhibition, who writes, "Unfortunately, the Exhibition confused taste, strengthened the belief that design and ornament were identical, and the results of that confusion persisted until the beginning of the First World War in 1914."

71. John R. Davis, *The Great Exhibition* (New York: Sutton, 2000), xi.

72. See Hermione Hobhouse, *The Crystal Palace and the Great Exhibition: Art, Science and Productive Industry: The History of the Royal Commission for the Great Exhibition of 1851* (London: Continuum, 2002), 45.

73. Ibid.

74. See *The Papers of Joseph Henry*, Introduction, Volume 8, The Smithsonian Years: January 1850–December 1853, available at http://siarchives.si.edu/history/jhp/introto8.htm#104.

75. Ibid., and see also Arthur P. Molella et al., eds., *A Scientist in American Life: Essays and Lectures of Joseph Henry* (Washington, DC: Smithsonian Institution, 1980), 53.

76. *The Papers of Joseph Henry*, Doc. 97.

77. Dalzell, *American Participation*, 22.

78. Ibid., 25. Dalzell continues on this point: "While, then, the American display at the Great Exhibition was organized under official sanction from the Federal and State governments, its chief impetus lay in the decision made by hundreds of private individuals," ibid.

79. *Springfield Republican*, November 27, 1850, as quoted in Dalzell, *American Participation*, 29.

80. Dalzell, *American Participation*, 35–36.

81. Quoted in Bonython and Burton, *The Great Exhibitor*, 142.

82. Davis, *The Great Exhibition*, 138.

83. Bonython and Burton, *The Great Exhibitor*, 131.

84. *Southern Quarterly Review*, N.S., I (July 1850), 301–3, as quoted in Dalzell, *American Participation*, 17.

85. See *Punch*, XX, "America in Crystal," 209; and 246: "A Hint for the American Non-Exhibitors," 1851, http://books.google.com/books/about/PUNCH_VOL_XX_1851.html?id=EOVbAAAAQAAJ.

86. Dalzell, *American Participation*, 39–44. See also Horace Greeley, *Glances at Europe* (New York: Dewitt & Davenport, 1851), 88–90. Greeley, speaking of Americans, argued the English favored classes "dread the contagion of our example."

87. Hobhouse, *The Crystal Palace*, 67.

88. From "Report of the New Jersey Commissioners of the World's Fair," *Journal of the Eighth Senate of the State of New Jersey* (Freehold, NJ, 1852): 77–79, in Dalzell, *American Participation*, 54–55.

89. See D. Eldon Hall, *A Condensed History of the Origination, Rise and Progress, and Completion of the Great Exhibition of the Industry of All Nations*, 39–43, in Dalzell, *American Participation*, 55.

90. *Punch* XX, 236.

91. Henry Clarke Wright, "American Slavery in the World's Fair in London," *Liberator* (Boston), February 28, 1851.

92. Paul Young, *Globalization and the Great Exhibition: The Victorian New World Order* (New York: Palgrave Macmillan, 2009), 194. For additional discussion of the globalization paradigm in relation to the exhibition, see Jeffrey Auerbach and Peter H. Hoffenberg, eds., *Britain, the Empire, and the World at the Great Exhibition of 1851* (Aldershot: Ashgate, 2008).

93. Bennett, "The Exhibitionary Complex," 92.

94. Paul Greenhalgh, *Ephemeral Vistas: The Expositions Universelles, Great Exhibitions, and World's Fairs, 1851–1939* (Manchester: Manchester University Press, 1988), 17.

95. See Russell Jacoby, *Social Amnesia: A Critique of Contemporary Psychology* (Boston: Beacon, 1975), 370.

96. See Kylie Message, *New Museums and the Making of Culture* (Oxford: Berg, 2006), 88–89.

97. Henry Mayhew, *1851: or, the Adventures of Mr. and Mrs. Sandboys and Family* (London: Mayhew, 1851), 131. For more discussion of the labor class and its relation to the Great Exhibition, see Peter Gurney, "An Appropriated Space: The Great Exhibition, the Crystal Palace and the Working Class," in *The Great Exhibition of 1851: New Interdisciplinary Essays*, ed. Louise Purbrick (Manchester: Manchester University Press, 2001),114–45.

98. See Gurney, "An Appropriated Space," 114–45.

99. Donald Preziosi, *Brain of the Earth's Body: Art, Museums, and the Phantasms of Modernity* (Minneapolis: University of Minnesota Press, 2003), 114.

100. Chapter 4 of this study takes on what could be conceived as a more sinister face-off of national pavilions at world's fairs in the middle of the Cold War.

101. See *Punch* XXI for several further instances of English appreciation for the U.S. section and American industrial know-how in general.

102. *The Liverpool Times*, as quoted in Charles T. Rodgers, *American Superiority at the World's Fair* (Philadelphia: John J. Hawkins, 1852), 89, and in Dalzell, *American Participation*, 51–52.

103. Dalzell, 53.

104. See Jeffrey Kastner, "National Insecurity," *Cabinet Magazine*, no. 22 (Summer 2006), 2, http://www.cabinetmagazine.org/issues/22/kastner.php.

105. Benjamin P. Johnson, *Report on the Industrial Exhibition* (London, 1851), 13.

106. Preziosi describes the Crystal Palace as "the first fully realized modernist institution" and "a dream from which we have yet to awaken," in *Brain of the Earth's Body*, 102, 97. See also Lara Kriegel, "After the Exhibitionary Complex: Museum Histories and the Future of the Victorian Past," *Victorian Studies* 48, no. 4 (2006): 689. Kriegel adds: "The displays in the Crystal Palace fed the belief that Europe was, indeed, the very apex of civilization," ibid.

107. Dalzell, *American Participation*, 18.

108. See Robert W. Rydell, *All the World's a Fair: Visions of Empire at American International Expositions, 1876–1916* (Chicago: University of Chicago Press, 1984), 8. See also Merle Curti, "America at the World's Fairs, 1851–1893," *American Historical Review* 55, no. 4, (July 1950): 833–56. For a larger discussion of America's shifting global identity during the latter half of the nineteenth century, see Frank A. Ninkovich, *Global Dawn: The Cultural Foundation of American Internationalism, 1865–1890* (Cambridge, MA: Harvard University Press, 2009). For a general study of cultural representation at world's fairs through national efforts during the nineteenth century, see, for instance, Wolfram Kaiser, "The Great Derby Race: Strategies of Cultural Representation at Nineteenth-Century World Exhibitions," in *Culture and International History*, ed. Jessica C. E. Gienow-Hecht and Frank Schumacher (New York: Berghahn, 2003), 45–59.

109. Cull, *The Cold War and the United States Information Agency*, 4. See also Michael H. Hunt, *Ideology and U.S. Foreign Policy* (New Haven: Yale University Press, 1987).

110. Archibald MacLeish in Ruth Emily McMurray and Muna Lee, *The Cultural Approach: Another Way in International Relations* (Chapel Hill: University of North Carolina Press, 1947), ix–x.

111. Ninkovich, *Diplomacy of Ideas*, 31.

112. The rationale for the establishment of this committee was threefold, according to USIA career officer Fitzhugh Green: "motivate Americans to enlist in the military forces, to produce munitions, to buy bonds; paint America positively in the perceptions of allies and neutrals; and weaken the enemy," in Fitzhugh Green, *American Propaganda Abroad: From Benjamin Franklin to Ronald Reagan* (New York: Hippocrene, 1988), 12. See also James Robert Mock and Cedric Larson, *Words That Won the War: The Story of the Committee on Public Information 1917–1919* (Princeton, NJ: Princeton University Press, 1939); George Creel, *How We Advertised America* (New York: Harper & Brothers, 1920); and Walter Lippmann, *Public Opinion* (New York: Harcourt, 1922).

113. Kennedy, in Katzenstein and Keohane, 53.

114. Ninkovich asserts that Elihu Root, supporter of the Carnegie Endowment, believed that "any system of international law—with or without sanctions—would need to be undergirded by a supportive framework of public opinion. This implied the need for an international communion of ideas and sympathies," in *Diplomacy of Ideas*, 10.

115. Ibid., 2–3.

116. See Blake, *History of American Life and Thought*, 489.

117. Franklin D. Roosevelt, inaugural speech. March 4, 1933. This was an about-face to Teddy Roosevelt's deep-seated doctrine that a nation prepared for war "is the surest guaranty for peace. Arbitration is an excellent thing, but ultimately those who wish to see this country at peace with foreign nations will be wise if they place reliance upon a first-class fleet of first-class battleships rather than on any arbitration treaty which the wit of man can devise." See Theodore Roosevelt, *Address of Hon. Theodore Roosevelt Before the Naval War College*, June 2, 1897.

118. The United States had demonstrated an active military and commercial interest in the region dating all the way back to the 1780s (see *Federalist Paper No. 11*, written in 1787, in which Alexander Hamilton expresses the need of American economic expansion in the West Indies). For a compendium of primary source material related to the variety of U.S. interventions in Latin America, see Robert H. Holden and Eric Zolov, *Latin America and the United States: A Documentary History* (New York: Oxford University Press, 2011).

119. The Roosevelt Corollary asserted a carte blanche, heavy-handed American interest in Latin America, in which military intervention was acceptable if deemed necessary by the United States.

120. Ninkovich, *Diplomacy of Ideas*, 28. Sumner Welles, on the other hand, "stressed his conviction that the State Department could do little more than fulfill the terms of the Buenos Aires convention." See also Ben M. Cherrington, "Cultural Ties That Bind in the Relations of the American Nations," *Modern Language Journal* 24,

no. 6 (March 1940): 403–9. Arndt discusses Cherrington's perhaps naïve definition of "cultural policy," noting that Cherrington "defended a purist definition, seeing cultural affairs as totally apolitical," from *First Resort of Kings*, xix.

121. The mandate for an official cultural diplomacy agency was unclear, according to Arndt: "The words 'policy' and 'cultural policy' also present problems. How cultural diplomacy relates to foreign policy has been debated since 1938 . . . by 1943 it was obvious that the word 'policy' was misleading and that cultural diplomacy had obvious political impacts; in fact, there were many meanings to 'policy,'" ibid.

122. Proof that Nazi ideological infiltration was successful to a point was the post–World War II escape of many Nazis to South America. See also Ninkovich: "The statist philosophies of the USSR, Germany, Italy, and Japan were reflected not only in their military and economic policies, and in their ruthless statecraft, but also in their adoption of cultural diplomacy as an explicit weapon in the arsenal of national power," *Diplomacy of Ideas*, 23.

123. See John Brown, "Arts Diplomacy: The Neglected Aspect of Cultural Diplomacy," in *America's Dialogue with the World*, ed. William P. Kiehl (Washington, DC: Public Diplomacy Council, George Washington University, 2006), 16, http://uscpublicdiplomacy.org/pdfs/061220_brown.pdf.

124. As Arndt attests: "The first American formal effort in cultural diplomacy was reluctantly undertaken by government at the strong insistence of the private sector, which was to be the prinicipal actor with minimal government assistance and interference." See Richard T. Arndt, "American Cultural Diplomacy: The U.S. Government Role," in *Exporting America: Essays on American Studies Abroad*, ed. Richard P. Horwitz (New York: Garland, 1993), 12.

125. Frank A. Ninkovich, "Currents of Cultural Diplomacy and the State Department, 1938–1947," *Diplomatic History* 1, no. 3 (July 1977): 216.

126. Brown, "Arts Diplomacy," 75. See also Ninkovich, *Diplomacy of Ideas*, and J. Manuel Espinosa, *Inter-American Beginnings of U.S. Cultural Diplomacy, 1936–1948* (Washington, DC: Bureau of Educational and Cultural Affairs, U.S. Department of State, 1976), for a general understanding of the institutionalization of U.S. cultural diplomacy, beginning with the anti-Nazi efforts in Latin America; also see Milton Cummings, *Cultural Diplomacy and the United States Government: A Survey* (Washington, DC: Center for Arts and Culture, 2003).

127. See Clarissa Ceglio, "The Wartime Work of U.S. Museums" (research report, Department of American Studies, Brown University, Providence, RI, 2010), http://www.rockarch.org/publications/resrep/ceglio.pdf.

128. "The Museum and the War," *Bulletin of the Museum of Modern Art* 10, no. 1 (Oct./Nov. 1942): 8.

129. Ceglio, "Wartime Work of U.S. Museums," 3.

130. See Robert Griffith, "The Selling of America: The Advertising Council and American Politics, 1942–1960," *Business History Review* 57 (Autumn 1983): 388–412; Frank Fox, *Madison Avenue Goes to War: The Strange Military Career of American Advertising, 1941–1945* (Provo, UT: Brigham Young University Press,

1975), 49–51; Harold B. Thomas, "The Background and Beginning of the Advertising Council," in *The Promise of Advertising*, ed. C. H. Sandage (Homewood, IL: Irwin, 1961), 15–58; Chester J. La Roche, Arthur Price, Arthur T. Robb, Ralph Coghlan, and Leonard Dreyfuss, "Should the Government Advertise?" *Public Opinion Quarterly* 6, no. 4 (Winter 1942): 511–36; Philip Salisbury, "Has Advertising Come of Age?" *Journal of Marketing* 8, no. 1 (July 1943): 25–32; for postwar domestic and foreign advertising activity, see, for instance: Drew Dudley, "Molding Public Opinion through Advertising," *Annals of the American Academy of Political and Social Science* 250 (March 1947): 105–12; J. A. R. Pimlott, "Public Service Advertising: The Advertising Council," *Public Opinion Quarterly* 12, no. 2 (Summer 1948): 209–19. See James Aulich, *War Posters: Weapons of Mass Communication* (New York: Thames & Hudson, 2007), 169–70.

131. Ibid., 169.

132. Ibid.

133. Ibid., 169.

134. Antonio Pedro Tota, *The Seduction of Brazil: The Americanization of Brazil during World War II*, trans. Lorena B. Ellis (Austin: University of Texas Press, 2009), 111–18.

135. Ibid., 118.

136. Press release 42401-24, Museum of Modern Art, April 1, 1942, http://www.moma.org/docs/press_archives/784/releases/MOMA_1942_0026_1942-04-01_42401-24.pdf?2010.

137. Press release 421008-64, Museum of Modern Art, October 8, 1942, http://www.moma.org/docs/ press_archives/828/releases/MOMA_1942_0070_1942-10-08_421008-64.pdf?2010.

138. "The Museum and the War," *Bulletin of the Museum of Modern Art* 10, no. 1 (Oct./Nov. 1942): 10. For a list of all MoMA exhibitions during World War II, see http://www.moma.org/ learn/resources/archives/archives_exhibition_history_list#1940. For general discussions of political and propaganda posters and their heritage, see also William R. Bird and Harry R. Rubenstein, *Design for Victory: World War II Posters on the American Home Front* (New York: Princeton Architectural Press, 1998).

139. Bennett, "The Exhibitionary Complex," 90.

140. For history on the CIAA, see Gisela Cramer and Ursula Prutsch, "Nelson A. Rockefeller's Office of Inter-American Affairs (1940–1946) and Record Group 229," *Hispanic American Historical Review* 86, no. 4 (2006): 785–806; and Office of Inter-American Affairs, *History of the Office of the Coordinator of Inter-American Affairs: Historical Reports on War Administration* (Washington, DC: U.S. Government Printing Office, 1947).

141. Peter H. Smith, *Talons of the Eagle: Dynamics of U.S.-Latin American Relations*, 2nd ed. (Oxford: Oxford University Press, 2000), 79. For another study that addresses American imperialist ambitions through cultural programs head-on, see Amy Kaplan and Donald Pease, eds., *Cultures of United States Imperialism* (London:

Duke University Press, 1993). For more on Rockefeller and the business side of his interests in Latin America, see Gerard Colby and Charlotte Bennett, *Thy Will Be Done: The Conquest of the Amazon; Nelson Rockefeller and Evangelism in the Age of Oil* (New York: HarperCollins, 1995).

142. Brown adds: "The use of high culture as a tool of influence was not among OWI's priorities, although it established libraries abroad under the USIS logo that stayed open after the war (and that the United States Information Agency, established in 1953, took over during the Cold War). The OWI was abolished in 1945," "Arts Diplomacy," 75–76. See also A. M. Winkler, *The Politics of Propaganda: The Office of War Information, 1942–1945* (New Haven, CT: Yale University Press, 1978).

143. Smith, *Talons of the Eagle*, 86.

144. Jonathan Crary, "Spectacle, Attention, Counter-Memory," *October* 50 (Autumn 1989): 96–107.

145. Bennett, "The Exhibitionary Complex," 93.

146. Kennedy, "Imagining America," 51.

147. See Erving Goffman, *The Presentation of Self in Everyday Life* (New York: Doubleday, 1959).

148. Bennett, "The Exhibitionary Complex," 73.

149. This concept of *unfinalizability*, popularized by Mikhail Bakhtin, hints that the meaning of America, particularly to its government leadership, was a moving target, and while the Declaration of Independence was a first step toward nationhood, it was also a leap of faith as to what identity America would embrace and project to a "candid world." America, it seems, had no identity of its own to declare.

CHAPTER TWO

Confusion Makes
Its Masterpiece

U.S. Participation in 1950s Trade Fairs

The exhibits which are to represent the U.S. at trade fairs this year must offer something more persuasive for propaganda purposes than mere products and spectacular effects. There may not be much time left to stop or slow down the wave of resentment rising against us in the neutralist and anti-western countries. This medium can and should be used to bring into focus a personal image of America. Every effort should be made to show visitors to our exhibits that, although our circumstances in life may differ, there exists a basic, human kinship between them and the American people.[1]

By and large, while other national exhibits gauged their extravaganzas to definite economic possibilities within the country, the American spectaculars were being put on in the best tradition of the Big Top. Thus, if they failed it was not for lack of showmanship, or even of clear American identification. The underlying problem emerged cleanly as one of how we are being interpreted.[2]

Just two years after the end of World War II and five years before he would be inaugurated the thirty-fourth president of the United States, in 1947 Dwight D. Eisenhower openly advocated for the creation of a government program that would teach foreigners about American culture. Kenneth Osgood insists that "the president believed deeply in the value of cultural exchange activities. . . . Testifying before the House, he advocated an information program that disseminated cultural information in terms 'readily comprehended by the people . . . in terms of ice boxes, radios, cars, how much did [Americans] have to eat, what they wear, when they get to go to sports spectacles, and what they have available in the way of art galleries and things like that."[3] Set against the backdrop of the Truman Doctrine, which advocated the containment[4] of Soviet aggression anywhere in the world, and the Marshall Plan, which aimed to rebuild the countries of Western Europe[5] (with the additional mandate of fending off Soviet ideological advances), the Smith-Mundt Act, signed into law by Harry S. Truman on January 27, 1948, would promulgate overseas information programs while making it illegal for the U.S. government to disseminate propaganda within its territorial borders.[6] As former executive director of the United States Advisory Commission on Public Diplomacy, Matt Armstrong justifies Congress's hastening of the Smith-Mundt bill to signed law as a result of the ratcheting up of Soviet Communist propaganda. The U.S.S.R.'s information machines at the time were, in essence, "drowning out the promise of the Marshall Plan."[7]

A year later the Hoover Commission would publish a report that advised that the current foreign information program be removed from the State Department and given its own independent identity. The planning for this new agency, based on the President's Committee on International Information Activities, would eventually give shape to Eisenhower's new information agency a few years later.[8] The late 1940s also witnessed the inauguration of an early instance of American cultural exhibitions as a tool of Cold War public diplomacy: the Marshall Plan exhibitions, which were small, traveling caravans that crisscrossed Europe in order to explain U.S. values and information in a creative and up-front fashion to a shell-shocked, post–World War II Western European population.[9] Europeans viewed American culture as one of material abundance and pleasurable consumption with the presence of healthy GIs distributing "chocolate, chewing gum, nylons, and other delicacies to the fraulein of their choice and often to her entire family," and the various publications—from magazines to trade union journals—that showed the United States in essentialist terms as the "land of plenty." The United States, according to historian Sara Lennox, "was not prepared to leave the task of informing a recovering Europe about the American Way of Life to lively European fantasies alone."[10] Exhibitions were concise, transportable tools to convey the positive intent of the Marshall Plan. The "Nylon War" popularized by David Reisman in a 1951 fictional account, expounded on "Operation Abundance," a propaganda strategy that would in reality prove prescient for the role that U.S. consumer culture would play in West Germany in order to thwart Soviet influence.[11] As Castillo points out, the Marshall Plan exhibitions of household goods that traveled through western European countries from 1948 through 1951 would set the precedent for the later government and private-sector partnership that would reach its peak in the *American National Exhibition* in Moscow (ANEM) in 1959: "Household goods exhibitions sponsored by the Marshall Plan in West Berlin recruited 'top-flight' civilian talents, including Edgar Kaufmann Jr., design curator at New York's Museum of Modern Art (MoMA)."[12] Kaufmann would later create the Good Design program at the Museum of Modern Art, which would help establish industrial designers like Arne Jacobsen, Finn Juhl, and particularly Charles and Ray Eames, who would become consultants to the government for future fairs and expos into the 1970s.[13]

By the early 1950s, Eisenhower abandoned his initial hope for a lasting peace with the Soviet Union and would "regard communism at home and abroad as America's leading threat," a menace "to be contained by social change, the achievement of economic security."[14] His inauguration in 1953 signaled a new approach to the issue that served as analog to national military concerns throughout his presidency: the U.S. economy. Despite Eisenhower's party identification, Blanche Wiesen Cook avows "petty rivalries, party rituals annoyed him. His vision was global." Eisenhower's ambition, moreover, was "bipartisan citizens for Eisenhower acclaiming his view of the future."[15] This view dwelt predominantly on the status of the Soviet Union and the spread of communism abroad. Only months into his first term as president, Eisenhower's economic worries were not unfounded, as "indicators pointed to an approaching downturn in the business cycle. . . . Democrats were already attacking the Administration's economic policies, while Eisenhower, in a nationwide radio and television address, charged that his critics were 'peddlers of gloom and doom.'"[16] Fortunately, Eisenhower had personally cultivated many business allies from his prepresidential days that would rise to the occasion to improve the economic reputation of the United States, both at home and abroad.

The Advertising Council

American industry, severely retrenched in the Depression of the 1930s, had been reinvigorated through the production of war materiel. Spared Europe's challenge of rebuilding a devastated industrial sector after the end of the Second World War, the U.S. economy had retooled itself for domestic production; by the 1950s, it was experiencing unprecedented growth. The products of industry and how they impacted on the lives of ordinary American citizens was a wholly valid subject.[17]

According to Cook, the "American Century," as coined by publicist Henry Luce, became "the public rhapsody of the postwar period" and was supported to such a wholehearted extent by the U.S. government and its institutional ally, the Advertising Council, that "to call the idea of the American Century arrogant or imperialist was to be a Communist dupe or traitor."[18] As a non-profit organization whose public campaigns during World War II rallied the U.S. advertising industry behind the American war effort, the Advertising Council proved highly influential to President Eisenhower as he navigated a new U.S. approach toward a global postwar economic policy.

After 1945, the War Advertising Council dropped its wartime signifier and became a corporatist brotherhood that sought a deeper alliance between business and government. Haddow confirms that "fraternal business organizations pulled together in order to ensure a renewed prosperity and to counter the perceived threat to business posed by both domestic New Deal programs and Soviet competition."[19] It also sought to establish, according to Griffith, "close, reciprocal relationships with the executive branch."[20] As an engine of persuasion to popularize notions of U.S. prosperity through major advertising campaigns, these public service announcements served a dual purpose. First, they would promote the advertising industry itself as "a responsible and civic-spirited industry," and, second, the U.S. capitalist system as productive for "a dynamic, classless, and benignly consensual society."[21] The peacetime goals, moreover, did not depart ultimately from those during the war. The Advertising Council, made up of hundreds of big business concerns, saw as its purpose the philosophically straightforward tactic of disproving totalitarianism and its suppression of the individual while championing free enterprise and American entrepreneurial drive. Further, Theodore Repplier, the council's executive director, was persuaded that "business," which had risen in prestige during the war, was "again being pictured as the 'villain' in the American drama. . . . Everybody agrees," he concluded, "that the American enterprise system needs 'reselling.'"[22]

The Eisenhower presidency would continue to welcome the growing involvement of powerful interest groups such as the Advertising Council in American foreign policy, including their advertising efforts with C.A.R. E., civil defense, and Radio Free Europe, in spite of, according to Griffith, its "highly selective view of American society."[23] This heavily influential group had at its disposal not only the ear of the executive branch but "the greatest aggregate means of mass education and persuasion the world has ever seen," a conveyance of propaganda which, as William Whyte asserts, was "naïve . . . psychologically un-sound . . . abstract . . . defensive, and . . . negative." Vital to understand, according to Griffith, was that this approach was "neverthe-less repetitive, pervasive and unchallenged, surrounding Americans in all walks of life with an omnipresent if distorted reflection of their society and thus helping shape, to a degree no less real for being difficult to measure, the political culture of postwar America."[24]

Perhaps the most significant contribution of the Advertising Council toward influencing foreign publics about the positive attributes of the U.S. capitalist system was the *People's Capitalism* exhibit campaign.[25] In short, as Cook attests, "The Soviet economic offensive required American economic expansion. It was supported by McCarthyism, domestic and international political warfare, and 'People's Capitalism.' Words to calm. Words to confuse. Words to mobilize public opinion for a world economic crusade."[26] As advertising specialists, the council understood the necessity to strategize in order to win future customers—in this case, future buyers who would buy into the American way—for their products or ideas. A February 9, 1956, memo from the Trade Fair Advisory Committee included a digest of member Ted Patrick's paper, in which he advises the objective, "To make clear the true nature of the United States economic system and our unique form of capitalism—'People's Capitalism,'" with the caveat that "it should be adopted to the extent that we practically should never use the word Capitalism itself."[27] The Annual Report of the Advertising Council for 1955–1956 pulled no punches in its self-praise of their "new approach to our overseas propaganda" which demonstrated "the peaceful evolution of the American economy into a system which benefits nearly all of the people."[28]

The council would prove a close ally to the president both in domestic and in foreign public relations campaigns. With frequent invitations to the White House throughout the duration of the Eisenhower presidency, which consisted mainly in developing strategies to convey the administration's and the council's shared economic goals, the council's advice on the evolution the *People's Capitalism* campaign was specifically "designed to show the world how in America the rewards of capitalism" were "shared with the workers," how "class lines [had begun] to disappear," and how "almost everybody became a capitalist."[29]

The Birth of the United States Information Agency

The transition from the Truman to the Eisenhower presidencies would also bring with it the push for America to conceive a formal plan for a new information agency. The Eisenhower administration observed early on the Achilles heel of American public diplomacy: civil rights violations in the South. Historian George Herring declares that U.S. race issues "became inextricably entangled with the Cold War. The persistence of virulent racism in the United States and its most blatant manifestation in rigid, legalized segregation in the

South gave the lie to U.S. claims for leadership of the 'free' world and became a stock-in-trade of Communist propaganda."[30] A second major concern of the administration were the ideological allegiances of nonaligned countries in the Middle East, Asia, and Africa, not to mention the neutralist movement claimed by India's Jawaharlal Nehru, Egypt's Gamal Abdel Nasser, and Yugo-slavia's Josip Broz Tito, which "posed major challenges for the great powers."[31] Boorstin declares:

> In the cliché-ridden "Battle for Men's Minds," perhaps our problem is not so much that peoples abroad have an "unfavorable image" of America while they have a more favorable image of life among our enemies. Some of our difficulty may be much simpler, and too obvious for us to notice. I suspect we suffer abroad simply because people know America through images. While our enemies profit from the fact that they are known only, or primarily, through their ideals. That is, through their professed goal of perfection.[32]

As will be discussed later in this chapter, ideological influence became a seemingly global issue in the cultural wars fought between the United States and the Soviet Union. Moreover, regional issues would force the United States to shape its cultural outreach to specific foreign audiences, sometimes with success, other times not.

The new administration would create the United States Information Agency, whose main mission was "to submit evidence to peoples of other na-tions by means of communication techniques that the objectives and policies of the United States are in harmony with and will advance their legitimate aspirations for freedom, progress and peace."[33]

Based on a similar operating principle as the wartime Office of War Infor-mation (OWI), the USIA would adapt consumer marketing techniques into the U.S. overseas propaganda machine, following the OWI's edict: "If you could sell it in Kalamazoo, you could sell it in Karachi."[34] These tactics, which included country studies, cultural analysis of world regions, and consideration of class, religion, and political disposition, would attain refinement in the USIA's attempts to nuance its approach to foreign populations.[35] As in the case of pushing back Nazi and fascist ideological influence in Latin America during World War II, Eisenhower's notion of "rolling back" Soviet influence included the genteel battle of wills through the display of capitalist versus communist lifestyles on a global scale. As asserted by Frances Stoner Saunders:

> Experts in the use of culture as a tool of political persuasion, the Soviets did much in these early years of the Cold War to establish its central paradigm as a cultural one. Lacking the economic power of the United States, and, above

all, still without a nuclear capability, Stalin's regime concentrated on winning "the battle for men's minds." America, despite a massive marshalling of the arts in the New Deal period, was a virgin in the practice of international *Kulturkampf*.[36]

This same year that witnessed the creation of the USIA would also take account of the death of Marshal Stalin, the Korean armistice, and at home the anticommunist paranoia spurred by Senator Joseph McCarthy. It would become clear that the real leader to surface in the post-Stalin shuffle was Nikita Khrushchev, who would spend the next four years consolidating his role as leader of the U.S.S.R., in part through his de-Stalinization programs.

The time was ripe for Eisenhower's new information agency to act, and it wasted no time in doing so. As USIA veteran Burnett Anderson observes, "The Information Agency was only four months and eight days old" when, on December 8, 1953, President Eisenhower formalized his wishes for the sharing of nuclear technology to "improve the material condition of peoples everywhere and enhance the prospect for peace"[37] in an address to the United Nations General Assembly. During the next two years, the USIA would convey the president's message through the *Atoms for Peace* exhibition that traveled the globe, from India to Italy, from Brazil to Britain. Its goal, to allay fears of the atomic bomb and to pressure indirectly the U.S.S.R. to an agreement concerning the safe management of nuclear technology, was realized as a public diplomacy triumph. The USIA's first semiannual congressional report stated that "the agency had given saturation—radio, press, newsreel, and other—coverage to the unfolding story, that more than 6 million people had already attended *Atoms for Peace* exhibits everywhere from Europe to Pakistan to India, and that more than a billion had seen, heard, or read about the U.S. proposal."[38] Ironically, while American schoolchildren watched the *Duck and Cover* film, released around this time by the Federal Civil Defense Administration to give instructions in surviving the detonation of a Soviet-launched atomic device, the success of this exhibition to deliver a more human side to the atomic arms race would initiate the long-term practice of museum-quality exhibitions as American foreign policy tools for the next forty years.[39] Though the introduction of the "friendly atom"[40] clearly served as a priority for the president in explaining American values to foreign publics, there was the additional objective to push an idealized image of American life, which the president sensed was misunderstood by overseas audiences. As Osgood adds:

Many foreigners believed in the barrenness of American culture. Most appeared to agree with Soviet propaganda that the "American people are preeminently a gadget-loving people produced by an exclusively mechanical, technological and materialist civilization." A vigorous and effective cultural program was necessary to dispel such notions, the agency argued, because cultural leadership was a prerequisite of world leadership.[41]

Indeed, the Eisenhower administration formed the Operations Coordinating Board (OCB),[42] the agency responsible for implementing national security policies among select government agencies, which, as Osgood suggests, "perceived a 'vastly increased and coordinated effort' by communist countries to use cultural exchanges and trade fairs as vehicles for propaganda" with the goal of winning hearts and minds.[43] A few months later the United States would take its first uncertain steps in countering Soviet cultural influence at the Bangkok trade fair in December 1953.

The hallmark of this cultural diplomacy model, as will be discussed in the next section, would be the alliance of government representatives with design expertise in tandem with the museum and industrial design community. The *American National Exhibition* in Moscow in 1959 would prove to be the apotheosis of this model.

The Office of International Trade Fairs

> The President told Congress last January this country generally has been conspicuous by its absence at past fairs. In the four years up to last December, Russia and her satellites put in an appearance at 133 fairs, the U.S. Government at none. The Reds used this absence as a vehicle for propaganda that America was interested only in war production while they pictured their countries as a workers' paradise and emphasized peace.[44]

In August 1954, President Eisenhower withheld five million dollars from his Emergency Fund for International Affairs, half of which was allocated to the Department of Commerce for official participation at international trade fairs, and the remaining funds given to the Department of State and the United States Information Agency (USIA) for "cultural programs and exploitation of the trade fair and cultural activities abroad." This was, essentially, the information agency's goal to "stimulate the presentation overseas of the best American industrial and cultural achievements in order to offset worldwide Communist propaganda charges that the United States has no culture and that its industrial production is oriented towards war."[45] Given permanent status by an act of the Eighty-Fourth Congress, its global mandate, according to the president, was "to tell adequately the story of our free enterprise system and to provide international trade promotion co-operation."[46] Peter Harnden, who was previously head of Marshall Plan exhibitions, was tapped to head the U.S. Office of Design and Production, which he would maintain in Paris, designing the first packaged exhibits for U.S. pavilions around the themes of *Atoms for Peace*, American suburban home living, and other topics. This office would close after the arrival of the new director of the OITF in 1956, Harrison T. McClung, who would bid out to industrial designers the design and construction of U.S. pavilions.[47]

The formal operational guidelines for American participation at international trade fairs were divided into three broad categories that consisted of exhibit theme, government policies that would be addressed in the exhibit, and basic "guide lines" that included "portrayal methods," "psychological criteria," and "individual company exhibitors."[48] The "Statement of Assumptions and Guiding Principles" was based on the notion that as a result of "widespread misunderstanding and misinterpretation abroad concerning the United States," the nation would enter into this cultural arena "in order to enhance American prestige abroad and take the initiative through positive—not negative or defensive—action in the field." Not least, additional guidelines prescribed "participation should be appropriate to the limits of the trade fair as a medium of expression," and this "must be carried out as far as possible by private industry, with the Government stimulating, assisting and supplementing industry's own efforts."[49] Ultimately, the final guideline smacked of American exceptionalism and read: "The underlying philosophy of the Trade Fair Program should be that our material well-being is an evolutionary product of our ideological concepts which foreign people can share through confidence in the United States, emulation or sympathetic affiliation."[50]

This final guideline engages the fundamental philosophy of the *People's Capitalism* campaign—as Haddow emphasizes, the narrow and essentialist vision of expressing the material abundance of American life. The trade fairs would, early on, after the shift toward engaging the assistance of world-class industrial and graphic designers, transcend the often "trite" goals of *People's Capitalism*.[51] In 1956, *People's Capitalism—A New Way of Living* was installed at the Bogotá Trade Fair in Colombia, where it was enthusiastically received. According to Cull, the exhibit provoked a strong Soviet reaction: "In the U.S.S.R., the editor of *Pravda* (and soon-to-be foreign minister) Dmitri Shepilov fumed that *People's Capitalism* made as much sense as 'fried ice,' and in the summer of 1956 the Kremlin commissioned economist Eugene Varga to refute the concept in two five-thousand-word articles for its international journal *New Times*. Moscow was worried."[52]

The challenge of conveying American ideals based solely on material abundance was not lost on the president or on the designers who would eventually take the reins of this program. In a prescient article by Jane Fiske Mitarachi, entitled "Design as a Political Force," the U.S. trade effort was viewed within the larger framework of U.S. soft power abroad:

> The situation facing the OITF overseas is not basically different from the one that has been faced by every American diplomatic mission abroad since the war—probably the most difficult political role any nation has ever faced. The U.S.A., as a world leader, is in a position to be feared but not liked. It is an accepted paradox that nobody really loves a leader, however much he may need or depend on him. When that leader also is the richest nation in the world, and everybody's benefactor to boot, it is all the more an object of resistance and resentment.[53]

The Apotheosis of Industrial Design for Government Use

This chapter now explores the ideological underpinnings of exhibition design that delivered the make-believe aspects of U.S. pavilions in trade fairs during the mid-1950s. Two distinct theories of exhibitions emerged leading up to and during World War II that would become harbingers to the type of exhibition design the U.S. government would support through trade fairs and world expos from the mid-1950s and beyond. These approaches, rooted in wartime information techniques and avant-garde aesthetics, were developed by two men: Misha Black, Principal Exhibitions Officer for the Ministry of Information in Great Britain during World War II,[54] and Herbert Bayer, a German member of the Bauhaus who came to the United States and started working on exhibits at the MoMA in 1938.[55] These designers shared disdain for the Nazi hysteria-inducing technique of propaganda exhibition, but this is where the similarities ended.

These two designers held antithetical views about how an exhibit should be mounted. Whereas Black, according to Masey, "declared that 'the essential function of propaganda exhibition is to implant, or sustain, a general idea in the mind of the visitor,'" an approach which "advocated strong emphasis on the use of 'actual physical objects' and demonstrations," it was Bayer who sought to "organize space through architecture and presentation of key ideas" in order to make "an impression on the visitor."[56] Both of these men became part of the discussion of how to get exhibits to communicate during and after World War II. As a wartime exhibits specialist, Black learned how exhibition design could be effective:

1. The task of every exhibition is to sell something, whether it is a new line of tea-pots or a plan for the regeneration of Western civilization.

2. Exhibitions are the most effective . . . when the sales message can be conveyed by a display of the actual objects it is intended to sell, by demonstration, or by objects which poignantly materialize an idea.
3. When the sales story excludes demonstration or display of objects, or models, then exhibitions become a secondary medium of use as an ancillary to other sales and propaganda methods.[57]

Black's work influenced the conversation about what exhibit design was. On the other hand, Bayer's Bauhaus roots indicated his idealized approach to the way exhibitions should communicate to the visitor. According to Chanzit:

> What is noteworthy about his designs is their emphasis on the exhibition hall as a *total environment* including, in addition to vertical walls, the entire space, which functions as a dynamic environment for the interaction between people and what is exhibited. In 1930 Bayer synthesized the principle that would guide his future direction in exhibition design: the concept of a "field of vision."[58]

The disagreements between these two designers stemmed from their respective approaches to communicating with audiences through exhibitions. While Bayer advocated moving people through an exhibition as a group, with one point of view, and showing them one display after another on a route of travel from which they cannot deviate, Black believed that some people may want to move differently in the space. He opted for letting people wander around. U.S. trade fair pavilions would benefit from both methods. Bayer's approach, which wanted a completely prescribed visitor experience, where visitors are moved like pieces in a chess match, would be balanced by the insertion of artifacts and demonstrations as promoted by Black. This conversation was picked up and driven at Aspen design conferences created by Walter Paepcke.[59] As Chanzit points out, "There is little doubt that the modern installations by Bayer and some of his contemporaries in America influenced the display methods of later American exhibitions and trade fairs."[60]

Iwona Blazwick discusses the early years of the MoMA exhibitions and their shaping by the modernist ethos of European artists and designers that included Bayer. This ethos, she argues, raised function and design to equal status as art, and while its utopian emphasis was quashed by "the dystopian realities of two world wars and the transition of revolution into totalitarianism," these exhibitions revealed how "the global economic and cultural power base shifted from Europe to America." These postwar displays that hinted at a particular type of domestic bliss, ultimately celebrated, in Blazwick's words, "a modernity of the present."[61]

The domestic design shows at the MoMA reflected this and reached their zenith in 1950 with the *Good Design*[62] exhibition featuring the work of Charles and Ray Eames and cosponsored by the Chicago Merchandise Mart. This annual exhibition, taken on by a different designer or design team each year, located its roots with, but transcended the concept of the famous *Machine Art* exhibit, curated by Philip Johnson, from before the war.

> The [*Good Design*] programme marked an even sharper break with the design standard established at MoMA by Johnson's "Machine Art"[63] exhibition of 1934, with its machine forms abstracted from reality and arranged to suggest timeless perfection. The general mood of "Good Design" was necessarily domestic. More to the point, all the objects were new to the market. However timeless good design might be in theory, in practice it involved perpetual novelty. . . . Kaufmann assumed that improvement would in turn eventually reach ordinary Americans.[64]

While curator Paola Antonelli argues that "the biggest challenge with design shows is to avoid the 'trade fair effect,'"[65] therein lies an irony that the overall scenographic approach to trade fairs and subsequent national pavilions at world megashows is indeed rooted in Philip Johnson's "extreme act of conceptualization," in which he took "springs and ball bearings and put them on white pedestals against white walls like sculpture."[66]

Mary Anne Staniszewski theoretically justifies the idea that *Machine Art* was much more than a mere exercise in conceptual art. It was, at its very core, a preamble to brilliantly designed trade fairs, complete with a catalogue that alerted visitors to the names of designers and their products and stores that carried this merchandise: "Studding the walls throughout the exhibition, in clear, legibly sized black lettering were the names of U.S. companies: Aluminum Company of America, U.S. Steel Corporation, Bingham Stamping and Tool, America Sheet and Tin Plate Company, American Radiator Company."[67] Much like a trade fair, visitors, according to Staniszewski, "transgressed museum codes of behavior and went so far as to handle and test the products, check prices, and attempt to make purchases. In other words, they were shopping."[68] But whereas Black's style of propaganda display could be interpreted as fostering an arena for cultural "shopping," the Bayerian approach—in which visitors were forced through a preset physical and ideological route—should be seen as one distinctly grounded in a variety of cultural slavery. To further explore this idea, it is important to draw on Bennett, who points out that the cultural technology of a state-sponsored exhibition enables an outside visitor to identify with power, to see it as, if not directly theirs, then indirectly so, a force regulated and channelled by society's ruling groups but for the good of all: this was the rhetoric of power embodied in the exhibitionary complex—a power made manifest not in its ability to inflict pain but by its ability to organize and co-ordinate an order of things and to produce a place for the people in relation to that order.[69]

In these settings, visitors could traverse simultaneously both the worlds of high art and, to reintroduce Veblen's term, conspicuous consumption, while, unbeknown to them, falling victim to what Bennett describes as what was original and unique to nineteenth-century expositions: "the ideological economy of their organizing principles" that redefined the processes of industry into "material signifiers of progress . . . a collective national achievement with capital as the great co-ordinator."[70]

These shows set in the Museum of Modern Art were, arguably, havens, dream worlds where both buyers and museum visitors could penetrate a fictive world that was otherwise nonexistent outside these glorified settings. As Walter Benjamin describes the commercial/ideological dark side of trade fairs:

> The world exhibitions glorify the exchange-value of commodities. They create a framework in which commodities' intrinsic value is eclipsed. They open up a phantasmagoria that people enter in order to be amused. The entertainment industry facilitates this by elevating people to the level of commodities. They submit to being manipulated while enjoying their alienation from themselves and from others.[71]

But what does this display of an artificial world (as the *ur*-image, albeit simulated, of America) mean to the consumer? What catalyzed the shift of cutting-edge design from the galleries of the Museum of Modern Art and the display windows of department stores to the U.S. pavilions in the farthest reaches of the globe? As will be discussed next, it becomes clear that hundreds of thousands of foreign visitors voluntarily entered the U.S. pavilions at these hundreds of trade fairs in the 1950s, fulfilling the principal idea underlying the exhibitionary complex: "a voluntarily self-regulating citizenry" that would, through these displays, align themselves with a distinct rhetoric of American values.

This chapter is also an effort to describe additional aspects of U.S. pavilions at a number of 1950s trade fairs that resonate with Bennett's exhibitionary complex. Bennett explains that the evolution of the display of national values via material culture within the cultural technology of the national pavilion is rooted in exhibition practices formally introduced at the Great Exhibition of 1851.[72] Preziosi concurs: "The Great Exhibition . . . in fact, crystallized and put into its proper place an imperial fantasy world or imaginary geography of all peoples and products, with the modern citizen-consumer . . . at and as its (imaginary) center."[73] The Great Exhibition, then, is unavoidably a direct referent to the battle of ideologies between two great powers, the United States and the U.S.S.R., in the various national pavilions they constructed throughout the Cold War, first at trade fairs and later at world expos. In a sense, echoing Preziosi, "we've never left this building."[74] Perhaps it is not hyperbole that Eco describes the visiting of trade fairs as "a devout pilgrimage to one of the sanctuaries of mass communication."[75] And what was conveyed to the masses at these events? These fairs would become a battleground of warring utopias—capitalist versus communist—in a ruthless game for global cultural supremacy.

How Harrison T. McClung Revolutionized U.S. Participation in Trade Fairs

As the program gained momentum, in its second year, the OITF was placed under the direction of former advertising executive Harrison T. McClung, and it soon showed a change of direction. Closing the Paris design office, OITF decided that design contracts should be put out for bid among designers and architects of varied experience. Even more significant, it decided to seek outside advice on its approach. Members of OITF contacted various professional groups, among them the Advertising Council and the American Society of Industrial Designers, asking them to form a committee to help them in reaching designers about bids.[76]

What ultimately spurred U.S. activity in trade fairs and cultural fairs alike was the Soviet Union's taking first prize at the Bangkok Constitution Fair in December 1953, an event that threw into high relief the outright absence of a U.S. pavilion. Eisenhower needed to find a solution to the Soviets' upper hand in the dozens of trade and cultural fairs around the world every year. As Cull asserts, "A joint effort between the USIA, the Department of Commerce, and 100 U.S. corporations prepared a lavish exhibit for the 1954 Bangkok fair called *The Fruits of Freedom*."[77] By January 1955, there was outright discussion of fairs as useful for propaganda means, as this letter to OITF fair director Roy Williams from Robert Warner emphasized, addressing the upcoming fairs in New Delhi, Djakarta, Bangkok, Damascus, Karachi and Cairo:

The problem facing us with these fall fairs in the Middle East and Far East is quite different from that in Europe. While it is extremely important that we remember the trade aspects of these fairs, the propaganda aspects here are of tremendous importance. Insofar as the value of U.S. prestige is concerned, and in our conduct of the cold war, I do not think there is any question but that these fairs are the most important in the world. . . . My recommendation is that we either put on shows which will assure us of coming out on top in every exhibit or we drop out. We cannot be in the position of taking second place to Russia or, worse, taking third place to Russia and Communist China in Asia.[78]

While the United States had participated in trade fairs before the creation of the OITF,[79] there was evidence that once both this new trade fair agency and the USIA (known as USIS abroad) were paired up to guide U.S. cultural exhibitions, early frictions ensued between these two government entities. Head of the Office of International Trade Fairs, Harrison T. McClung, evokes this tension in a letter dated April 21, 1955 to Robert Warner, Acting Director, Office of International Trade Fairs:

With the exception of the theme for the Karachi fair, we are expecting USIS Public Affairs Officers to give us suggestions for themes for the Far and Middle Eastern Fairs. To date, we have not decided on any theme for these fairs and we would like to work these out as soon as possible, since we cannot proceed with procurement without central themes. Therefore, will you look into this matter so we may finalise this phase of our fair planning. We should ship exhibits to Jakarta no later than May 15.[80]

However, it is keenly evident that the collaboration with private-sector creative forces eventually gave the exhibitions a fighting chance for success. A harbinger to this attitude showed up early, as it appeared OITF personnel clashed with USIS at Bangkok in 1954. In a letter from OITF Director Roy Williams to Bob Warner dated January 12, 1955:

Insofar as Asia is concerned, there must be a clarification as regards authority. We must never again have two competing elements on a fairground as we did in Bangkok. It can only result in one part of the exhibit suffering seriously at the expense of the other. My suggestion would be that the fair managers and you and I in Asia be given full responsibility for putting on the exhibits but that the head of USIS in each area be given veto power.[81]

The United States had clearly enjoyed hit-or-miss success at fairs in the early to mid-1950s,[82] though a pivotal moment in the evolution of the trade fair program came when Roy Williams, the original head of the Office of

International Trade Fairs, left the position in the spring of 1956 and was replaced by Harrison T. McClung, who had briefly served as USIA consultant for trade fairs under Williams.[83] As Jack Masey asserts: "He [McClung] is one of the unsung heroes of this story, coming from the advertising mecca of Madison Avenue to head up OITF. McClung's idea was to go out and get professional industrial designers to do trade shows."[84] This is an important point to understand. The underlying reason the OITF's Paris design office, which up until this point had been responsible for the design and fabrication of U.S. trade fairs, was shut down at this time was because the Soviets were enjoying significant success with their shows in the nonaligned nations, which included displays of model homes and kitchens. As the *New York Times* speculated:

> In recent years the Soviet Union, and to a lesser extent also Communist China and the Eastern Europe satellites, have been demonstrating that such fairs can be effectively employed to spread propaganda, about the "advanced" economies of Communist countries and the "abundance" of goods therein. The fact that many of these fairs in recent years have had little American representation, or none at all, has materially aided the Soviet propaganda.[85]

McClung was from the outset a fierce advocate of using professional industrial designers, and this is, according to Masey, the beginning of the Cold War–era trajectory in which the U.S. government—first through the Department of Commerce and later through a partnership between Commerce and the USIA—opened the doors wide for experimental design for its propaganda. But why did McClung decide to find outside designers to help with the U.S. mission of its trade fair program? McClung had been, after all, quite familiar with U.S. attempts at cultural exhibitions in the early Cold War as well as the goals of the Advertising Council as a former advertising executive and as director of special media of the Citizens Committee for Eisenhower. It was McClung's mostly unilateral decision, in the end, to hand over to the industrial design profession Ike's directive of pushing economic policies through cultural means.

Essentially, no one inside the government, aside from a few individuals like McClung and Masey, knew what to do with exhibiting "America" at these events. And as designer Beverly Payeff-Masey offers: "We ended up showing what the designers wanted to show, because of the urgency of the Cold War."[86] In other words, because of the urgency to compete with the Soviets at international fairs, designers actually began to make decisions about the content. This is similar to the previously mentioned exhibitionary episodes discussed in the introduction of this study: the mastodon story, the U.S. pavilion at the Great Exhibition of 1851, and the MoMA poster displays, in that although there was an official government body overseeing these events, it was still the ingenuity of the private sector that made the strides toward unique success in these exhibits. This paradox of leadership over the content and message of the U.S. trade fair participation is addressed by Payeff-Masey, who believes

> it makes sense that you would need a particular type of person to put these things together. And we should remember that industrial design at this time was not as we know it today. It was an emerging discipline. The American exhibitions actually helped this design discipline emerge just as the designers helped the exhibitions proceed. So, it's really an interesting juxtaposition. And so there's this tension that goes all the way through the story of U.S. cultural exhibitions abroad.

The core themes of *Atoms for Peace* and *People's Capitalism*, for example, around which exhibits would be created, would allow American manufacturers to show their wares. While these themes would provide guidance for the content of the exhibits, the dominant by-product of the transition from Roy Williams to Harrison T. McClung would be the advent of the paradox in management surrounding the message these exhibits would carry. Ultimately, this is the point at which the designers who were not part of the bureaucracy took over, holding free rein over the appearance of these fairs that, over time, were not pushed by policy makers anymore. Mitarachi describes the U.S. participation at trade fairs leading up to 1956:

> The first American exhibits, at the end of 1954 and 1955, were designed and/ or supervised by the Office of Design and Production, maintained in Paris by the Office of International Trade Fairs; Roy Williams was then Director of the OITF. The exhibits . . . demonstrated a consistently tasteful, modern style, and showed much of the same material. A typical display at the Paris Fair, for instance, included a house (decorated by House Beautiful) in which "mother" prepared meals in a modern kitchen equipped with freezer, garbage disposal unit, dishwasher, mixer, and other gadgets. "Father" puttered with the car in the carport, worked with power tools in the home shop.[87]

The U.S. Government Becomes an Exhibit Design Client

In 1956, the Paris design office of OITF, manned by Peter Harnden, would close with design contracts put out for bid among several up-and-coming industrial designers and architects. As Masey points out, "OITF asks the Advertising Council and the American Society of Industrial Designers to select the designers who will be invited to bid on contracts to be held in numerous sites around the world."[88] Mitarachi echoes this idea, in that these designers, who worked with OITF staffers to come up with themes for these new fairs that emerged in 1956, were hired as "problem solvers" in "visual communication." This handing over to designers almost wholeheartedly Ike's mandate to show the positive aspects of American foreign policy and public life through trade fairs placed the designers and their decisions at the forefront of how foreign audiences saw the United States. This "approach to problem-solving," as Mitarachi suggests, fell squarely on the shoulders of designers, and became "undoubtedly one of the most serious responsibilities that the design profession has ever assumed."[89]

In addition, the 1956 fairs that emerged from this new dynamic of designers who were driving the content of the exhibitions were all created under "breakneck conditions."[90] As Mitarachi explains, "Bid guesswork was just the first of their problems. The preliminary surveys, averaging several days to a week, permitted consultation with embassy officials, but the pressure of the schedule—with some contracts signed 60–70 days prior to the opening dates—did not make it easy to do basic research about national attitudes and problems."[91] What would ensue, moreover, would be a severe lack of institutional control at USIA, in part because of the fierce time constraints on delivering the highly complicated pavilions and their contents to points around the world. More importantly, Masey states, "Policy wonks had no interest in meddling with design questions and exhibition people did not report to those responsible for pushing policies."[92]

America Visits an "Uneasy Country": The Fair That Changed It All[93]

To give each viewer one single major impression:
ALL FACETS OF THE AMERICAN SYSTEM ARE
BASED ON RESPECT FOR THE INDIVIDUAL [sic].

Inherent in this impression is the conviction that America's actions are consistently motivated by the moral principle of respect and concern for the rights, welfare, and dignity of individuals of all nations as well as its own.[94]

By 1956, U.S. pavilions at international trade fairs would follow a visual and ideological balance of both Black's and Bayer's display styles tempered with the clean, simple modernism of the international style that was first introduced by the Museum of Modern Art in the early 1930s. This exhibitionary assault of fantasy houses, cars, and other products, displayed in avant-garde architectural structures, broadcast to audiences around the world a make-believe American utopia of "domestic simulacra."[95] Castillo points out that early 1950s fairs showed recreated scenes of blissful domestic life in the United States with real Americans.[96] While well-known industrial designers had been enlisted to help put together fairs in 1955 and earlier, it was the harnessing of this support through competition bidding with which Harrison McClung would redefine and give structure to what had been in its short life span the haphazard way the OITF approached fairs.

The fall of 1956 would witness an array of fairs in countries the United States needed to win over through soft diplomacy methods, particularly through trade fairs. McClung's formula of inserting designers, architects, and museum professionals was in full swing. The American pavilion in Izmir, Turkey, whose theme celebrated "150 Years of U.S. Industrial Progress," featured a pavilion designed by Lothar Witteborg and Henry Gardiner, from the Museum of Natural History.[97] The welcome letter drafted by the White House on August 15, 1956, declared: "The Fair will accelerate the march of progress toward a fuller and more satisfying life for all people," through "the energy and spirit of the Turkish people" that "will assure the steady and prosperous development of the Turkish nation."[98] The Third International Fair in Damascus hosted a U.S. pavilion with the theme of "Free Men Can Be Friends," which featured miscellaneous light industry and agricultural technological displays and was organized by William T. Snaith, managing partner at Loewy Associates.[99] The fair, which most aptly characterizes this period of American ingenuity at these international events, was ironically not a true trade fair but one more focused on world cultures. The Jeshyn International Fair in Kabul, Afghanistan, featured the theme, "Progress through Peace." Organized by Masey and displayed from August 24 through September 7, 1956, this U.S. effort would decisively confirm the use of private architectural and industrial design at all future fairs. However, it is arguable whether this event would reveal more about the utopian visions of individual designers than anything remotely related to policy wonks that, according to Masey, wanted nothing to do with these events.

Though Buckminster Fuller's geodesic domes were first brought to international attention at the 1954 Milan Triennale,[100] he had already made an impression with these structures at the inaugural Aspen industrial design conference in 1952. Fellow attendees included Walter Dorwin Teague, Alfred Knopf, and Nikolaus Pevsner, who himself puzzled over "Bucky" Fuller, who, to him, was a "bit of a medicine man," who had "spent some twenty-five years perfecting geodesic domes, domes of ever lighter materials carrying ever heavier loads."[101] Iterations of these domes would show up at U.S. trade fairs and world expos for the next ten years.

Masey, an original member of George S. Patton's "ghost army" during World War II, "inflating Sherman tanks by mouth" before evolving into an exhibitions designer for the USIA, found himself forced by strong political pressure and strict time constraints to deliver a compelling pavilion to represent America at the International Jeshyn Fair in Kabul in the fall of 1956. What led Masey to Bucky Fuller makes sense: after the war, Masey studied at Yale on the G.I. Bill, working summers at *Architectural Forum* magazine, doing stories about Fuller. In 1951, while working at an architecture firm, Masey received a phone call from the State Department, enlisting him to staff an information program post in India, where for the next five years Masey developed small traveling exhibits to explain the United States to Indians. Since he was the South Asian representative within the USIA, he was contacted to rescue the U.S. participation at Kabul after the British Embassy in Kabul called the U.S. State Department and urged American participation in the Jeshyn International Fair because, at six weeks out, the Soviet Union and its satellite states were reportedly attempting to make a big impression.

The year before, Roy Williams, who was still director of the new OITF, stressed the importance of U.S. participation in "the annual Afghan Independence Fair to be held in Kabul in August," emphasizing that the United States has been "deeply concerned over the problem of Soviet economic penetration of Afghanistan—a situation which had become acute in the past year."[102] In fact, flyovers had been conducted of the fairgrounds, and it became obvious that the Soviets had already developed a large footprint there. It was at this point that McClung asked Masey to find a designer who can go to Kabul to take this on. As there was nobody inside the government who could effectively offer a design on such short notice, this ends up being the story of Bucky Fuller and his domes that would travel to trade fairs in the coming years: "And then I had this lightning bolt. So I call my boss back in Washington [William J. Handley, Near East Area Director of USIA], and say, 'Bill, I had a brainstorm, and I don't know if this is even possible, but there's one guy who I think can do this.' He said, 'Who?' I said, 'Buckminster Fuller.' 'Who the hell is that?' I said, 'This guy is a genius. He's invented this thing called a geodesic dome.'"[103]

After a hasty phone call to Fuller, Masey called an impromptu meeting at the Biltmore Hotel in New York City on May 23, 1956, where he vented concern over the "anticipated slickness of Iron Curtain pavilions"[104] at Kabul. After two days of negotiations, Masey and Fuller agreed to plan to deliver a custom-made dome to Kabul within six weeks. Fuller was enthusiastic about going into Kabul because he was familiar with the work of H. J. Mackinder, a geographer who posited the theory that if one wanted to control the world, one had to control the heartland, and the heartland was Afghanistan. Fuller was enamored with this theory and told Masey, "I'm going there, this is the heartland."[105]

After calling an architect in Germany who could design the interior of the dome, Masey organized the dome and all its contents—the "crap" from the trade fair circuit, which was currently on display at a trade fair in Bangkok and included a bouncing ball-bearing display, a Borden talking chicken, a talking cow, a television display, and so forth—to Kabul (figures 2.1–2.3).

Figure 2.1.   The "Talking Chicken" display at the U.S. Pavilion, Jeshyn International Fair, Kabul, Afghanistan, 1956.
Courtesy, Jack Masey Collection.

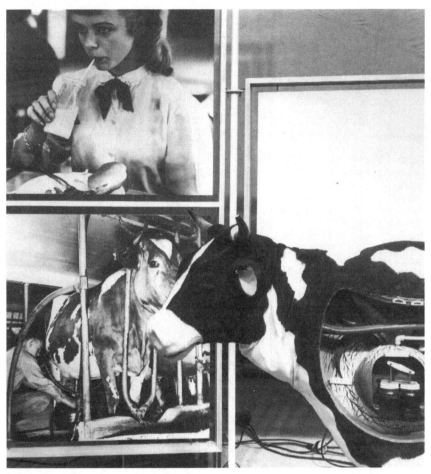

Figure 2.2. The "Talking Cow" display at the U.S. Pavilion, Jeshyn International Fair, Kabul, Afghanistan, 1956.
Courtesy, Jack Masey Collection.

Fuller's representatives, Jefferson Davis Brooks and John Dixon, flew out to Kabul, after switching to tiny planes because of the nature of the Kabul landing strip, which, as Masey points out, "is in a bowl, in the Hindu Kush mountain range. The foothills of the Himalayas."[106]

What happened next was emblematic of the "breakneck speed" of organizing and delivering these pavilions, as Mitarachi mentions. Three days before the opening, the U.S. pavilion had nothing but an eight-inch concrete slab poured. Masey himself admits, "There's nothing else, and, it is obvious that the U.S. may not succeed this time." The representative from the OITF, Tom

Figure 2.3.   The television exhibit in the U.S. Pavilion, Jeshyn International Fair, Kabul, Afghanistan 1956.
Courtesy, Jack Masey Collection.

Hall Miller,[107] witnessed the putting up of the dome, which took forty-eight hours (figures 2.4–2.7). Masey describes the scene: "The whole fairground is surrounding us. The Russians are there. The Chinese are there. They're watching, not believing their eyes, the American ingenuity. American genius."[108] Despite the apparent success at American entrepreneurial drive in delivering an exciting U.S. pavilion on time, ultimately, much can be read into this letter from Jack Masey to Harrison T. McClung, September 6, 1956:

> The bouncing ball bearing; the Lionel model trains; the talking cow and the talking chicken are all very amusing gimmicks, but it is doubtful whether they are going to change men's minds about the United States. At best, they are great crowd drawers and this is fine if the Fair Program has no other motive but to entertain. Entertain we must in Southeast Asia but I think we must have substance, too. Without it, I see little value in participating in Southeast Asian fairs at all.[109]

Figure 2.4.   Afghan workers assist in erecting Buckminster Fuller-designed dome for U.S. Pavilion at Jeshyn International Fair, Kabul, Afghanistan,1956.
Courtesy, Jack Masey Collection.

The dome would prove to be portentous and preternatural. It was an inexpensive dazzler. It also came about as a result of a phenomenon mentioned earlier in this chapter: the design expertise that enlisted the help of outsider Fuller came from within the government. "I've been in the business of deceit forever," Masey jokingly added.[110] And it was McClung who, in a December 1, 1956, report, outlined his recommendations for portable, easy-to-use exhibition hardware that could be installed and deinstalled for potential use in international trade fairs (figures 2.8–2.9). The report reveals McClung's roots in advertising and his "pitch" for what would become two of the most widely used structural technologies in the twentieth century: geodesic domes and Unistrut building materials.[111]

Figure 2.5. Workers constructing Fuller dome for U.S. Pavilion, Jeshyn International Fair, Kabul, Afghanistan, 1956.
Courtesy Jack Masey Collection.

Figure 2.6.   Workers begin applying the covering for the Fuller dome at the U.S. Pavilion, Jeshyn International Fair, Kabul, Afghanistan, 1956.
Courtesy Jack Masey Collection.

Figure 2.7.   The U.S. Pavilion nearing completion, Jeshyn International Fair, Kabul, Afghanistan, 1956.
Courtesy, Jack Masey Collection.

Figure 2.8.   The entrance to the U.S. Pavilion, Jeshyn International Fair, Kabul, Afghanistan, 1956.
Courtesy, Jack Masey Collection.

Figure 2.9.   The entrance to the U.S. Pavilion, from the inside looking out, featuring portrait of President Eisenhower and the New York skyline, with welcome message from the president.
Courtesy, Jack Masey Collection.

By early 1957, USIA had its own exhibits office run by Masey as a result of the success of the 1956 fairs. Masey concludes: "So what happened was, after Kabul, the office of trade fairs (OITF) was slowly wiped off the face of the earth and USIA took over. So this is like the changing of the guard. You had Commerce in there for a while, but then we got bored with trade fairs. We didn't want to do them anymore. No more trade fairs. And that's when USIA took over."[112]

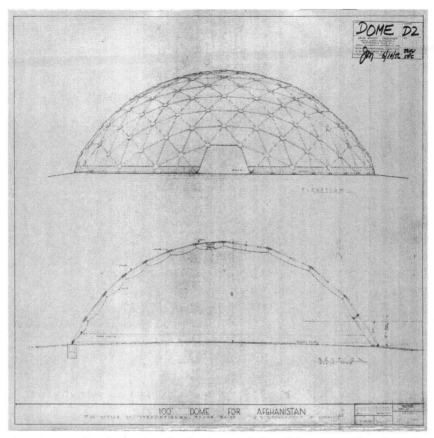

Figure 2.10. Elevation section drawing by Geodesics of the U.S. Pavilion dome designed by Buckminster Fuller, 1956.
Courtesy, Jack Masey Collection.

Conclusion—A Look at American Imperial Idioms[113]

The alliance struck among government agencies and the private sector over international exhibitions would prove providential in the way America showed itself to the world. This partnership elicits ongoing themes that inform the trajectory of the exhibitions that reflected their organizers' "need to be understood as vehicles intended to win popular support for national imperial policies."[114]

As Pulos explains, dreams of utopia, of infallible societies, have been expressed through world fairs and national pavilions, particularly the 1939 New

York World's Fair and its *Futurama* pavilion that envisioned a harmoniously laid-out future urbanscape. By offering a perfected vision of American life through the one-off fantasy pavilions perpetrated by government-sanctioned industrial designers and architects, what was really being offered was, in essence, an escapist vision, an impossible world that a visitor could see momentarily at a trade fair but never truly inhabit.[115] Bennett shows that while the Great Exhibition inspired later world's fairs' "displays of elaborate projects for the improvement of social conditions in the areas of health, sanitation, education, and welfare," these subsequent exhibitions embodied

> Utopian principles of social organization which . . . would eventually be realized in perpetuity. As world fairs fell increasingly under the influence of modernism, the rhetoric of progress tended, as Rydell puts it, to be "translated into a Utopian statement about the future," promising the imminent dissipation of social tensions once progress had reached the point where its benefits might be generalized.[116]

As several government documents have shown, one ideological thrust of the organizers of the U.S. trade fair pavilions was to have visitors identify with the very power that would ultimately dominate them ideologically. In a Bayerian twist, visitors who coursed through the established routes of meticulously themed pavilions would be able, in the end, "to identify with power, to see it as, if not directly theirs, then indirectly so, a force regulated and channelled by society's ruling groups but for the good of all: this was the rhetoric of power embodied in the exhibitionary complex—a power made manifest . . . by its ability to organize and co-ordinate an order of things and to produce a place for the people in relation to that order."[117]

The leitmotif of experimental architecture, the most well-known example being the Fuller dome first introduced by Masey at the 1956 Kabul fair, would become, citing Samuel Taylor Coleridge's well-known paean to Kubla Khan, "a miracle of rare device" at several U.S. pavilions at international trade fairs.

To return briefly to nineteenth-century precedents to 1950s U.S. trade fair pavilions, it is useful to quote Bennett, who, citing Pearson, urges an understanding that through the "state's role in the promotion of art and culture," the influence needed to "making extended populations governable" worked "by entertainment rather than by disciplined schooling; and by subtlety and encouragement." In other words, the U.S. trade fair pavilion, through its seduction of foreign visitors, ultimately "depended on their voluntary participation."[118] Architecturally, the Fuller dome would seduce visitors as a symbol understood both as a structural and cultural marvel and, from the perspective of the exhibitionary complex, as what Preziosi might call "another structural descendant of the great Crystal Palace."[119]

As Masey points out, the Kabul dome arrived at the eleventh hour, costing $100,000 and taking forty-eight hours to erect, with the help of Afghani laborers who would remark that the dome was similar to the mobile tent structures—yurts—they used in Afghan daily life. A description of an encounter that occurred in the dome during the fair: As Masey was training twenty English- and Farsi-speaking guides to explain the dome's contents to visitors, he was approached by one of his American assistants, who said, "Jack, there are five representatives from the Chinese pavilion who want to see you." They entered the dome. They looked up, and their average age, according to Masey, was thirty to thirty-five. One of the group approached and with an American accent said, "Hi. You may be confused. All of us used to be Americans." As Masey clarifies, "They were very excited about what was happening in China, and so they all went to China. They were all now Chinese citizens." And the leader of the group continued: "But I gotta tell you something." Looking around the building, he said, "We can now see what we left in America." As Masey concluded: "It blew my mind. They were crushed. And they asked if they could draw it. I said, 'Of course, and if I can get my hands on a set of drawings, I'll send them to you. I know Mr. Fuller, and, the fact that you're interested in this structure, he would love this.' They had never heard of him, but wanted to know whom the 'genius' was who made this. They were engineers back in China."[120]

Kabul, in the end, is an ideal example of how the exhibitionary complex applies both to individuals and to groups. Masey established a routine, first in India in 1955, of having local bilingual citizens explaining U.S. values and ingenuity in the vernacular to their own people. Speeches given by local bilingual Afghans to the U.S. pavilion visitors included this phrase: "The very dome which houses these exhibits . . . is a demonstration of the degree of industrial progress attained in the U.S. . . . It emphasizes the marriage of aesthetics and technology—two very vital phenomena which are symbolic of a people who believe that only through peace can there be progress."[121]

This practice would later find traction in the use of young, attractive, bilingual American guides to explain similar material to Soviet citizens, starting at the *American National Exhibition* in Moscow in 1959. Though this study is not focused on detecting the emotional and intellectual tenor of foreign visitors to the U.S. trade fair pavilions, the reaction of the Chinese engineers informs Bennett's concept of "the soft approach" to winning hearts and minds through the mechanism of the exhibitionary complex.

The following chapter will further explore the concept of Bayer's "total environment" theory as it relates to the spectacular aspects of the 1959 *American National Exhibition* in Moscow, an event that could be alternatively described as an American *gesamtkunstwerk*. Invoking Guy DeBord, who describes the spectacle as "a form of drama, a form of theater, and a craze of information flows, music, entertainment, and other strategies intended to attract consumers from all walks of life," Jonathan Matusitz explains that these specific venues are in the end less about refrigerators, stoves, and furniture and more about the unattainable and unreplicable experience of the spectacle itself.[122]

By 1957, the USIA had pledged deeply into the overseas trade fair program, constructing pavilions and designing exhibits to build trade and friendships throughout the world. What becomes more evident in the following chapters are the problems the designers face in trying to get this work done. These individuals who are not part of the government's public diplomacy bureaucracy continue making unilateral decisions and are enabled by the USIA's own in-house operation. As this chapter explains, this is the point of great change in exhibitions abroad.

While this chapter has been devoted to the ways the United States was an image maker as it self-styled itself through national pavilions at trade fairs during the mid-1950s, it is important to see the inversion of this idea, in that in the competition for the hearts and minds of millions of foreign visitors, the United States can also be seen as an image breaker. Historian David Freedberg discusses the political aspects of image breaking, the pulling down of symbols of repressive individuals and regimes. He studies politically motivated iconoclasm, or "the shuffling off the imperialist yoke," with later twentieth-century examples. Freedberg writes, "To pull down the images of a rejected order or an authoritarian and hated one is to wipe the slate clean and inaugurate the promise of utopia."[123] As the Soviets dominated trade fairs for years, the U.S. arrival on the scene was as the iconoclast that destroys the old to bring in the new. Once again, this battle for hearts and minds was in another sense the battle of one utopian dream against another, and it would remain, through the 1970s, in the hands of designers. As Mitarachi stresses:

> In throwing the problem open to designers, it not only gave members of the profession a good chunk of government work; it also gave them a new kind of responsibility for presenting America, and in some cases formulating America's approach to other nations. Designers were being asked to be propagandists; design became a tool of communication and the visual composition of an exhibition a secondary problem.[124]

It could be argued that McClung and the revolution in trade fair design that he sparked turns the exhibitionary complex on its ear. But no, it was still an ordering mechanism that carried with it the imprimatur of the United States government. U.S. pavilions became a type of, in the words of Preziosi, epistemological technology that visitors (shoppers and slaves) responded to because it was a potent, contrived, and at times specious representation of America. Fictional or not, this image of America, engaged to win hearts and minds the world over, continued to fulfill a distinctly hegemonic function.

Notes

1. See "USIA Recommendations for Trade Fairs," in NA RG489, Records of the International Trade Administration, Bureau of Foreign Commerce, Office of International Trade Fairs, Correspondence and Reports, 1954–1958, OCB Agenda, Quarterly Reports, Box 4, Folder: "Policy, 4/55–7/56."

2. Jane Fiske Mitarachi, "Design as a Political Force," *Industrial Design* (February 1957): 13.

3. As quoted in Kenneth Osgood, *Total Cold War: Eisenhower's Secret Propaganda Battle at Home and Abroad* (Lawrence: University of Kansas Press, 2006), 217–18.

4. On February 27, 1947, Assistant Secretary of State Dean Acheson, in an Oval Office meeting with President Truman, Secretary of State George Marshall, and a congresssional delegation headed by Senator Arthur Vandenberg, described in plain terms the polarization of power between the free West and the communist East: "Only two great powers remained in the world . . . United States and the Soviet Union. We had arrived at a situation unparalleled since ancient times. Not since Rome and Carthage had there been such a polarization of power on this earth. . . . For the United States to take steps to strengthen countries threatened with Soviet aggression or Communist subversion . . . was to protect the security of the United States—it was to protect freedom itself." In Henry Kissinger, *Diplomacy* (New York, Simon & Schuster, 1994), 451–52.

5. See Klaus Knorr's theory of "patronal leadership," when, after World War II, the U.S. aid sent to Europe and Japan enabled an American status which Keohane calls "hegemonic leadership," in Robert O. Keohane, *After Hegemony: Cooperation and Discord in the World Political Economy* (Princeton, NJ: Princeton University Press, 1984), 128. These exchanges, in which the recipient receives more than it gives, results in a goods-for-influence scenario, which further strengthens the hegemon and engages what Albert Hirschman (1945/1980) calls the "influence effect," as cited in Keohane, ibid., 139.

6. Smith-Mundt, otherwise known as the U.S. Information and Educational Exchange Act, Public Law 80-402 (1948).

7. See Matt Armstrong, "A Brief History of the Smith-Mundt Act and Why Changing It Matters," *www.MountainRunner.us* (blog), February 23, 2012, http://mountainrunner.us/2012/02/history_of_smith-mundt/#more-3174.

8. *The United States Information Agency: A Commemoration* (Washington, DC: U.S. Department of State, 1999), 15. As Osgood concurs, both the Fulbright and Smith-Mundt Acts "formalized the government's interest in educational and cultural exchanges, but these activities were explicitly separated from government propaganda, at least on paper. Cultural affairs were to promote 'increased understanding' rather than support for U.S. foreign policy goals" (218–19). For a deeper discussion of the state of U.S. international information programs during the transition from the Truman to Eisenhower administrations, see Nicholas J. Cull, *The Cold War and the United States Information Agency: American Propaganda and Public Diplomacy, 1945–1989* (Cambridge: Cambridge University Press, 2008), 39–41. See also Melvyn P. Leffler, *A Preponderance of Power: National Security, the Truman Administration, and the Cold War* (Palo Alto, CA: Stanford University Press, 1992), 181: "In mid-1947, [George] Kennan and his colleagues agreed that their most important task was to launch the Marshall Plan and co-opt western Germany. They had to defeat Communist efforts and the Kremlin's hopes to lure Western Europe into the Soviet orbit."

9. It would be designer Peter Harnden, with assistance by Philip George, who planned and deployed these exhibitions. Harnden, headquartered in Paris, later became Chief of Design and Production for the U.S. trade fair entries in the 1950s. Beverly Payeff-Masey, researcher for *Cold War Confrontations*, tells that the Marshall Plan exhibits were written word for word by policy people: "They couldn't go out unless they were literally combed over for content, by people in the government. And Phil was the guy who went out there moving trucks, barges, and so forth." Beverly Payeff-Masey, in discussion with author, New York City, August 23, 2010.

10. See Sara Lennox, "Constructing Femininity in the Early Cold War Era," in *German Pop Culture: How "American" Is It?*, ed. Agnes C. Mueller (Ann Arbor: University of Michigan Press 2007), 74–75.

11. Greg Castillo, "Domesticating the Cold War: Household Consumption as Propaganda in Marshall Plan Germany," *Journal of Contemporary History* 40, no. 2 (April 2005): 261.

12. Ibid., 263.

13. See Peter Hall, "A Good Argument," *Metropolis Magazine*, March 2009, http://www.metropolismag.com/March-2009/A-Good-Argument/.

14. Blanche Wiesen Cook, *The Declassified Eisenhower: A Divided Legacy of Peace and Political Warfare* (New York: Penguin, 1984), 81. See also James Reston, "Eisenhower Plans Key Staff to Guide 'Cold War' Policy," *New York Times*, January 11, 1953, 53. For further understanding of the political zeitgeist of this period, see Henry A. Kissinger, "Reflections on American Diplomacy," *Foreign Affairs* 35, no. 1 (Oct. 1956): 37–56. Lizabeth Cohen has described a distinctly American "consumer's republic," which after World War II "promised great prosperity through yoking employment and economic growth to high consumer demand," thereby providing

the United States "a ready weapon in the political struggles of the Cold War." For the original source, see Lizabeth Cohen, *A Consumers' Republic: The Politics of Mass Consumption in Postwar America* (New York: Vintage, 2004), 124.

15. Cook, *Declassified Eisenhower*, 74–75.

16. Robert Griffith, "The Selling of America: The Advertising Council and American Politics, 1942–1960," *Business History Review* 57, no. 3 (Autumn 1983): 405. On business ideology in the 1950s, see also Francis X. Sutton et al., *The American Business Creed* (Cambridge, MA: Harvard University Press, 1956).

17. Jack Masey and Conway Lloyd Morgan, *Cold War Confrontations: U.S. Exhibitions and Their Role in the Cultural Cold War* (Baden, Switzerland: Lars Müller, 2008), 155.

18. Cook, *Declassified Eisenhower*, xxii.

19. Robert H. Haddow, *Pavilions of Plenty: Exhibiting American Culture Abroad in the 1950s* (Washington, DC: Smithsonian Institution, 1997), 4. See, also for background on the Advertising Council, Frank W. Fox, *Madison Avenue Goes to War: The Strange Military Career of American Advertising, 1941–45* (Provo, UT: Brigham Young University Press, 1975), 22, 49–55. On the early history of the Advertising Council, see especially Harold B. Thomas, "The Background and Beginning of the Advertising Council," in *The Promise of Advertising*, ed. C. H. Sandage (Homewood, IL: Irwin, 1961), 15–58. For the transition of the wartime Advertising Council's peacetime influence on the executive branch and vice-versa, see Wendy L. Wall, *Inventing the "American Way": The Politics of Consensus from the New Deal to the Civil Rights Movement* (Oxford: Oxford University Press, 2008); and Griffith, "Selling of America," 392, 394: "The Advertising Council," observed James Young, was an "and/or" organization. "It believes that there are some things in the public interest that business is best fitted to accomplish, some which government is best equipped to accomplish, and some which government and business, working together, can best get done." See also Chester J. LaRoche to Harry S. Truman, July 11, 1947, in White House Central Files (WHCF), President's Personal File (PPF 2151), Truman Papers, Independence, Missouri.

20. Griffith, "Selling of America," 388.

21. Ibid.

22. Ibid., 392.

23. Ibid., 412. Griffith discusses Ike's attempts as early as 1948 to push the Advertising Council "to sell . . . an understanding of the free enterprise system," 404. See also Kenneth Osgood, from March 10, 2008, lecture at the Miller Center for Public Affairs, YouTube video, 5:09, posted by MaAmericanpresident, March 10, 2008, http://www.youtube.com/watch?v=0rBdjBZooas: "I was surprised to discover how far-reaching the global battle for hearts and minds was . . . the imperative of shaping, influencing, and manipulating public opinion affected an extraordinary range of activities relating to U.S. foreign relations. Trade and economic aid, space exploration and scientific research, atomic energy and disarmament, book publication and translation, educational exchanges, cultural interactions, and the day-to-day operations

of American diplomats abroad." The real battles, Ike emphasized, were political, economic, and psychological. And he made this case quite forcefully in the January 1958 State of the Union address. And he said the Soviets were waging total Cold War: "What makes the Soviet threat unique in history is its all-inclusiveness." See the Introduction, note 29 for complete reference.

24. Griffith, "Selling of America," 412.

25. For ample discussion of the *People's Capitalism* campaign, see Kenneth Osgood, *Total Cold War: Eisenhower's Secret Propaganda Battle at Home and Abroad* (Lawrence: University of Kansas Press, 2006); Haddow, *Pavilions of Plenty*; and Cull, *The Cold War and the United States Information Agency*.

26. Cook, *Declassified Eisenhower*, 311. See also Victoria de Grazia, *Irresistible Empire: America's Advance through 20th-Century Europe* (Cambridge, MA: Belknap, 2005), 350–53. Griffith affirms: "If consensus did indeed characterize America's national culture in the 1950s, it was perhaps to a degree we have not fully appreciated, a consensus manufactured by America's corporate leaders, packaged by the advertising industry, and merchandised through the channels of mass communication," in "The Selling of America," 412.

27. NA RG489 Records of the International Trade Administration, Bureau of Foreign Commerce, Office of International Trade Fairs, Correspondence and Reports, 1954–1958, Box #1, Folder: "The Advertising Council."

28. Ibid., August 13, 1956, Annual Report [to Mr. James M. Lambie, Jr., White House, Special Assistant in The White House Office handling advertising liaison, from Ted Repplier, The Advertising Council].

29. Griffith, "The Selling of America," 405.

30. George C. Herring, *From Colony to Superpower: U.S. Foreign Relations since 1776* (Oxford: Oxford University Press, 2008), 655.

31. Ibid., 652. For an analysis of the Soviet cultural approach to non-Western and nonaligned countries, see chapter 7 of Frederick C. Barghoorn, *The Soviet Cultural Offensive: The Role of Cultural Diplomacy in Soviet Foreign Policy* (Princeton, NJ: Princeton University Press, 1960), 188–225.

32. Daniel Boorstin, *The Image: Or What Happened to the American Dream* (New York: Atheneum, 1961), 243.

33. Directive Approved by the President for the Guidance of the United States Information Agency, October 28, 1953, Eisenhower, *Public Papers of the Presidents, 1953*: 728; Streibert to Eisenhower, October 27, 1953, *Foreign Relations of the United States, 1952–1954*: 1755.

34. Wilson P. Dizard, *Inventing Public Diplomacy: The Story of the U.S. Information Agency* (Boulder, CO: Lynne Rienner, 2004), 19.

35. Another precedent that wartime information activities established was, according to Dizard, the use of public opinion surveys to assess public attitudes toward American foreign policies: "The corollary to this proposition was that results could be used to develop appeals that would influence public opinion. . . . Harold Lasswell, the acknowledged leader of the group, summed up their basic approach when he

defined mass communications as answering the questions, 'Who says what, in what channel, to whom, and with what effect?' These theoretical findings became the guidelines for U.S. overseas cultural and information operations over the next half-century," ibid.

36. Frances Stonor Saunders, *Who Paid the Piper: The CIA and the Cultural Cold War* (London: Granta, 1999), 17. Source as noted: Gregory Bateson, Research and Analysis, OSS, to General Donovan, August 18, 1945 (CIA.HSC/RG263/NARA). For additional research on the CIA's involvement in the realm of cultural diplomacy, see Hugh Wilford, *The Mighty Wurlitzer: How the CIA Played America* (Cambridge, MA: Harvard University Press, 2008).

37. Burnett Anderson, in Hans N. Tuch and G. Lewis Schmidt, eds., *Ike and the USIA: A Commemorative Symposium* (Washington, DC: U.S. Information Alumni Association, Public Diplomacy Foundation, 1991), 24. See John Gunther, *Inside Russia Today* (New York: Harper, 1957), 388: "When, however, the Soviet Union broke the American monopoly on atomic bombs in 1949, and in particular when its first hydrogen bomb was successfully exploded in 1953, the balance of power in the world was irremediably changed." See also Chris Tudda, *The Truth Is Our Weapon: The Rhetorical Diplomacy of Dwight D. Eisenhower and John Foster Dulles* (Baton Rouge: Louisiana State University Press, 2006), 87–88. For Tudda, the *Atoms for Peace* concept "grew out of the recommendations made by the Operation Candor panel as well as the successful testing of a hydrogen bomb by the Soviets in August" and that the speech was "predicated on exposing the post-Stalin peace campaign and elevating the U.S. position as the foremost champion of peace and disarmament."

38. Ibid., 25. See also Stewart Alsop, "Eisenhower Pushes Operation Candor," *Washington Post*, September 21, 1953, http://www.eisenhower.archives.gov/research /online_documents/atoms_for_peace/Binder20.pdf.

39. The FDCA would later create the film *Operation Ivy* not as a film prescribing actions to take in the case of a thermonuclear attack but merely as an educational tool for audiences curious about the early experiments with hydrogen bomb technology.

40. See, for instance, F. Barrows Colton, "Man's New Servant: The Friendly Atom," *National Geographic Magazine* (January 1954): 86–87; Henry A. Dunlap and Hans N. Tuch, *Atoms at Your Service* (New York: Harper and Brothers, 1957).

41. Osgood, *Total Cold War*, 217.

42. Dwight D. Eisenhower. "Executive Order 10483—Establishing the Operations Coordinating Board," September 2, 1953, PPP, Washington, DC.

43. Osgood, *Total Cold War*, 216–17.

44. See March 9, 1955, Bulletin from American Association of Advertising Agencies on plans for exhibits at international trade fairs in 1955 and 1956, in NA RG40, General Records of the Department of Commerce, Office of International Trade Fairs, Public and Industry Relation Records, 1955–1956, Box 1, Folder "OITF-Public Information File, Correspondence, 1955, A."

45. U.S. Department of Commerce memorandum, October 22, 1956, in NA RG489, Records of the International Trade Administration, Bureau of Foreign Commerce,

OITF, Correspondence and Reports, 1954–1958, OCB Agenda—Quarterly Reports, Box 4, Folder "Personal, McClung, May 56–Oct 56." See also Osgood, *Total Cold War*, 214–15.

46. *Billboard Magazine*, July 8, 1957, 66.

47. See Arthur J. Pulos, *The American Design Adventure, 1940–1975* (Cambridge, MA: MIT Press, 1988), 243.

48. *Operating Guide for U.S. Government Personnel and Contractors Planning Exhibits at International Trade Fairs*, USIA Historical Collection, State Department, 1954.

49. See also August 13, 1953, memorandum from William L. Clark to Richard A. Humphrey: "While it is recognized that the majority of these fairs or expositions were 'trade' or 'industrial' fairs, it was believed that American business might be induced to cooperate in a series of joint business-government exhibits at these fairs, thereby minimizing the cost of government participation." In Information Center Service folder, U.S. Information Agency, USIA Historical Collection.

50. *Operating Guide for U.S. Government Personnel.*

51. See Haddow, *Pavilions of Plenty*, 62.

52. Cull, *The Cold War and the United States Information Agency*, 118.

53. Mitarachi, "Design as a Political Force," 3.

54. On January 1, 1943, Black partnered with Herbert Read in the creation of the Design Research Unit, whose main goal "is to present a service so complete that it could undertake any design case that might confront the State, Municipal Authorities, Industry and Commerce," in Avril Blake, *Misha Black* (London: Design Council, 1984), 30.

55. Bayer would by 1946 join the Container Corporation of America as art director at Walter Paepcke's invitation. Paepcke's Aspen Institute would subsequently give Bayer and the nascent community of U.S. industrial designers a haven to share their ideas on design and the arts. See Gwen F. Chanzit, *From Bauhaus to Aspen: Herbert Bayer and Modernist Design in America* (Boulder, CO: Johnson Books / Denver Art Museum, 2005), 155.

56. See Masey and Morgan, *Cold War Confrontations*, 14, 165.

57. Misha Black, ed. *Exhibition Design* (London: Architectural Press, 1950), 30.

58. Chanzit, *From Bauhaus to Aspen*, 112; George Nelson, ed., *Display* (New York: Whitney, 1953), 110.

59. Nelson discusses this philosophical rift concerning the control of crowds through exhibit spaces. For Bayer, he states, "An exhibition has a story to tell. The story begins at the entrance and ends at the exit, and it should be seen—just as a book is read—in its proper sequence," in *Display*, 116. See also Haddow, *Pavilions of Plenty*, introduction, chapters 2 and 8; James Sloan Allen, *The Romance of Commerce and Culture: Capitalism, Modernism, and the Chicago-Aspen Crusade for Cultural Reform* (Chicago: University of Chicago Press, 1983), chapters 1 and 2. On design concepts generated from the Aspen conferences, see Reyner Banham, ed., *The Aspen Papers: Twenty Years of Design Theory from the International Design Conference in Aspen* (New York: Praeger, 1974). The design for this book comes, perhaps not so

ironically, from Chermayeff & Geismar Associates, one of the firms that would be responsible for later design of the U.S. pavilion at Expo 67 in Montreal.

60. Chanzit, *From Bauhaus to Aspen*, 145. For more on the arrival of design emigrés to the United States from Europe in the interwar years as the catalyst that pushed both American industrial design and, more relevantly, exhibition design into a new dynamism that would reach its apex in the postwar years of museum and trade fair displays, see Chanzit, 144; Pulos, *The American Design Adventure, 1940–1975*.

61. Iwona Blazwick, "Temple/White Cube/Laboratory," in *What Makes a Great Exhibition?*, ed. Paula Marincola (Philadelphia: Philadelphia Exhibitions Initiative, 2006), 124. For more general studies of the MoMA's history, see, for instance, A. Conger Goodyear, *The Museum of Modern Art: The First Ten Years* (New York: Museum of Modern Art, 1943); Russell Lynes, *Good Old Modern: The Museum of Modern Art* (New York: Atheneum, 1973); and Mary Anne Staniszewski, *The Power of Display: A History of Exhibition Installations at the Museum of Modern Art* (Cambridge, MA: MIT Press, 1998). For the organic design competitions at the MoMA in the 1940s, which form part of this trajectory toward the trade fairs, see Peter Blake, *No Place Like Utopia: Modern Architecture and the Company We Kept* (New York: Norton, 1993), 72–173. For more discussion of modernism and the concept of the American Century, see Jeffrey L. Meikle, *Design in the USA* (Oxford: Oxford University Press, 2005), 136.

62. See Nelson, *Display*, 128–30.

63. In 1934, Philip Johnson organized the *Machine Art* exhibition at the MoMA. See Museum of Modern Art, *Machine Art: March 6 to April 30, 1934, Sixtieth Anniversary Edition* (New York: Abrams, 1994) and "The Talk of the Town: Machine Art," *New Yorker*, March 17, 1934, 18. For discussion of the transition of industrial design to high art and museum-quality display both in museums and in trade, see Norman Bel Geddes, "Toward Design," *Advertising Arts* (March 1933): 9–11; J. Stewart Johnson, *American Modern 1925–1940: Design for a New Age* (New York: Abrams, 2000); Roland Marchand, *Advertising the American Dream: Making Way for Modernity, 1920–1940* (Berkeley: University of California Press, 1985); and Walter Dorwin Teague, "Rightness Sells," *Advertising Arts* (January 1934): 25–26.

64. Meikle, *Design in the USA*, 149. See also, Nelson, *Display*, 129–43.

65. Paola Antonelli, "Design and Architecture: Paola Antonelli Interviewed by Bennett Simpson," in *What Makes a Great Exhibition?*, ed. Paula Marincola (Philadelphia: Philadelphia Exhibitions Initiative, 2006), 87. For discussion surrounding the 1934 *Machine Art* exhibit, see A. Philip McMahon, "Would Plato Find Artistic Beauty in Machines?" *Parnassus* 7, no. 2 (February 1935): 6–8. The author touches on the innate beauty of geometry wherever it arises, be it in nature or in man-made machines. See also Edward Alden Jewell, "The Realm of Art: The Machine and Abstract Beauty," *New York Times*, March 11, 1934, Arts 2.

66. Antonelli, "Design and Architecture," 86. See also Bruce Altshuler, ed., *Salon to Biennial—Exhibitions That Made Art History*, vol. 1, *1863–1959* (London: Phaidon, 2008), 17. "The adoption of the white cube as an international standard for the

display of modern and contemporary art can be credited largely to the exhibitions mounted during the 1930s at the Museum of Modern Art in New York by founding director Alfred H. Barr, Jr. But it was on a study trip to Germany in the late 1920s that Barr came upon the kind of display that he would adapt for the MoMA when it was established in 1929." On Alfred Barr's connection to and enthusiasm for modern architecture and industrial design, see Blake, *No Place Like Utopia*, 128, 147.

67. Staniszewski, *The Power of Display*, 159.

68. Ibid.

69. Bennett, "The Exhibitionary Complex," 80.

70. Ibid.

71. Walter Benjamin, *Reflections: Essays, Aphorisms, Autobiographical Writings*, ed. Peter Jemetz, trans. Edmund Jephcott (New York: Harcourt Brace Jovanovich, 1978), 152.

72. Bennett asserts that two shifts in how exhibitions were treated, starting with the Crystal Palace, were the shift from exhibiting "the *processes* to the *products* of production," and the evolution of "the principles of classification based on nations . . . in the form of national courts or display areas," in "The Exhibitionary Complex," 94–95.

73. Donald Preziosi, *Brain of the Earth's Body: Art, Museums, and the Phantasms of Modernity* (Minneapolis: University of Minnesota Press, 2003), 113.

74. Ibid., 114.

75. Umberto Eco, "Two Families of Objects," in *Travels in Hyperreality: Essays*, trans. William Weaver (San Diego: Harcourt, 1986), 183. See also Paul A. Taylor, "Hyperreality," in *The Wiley-Blackwell Encyclopedia of Globalization*, ed. George Ritzer (Oxford: Blackwell, 2012). This author writes: "The crucial feature of hyperreality is the notion that previous traditional notions of an authentic 'pure' reality are no longer tenable. It refers less to an inability to distinguish between what is fake and what is real (which presupposes at least an ongoing possibility that the distinction can still be made) and more to the need to recognize that the distinction is now impossible to make because global media technologies have irredeemably altered the very texture of cultural reality."

76. Mitarachi, "Design as a Political Force," 3.

77. Cull, *The Cold War and the United States Information Agency*, 113–14. For discussion on how State, Commerce, and USIA set out to balance their roles in the trade fair program, see NA RG489 Records of the International Trade Administration, Bureau of Foreign Commerce, Office of International Trade Fairs, Correspondence and Reports, 1954–1958, Exhibit Proposals—Industry Letters, Box 2, Folder "Policy, 11/55–7/56," specifically "Agreed Policy Guide Lines for International Trade Fair Program," which is signed by USIA Director Theodore Streibert and Secretary of Commerce Sinclair Weeks.

78. NA RG40 General Records of the Department of Commerce, Office of International Trade Fairs, International Trade Fairs Historic Document File, 1957, Box 1, Folder "Trade Fair Program, Miscellaneous Correspondence thru 4/30/55, OITF,"

January 12, 1955, letter to Roy F. Williams from Robert Warner, 1. See January 27, 1955, letter to Don D. Canfield, Consultant on Trade Fairs, from Roy F Williams, Director, Office of International Trade Fairs, on Frankfurt and Hannover fairs, in same folder, which references in similar fashion exhibits designer Peter Harnden's striving for making fairs a success.

79. See Greg Castillo, "Domesticating the Cold War: Household Consumption as Propaganda in Marshall Plan Germany," *Journal of Contemporary History* 40, no. 2 (April 2005): 261–88; also Jack Masey, in discussion with author, interview, New York City, August 23, 2010: "In the early 1950s, Commerce was going to a ton of shows through Asia, including Bangkok, Tokyo, you name it. Throughout Europe. The Marshall Plan countries. All of this was going on. But with not-so-good stuff, unfortunately."

80. See memorandum, Harrison T. McClung, whose official title was "coordinator of trade fairs," U.S. Information Agency to Robert Warner, Acting Director, Office of International Trade Fairs, April 21, 1955, in NA RG40 General Records of the Department of Commerce, Office of International Trade Fairs, International Trade Fairs Historic Document File, 1957, Box 1, Folder "Trade Fair Program, Miscellaneous Correspondence thru 4/30/55, OITF." An earlier memorandum in this folder, also to Bob Warner, dated February 20, 1955, demonstrates McClung's collegiality with the director of trade fairs as well as McClung's presence at trade fairs throughout the Far East, Middle East, and Europe as OITF's public diplomacy consultant. Between March 10 and April 2, 1955, McClung's itinerary took him from DC to New York to London to New Delhi to Karachi to Damascus to Beirut to Cairo to Rome to New York to DC.

81. NA RG40 General Records of the Department of Commerce, Office of International Trade Fairs, International Trade Fairs Historic Document File, 1957, Box 1, Folder "Trade Fair Program, Miscellaneous Correspondence thru 4/30/55, OITF," 2.

82. See "Cinerama in Damascus," *Life*, September 27, 1954, 22. For compelling discussion of regional strategy for U.S. pavilions at international trade fairs, see also December 22, 1954, letter from Victor C. Algrant (FOA or OCB Work Group on Trade Fairs) to Samuel W. Anderson (Assistant Secretary of Commerce for International Affairs). Subject: Ad Hoc Reports, in NA RG40 General Records of the Department of Commerce, Office of International Trade Fairs, International Trade Fairs Historic Document File, 1957, Box 1, Folder "Trade Fair Program, Miscellaneous Correspondence thru 4/30/55, OITF." From an industrial design standpoint, before the change in OITF management occurred with the arrival of McClung, see "The United States goes to Market in Trade Fairs," *Industrial Design*, June 1955, 12.

83. See memo from Commerce Secretary Sinclair Weeks, May 3, 1956, announcing the hire of McClung, in RG489, Records of the International Trade Administration, Bureau of Foreign Commerce, Office of International Trade Fairs, Correspondence and Reports, 1954–1958, OCB Agenda—Quarterly Reports, Box 4, Folder: "Personal, Mr. McClung, May 56–Oct.56." See same folder May 15, 1956, letter from McClung to Roy Williams, which states, "With considerable trepidation and much

humility I will try to go on from where you left the program. It is a good program. It is necessary to our national effort in behalf of free people all over the world."

84. Beverly Payeff-Masey, interview, August 23, 2010.

85. *New York Times*, February 15, 1954.

86. Payeff-Masey, interview, August 23, 2010.

87. Mitarachi, "Design as a Political Force," 3. For background to mid-1950s trade fair advisory groups, see "Preliminary Report of Ad Hoc to the Inter-Agency Advisory Group for the Trade Fair Programs" in NA RG489, Records of the International Trade Administration, Bureau of Foreign Commerce, Office of International Trade Fairs, Correspondence and Reports, 1954–1958, Box 1, Folder "Ad-Hoc Group Reports."

88. Jack Masey, interview, August 23, 2010.

89. Mitarachi, "Design as a Political Force," 15–16. See also Pulos, *The American Design Adventure*, 243.

90. Mitarachi, "Design as a Political Force," 14.

91. Ibid.

92. Masey, interview, August 23, 2010.

93. Mitarachi: "The U.S.A. wants and needs to establish its influence in politically uneasy countries, to promote capitalism as a system superior to communism. The first goal, then, is eminently political despite its commercial garb." "Many visitors in underdeveloped countries can appreciate Russian achievements because they identify themselves with people who have recently overcome physical and economic handicaps. The same achievements by Americans look like the work of a privileged nation with which they have no personal identification," "Design as a Political Force," 4.

94. From subsection "Specific Objectives of Each Central Exhibit," *Operating Guide for U.S. Government Personnel and Contractors Planning Exhibits at Interantional Trade Fairs*, U.S. Department of Commerce, Office of International Trade Fairs, USIA Historical Collection, U.S. State Department, 1954, 6.

95. See Greg Castillo, *Cold War on the Home Front: The Soft Power of Midcentury Design* (Minneapolis: University of Minnesota Press), xxiii. Here, he invokes Beatriz Colomina's term of "exhibitionist houses," which "inhabited exhibition spaces of publication, memory, and fantasy." Peter Blake contends that the MoMA's "attitude toward architecture bore very little relationship to . . . the Modern Movement," which, in Blake's view, "was a politically radical commitment to enhancing the human condition—a way of dealing with predictably desperate problems of excessive urbanization and universal overpopulation." See Blake, *No Place Like Utopia*, 147.

96. See also Greg Castillo, "Marshall Plan Modernism in Divided Germany," in *Cold War Modern: Design 1945–1970*, ed. David Crowley and Jane Pavitt (London: V&A Publishing, 2008), 66–71.

97. See Mitarachi, "Design as a Political Force," 6.

98. See NA RG40 General Records of the Department of Commerce, Office of International Trade Fairs, International Trade Fairs Historic Document File, 1957, Box 1, Folder "Trade Fair Program: Descriptions of Individual Fairs."

99. Ibid., Folder "Damascus."

100. See *Industrial Design* magazine, August 1954, for a discussion of domes as the saving grace of the otherwise lackluster U.S. showing at the event; Pulos, *The American Design Adventure*, 252–53.

101. See Nikolaus Pevsner, "At Aspen in Colorado," in *The Aspen Papers: Twenty Years of Design Theory from the International Design Conference in Aspen*, ed. Reyner Banham (New York: Praeger, 1974), 15–18; and Meikle, *Design in the USA*, 170.

102. See Masey Archive, Letter, Kabul 1956, Jeshyn International Fair, Box 1. See also Peggy and Pierre Streit, "The Bear That Walks the Afghan Streets," *New York Times*, March 11, 1956, 219. For an appraisal of the U.S. approach to economic expansion via foreign aid in Afghanistan, see also Peggy and Pierre Streit, "Lesson in Foreign Aid Policy," *New York Times*, March 18, 1956. For two additional articles that shed light on U.S. economic influence in Afghanistan as a method to thwart Soviet expansion, see Peter G. Franck, "Economic Progress in an Encircled Land," *Middle East Journal* 10, no. 1 (Winter 1956): 43–59; and Willard L. Thorp, "American Policy and the Soviet Economic Offensive," *Foreign Affairs* 35, no. 2 (January 1957): 271–82. For a particularly exciting article that addresses the attitudes of nonaligned nations in Asia and the challenge of allegiance to the capitalist vs. the communist school of thought, see M. R. Masani, "The Mind of Asia," *Foreign Affairs* 33, no. 4 (July 1955): 548–65.

103. Masey interview, August 23, 2010. Meikle points out that Fuller held a contentious view of industrial design, calling it "the greatest betrayal of mass communication integrity in our era," but emphasizes that Fuller later enunciated a hope that industrial design was "capable of bringing the human race to 'an utterly new omnisuccessful relationship to the universe,'" in Jeffrey L. Meikle, *Twentieth Century Limited: Industrial Design in America, 1925–1939* (Philadelphia: Temple University Press, 1979), 55–56. There is a wealth of material on the story of Fuller's geodesic domes and his other "utopian" experiments. See R. Buckminster Fuller, *Utopia or Oblivion: The Prospects for Humanity*, ed. Jaime Snyder (Baden, Switzerland: Lars Müller, 2008); Shoji Sadao, "A Brief History of Geodesic Domes," in *Buckminster Fuller: Anthology for the New Millennium*, ed. Thomas T. K. Zung (New York: St. Martin's, 2001); K. Michael Hays and Dana Miller, *Buckminster Fuller: Starting with the Universe* (New York: Whitney Museum of American Art; New Haven, CT: Yale University Press, 2008), 7–19; Linda Sargent Wood, *A More Perfect Union: Holistic Worldviews and the Transformation of American Culture after World War II* (Oxford: Oxford University Press, 2010), 53–81.

104. See Masey diary, Masey Archive, Kabul 1956, Jeshyn International Fair, Box 1.

105. See R. Buckminster Fuller, *Critical Path* (New York: St. Martin's, 1981), 193–96; H. J. Mackinder, "The Geographical Pivot of History," *Geographical Journal* 23, no. 4 (April 1904): 421–37. For a more scholarly counterpoint to this theory, see, for instance, Milton Bearden, "Afghanistan, Graveyard of Empires," *Foreign Affairs* 80, no. 6 (November/December 2001): 17–30.

106. Masey, interview, August 24, 2010. McClung himself would report that "the logistics of this Fair were almost beyond belief. The passes were flooded a good part of the time and generally it was impossible to get any airlifts from Karachi to Kandahar," 2, in NA RG489, Office Memorandum, Harrison T. McClung, Director, Office of International Trade Fairs, to Robert Warner, Assistant Director for Near East and Far East, September 4, 1956, International Trade Administration Bureau of Foreign Commerce, Office of International Trade Fairs, Reports 1954–1958.

107. See NA RG489 Records of the International Trade Administration, Bureau of Foreign Commerce, Office of International Trade Fairs, Correspondence and Reports, 1954–1958, Kabul 1956—Osaka 1956, Box 13, Folder "Kabul Fair, Afghanistan, January 56–September 57," letter from Tom Hall Miller to Robert Warner Deputy Director, OITF, Dept. of Commerce, and memo from Warner to McClung on the challenges of the fair. From the same folder, see McClung's meeting with Masey in June 12, 1956, letter.

108. Masey, interview, August 24, 2010.

109. Masey files, 2. See also NA RG40 General Records of the Department of Commerce, Office of International Trade Fairs, International Trade Fairs Historic Document File, 1957, Box 1, Folder "Kabul 1956."

110. Masey, interview, August 24, 2010.

111. Harrison T. McClung, *Portable Demountable Trade Fair Pavilions: A Research Project for Office of International Trade Fairs, United States Department of Commerce*, by C. M. Shaw Associates, December 1, 1956, RG489 Records of the International Trade Administration, Bureau of Foreign Commerce, Office of International Trade Fairs, Correspondence and Reports, 1954–1958, Box #1, Folder: "Design Contracts, 10/54–4/56."

112. Masey, interview, August 24, 2010. For more analysis of the Kabul fair, see David Cort, "Darkness under the Dome," *Nation*, March 1, 1958, 187–88; "'Dome' Takes to Air," *News and Observer* (Raleigh), July 16, 1956. See also Masey and Lloyd Morgan, *Cold War Confrontations*, 34–87; Haddow, *Pavilions of Plenty*, introduction, specifically 16–17, chapter 1, chapter 2, 61–62.

113. The term "imperial idioms," meant as aesthetic devices used by and for ruling governments, is borrowed from Penelope J. E. Davies, *Death and the Emperor: Roman Imperial Funerary Monuments from Augustus to Marcus Aurelius* (Austin: University of Texas Press, 2004), 79–92.

114. See Robert W. Rydell, John E. Findling, and Kimberley D. Pelle, *Fair America: World's Fairs in the United States* (Washington, DC: Smithsonian Institution, 2000), 5.

115. See Arthur J. Pulos, "United States: The Wizards of Standardized Aesthetics," in *History of Industrial Design: 1919–1990, The Dominion of Design*, ed. Carol Pirovano (Milan: Electa, 1991), 168. See also Marco Duranti, "Utopia, Nostalgia and World War at the 1939–40 New York World's Fair," *Journal of Contemporary History* 41, no. 4 (October 2006): 663–83.

116. Bennett, "The Exhibitionary Complex," 95. Boorstin reiterates the power of the image of a perfect society: "The image—limited, concrete, and oversimplified—inevitably seems narrow and unadaptable. Because it is a projection of ourselves, it declares our conceit. Images always seem more static and rigid than ideals. Utopianism has a happy fluidity and vagueness," in *The Image*, 244.

117. Bennett, "The Exhibitionary Complex," 76.

118. Ibid., 99. For a fascinating discussion of the symbols of domes as icons of imperialism, see Oleg Grabar, "From Dome of Heaven to Pleasure Dome," *Journal of the Society of Architectural Historians* 49, no. 1 (March 1990): 15–21.

119. See Preziosi, *Brain of the Earth's Body*, 134.

120. Masey, interview, August 24, 2010.

121. As quoted in Alex Soojung-Kim Pang, "Dome Days: Buckminster Fuller in the Cold War," in *Cultural Babbage: Technology, Time and Invention*, ed. Francis Spufford and Jenny Uglow (London: Faber and Faber, 1996), 187.

122. See Jonathan Matusitz, "Cathedrals of Consumption," *Wiley-Blackwell Encyclopedia of Globalization*, ed. George Ritzer (Oxford: Blackwell, 2012), doi:10.1002/9780470670590.wbeog064.

123. David Freedberg, *The Power of Images: Studies in the History and Theory of Response* (Chicago: The University of Chicago Press, 1989), 390.

124. Mitarachi, "Design as a Political Force," 3.

CHAPTER THREE

A "Carefully Planned Bombardment"

The American National Exhibition in Moscow, 1959

The basic signifying currency of the exhibitions, of course, consisted in their arrangement of displays of manufacturing processes and products. Prior to the Great Exhibition, the message of progress had been carried by the arrangement of exhibits in, as Davison puts it, "a series of classes and sub-classes ascending from raw products of nature, through various manufactured goods and mechanical devices, to the 'highest' forms of applied and fine art." . . . The effect of these developments was to transfer the rhetoric of progress from the relations between stages of production to the relations between races and nations by superimposing the associations of the former on the latter.[1]

While the previous chapter focused on trade and cultural exhibitions that played to audiences around the world during the mid-1950s, this chapter revisits the *American National Exhibition* in Moscow (ANEM), which for six weeks in the summer of 1959 showed nearly three million Russians various aspects of the American way of life. Though the ANEM has received significant attention from a number of scholars,[2] academic work on the subject has not acknowledged the strong indications of the exhibitionary complex that this event embodies. Was the ANEM an example of what Preziosi would call "another solution to the formatting of ethnicity, progress, evolution, artistic development, and cognitive specificity," such as that found in the Crystal Palace?[3] This chapter begins with a discussion of what served as the main source of political contention between the United States and the Soviet Union at the time of the U.S.-U.S.S.R. Cultural Exchange Agreement

97

of January 27, 1958, and the Protocol Agreement of September 10, 1958, which outlined the plan for a mutual exchange of exhibitions. According to the *Review of the American National Exhibition in Moscow*, drafted by the general manager of the exhibition, Harold C. McClellan, the September 1958 agreement "provided for the first time since 1917 a specific understanding through which national exhibitions would be exchanged between the two countries."[4] The October–November meeting in Moscow and the December meeting in Washington between U.S. and U.S.S.R. representatives in 1958 would confirm the negotiations that had transpired throughout the year. In spite of the Sputnik launch in 1957 and Khrushchev's announcement of his Seven-Year Plan for economic growth of the Soviet Union, a much more sinister event would overshadow U.S. foreign-policy concerns.

The Berlin Crisis

At the end of World War II, the Allied Powers divided a defeated Germany into four occupied zones. Analogously, the city of Berlin was split into four sectors and administered by the United States, Great Britain, France, and the Soviet Union. Less than a year later, disagreements over the administration of postwar Europe would lead to the end of the joint supervision of Berlin, making it a Cold War trouble spot over the next forty-five years.[5] On March 5, 1946, during a visit to Westminster College in Fulton, Missouri, former British prime minister Winston Churchill spoke of "these anxious and baffling times," in reference to the mutual fear and suspicion brewing between the emerging superpowers of the United States and the U.S.S.R.

Not surprisingly, after the 1947 establishment of the Federal Republic of Germany and the German Democratic Republic, Berlin would become a powerful symbol of the clash between the capitalist West and the communist East. According to authors Jack Masey and Conway Lloyd Morgan, it would serve as a "source of affront to the Soviets, this island of capitalism within their sphere of influence. For the others, it was both the tangible reminder of their victory and an ideal observation post for looking over the enemy's shoulder, a base for espionage and intrigue, a testing ground of Cold War tactics."[6] Despite Churchill's strong advocacy for the "grand pacification of Europe," it soon would become obvious that a divided Berlin mirrored the larger, more perplexing reality that an "iron curtain has descended across the continent."[7]

On June 20, 1948, the Western Allies introduced the new Deutsche Mark in their sectors, thereby replacing the defunct Reichsmark in an ongoing effort to jump-start the postwar German economy. Nestled deep in the Soviet sector of East Germany, the still-united Berlin would become divided by the Soviets, who declared the British and the Americans had enacted an economic policy without first consulting the U.S.S.R. Days later the Soviets reacted by imposing a complete blockade of western Berlin, cutting off all access by road, rail, and water. Historians argue whether the U.S.S.R. was hoping for a land grab in order to absorb the western sectors of the city into their sphere of influence. This was not to be. The U.S. countermeasure, an airlift, would serve as the lifeline to the western portion of the city, with more than 270,000 flights in total delivering food and fuel to the besieged city. In May 1949, Stalin lifted the blockade, and the West's "propaganda by deed"[8] cemented West Berlin's status as a symbol of freedom in a city that would remain politically divided until the fall of the Berlin Wall in 1989.

The United States would adopt an official stance toward the Soviet presence in Eastern Europe with the help of one of its Moscow-based diplomats, George Kennan. His "Long Telegram," a cautionary analysis and profile of Soviet foreign-policy objectives, was written at the behest of the U.S. State Department, who wanted insights into the Soviet Union's rejection of the World Bank and International Monetary Fund. This document would set the foundation for America's policy of containment vis-à-vis the U.S.S.R. for the duration of the Cold War. Throughout the telegram, Kennan persuasively asserted that the Soviets held an innately antagonistic disposition toward capitalist countries, did not seek "permanent peaceful coexistence," and suffered from "a neurotic view of world affairs."[9]

This landmark document would also clarify the plight of Soviet Russians who had in a single generation suffered Stalin's Great Purge and the equally devastating effects of World War II. Kennan believed, perhaps rightly, that not only "have [the] mass of Russian people been emotionally further removed from doctrines of Communist party than they are today," but that apparent Soviet expansionist aggression did not reflect the will of the citizenry:

> First, it does not represent the natural outlook of the Russian people. Latter are, by and large, friendly to the outside world, eager for experience of it, eager to measure against it talents they are conscious of possessing, eager above all to live in peace and enjoy fruits of their own labor. Party line only represents thesis which official propaganda machine puts forward with great skill and persistence to a public often remarkably resistant in the stronghold of its innermost thoughts. But party line is binding for outlook and conduct of people who make up apparatus of power—party, secret police and Government—and it is exclusively with these that we have to deal.[10]

However, concern for a distant and unreachable Soviet public would be muted for the next ten years while the United States and the U.S.S.R.

continued to spar over the rest of humanity they deemed vulnerable to the other's ideological influence.[11]

Kennan's diplomatic vision of managing the Soviets through political, economic, and military pressures would soon be eclipsed by a harsher approach to Soviet containment. Meanwhile, in 1950, Paul Nitze, director of planning for the State Department, authored the hawkish NSC-68 document that strategized a fierce military superiority over the Soviets.

It should be remembered, however, that both Kennan and Nitze worked toward the foreign-policy goals of the Truman administration. Eisenhower, in a departure from what many Republicans saw as the failure of containment policy to thwart the Soviet threat under Truman, promoted a campaign of ideological "liberation" specifically for those people suffering in the Soviet-bloc countries.[12] While in campaign mode in 1952, Eisenhower underscored, "The American conscience can never know peace until the millions in Soviet satellites are restored again to be masters of their own fate."[13]

In June of 1953, East Berlin construction workers would strike in protest of state-mandated work quotas. The uprising, brutally crushed by Soviet troops, would lead to the opening of refugee camps in West Berlin, which offered safe haven to those fleeing Soviet repression. From 1949 through 1961, almost three million people would leave their homes in East Germany to escape to West Berlin. By the late 1950s, the East German "brain drain" would become the dominant political issue between the United States and the Soviet Union. The lack of any decisive response, military or otherwise, from the West assured the Soviet Union of, in the words of historian Frank Ninkovich, "the existence of a shared understanding between the superpowers about their respective spheres of influence in Europe and on the desirability of not disturbing the status quo."[14]

The Exhibition: Of What Was This a Consequence?

Prior to the Geneva Summit in 1955, there was little hope of the United States to share its culture directly with Soviet citizens. Yale Richmond addresses a seldom discussed but fascinating chapter of U.S.-Soviet relations, in that since the Bolshevik Revolution in 1917, Lenin, Trotsky, and Stalin "chose technological America as their model."[15] The Four-Power Summit Conference in Geneva offered the chance for President Eisenhower and Premier Khrushchev to meet face to face to deal with what would become the dominating issues of the Cold War at the end of the 1950s: "European security in Germany, disarmament, and the development of contacts between East and West."[16] Cull asserts:

Given Eisenhower's appreciation of the power of culture in international affairs, it was only to be expected that any opportunity to gain a foothold in the U.S.S.R. would be seized. As early as the Geneva Summit of 1955, the United States, the United Kingdom, and France proposed a seventeen-point program of Soviet concessions to allow such things as freer exchange of information, tourism, and an end to jamming. The Soviets rejected any multilateral accord on culture but seemed open to bilateral agreements. They showed themselves willing by inviting *Porgy and Bess* to Moscow and Leningrad. The United States codified its wish for cultural exchange as a method of influencing Soviet society in the policy document NSC 5607 of 29 June 1956. . . . A door was opening.[17]

A month later, Jack Masey had the opportunity to walk Khrushchev through the John Vassos–designed American pavilion of the Indian Industries Fair, sponsored by the Federation of Indian Chambers of Commerce and Industry, which ran in New Delhi from October 29, 1955, through January 1, 1956 (figure 3.1). Masey speculates that the American pavilion in India would serve as an entrée to American culture that would lead the Soviet leader three years later to agree to a blockbuster U.S. exhibition in Moscow. It was there at the ANEM in 1959 that Khrushchev announced his willingness to stage "a littler corner of America in Moscow" because he wanted his people to "see the American exhibition as an exhibition of our own achievements in the near future."[18] The American pavilion in India four years earlier featured the fruits of the *Atoms for Peace* program, sponsored by the United States This very detailed exhibit for the Indian public, explaining how nuclear energy can serve peaceful purposes, included a dazzling section called "Magic Hands," which featured "one animated mechanical device never before seen in India which can work miracles—or near miracles, anyway. Make it write, pour, unravel, and tighten. Add a beautiful woman, and you have got a devastating exhibit."[19] The description of the "Magic Hands" further mentions: "Obsessed with animation for its own sake, Indian audiences packed this exhibit more than any other at the Atomics Section, returning again and again for additional glimpses of the mechanical hands at work—and, of course, the operators"[20] (figure 3.2).

This exhibit also became the proving ground for the use of local guides that the USIA would employ at later trade and cultural fairs (figures 3.3–3.4). Masey concurs:

In 1955, you had Washington coming up with this. There was Ike's speech before the UN that we have the atom and it has to work for humanity. I was in New Delhi at the time, and I thought hey, I'd like that for India. The Indians were getting into international fairs. Asia was coming to life. So, I hired a force

Figure 3.1.   Crowds waiting to enter the U.S. Pavilion at the Indian Industries Fair, New Delhi, 1955.
Courtesy, Jack Masey Collection.

Figure 3.2.   The Magic Hands demonstration at the U.S. Atomics Exhibit, Indian International Fair, New Delhi, 1955.
Courtesy, Jack Masey Collection.

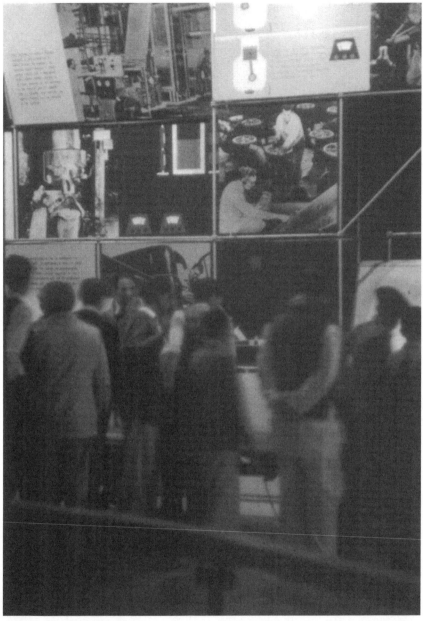

Figure 3.3.   Guide and visitors at the U.S. Atomics Exhibit, Indian Industries Fair, New Delhi, 1955.
Courtesy, Jack Masey Collection.

Figure 3.4.   Guide and visitors at the U.S. Atomics Exhibit, Indian Industries Fair, New Delhi, 1955.
Courtesy, Jack Masey Collection.

of 75 young Indians [figure 3.5]. And having been in India already for a year or two, I was intent on giving those Indians a break who wanted jobs who hadn't worked much before. You had to speak English, you had to speak Hindi, since it was the official language, plus two other Indian dialects. They were fabulous.[21]

Masey would tour not only Khrushchev through the American pavilion but Indian prime minister Nehru as well, who stopped to chat with the Indian student guides and discuss their knowledge of atomic physics, with which he was very impressed (figures 3.6–3.7).

Importantly, the American pavilion at the Indian Industries Fair in New Delhi would reinforce what Masey already knew from his previous four years of experience in India putting up U.S. exhibits across the subcontinent: the availability or lack thereof of congressional funding for exhibitions and the significantly daunting conditions that prevailed in most of the countries where the United States and the U.S.S.R. were vying for influence. As Payeff-Masey asserts,

The major insight gained in India in 1955, which included the trouble of constructing the labor-intensive "pillbox" that was the American pavilion in New

Figure 3.5.   Jack Masey (front row left) with team of guides for U.S. Pavilion at Indian Industries Fair, New Delhi, 1955.
United States Information Agency (USIA).

Delhi, was based on Masey's praise of the simple, aesthetically-pleasing and easily erectable Czech pavilion. This design approach used by the Czechs would allow pavilion buildings to expand or contract organically in size (as needed, depending on availability of money or materiel) without losing the aesthetic quality of the design. Believing that the creation of an impressive pavilion did more politically for the U.S. abroad vis-à-vis the Soviets than the sale of sewing machines at trade fairs, Masey understood that this approach would allow designers to be simultaneously on the offense for aesthetic quality while on the defense against funding cuts and lack of skilled labor. This approach would be evident in how the American pavilions would be produced in the following decades.[22]

Masey finishes his discussion of the Khrushchev visit by offering a rationale for why the Soviets wanted to engage in cultural exchange agreements the following years:

Figure 3.6. Jack Masey (left) conducts a tour for Nikita Khrushchev (center) and Niko-lai Bulganin (right) of the U.S. Pavilion at the Indian Industries Fair, New Delhi, 1955. United States Information Agency (USIA).

I'll tell you where I think this is of consequence. This is 1955, and party secretary Khrushchev's been taken through this exhibit of American atomic energy. And here is what I think happened and what leads to 1959: it was the Soviets' idea to exchange national exhibitions. It wasn't ours. He [Khrushchev] wanted to know what was going on. I have this nutty theory: he saw American know-how in '55. He was there, and we signed an agreement with the Soviets for 1959, it was "we should show science, technology, and culture." We reversed everything! We had culture, and virtually no science, and a tiny bit of technology. But this is what Khrushchev was thinking of: I want the Russian people to see what's ahead for them. And so I think his visit to the U.S. pavilion in New Delhi plays a role.[23]

In a Cold War rendition of Rudyard Kipling's "Great Game," the American pavilion in India would make an impression, both on "nonaligned" Indians as well as on Khrushchev. This mid-twentieth-century version of ideological frontierism in an ideologically neutral landscape aimed to win over Indians. Its unforeseen benefit was to seduce the leader of its adversary himself: Nikita Khrushchev.[24]

Chronologically, the 1956 policy document fortuitously followed Khrushchev's "Secret Speech to the Closed Session of the Twentieth Party Congress" on February 25, 1956. In it he denounced Stalin, and the Soviet Union

Figure 3.7. Jack Masey (left) leads Indian prime minister Jawaharlal Nehru through the
U.S. Pavilion, Indian Industries Fair, New Delhi, 1955.
United States Information Agency (USIA).

would enter a time period known as the "Khrushchev Thaw." Further, the rationale for East-West exchanges would near official status in a statement of policy by the National Security Council on June 29, 1956:

a. To promote within Soviet Russia evolution toward a regime which will abandon predatory policies, which will seek to promote the aspirations of the Russian people rather than the global ambitions of International Communism, and which will increasingly rest upon the consent of the governed rather than upon despotic police power.

b. As regards the European satellites, we seek their evolution toward independence from Moscow.[25]

In 1957, after Congress removed the fingerprinting provision of the Immigration and Neutrality Act from five years prior, relations between the Cold War adversaries had shifted, according to veteran American diplomat Walter Roberts, from "the freezer to the refrigerator."[26] A year later, the "Agreement between the United States of America and the Union of Soviet Socialist Republics on Exchanges in the Cultural, Technical and Educational Fields" was officially enacted.[27] One of the key points of this negotiation was the shared cultural programming of the United States and the Soviet Union. Most importantly, the negotiations allowed for direct contact between Americans and Russians, an unprecedented element of the treaty that the Soviets had tried to avoid. As Richmond examines,

> The early years of exchanges were the learning years, when two vastly different societies had to learn how to work together. The watchwords on both sides were control, strict reciprocity and suspicion. It was a very frustrating and time consuming experience, but it served to establish procedures and patterns which, for better or worse, were to govern the future of these exchanges.[28]

In the long tradition of world's fairs dating back to the Great Exhibition of 1851, the Universal and International Exposition in Brussels in 1958—the first world's fair following World War II—demonstrated yet another opportunity for nation-states to show the best that their cultures had to offer. The U.S. pavilion was designed in anticipation of the strong showing by both the Soviet Union and the People's Republic of China.[29] Like the U.S. participation at trade and cultural fairs in the mid-1950s, the American section included an atomic energy display, fashion shows, film screenings, an American "streetscape," and contemporary abstract art.[30] But this exhibitionary event was sponsored wholly by the U.S. State Department, which included an advisory board that featured the likes of industrial design legends Walter Paepcke, Walter Rostow, and others. In the end, the USIA itself had little direct involvement in the organization of the American pavilion. Overall, the lavish, cutting-edge architecture, provided by legendary American architect Edward Durrell Stone, was, as Masey puts it: "the quintessential American fairyland"[31] (figures 3.8–3.11). This world's fair would serve, arguably, as an exercise leading up to the *American National Exhibition* in Moscow—an exhibition that would employ a number of these same elements—a year later.

A controversial inclusion in the U.S. pavilion in Brussels was the *Unfinished Business* exhibit designed by American Leo Lionni, a conceptual experience that revealed outright the unresolved social problems plaguing America at the time, namely race relations (figures 3.12–3.13). Spurred by the Soviets' vocal disapprobation of the school desegregation crisis in Little Rock, Arkansas, USIA planners effectively portrayed America as a nation that understood its work as a global superpower was not yet finished. The

Figure 3.8.   The U.S. Pavilion designed by architect Edward Durrell Stone, at the Brussels Expo, 1958.
Courtesy, Jack Masey Collection

Figure 3.9.   Interior of the U.S. Pavilion at Brussels, 1958.
National Archives and Records Administration (NARA)

walk-through gallery space featured American guides who answered the difficult questions about the pressing racial issues at home. Surveys showed that Europeans appreciated the candor and overall message of the display: America may not be perfect, but it is making progress. As Masey adds,

> Well, you see, '58 was something miraculous, because a good design came out of something called a committee. Regrettably, they went all the wrong directions, as I saw it. I became very good friends with Peter Harnden, who was one of the designers. He was really having trouble with Washington because they had formed a committee already. And what, of course, grew out of that was something interesting. The guy who dreamed up *Unfinished Business* was a politico, a part of the committee. This guy says, "we know the Soviets are going to be coming in and trying to take us apart. . . . We know we're going to be attacked for race relations. Let's head 'em off at the pass. Let's do something!" So, intellectually, it's brilliant. Let's do a political statement, which is always dangerous, and which this wasn't supposed to be. We know the Soviets are coming after us, and, in anticipation of that, say, "yes, we do have racial problems, but, and this is a big 'but!'"[32]

As Masey asserts, the political statement which sounded reasonable among exhibition designers sitting around a table, the *Unfinished Business*

Figure 3.10.   Graphics streetscape in the U.S. Pavilion at Brussels, 1958.
Courtesy, Chermayeff and Geismar.

Figure 3.11.   Fashion show in the U.S. Pavilion, Brussels, 1958.
National Archives and Records Administration (NARA).

Figure 3.12.   Photo mural depicting multiracial harmony in the *Unfinished Business* exhibit, U.S. Pavilion, Brussels Expo, 1958.
National Archives and Records Administration (NARA).

Figure 3.13.   View of exterior of the *Unfinished Business* exhibit, designed by Leo
Lionni, at the U.S. Pavilion, Brussels Expo, 1958.
Photographer: Leo Lionni.

portion of the American pavilion would prove in the end a political calam-
ity: "When you do a political show, there are political ramifications. Where
might objections come from? This was something they never even thought
about."[33] The objections came from Southern senators who drafted written
protests to the State Department, objecting to the airing of America's "un-
washed laundry" at an international forum, especially a high-stakes venue
such as a world expo at a critical juncture in the Cold War (figure 3.14).
Masey continues:

> Their argument was that we were not showing the other side of the issue, the
> rights and prerogatives of the states of the South. They were crazy (laughing)
> . . . they basically said: "Why not show the positives of segregation?" So, you
> know what happened? The State Department panicked. And I mean pan-
> icked. They started making changes in the show. So, the Undersecretary of
> State announces, "we are changing the exhibit because of shoddy craftsman-
> ship." This is a lie. A blatant lie. Which meant, "take the bad stuff out." And
> find a replacement. If we used the *Unfinished Business* at Moscow '59, Pravda
> would've loved it: "See, there are newspapers here saying there are race riots."
> We've said we knew this all along. But at '59, we made a point to answer all

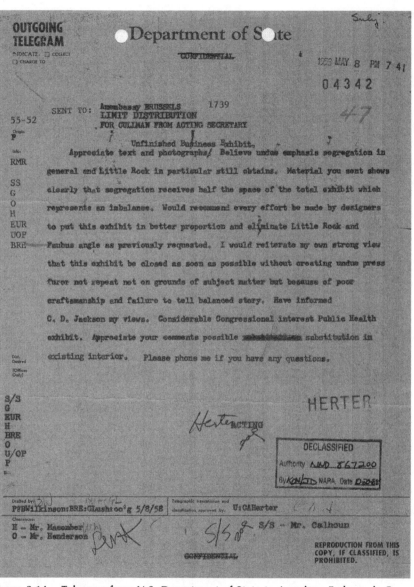

Figure 3.14. Telegram from U.S. Department of State to American Embassy in Brussels regarding the closure of the *Unfinished Business* exhibit at the U.S. Pavilion due to pressure from some members of the U.S. Congress.
National Archives and Records Administration (NARA).

the political questions through the Eames film, the guides, the IBM information machine, and so on.[34]

The monumental work of representing America overseas at the Brusssels Expo would soon be adapted for the first official cultural exhibition exchange under the new agreement with the Soviets the following year. But what would America show of itself in Moscow, the capital of its ideological competitor? What would appeal to the Soviet public? As Russian scholar Isaiah Berlin cogently described it, "For Soviet society is organized not for happiness, comfort, liberty, justice, personal relationships, but for combat. Whether they wish it or not the drivers and controllers of this immense train cannot now halt it or leap from it in mid-course without risk of destruction."[35]

Conceptual Antecedents to the *American National Exhibition* in Moscow

Arguably, the cultural DNA for the creation of the ANEM came directly from the 1950s trade and cultural fairs and the design and marketing theory that supported them. In a way, the ANEM was business as usual, except that this event would prove to be the largest effort the U.S. government would undertake in the Soviet Union itself during the Cold War. The *American National Exhibition* in Moscow was, according to Castillo, the culmination of an aesthetic and ideological trend that began with Marshall Plan exhibitions of U.S. domestic products, an exhibiting practice perfected among the trade fair pavilions of the mid-1950s. The Kremlin had, in essence, "sanctioned an American consumer spectacle in Moscow, the Soviet capital and ideological heart of global communism," raising the question, "Was this a myopic blunder, or could it have been part of a Promethean scheme to steal the secrets of consumer modernity from its capitalist master?"[36]

Observing American design and commodity culture's influence in Europe following the Second World War, Victoria De Grazia comments on the social effects of cleverly designed commercial products in what she describes as "the hegemony of American consumer culture over European consumer civilization."[37] Invoking Baudrillard's theory that "a new consumer product created a wide if inauthentic sense of community among its users, only to turn them inward into an atomized, intensely private, depoliticized world," she alleges that social critics in general abandoned allegiance to Marx's "fetishizing of commodities," which was unable "to decipher the signs and signifiers of this new 'hyperreality.'"[38] The *American National Exhibition* in Moscow would demonstrate the zenith of this mechanism of selling the *hyperreal* that had been used throughout U.S. trade fair pavilions around the world in the mid-1950s. As Haddow points out, "Appliance exhibits, model homes, modern kitchens, television, hi-fi, and movie demonstrations were sent abroad to dazzle audiences and win friends for the American way. Uniting the 'free world' against the Communists meant teaching consumerism and family values."[39] This "people's capitalism" in action, originally deployed in the post–World War II sociopolitical world in order to keep allies and sway nonaligned countries to America's mode, would now be activated in the geographical heart of America's ideological enemy. It would be the theme of hyperreality in the form of Charles and Ray Eames's film *Glimpses of the USA*, fashion shows, American women "at work" in their model kitchens, and even the presence of bilingual American guides, that would prove to be the exhibition's dominant propaganda tools. These interactive elements to the exhibition would offer Soviet visitors the opportunity to forgo verisimilitude to witness a version of American life that exists, arguably, only in a highly stylized and simulated environment.

Several authors have addressed the concept of hyperreality as it conveniently folds into discussions of hyperconsumption, enabling what Gilles Lipovetsky calls both "a civilization of paradoxical happiness" and "a civilization of desire." [40] This paradigm references Veblen's discussion of *conspicuous consumption* and the transclass need both for feeling part of a secure social group by virtue of one's material possessions as well as notions of ostentation that are spurred by the continual renewal of product designs and the artificially induced demands for newer, more abundant products.

John Berger, in his study of signs embedded in traditional Western cultural aesthetics, argues that as spectator-buyers struggle to make sense of "the interminable present of meaningless working hours," their only refuge is in "a dreamt future in which imaginary activity replaces the passivity of the moment."[41]

A third dominant theme evident in most discussions of trade fairs is what Bennett, quoting Walter Benjamin, calls "places of pilgrimage to the fetish Commodity."[42] Eco similarly calls trade fairs the "great kermesse of triumphant merchandise."[43] Whereas American household products were themselves finite commodities, it was the idea behind them—the myth of a more leisurely life, an American life, a better life—that was the real message in the U.S. trade fairs of the 1950s and aspects of the ANEM later.

As sociologist Piergiorgio Degli Esposti theorizes, "We are dealing with a world in which economy has been transmuted into culture and culture into the transient and disposable world of goods . . . where 'fantasies can be far more important and rewarding than reality' . . . which, through their proliferation of settings, allow the formation of a 'society of simulation,'" invoking Baudrillard's definition of simulacra, "where boundaries between the imaginary and the real have eroded."[44] Again, it was Baudrillard who, writing on the simulacra, claims that Disneyland is but the quintessential example of a falsely portrayed America and that the theme park itself, a microcosmic utopia, usurps any semblance of a real America and instead offers up a "digest of the American way of life, panegyric to American values, idealized transposition of a contradictory reality."[45] Likewise, the living dioramas of American goods being used by "real" Americans in picture-perfect scenographies at the ANEM strongly resemble the "imaginary stations" that Baudrillard and others indict as mythomaniacal snapshots of America that lack verisimilitude.

Esposti draws further parallels between Debord's concept of the spectacle and Ritzer's indictment of the utopian urge that underpins the "cathedrals of consumption," concluding that "the re-enchantment of the cathedrals of consumption depends on their growing increasingly spectacular."[46] These fairs and their highly conceptualized realities became "cathedrals of consumption," though the spectacular lifestyles they frame within the exhibition context transcend mere consumption.

George Nelson

Among the designers who, early on, jumped on the display bandwagon was architect, writer, and industrial designer George Nelson, who began to invent systems for traveling shows that would later be expanded in scope for larger shows, like the *American National Exhibition* in Moscow in 1959. His office had in 1957 designed three pavilions for the USIA's *Education for Theatrical Design* show at Brazil's São Paulo biennial. The firm had also been enlisted to develop a nuclear energy exhibit for the ANEM, but the project was canceled at the drawings phase. However, Nelson would be contacted at the end of 1958, presumably following the confirmation of the cultural-exchange agreement, as a potential contributor to the ANEM. As Abercrombie makes clear, "No one then suspected that Nelson's role would grow to encompass the design of the whole show, which was to be one of the most visible and most acclaimed exhibitions of the era."[47] Nelson's philosophical approach would prove significantly more substantial than the gossamer-thin veneer of his see-through umbrella designs from the mid-1950s, though this particular design would evolve into similar towering structures later at Moscow in 1959.[48] The government had already developed practical solutions to problems of display and disposability with traveling cultural exhibitions.[49] These early efforts at developing lightweight, visually compelling though temporary exhibition infrastructures reflected not only a utilitarian urge to streamline the production of traveling cultural shows for the government. These transportable design structures yielded further insights into the inner workings of the designers' approaches to the task. As Abercrombie explains, "George Nelson endeavored to design imaginary landscapes. He wanted to design for an American society to come, a society that could have become the new society, invaded by prosperity, by the certainties of technology, invaded by optimism—a relaxed society, a society capable of playing, a society capable of humour, and above all a society without fear."[50] Nelson himself admitted the seeming avant-gardism of which he and design peers like the Eameses and others were offering the world at the time were truly predated by earlier exhibitions, including the Great Exhibition of 1851:

> It is an odd thing, but true, that when one begins to trace developments in architecture, structure, interior design and related areas, the old expositions turn out to be remarkably accurate guides to future ways of doing things. Paxton's Crystal Palace, built in 1851, was a prefabricated structure entirely done in metal and glass, and its implications are not fully exhausted a century later.[51]

This creation of what Nelson called "a civilization of super-comfort" was able, following the horrors and sacrifice of World War II, to achieve a "volume of production no one could have even conceived a generation ago," that forever altered the traditional economic formula of haves and have-nots and "converted it into a diamond where the big purchasing power is spread over an enormous number of middle-class people." It would be this now-empowered proletariat who would provide a market or "a vast demand for television sets, refrigerators in which the ice cubes are made without trays, air conditioning and outboard motors" that, Nelson admitted, though it "does not represent the highest objective society has ever set for itself . . . does not make it vicious."[52] Designer Ettore Sottsass Jr. offers in hindsight a perhaps more thoughtful explanation for the industrial design field's elevation to an all-pervasive part of society:

> I truly believe that in those years George Nelson, and his very few traveling companions, were trying to offer the whole of America—the whole noisy, breathless America, the greedy, ferocious America, the uncertain America—a new proposal; that they were trying to offer the design for a new metaphor for a new society, a society that for better or worse would be increasingly conditioned by the narrow mechanisms of the "industrial civilization."[53]

Though the Soviet audiences would become intimately familiar with the display of American products—"the forbidden fruits of the West"[54]—it would be the diverse approach to the recreation of life in America, through various types of simulacra that would position visitors "at the threshold of greater things to come."[55] As Bennett demonstrates, exhibitions predicated on the model of world's fairs "located their preferred audiences at the very pinnacle of the exhibitionary order of things they constructed" and "came to function as promissory notes in their totalities, embodying, if just for a season, Utopian principles of social organization which, when the time came for the notes to be redeemed, would eventually be realized in perpetuity."[56] The organizers of the ANEM held no such illusions, however.

Domestic Goods and Beyond: Origins of an American *Gesamtkunstwerk*

The official goal of the *American National Exhibition* in Moscow was to actualize the U.S.-U.S.S.R. cultural agreement of 1958.[57] According to American diplomat Hans Tuch, it served to present the Soviet public with a complete picture of American society.[58] On another level, it served as an offensive weapon to show how the "Americanness" of everything from architecture and automotive engineering to modern art and mass-produced kitchens was superior to the Soviet version. The designers of the exhibition knew well that the Soviet Union could boast an advantage in the fields of rocketry and physics—the launch of Sputnik two years before solidly positioned the Soviets as front-runners in the "space race."[59] The U.S. show in Moscow would thus have to address what historian David Caute calls the "Soviet sensitivity about economic efficiency, technological advance, production statistics, and housing standards," which Western students of Soviet communism identified as a Russian inferiority complex. Caute asserts: "Even in the age of the H-Bomb, the Sputnik, and the supersonic Ilyushin, the Soviet state was forever struggling against underdevelopment, both real and feared, reinforced by self-imposed insulation against the global market. The Western press relentlessly mocked hyperbolic Soviet claims to have invented the world and everything in it."[60]

The visitors' entrance hall at the ANEM consisted of an enormous geodesic dome based on the Buckminster Fuller design that had proved a success at the United States pavilion at the Jeshyn International Fair in Kabul, Afghanistan, three years earlier and at numerous subsequent fairs around the world since then (figures 3.15–3.16). Jack Masey, chief of design and construction of the ANEM, and his team considered it an appropriately ostentatious reference point from which the Soviet visitors could then explore the exhibition: "It was decided that the dome would be the central statement, functioning as a kind of 'information machine.'"[61]

Tasked by exhibition organizers to "create a visual proof of the abundance of American society,"[62] in which "the number of images to be seen had to be too many to comprehend individually, but not so many that the information

Figure 3.15: . Detail of the Kaiser-Fuller dome during construction at the American National Exhibition in Moscow, 1959. Photographer: Lucia DeRespinis.

Figure 3.16. Visitors enter the dome at the American National Exhibition in Moscow, 1959.
United States Information Agency (USIA)

would be confusing or hard to follow,"[63] the Eameses were already expert in delivering elegant propaganda cinema to American exhibitions abroad. Their animated *Information Machine* film, created for the 1958 Brussels World's Fair, had impressed visitors the year before. Designer Peter Blake describes what the visitors saw upon entering the dome:

> The story told in film was simple: two typical days in the life of America—a typical weekday and a Sunday. The images, always in tandem, were of ordinary things: people waking up, having breakfast, going off to school or to work, having lunch, coming home, and so on. There were scenes of play, of worship, of art shows, of sports, of traffic jams (and interminable highway intersections), of travel—trains, buses, planes—of innumerable details that added up to a rather routine travelogue of the U.S.A.[64]

The display of the live-action film *Glimpses of the USA*[65] on seven twenty-foot-by-thirty-foot screens provided the Soviet audience with an experience of the operatic, in which "the impending shift from material to immaterial was forecast."[66] It was indeed this shift from the materialism of goods to the immaterialism of information that reflected the larger social trends of the era (figures 3.17–3.18). Hélène Lipstadt points out the contrarian aspirations of USIA

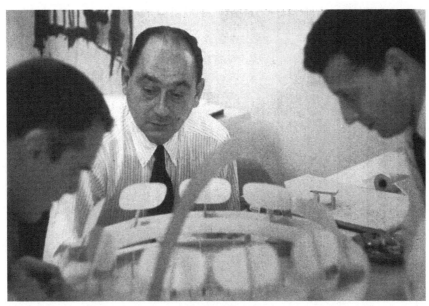

Figure 3.17. Charles Eames, George Nelson, and Jack Masey (left to right) discuss a model of the interior of the dome at the American National Exhibition in Moscow, including the potential placement of the seven screens for the Eames-directed *Glimpses of the USA* film. United States Information Agency (USIA).

Figure 3.18.   Russian visitors catch their first glimpse of *Glimpses of the USA*, the film directed by the Eames Office for the American National Exhibition in Moscow, 1959. © 2014 Eames Office LLC (www.eamesoffice.com).

Director George Allen, whose conventional—and commercial—approach to the overall message of the ANEM embraced the multiscreen format since it was "one really effective way to establish the credibility for a statement that the products on view were widely purchased by the American people."[67] But the film, played sixteen times a day, showed above all, in the words of Buckminster Fuller, who wrote in 1973, "the loving side of American life, that everyone [sic] of the packed Russian audience could be seen at the end with eyes full of tears of [sic] the kinship of human beings."[68] The entire creative process that went into the making of the film occurred in Los Angeles, thousands of miles away from the Eameses' client, the USIA. As Lipstadt argues, it was no mistake that the final print of the film was not shared with Masey, Nelson, and the "USIA's Sovietologists" until the night prior to the opening of the exhibition. This subtle gesture toward absolute creative control over their projects, however, would help the Eameses to maintain their "ideological innocence" and would set the precedent for future collaborations between Charles and Ray Eames and government agencies[69] (figure 3.19).

The dome also housed the IBM information machine, which was programmed to answer more than a thousand questions about American culture. This Plato's Cave of manipulated or preset information articulated a very particular American social landscape and was engaging, reinforcing, and meaningful. It was, in essence, the entrée to the total experiential environment—an

Figure 3.19.   Charles and Ray Eames enjoy the opening day of the American National Exhibition in Moscow, 1959.
United States Information Agency (USIA).

American *gesamtkunstwerk*—that conjured the ideal of the "total work of art" that Richard Wagner described first in July of 1849, in the first of three essays called "Art and Revolution."[70] This total work of art, the *gesamtkunstwerk*, would reflect the essence of the unified parts of the ancient Greek tragedy as well as improve upon the popular, more modern evolution of the musical drama: opera.[71]

This romantic ideal of the total creative work that would engage and instruct and entertain audiences with its hallmarks of the hyperreal would, for several industrial designers, find traction in the university fine arts curriculum designed by the team of George Nelson, Alexander Girard, and Charles Eames in 1952. As Eames's research assistant Jehane Burns states: "In 1952, with Alexander Girard and George Nelson, they combined multiple projection for the first time with slides, live narration, and even piped-in smells, in 'A Rough Sketch for a Sample Lesson for a Hypothetical Course'—an attempt to see how much information could be effectively conveyed in an hour."[72]

Invited by the head of the university's department of fine arts, Lamar Dodd, this residency by Nelson, Girard, and Eames to the University of Georgia in Athens would address "some problems of educational policy."[73] In an ironic turn, when asked by Nelson why he and his fellow designers—who had no previous experience in curriculum design—were given free rein to develop a course on teaching creativity, he was told, "That's why we want you."[74] This artistic synesthesia or *gesamtkunstwerk* of an array of media would be the genesis of what becomes the film in Moscow, the precursor to *Glimpses of the USA* and for the dioramic approach to exhibitions from the mid-1950s through the 1970s. This "bombardment style" or "saturation"[75] of communicating through exhibitions is echoed in Preziosi, who refers to the Crystal Palace exhibition of 1851 as a form of a *gesamtkunstwerk* in the service of imperialist aims.[76] This instructional course on how to teach creativity began with the designers' intention "of communicating something specific, the shortest time taken to do this—without loss of comprehension or retention."[77] In addition to a sixteen-millimeter projector, three slide projectors, tape recorders, three screens, boxes of films, slides, and magnetic tape, Girard's part of the exhibit "arrived in a series of mammoth packing cases and he also brought a collection of bottles of synthetic smells, to be introduced into the room via the air conditioning system at various points in the show."[78]

While the emphasis of what became known as the Art X course was how to communicate messages—through what was arguably a make-believe apparatus—Nelson points out that "the idea was to develop high-speed techniques for exposing the relationships between seemingly unrelated phenomena. This meant films, slides, sounds, music, narration—the familiar world of audio-visual aids—and it soon became clear that we were committed to a job which might easily demand the resources of a Hollywood production unit."[79]

Whereas the Art X curriculum was made to solve problems of communication in the teaching of creativity, the Eames film at the ANEM was, according to Peter Blake, "a spectacular piece of highly sophisticated propaganda. Sweet, innocent, possibly naïve, obviously one-sided. There were no images of crime, of poverty, of racial tension, or of the kind of inequity that would characterize America in the yuppie decade of the 1980s. It was a multimedia vision of a latter-day Norman Rockwellian America—and it worked."[80] *Glimpses of the USA* would echo, from a distinctly American point of view, the 1955 the Museum of Modern Art's *Family of Man* exhibition. This static display of more than five hundred photographs from sixty-eight countries was hailed by American poet Carl Sandburg, who wrote, "If the human face is the 'masterpiece of God' it is here then in a thousand fateful registrations."[81] Following the original exhibition's success in New York, the USIA adopted the show and toured it in various formats on a goodwill tour to forty countries over the next six years. This, too, would be on display at the ANEM, as would Walt Disney's *Circarama* film, a 360-degree spectacle that reflected Disney's own interpretation of life in the United States.[82]

Before exiting the dome, visitors were invited to approach the IBM-sponsored display, which featured a computer programmed to answer questions about the United States, including topics that illustrated some of the less palatable truths of American society (figure 3.20). Examples from the first few days of the exhibition included:

> *What is the price of American cigarettes?* It varies from twenty to thirty cents. The average semiskilled worker earns enough money in one hour to buy about eight packages.
>
> *What is meant by the American dream?* That all men shall be free to seek a better life, with free worship, thought, assembly, expression of belief, and universal suffrage and education.
>
> *How many Negroes have been lynched in the United States since 1950?* Seven deaths—six Negroes and one white—have been classified as lynchings since 1950 by the Tuskegee Institute, a Negro college. Responsible Americans condemn lynching and the perpetrators are prosecuted.
>
> *What is the average income of the American family?* $6,100 in 1957.

Next on the tour was the Glass Pavilion that featured the exhibits of American products. Corporate sponsors included RCA, Pepsi-Cola, Dixie Cup Co., IBM, and Cadillac. Here visitors encountered thematic sections of the

Figure 3.20.   Russian visitors engage with the IBM RAMAC computer to ask questions
about the United States, American National Exhibition in Moscow, 1959.
National Archives and Records Administration (NARA).

exhibition that included the interior of a model apartment, pots and pans, books and magazines, nylons, beauty kiosks, a fashion show, and American cars (figures 3.21–3.22). Americans working at the exhibition reported the expected daily attrition of Levi's jeans and reading materials, including Bibles and Sears Roebuck catalogues.[83] Sergei Khrushchev, a panelist at the George Washington University conference commemorating the fiftieth anniversary of the ANEM on July 23, 2009, visited the exhibition with his father on the day of the "kitchen debate." He succinctly recalls his first impressions: "There was a huge expectation and we didn't know what would be there. Books you can touch and open. Everybody remembered Pepsi-Cola, but it smelled like shoe wax. Our life was not a consumer society but a sacrifice society for the future."[84]

The Glass Pavilion would uncannily echo an earlier crystal structure from 1851 (figure 3.23). As *Life* pointed out, "Airy panels of transparent color, set in bold geometric patterns, separate exhibits of dishes and cooking utensils. Visitors saw this spectacle from balconies."[85]

One of the more compelling subplots from the exhibition was the presence of American fine art and its reception by the Soviet visitors. Curated by a jury of art professionals selected by the USIA, including Lloyd Goodrich, the

Figure 3.21.   A model living room in the Glass Pavilion, designed by industrial designer Lucia DeRespinis, American National Exhibition in Moscow, 1959.
United States Information Agency (USIA).

director of the Whitney Museum of American Art, the display was to show a selection of the best American art from the late nineteenth century up to the present. Well aware that current Soviet trends in artistic aesthetics veered heavily toward Socialist realism—not to be confused with social realism, a school of art that celebrated a forthright depiction of working-class realities—the jury proceeded to corral a diverse assortment of American art that could "match the Russians technically, could treat their subjects with imagination, were free to experiment with treatment and style, and could express themselves according to their own personal convictions and whims."[86] President Eisenhower, himself a layman painter, declared certain works chosen, such as

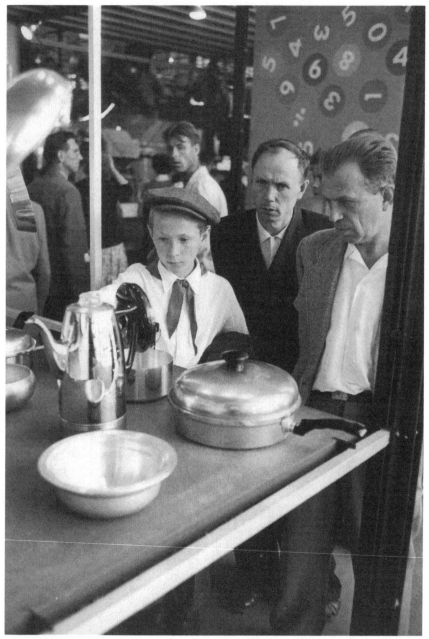
Figure 3.22.   Russian visitors inspect American pots and pans, American National Exhibition in Moscow, 1959.
United States Information Agency (USIA).

Figure 3.23.   Glass Pavilion, evening, American National Exhibition in Moscow, 1959.
United States Information Agency (USIA).

Jackson Pollock's "Cathedral," Jack Levine's "Welcome Home," and Gaston Lachaise's "Standing Woman" as challenging to traditional aesthetics.

Having already quelled an attempted witch hunt by representatives of the House Un-American Activities Committee who saw communist tendencies among U.S. contemporary artists, the jury agreed, at the president's bidding, to add works from America's pre–World War I artists, which included paintings by Childe Hassam, George Caleb Bingham, and John Singer Sargent. Historian Michael L. Krenn argues that though some Soviets, including Khrushchev, felt the abstract art was worthless since it failed to respond to the education of the proletariat, the mandate of Socialist realism, overall the American art display at Sokolniki Park made visitors think more philosophically about life and attitudes in the United States: "In Moscow there was no doubt among the Russians who viewed the exhibit that it was completely and definitively American. For the crowds that gathered around the paintings in Moscow, it was really more of a question of exactly what *kind* of America was on display."[87]

Indeed, at the very least, abstraction in art symbolized in the words of Frank Getlein, art critic for the *New Republic* who visited the show, the freedom of artistic expression all artists enjoyed in the United States.[88] Unreflective of any particular American reality, aside from freedom of expression, the abstract expressionism, at the ANEM and elsewhere, served as the purest example of what Clement Greenberg heralded, "American action painting."[89] Though the American art exhibition remained a source of contention and even derision among visitors, organizers deemed it a success (figure 3.24). Importantly, it countered the Stalinist-era aesthetic that continued to champion communist ideals of life in the factory and field, military heroes, and state leaders until the fall of the Berlin Wall in 1989.

Other elements of the ANEM included a complete and operational RCA television studio and a model American home, dubbed "Splitnik," since it was divided down the middle to provide a path for the millions of visitors over the six-week run of the exhibition. This installation also included the kitchen that would, unsuspectingly, host one of the great rhetorical battles of the Cold War. The exhibition designers had no way of predicting the importance of one of these products of industry—the ready-made kitchen unit by General Electric—and the vital role it would play in Cold War public diplomacy.

Figure 3.24.   A dubious Russian visitor tours the U.S. art show at the American National Exhibition in Moscow, 1959.
United States Information Agency (USIA).

Domestic Simulacra as
Ethnographic Village: Americans on Display

What was offered by the USA to the people of the Soviet Union was more than a cornucopia of consumer goods: the American Exhibition was an attempt to create a kind of "tourism in reverse" experience . . . one that focused on the individual citizen—how he goes shopping, how he has his hair cut, what the inside of his home is like, what he does for work and what he does for fun. In short, what everyday life is like for many millions of people who live in the U.S.[90]

At the end of the 1950s, Russians were no strangers to American culture. The desire to learn about the United States, the main rival of the U.S.S.R., trumped caution, however, as Masey and Morgan point out: "The Russians' insatiable curiosity about Americans—and all things American—is understandable given the demonization of the USA in the Soviet press, the lack of contact with foreigners in general, and the boredom of everyday life under the Soviet system."[91] For years there had been a broad cross-section of Soviet society listening to Voice of America radio broadcasts that escaped government jamming and a readership avidly devouring the USIA's *Amerika* magazine, both which gave, at best, a partial view of the life and times of U.S. culture. In the year leading up to the arrival of the *American National Exhibition* in Moscow, U.S. cultural infiltration in the Soviet Union included the politically charged visits by American musicians Van Cliburn, the young Texan who became the first American to win the Tchaikovsky International Piano Competition, and Paul Robeson, the left-leaning African-American basso profundo who captured the hearts of the Soviet citizenry. Other cultural visitors from the United States at the time confirmed Russian enthusiasm for all levels of American culture, as was demonstrated by the warm reception on separate occasions of both Bob Hope and the Harlem Globetrotters.[92]

According to Masey, the Soviet visitors would receive a healthy dose of a particular brand of American culture. He emphasizes that "we wanted to rub their noses in it,"[93] that the planners of the *American National Exhibition* in Moscow sought to provide the Soviet citizenry the starkly unsubtle reminder that the capitalist lifestyle was exceedingly more comfortable than daily existence under communism.[94] Further, it is arguable that, in the framework of Bennett's exhibitionary complex, the presence of the Soviet visitors themselves echoed the exhibition of primitive peoples at nineteenth-century world's fairs. In his discussion of the exhibitionary complex, Bennett cites

Charles Darwin's quest for "representing the fractured unity of the human Species" which, according to Bennett, "was achieved by the representation of 'primitive peoples' as instances of arrested development, as examples of an earlier stage of species development which Western civilizations had long ago surpassed." Though the Soviet citizenry clearly did not resemble a prehistoric people, they were, in the context of the ANEM, "denied any history of their own" and were, in essence, "dropped out of the bottom of human history in order that they might serve, representationally, as its support—underlining the rhetoric of progress by serving as its counterpoints."[95] Mitarachi reminds that for the trade fairs of the mid-1950s, U.S. organizers had understood that "most Fairs, open to the public, are a good free show for the people. They are attended both by businessmen and by workers and farmers and others who, having virtually no hope of owning the goods on display, come out of curiosity—an impressionable curiosity. What they see may represent to them either fantasy or frustration."[96] This mindset, in no uncertain terms, was also applied by ANEM organizers, many of who worked on the exhibitions that Mitarachi refers to above.

From a point of view of the history of collecting and display, it is important to revisit Castillo's theory that the ANEM marked a coda to an era of the outright display of domestic objects within "lifelike" dioramas. Matthew Roth discusses the dioramas in which objects are embedded as fabrications that "add a layer of aesthetic enjoyment to the gallery experience on top of the direct perception"[97] of the objects themselves. These object-rich exhibits at the ANEM, such as the GE House and the Glass Pavilion, replete with consumer goods, would in the future downshift to fewer artifacts on display, which did not, as the next chapter examines, take away from the profound, however subtle, ideological/imperial agenda implicit in the overall exhibitions themselves.

Baudrillard, on the subject of collecting, explains that the origin of the word "object" refers directly to "anything which is the cause or subject of passion. Figuratively and most typically: the loved object."[98] One should not lose sight, however, of what was on display, or at least what the thematic emphasis was throughout the run of trade fairs and the ANEM itself. These exhibitions that showed kitchens, cars, clothing, and architecture represented at this time what De Grazia would call "technologies of empire." They, in essence, helped perpetrate "the jealousy complex" that Baudrillard attests is the condition when "possession derives its fullest satisfaction from the prestige the object enjoys in the eyes of other people, and the fact that they cannot have it."[99]

Precedents for "living dioramas" at world's fairs date back to the nineteenth century. As Curtis Hinsley describes the throngs of humanity coursing through the Chicago Midway in 1893, the "flow of human traffic occupied the center of the picture."[100] Bennett's interpretation of these dioramas borrows from Rydell, whose exploration of American world fairs "provides the most detailed demonstration of the active role played by museum anthropologists in transforming" the exhibition space itself "into living demonstrations of evolutionary theory by arranging . . . peoples into a 'sliding-scale of humanity.'"[101] The ANEM also, in a way, accomplished "object lessons of evolutionary theory" in a much more muted, subtler fashion. This practice of contrasting peoples for imperialist purposes succeeds, from Bennett's point of view, in "underlining the exhibitionary rhetoric of progress by serving as visible counterpoints to its triumphal achievements."[102] While it was indeed the Soviet government that hosted the *American National Exhibition* in Moscow, it was the United States itself that controlled the exhibition space. Once more conjuring Bennett, it was in this display of power through culture "that relations of knowledge and power continued to be invested in the public display of bodies, colonizing the space of earlier freak and monstrosity shows in order to personify the truths of a new regime of representation."[103]

The fashion shows staged daily also conveyed the message that the United States far outpaced the U.S.S.R. in creature domestic comforts and overall quality of life (figures 3.25–3.27). As Masey points out, the fashion shows featuring American models was all "show business," since "you had gorgeous American chicks wearing fabulous outfits. And the Soviets were mesmerized. They'd never seen anything like it. Here, they were more transfixed with the people than what they were wearing."[104] Haddow acknowledges that the make-believe aspect of "unnaturally thin" models upheld the altogether erroneous message that "American women in Moscow seemed to have it all—slim figures, beauty products, convenient appliances and robotic servants, rock-and-roll plaids for daughter and ball gowns for Mom."[105] These dramatic representations of happy single ladies and celebrating couples—particularly the "wedding scene" in the fashion show—enjoying the material largesse of American culture bolstered the notion that the "most significant contribution to the growth of democracy made by twentieth century America has not been in politics or government but in the widespread distribution of material goods. The Sears, Roebuck catalog might be called the Magna Carta of our civilization and—some cynics might add—its Bible, too."[106] Indeed, the rhetoric of housework would become a point of contention at the ANEM in the well-documented Kitchen Debate between Khrushchev and Nixon.[107] *New York Times* columnist Harrison Salisbury would dub this encounter the "Sokolniki Summit."[108]

During their tour of the ANEM on opening day, the goodwill that began in the RCA television studio would soon ebb negatively toward a verbal

Figure 3.25. American model participating in a fashion show, American National Exhibition in Moscow, 1959.
Photographer: Mary Lou Leach, Courtesy, Jack Masey Collection.

Figure 3.26. Russian visitors watch American models in a fashion show, American National Exhibition in Moscow, 1959.
United States Information Agency (USIA).

Figure 3.27. Women's lingerie fashion show, American National Exhibition in Moscow, 1959.
Courtesy, Jacqueline Nelson.

battle over whose people—the Soviets versus the Americans—enjoyed a better quality of life (figure 3.28). While Khrushchev acknowledged the advances made by the United States in the sphere of domestic living, it would be Nixon who pointed beyond the washing machines and GE ovens to the chief benefit of modern industry for the masses: the power to choose.

However, the Soviet leader would remark—while cornered by Vice President Nixon in the General Electric kitchen at the *American National Exhibition*—that the modern conveniences Americans seem to delight in are nothing more than real versions of Charlie Chaplin's infamous eating machine, useless contrivances that take away from the quality of life.[109] Pulos maintains that while Nixon argued "the kitchen was evidence of how Americans were liberating their women," Khrushchev "retorted that it was

Figure 3.28.   Khrushchev and Nixon discuss the merits of the quality of living in the Soviet Union and the United States in the RCA television studio, American National Exhibition in Moscow, 1959.
National Archives and Records Administration (NARA).

just another capitalist tool."[110] Political bluster aside, this attitude toward the American way of life was exactly what Eisenhower wanted his public diplomacy to defend against, that the United States and its people were merely a shallow, gadget-obsessed people, with little cultural sense other than a predilection for the latest commercial product that could improve one's domestic life. William Safire offers a lucid appraisal of the meeting of Vice President Nixon and Premier Khrushchev at the exhibition:

> So, here you have all these things happening that you look back on now in a kind of golden fog. But the golden fog we look back on was a real war between communism and capitalism. And that's why when these two strong men met, they were deadly serious. They could kid around and talk about refrigerators and things like that, but there was a clear warning on the table from the Soviet Union that they were going to close off Berlin.[111]

Nina Gilden Seavey, Director of the Documentary Center at George Washington University and a speaker at the conference "From Face-off to Facebook: From the Nixon-Khrushchev Kitchen Debate to Public Diplomacy in the 21st Century," which took place on July 23, 2009, marking the fiftieth anniversary of the exhibition, characterized the tone of the meeting of Nixon and Khrushchev at the ANEM as remarkably symbolic of the "forty-year-old winter between the U.S. and the U.S.S.R." She described the behavior of these two leaders, particularly during their ideological sparring that led them from the RCA television studio installation to the model kitchen, as follows: "We fought and then we embraced . . . we fought and then we embraced . . . this became a symbol of our relationship."[112] During his visit to the exhibition at Sokolniki Park, Khrushchev himself would playfully brand his exchange with Nixon as "a communist spokesman dealing with a capitalist lawyer." Such levity, however, masked a looming international crisis of chief importance to the Cold War superpowers. According to Safire,

> The problem at that time was Berlin. And the key to Khrushchev was to solve his Berlin leak, the leak of the talent of East Germany back into West Germany. And people were leaving all the time through Berlin. And this was a running sore, as it were, because all the brains and all the entrepreneurial excitement were feeding out through Berlin. And so his threat at the time was to turn over operations of entry and exit of Berlin to the East German government. Sure enough, a year later, the Berlin wall went up.[113]

Safire himself overheard much of the rhetorical jousting between Nixon and Khrushchev. Also present was the entourage of reporters who leaped at the opportunity to document the impromptu, now legendary exchange. Nixon apparently had felt slighted by the Soviet premier's comment moments earlier in the television studio that "in another seven years, we will be on the same level as America. When we catch you up, in passing you by, we will wave to you." Looking to gain a foothold in the argument, the American vice president's team redirected the official tour of the exhibition so that it would bottleneck in the middle of the model home. Safire, on hand to publicize the efficiency of the polished and glittering domestic appliances enjoyed by average Americans, was responsible for taking one of the iconic photos of the two principals as they found themselves trapped—to Nixon's delight and Khrushchev's discomfort—in the General Electric kitchen (figure 3.29).

In front of dozens of onlookers, Nixon leaned into the display and took the Soviet premier to task, proclaiming the ingenuity of home design in the United States capable of improving the lives of millions of Americans. Eyewitnesses reported some selected portions of the Kitchen Debate:[114]

> Nixon: I want to show you this kitchen. It is like those of our houses in California. [Nixon points to dishwasher.]

Figure 3.29. Khrushchev and Nixon conduct their face-off in the General Electric kitchen, American National Exhibition in Moscow, 1959.
KEYSTONE/AP Photo: Associated Press.

Khrushchev: We have such things.

Nixon: This is our newest model. This is the kind which is built in thousands of units for direct installations in the houses. In America, we like to make life easier for women.

Khrushchev: Your capitalistic attitude toward women does not occur under communism.

Nixon: I think that this attitude towards women is universal. What we want to do is make life more easy for our housewives. This house can be bought for $14,000. Let me give you an example that you can appreciate. Our steelworkers, as you know, are now on strike. But any steelworker could buy this house. They earn $3 an hour. This house costs about $100 a month to buy on a contract running 25 to 30 years.

Khrushchev: We have steelworkers and peasants who can afford to spend $14,000 for a house. Your American houses are built to last only 20 years so builders could sell new houses at the end. We build firmly. We build for our children and grandchildren.

. . . .

Khrushchev: The Americans have created their own image of the Soviet man. But he is not as you think. You think the Russian people will be dumbfounded to see these things, but the fact is that newly built Russian houses have all this equipment right now.

Nixon: Yes, but—

Khrushchev: In Russia, all you have to do to get a house is to be born in the Soviet Union. You are entitled to housing. . . . In America, if you don't have a dollar you have a right to choose between sleeping in a house or on the pavement. Yet you say we are the slave to Communism.

. . . .

Khrushchev: On politics, we will never agree with you. But this does not mean that we do not get along.

Nixon: You can learn from us, and we can learn from you. There must be a free exchange. Let the people choose the kind of house, the kind of soup, the kind of ideas that they want.

Soon after these comments were made, the face-off in the kitchen subsided, and both protagonists reverted to the goodwill that became the hallmark for the cultural exchange agreement between the United States and the U.S.S.R. It would become glaringly clear, however, that what Khrushchev and Nixon were saying on that fateful afternoon in Moscow represented much more than the strong wills of expert politicians from opposite sides of the ideological fence. As journalist Marvin Kalb explains, "Russia was at a pivotal moment in its history. Moving on from Stalin, this exhibition was opening the door to the world for many Soviets. What Khrushchev and Nixon were saying was so reflective of what their two countries represented, or wanted to represent."[115]

At the end of his visit to the Soviet Union, Nixon was able during a television and radio address to talk directly to the Soviet people. This separate media event gave the Russians an opportunity to hear about American values directly from a high-ranking U.S. leader.[116] As Safire notes:

It didn't change Russian public opinion, but it made people think that maybe the enemy is only an adversary. And maybe frankly, some of the things they've got going over there [in the U.S.] will help a steelworker have a home and not the same home as every other steelworker. That's what I see as the fundamental importance of that exhibition and that confrontation in the kitchen.[117]

Nixon put a positive spin on not only the American identity but on the Cold War itself. While echoing Eisenhower's lament over the mutual suspicion between the superpowers that had reached critical levels leading up to the exhibition, specifically over the Berlin question, the vice president could be heard championing cultural exchange—specifically people exchange—as a means for lessening tensions between the Americans and the Soviets. This was a time when neither the United States nor the U.S.S.R. could foresee a peaceable outcome for their warring political systems. It would be the interaction of people from both systems (American guides and Russians citizens) that would illustrate the indelible, and fragile, human realities underlying the conflict.

The American Guides

> Some seventy-five American guides, including both male and female, fluent in Russian and headed for professional careers, explained to their Soviet counterparts that the amenities and consumer products on display not only kept American women beautiful, they also helped build careers in the traditionally male business world.[118]

Historians of Cold War history have given due weight to the domestic politics of producing this challenging exhibition, to the spectacle of modern design on display, and of course to the dramatis personae of the Kitchen Debate. However, only recently have cultural historians explored in greater depth the effect that real Americans, mostly in the form of exhibition guides, had on the Russian visitors. As representatives of the United States, these cultural ambassadors formed the backbone of the six-week, multivenue spectacle that aimed to offer a glimpse of American life to a Soviet citizenry wary of the West. Tuch describes the effect of the young American guides at the Moscow exhibition: "What made the show comprehensible to Soviet visitors were the Russian-speaking American guides. They showed the literal face of America. We must first understand the culture, the language, the history, the psychology, and the motives of the people with whom we wish to communicate. We learned, and we communicated."[119] These docents were often subjected to a range of hostile questions about the United States on such subjects as racism, violence, and the lack of American initiative on space exploration. Indeed, the theme of "information machine" continued through the live exhibits of these Russian-speaking U.S. citizens. It was this human element that offered Moscow's urban population a genuine connection with a side of American life they could not have known otherwise. Their interactions were not without risk, as Masey attests:

> There was a lot of harassment of our guides at the Moscow show in '59. The KGB, if they could set you up with something, embarrass you with something,

they would do it. The guides were told that there was absolutely no fraterniza-tion with Russian visitors. You can make friends with people. You can meet them in public. But privacy is out of the question. You were not allowed to carry any sensitive material on you at anytime, nor were you allowed to take anything anyone might want to give you. For instance, someone could hand you a paper that are state secrets and then you're framed.[120]

Guide George Feiffer offers a different take on the work of the guides: "We continued to see Russia as Stalinist, but it was not Stalinist. It was on the way to improving, slowly, staggeringly to a richer, more humane society. They needed encouragement, not a slap in the face. We slapped them in the face."[121] Guide Linda Gottlieb, in a reference to Edward R. Murrow's idealiza-tion of public diplomacy as person-to-person contact, remembers, "Many felt *we* were those last three feet."[122]

President Eisenhower reflected in his memoirs on the importance of the American guides at the ANEM:

> Our Moscow exhibition served a constructive purpose by bringing thousands upon thousands of Soviet men, women, and children face to face with the products of American industry and above all with American citizens. I was particularly impressed with reports of the group of outstanding United States college students who served as guides and who day after day stood up and in fluent Russian fielded questions of the greatest diversity about life in the United States. In fact, these bright young men and women so impressed their hearers that when some trained Communist agitators began infiltrating the crowd and throwing loaded questions, friendly Russians in the audience would help out by supplying answers in loud whispers.[123]

From Moscow to Expos: The Impact of the *American National Exhibition* on the USIA

Tomas Tolvaisas interprets the *American National Exhibition* in Moscow as the spark of a trajectory in which the United States, through subsequent ex-hibitions, would enjoy easy access to great numbers of the Soviet population after 1959.[124] Tolvaisas suggests the ANEM be seen as "a great communica-tor" for it "set a foundation for the following exhibitions that visited the Soviet Union through 1991. Due to budget constraints, smaller exhibitions would follow, travel throughout the U.S.S.R. and be shown throughout Eastern Europe, at trade fairs or solo exhibitions. These other exhibitions were bridge-builders between 1959 and the 21st century."[125] As the Soviet Union continued its effort at de-Stalinization under Khrushchev, Russians found themselves at a poignant moment in their history. Not only did this exhibition open the U.S.S.R. and its citizens to "American" realities, it also showed the human face behind the politically divisive, state-sponsored rhetoric. What followed the ANEM were these smaller thematic exhibitions that would tour the U.S.S.R. for thirty years—from 1961 until 1991. According to Masey,

> It still baffles everybody as to why the Soviets agreed to thirty years of punishment, especially when we all know that the Soviet exhibitions that traveled to the US during this time were seen by comparatively few Americans. Nobody cared. While in the Soviet Union, visitors mobbed every single American exhibit that traveled there. We packed 'em in, even though we were the enemy. We were the bad guys. And changes of presidency. Changes in the Soviet Union. These didn't affect this exchange.[126]

These smaller shows were, in a way, an answer to Eisenhower's concern about "a different kind of war," the "the massive economic offensive," Ike explained, "that has been mounted by the communist imperialists against free nations."[127] The USIA would follow Masey's recommendation after 1959 that each show—typically between four thousand and twelve thousand square feet—be limited to a single theme. After visiting the Soviet embassy in Washington, D.C., a deal was struck with the Soviets who showed interest in exchanging little traveling shows on different subjects. The first American show that traveled to the U.S.S.R. was devoted to plastics in the American home and in industry, since the Soviets continued to want to better understand technology in the United States. According to Masey, "They didn't realize we were going to have a whole apartment made virtually entirely of plastic, with fabulous chairs, fabulous tables, kitchenware, and so forth. Hey, we are who we are. Why should we underplay what we do?"[128] Additional thematic shows included *Technical Books*, a popular exhibition among Soviet audiences in that many scientists showed up. "This is what they really wanted out of us. No propaganda. But we snuck it in. Even in *Technical Books* we had books on film, books on movies, and so on," Masey states. Other shows from the early 1960s included *Transportation: USA, Medicine: USA, Graphic Arts: USA, Communications: USA*, and *Architecture: USA*. Architecture curator Arthur Drexler at the Museum of Modern Art designed the architecture exhibition. This show displayed a conceptual model for a modern U.S. city and included backlit color transparencies mounted on kiosks a foot thick and ten feet high. Some featured skyscrapers; some showed airports and private homes. Everything glowed.

These shows traveled to the farthest reaches of the Soviet Union, and, after 1959, most of the decisions were largely made by designers, not policy people. Ivan Chermayeff, one of the designers on the *Graphic Arts* exhibition, emphasizes the importance of these exhibitions that toured the Soviet Union exclusively: "These tinker toy exhibits that you could ship from place to place and set up very easily were simple stuff. There was an appetite to see what else was going on in the world. They were more deprived, the Russians, than we were. They wanted us there, so it was not controversial in political terms. If it were political, they wouldn't have wanted us to be there."[129]

This history of designers driving the content for national exhibitions would continue with the world expo pavilions that will be addressed in the next chapter. According to Masey, "The USIA saw design as kind of a little barnacle out there until it really delivered something remarkable."[130] As Payeff-Masey asserts,

This is the maturing of a way of communicating that was developed by things they [the designers] did outside USIA, but also within USIA. There was a maturity of American industrial designers, who were given the opportunity, mostly in the 60s, that allowed them to flourish and to have an audience, an influence that went well beyond the realm of public diplomacy into not only how the world saw the United States but how the world designed itself, the objects it was using.[131]

While cultural infiltration into the Soviet Union would continue on a regular schedule until the early 1990s, a version of Ike's "evolutionary approach"[132] to weaken communism, it would be the return to category one world's fairs in 1967 and 1970 that would offer the platform for the ascendancy of U.S. cultural exhibitions abroad.

Notes

1. Tony Bennett, "The Exhibitionary Complex," *New Formations* 4 (Spring 1988): 93–94.

2. See, for example, Walter L. Hixson, *Parting the Curtain: Propaganda, Culture, and the Cold War, 1945–1961* (New York: St. Martin's, 1997), chapters 6–8; Jack Masey and Conway Lloyd Morgan, *Cold War Confrontations: U.S. Exhibitions and Their Role in the Cultural Cold War* (Baden, Switzerland: Lars Müller, 2008), 152–283; Greg Castillo, *Cold War on the Home Front: The Soft Power of Midcentury Design* (Minneapolis: University of Minnesota Press, 2010), 139–70. For personal and eyewitness takes on the ANEM, see Peter Blake, *No Place Like Utopia: Modern Architecture and the Company We Kept* (New York: Norton, 1993), 228–48; and Hans

M. Tuch and G. Lewis Schmidt, eds., *Ike and the USIA: A Commemorative Symposium* (Washington, DC: U.S. Information Alumni Association, Public Diplomacy Foundation, 1991), 35–40.

3. Donald Preziosi, *Brain of the Earth's Body: Art, Museums, and the Phantasms of Modernity* (Minneapolis: University of Minnesota Press, 2003), 133.

4. See Harold C. McClellan, *A Review of the American National Exhibition in Moscow, July 25–September 4, 1959,* USIA Historical Collection, State Department, Washington, DC, 2. See also *United States Treaties and Other International Agreements,* 3975, 9 (1958), 13–39.

5. See L. H. Gann and Peter Duignan, "World War II and the Beginning of the Cold War," Hoover Essays No. 14, Hoover Institution on War, Revolution and Peace, Stanford University, 1996. Here Gann and Duignan discuss four schools of thought that attempt to explain the birth of the Cold War.

6. Masey and Morgan, *Cold War Confrontations,* 90.

7. Winston Churchill, speaking at Westminster College, Fulton, Missouri, March 5, 1946.

8. See Nicholas J. Cull, *The Cold War and the United States Information Agency: American Propaganda and Public Diplomacy, 1945–1989* (Cambridge: Cambridge University Press, 2008), 46.

9. On the subject of the Soviet psyche, Isaiah Berlin states: "One of the most arresting characteristics of modern Russian culture is its acute self-consciousness. There has surely never been a society more deeply and exclusively preoccupied with itself, its own nature and destiny," in "The Silence of Russian Culture," *Foreign Affairs* 36, no. 1 (October 1957): 1. He continues: "Between 1932 and, say, 1945 or indeed 1955, it would not be too much to say that—outside natural science—scarcely any idea or piece of critical writing of high intrinsic value was published in Russia, and hardly any work of art—scarcely anything genuinely interesting or important in itself and not merely as a symptom of the regime or of the methods practiced by it, that is to say, as a piece of historical evidence," ibid., 14.

10. Telegram, George Kennan to George Marshall ["Long Telegram"], February 22, 1946. Harry S. Truman Administration File, Elsey Papers, Harry S. Truman Library. For the Russian perspective on U.S. postwar foreign policy, see the Novikov Telegram of September 27, 1946, in which Soviet diplomat to the U.S. Nikolai Vasilevich Novikov offers a "response" to the top-secret Kennan telegram. See also Kenneth M. Jensen, ed., *Origins of the Cold War: The Novikov, Kennan, and Roberts "Long Telegrams" of 1946* (Washington, DC: United States Institute of Peace, 1991).

11. The Voice of America radio broadcasts did at this time have an effect on listeners behind the Iron Curtain. For more on this subject, see Cull, *The Cold War and the United States Information Agency,* several sections.

12. See, for instance, Peter G. Boyle, *American-Soviet Relations: From the Russian Revolution to the Fall of Communism* (London: Routledge, 1993), 120–21. Boyle cites Walter Lippmann, who criticized the strategy of containment: "Moscow, not Washington, would define the issues, would make the challenges, would select the ground

where the conflict was to be waged and would choose the weapon." From Walter Lippmann, *The Cold War* (New York: Harper, 1947), 9.

13. *New York Times*, August 26, 1952.

14. See Frank A. Ninkovich, *The Wilsonian Century: U.S. Foreign Policy since 1900* (Chicago: University of Chicago Press, 1999), 201. Masey and Morgan perhaps sum up this dynamic more succinctly: "If the cultural Cold War had a front line, Berlin was on it," *Cold War Confrontations*, 90. For a discussion of Khrushchev's motives during the peak of the Berlin Crisis (1958–61), see, for instance, Petr Luňák, "Khrushchev and Berlin Crisis: Soviet Brinkmanship Seen from Inside," *Cold War History* 3, no. 2 (January 2003): 53–82.

15. See Yale Richmond, *Cultural Exchange and the Cold War: Raising the Iron Curtain* (University Park: Pennsylvania State University Press, 2003), 6. According to Richmond, "The welcome mat was out for American know-how, and by 1930 the Soviet Union had agreements on technical cooperation with more than forty of the largest American corporations, including Ford, General Electric, and Dupont, whose efforts contributed to the success of the First Five-Year Plan." This interest and adherence to American industrial models fits with Jack Masey's theory about Khrushchev's wanting "cultural" exchange with the United States. Perhaps it was merely a want to continue technological insights into American industries. However, by the late 1930s, Stalin's "Great Terror" had all but closed the door for any type of exchange with the West.

16. See, for instance, Gunter Bischof and Saki Dockrill, eds., *Cold War Respite: The Geneva Summit of 1955* (Baton Rouge: Louisiana State University Press, 2000). For Ike's read of the situation, see Dwight D. Eisenhower, *The White House Years: Mandate for Change, 1953–1956* (Garden City, NY: Doubleday, 1963), 526–27. See also page 529 for Ike's frustration with the "Soviet duplicity" in their repudiation of "every measure to which they had agreed in July at the follow-up to the Geneva conference, the October 1955 Foreign Ministers' conference." For post-Geneva Soviet propaganda activities, see also NA RG306 U.S. Information Agency, Office of Research, Entry # P 160: Special Reports (S); 1953–1997, S-16-55 THRU S-2-56, Container #9, ARC# 5664216, "Post-Geneva Communist Propaganda: USSR."

17. Cull, *The Cold War and the United States Information Agency*, 161. See also Yale Richmond, *U.S.-Soviet Cultural Exchanges, 1958–1986: Who Wins?* (Boulder, CO: Westview, 1987), 133–39; Hans M. Tuch, *Communicating with the World: U.S. Public Diplomacy Overseas* (New York: St. Martin's, 1990), chapter 9; Kenneth Osgood, *Total Cold War: Eisenhower's Secret Propaganda Battle at Home and Abroad* (Lawrence: University of Kansas Press, 2006), chapter 6; Laura Belmonte, *Selling the American Way: U.S. Propaganda and the Cold War* (Philadelphia: University of Pennsylvania Press, 2008), 67–69; Eisenhower, *Mandate for Change*, chapter 21. For a contemporary discussion of the Geneva Summit, see John C. Campbell, "Negotiation with the Soviets: Some Lessons of the War Period," *Foreign Affairs* 34, no. 2 (January 1956): 305–19; and, Circular Letter from the Acting Director of the United States Information Agency (Washburn) to all USIS Posts, August 24, 1955, Department of State,

USIA/IOP Files: Lot 59 D 260, Director 1953–56, Confidential, as cited in *FRUS*, 1955–1957, Volume 9, Page 526. In this letter, Director Washburn states: "The new spirit of amity dramatically proclaimed at the Geneva 'Summit' Conference will very likely induce questions to you and your staff by American and other visitors along the line of, 'Now that East and West seem to have seen each other's point of view, why is a U.S. information program necessary? Shouldn't it be reduced or eliminated? Isn't the anti-Communist aspect of your program now in direct conflict with current American foreign policy? . . . First, it must be clearly understood that the United States is not in the information business solely as a result of the Communist threat. . . . The fact is that this country, willingly or not, is now and will continue to be involved in every world question of any magnitude.'"

18. Khrushchev, as quoted in *Time* magazine, August 3, 1959, 15.

19. See from Masey Archives USIA report on U.S. participation in the Indian fair, by Thomas E. Flanagan, Counselor for Public Affairs, dated February 2, 1956, which includes comparisons between "Free World" vs. "Iron Curtain" participants at the Indian fair. For example, the Free World national pavilions occupied 211,400 square feet while those of the Iron Curtain countries held 201,305 square feet. The main problem leading up to the launch of the exhibit was the projected visitor traffic flow. As the report demonstrates, it was decidedly Bayerian: "The first problem was coped with in a highly satisfactorily manner by establishing a one-way snake-like traffic through the exhibit from entrance to exit."

20. Ibid.

21. Masey, interview, August 24, 2010. For a general discussion of U.S.-India relations, post–World War II, see Andrew J. Rotter, "Feeding Beggars: Class, Caste, and Status in Indo-U.S. Relations, 1947–1964," in *Cold War Constructions: The Political Culture of United States Imperialism, 1945–1966*, ed. Christian G. Appy (Amherst: University of Massachusetts Press, 2000), 67–85.

22. Payeff-Masey, interview, August 24, 2010. See also the Final Report for the American pavilion (Masey Archives) at the Indian Industries Fair, January 1956, which lays out this discussion in greater detail.

23. Masey, interview, August 24, 2010. For more on the *Atoms for Peace* exhibit in New Delhi, see Cull, *The Cold War and the United States Information Agency*, 104. In addition, this was not the first foray of U.S. public diplomacy in India. For an earlier instance, see Eric D. Pullin, "'Noise and Flutter': American Propaganda Strategy and Operation in India during World War II," *Diplomatic History* 34, no. 2 (April 2010): 275–98.

24. For USIA-sponsored intelligence on India prior to the Indian Industries Fair, see "IRI Intelligence Summary: Analysis of Public Opinion Poll in India, October 13, 1955," in NA RG306 Records of the USIA, Office of Research and Intelligence, Intelligence Bulletins, Memorandums and Summaries; 1954–1956, 1955: IS-66 thru 1956: IS-3.3, Box 6, Folder "IS-89-55," specifically page 5. See also "Report of the Soviet Economic Offensive in India" as an example of worldwide study of Soviet aid to nonaligned countries (pair with article on Soviet economic offensive at home).

Senator John F. Kennedy himself voiced a strong opinion in favor of India developing itself as a "middle power broker nation." See John F. Kennedy, "A Democrat Looks at Foreign Policy," *Foreign Affairs* 36, no. 1 (October 1957): 44–59; see also P., "Middle Ground between America and Russia: An Indian View," *Foreign Affairs* 32, no. 2 (January 1954): 259–69. Vital for understanding U.S. nervousness in dealing with Indian Industrial Fair, in NA RG306 Records of the USIA, Office of Research and Analysis, Research Reports, 1956–1959, 1957: P-76 thru 1958: p-2.1, Box 4, Folder "P-87-57." For mention of Indian fair and others from an American business perspective, see W. Walter Williams, "It's Fair Weather," *Rotarian*, December 1955, 17.

25. NSC 5607, "East-West Exchanges." National Security Council statement of policy, June 29, 1956; declassified and released under the Freedom of Information Act, December 24, 1984.

26. Walter Roberts, introductory comments, "From Face-off to Facebook: From the Nixon-Khrushchev Kitchen Debate to Public Diplomacy in the 21st Century" (conference, George Washington University, Washington DC, July 23, 2009).

27. See Richmond, *Cultural Exchange and the Cold War*, chapter 3. See also MC468, Box 227, Folder #32, "General Reports, US-USSR Block Exchanges, 1950–1970," Bureau of Educational and Cultural Affairs Historical Collection (CU), Special Collections, University of Arkansas, Fayetteville. This folder contains a January 27, 1958, memo on "Joint US-USSR Communique on Agreement on Exchanges," including a section on exhibitions. For insight into the attitudes of the players responsible for this agreement, see June 9, 1958, progress report on U.S.-Soviet Exchange Agreement, in MC468, Box 228, Folder #7, "Exchanges with the USSR, General, 1958–59."

28. Richmond, *U.S-Soviet Cultural Exchanges, 1958–1986*, 9.

29. See United States Information Agency, Office of Research and Intelligence, Report, "Communist Propaganda and the Brussels Fair," January 22, 1958, in NA RG306 Records of the USIA, Office of Research and Analysis, Research Reports, 1956–1959, 1958: P-3 thru 1958: P-30, Box 5, Folder "P-6-58." See commentary on page 2 that mentions how the Soviets highlighted their heavy industrial breakthroughs at the expense of showing their weakness in producing consumer goods.

30. For a useful interpretation of how the U.S. and Soviet efforts "contested their claims for modernity" at the Brussels World Fair, which opened on April 17, 1958, see Susan Reid, "The Soviet Pavilion at Brussels '58: Convergence, Conversion, Critical Assimilation, or Transcultural?" (working paper, Woodrow Wilson International Center for Scholars, Cold War International History Project: Working Papers Series, Working Paper 62, December 2010), 9.

31. Jack Masey, "21st-Century World's Fairs" (lecture, National Building Museum, October 25, 2010), http://www.nbm.org/media/audio/21st-century-worlds -fairs-3.html.

32. Masey, interview, August 24, 2010.

33. Ibid.

34. Ibid.

35. Berlin, "The Silence of Russian Culture," 24.

36. See Greg Castillo, "Domesticating the Cold War: Household Consumption as Propaganda in Marshall Plan Germany," *Journal of Contemporary History* 40, no. 2 (April 2005): 262; and by the same author, *Cold War on the Home Front*, 140.

37. Victoria De Grazia, *Irresistible Empire: America's Advance through 20th-Century Europe* (Cambridge, MA: Belknap, 2005), 557. See also Rob Kroes, "Imaginary America in Europe's Public Space," in *The Americanization of Europe: Culture, Diplomacy, and Anti-Americanism after 1945*, ed. Alexander Stephan (New York: Berghahn, 2006), 345–46.

38. De Grazia, *Irresistible Empire*, 424. See also Jean Baudrillard, *Le système des objets* (Paris: Gallimard, 1968), 249–52; and, by the same author, *Consumer Society: Myths and Structures* (Thousand Oaks, CA: Sage, 1998).

39. See Robert H. Haddow, *Pavilions of Plenty: Exhibiting American Culture Abroad in the 1950s* (Washington, DC: Smithsonian Institution, 1997), 37.

40. See Gilles Lipovetsky, *Hypermodern Times* (Cambridge: Polity, 2005). For an excellent source on hyperconsumption as it lends itself to the idea of simulated, utopian, and make-believe realities for the consumer, see Jean Baudrillard, "Simulacra and Simulations," in *Jean Baudrillard: Selected Writings*, ed. Mark Poster (Palo Alto: Stanford University Press, 1988), 166–84. Several works by George Ritzer allow a fascinating entry point into how the doctrines of American consumer culture have taken hold, particularly in discussions of the globalization of their influence. See, for instance, George Ritzer, *The McDonaldization of Society: An Investigation into the Changing Character of Contemporary Social Life* (Thousand Oaks, CA: Pine Forge, 1993).

41. John Berger, *Ways of Seeing* (London: Penguin, 1972), 149.

42. Bennett, "The Exhibitionary Complex," 94. See also Richard Latham, "Communication of Values through Design," in *The Aspen Papers: Twenty Years of Design Theory from the International Design Conference in Aspen*, ed. Reyner Banham (New York: Praeger, 1974), 90–91: "These working-class families had tried to assemble, from the multitude of goods offered to them by designers and manufacturers, some picture of what they are. The picture was full of horror and disharmonies to anyone trained in visual values. But beneath each of those physical symbols—the lace coverlet and chenille scatter rugs and chrome dinette furniture—there was a real emotional need for the purchase. . . . But the needs and impulses are quite real, and who dares to scoff—without first comprehending those needs—or to insist that they substitute another set of symbols?"

43. Umberto Eco, "Two Families of Objects," in *Travels in Hyperreality: Essays*, trans. William Weaver (San Diego: Harcourt, 1986), 183.

44. Piergiorgio Degli Esposti, "Hyperconsumption," in *The Wiley-Blackwell Encyclopedia of Globalization*, ed. George Ritzer (Oxford: Blackwell, 2012).

45. See Baudrillard, "Simulacra and Simulations," 174–75. For another thoughtful discussion of the simulacrum, see Michael Camille, "Simulacrum," in *Critical Terms*

for Art History, 2nd ed., ed. Robert S. Nelson and Richard Shiff (Chicago: University of Chicago Press, 2003), 35.

46. As quoted in Esposti, "Hyperconsumption," 2.

47. See Stanley Abercrombie, *George Nelson: The Design of Modern Design* (Cambridge, MA: MIT Press, 2000), 159.

48. For conceptual precursors to the 1959 "umbrellas," see George Nelson, ed., *Display* (New York: Whitney, 1953), 41–43.

49. Harrison T. McClung later would spend much time with identifying ideal methods for developing temporary traveling shows based on the display techniques of these industrial designers. See McClung, "Portable Demountable Trade Fair Pavilions: A Research Project for Office of International Trade Fairs," United States Department of Commerce, by C. M. Shaw Associates, in NA RG489 Records of the International Trade Administration, Bureau of Foreign Commerce, Office of International Trade Fairs, Correspondence and Reports, 1954–1958, Box 1, Folder "Design Contracts, 10/54–4/56."

50. Abercrombie, *George Nelson*, ix–x.

51. Nelson, *Display*, 9.

52. George Nelson, "Design as Communication," *Industrial Design* (April 1954): 40.

53. Ettore Sottsass Jr., as quoted in Abercrombie, *George Nelson*, ix.

54. Cull, from a response to author's July 29, 2009 blog, "Summer of 'Splitnik': Remembering the American National Exhibition in Moscow," *CPD Blog*, http://uscpublicdiplomacy.com/index.php/newswire/cpdblog_detail/summer_of_splitnik_remembering_the_american_national_exhibition_in_moscow/.

55. Bennett, "The Exhibitionary Complex," 95.

56. Ibid. See also Cristina Marie Carbone, "Building Propaganda: Architecture at the American National Exhibition in Moscow of 1959," (PhD diss., University of California, Santa Barbara, 2001).

57. For play-by-play of meeting, see NA RG306 Records of the USIA, Records relating the *American National Exhibition*, Moscow, 1957–59, Airgrams and Cables through Radio and TV Coverage, Box 1, Folder "Negotiations-Moscow-Oct-Nov 1958."

58. Hans Tuch, from panel discussion at "From Face-off to Facebook: From the Nixon-Khrushchev Kitchen Debate to Public Diplomacy in the 21st Century" (conference, George Washington University, Washington, DC, July 23, 2009). The Soviets would stage their own exhibition, as per the agreement, in New York. See USIA, Office of Research and Analysis, "Soviet Exhibition in New York, May 7, 1959," in RG 306 Records of the USIA, Office of Research and Analysis, Research Reports, 1956–1959, 1958: P-3 thru 1958: P-30, Box 6, Folder "P-28-59."

59. See Robert Zieger, "The Paradox of Plenty: The Advertising Council and the Post-Sputnik Crisis," *Advertising & Society Review* 4, no. 1 (2003).

60. David Caute, *The Dancer Defects: The Struggle for Cultural Supremacy during the Cold War* (Oxford: Oxford University Press, 2003), 35–36.

61. Masey and Morgan, *Cold War Confrontations*, 162.

62. Ibid., 179.

63. See John Neuhart, Marilyn Neuhart, and Ray Eames, *Eames Design: The Work of the Office of Charles and Ray Eames* (New York: Abrams, 1989), 239. See also Beatriz Colomina, "Enclosed by Images: The Eameses' Multimedia Architecture," *Grey Room*, no. 2 (Winter 2001): 5–29.

64. Blake, *No Place Like Utopia*, 241.

65. See Jeffrey Meikle, *Design in the USA* (Oxford: Oxford University Press, 2005), 171–72. Here, Meikle states that the "Eames's multimedia show prefigured a future as yet unglimpsed," where "viewers were bombarded by a montage of 2,200 still and moving images depicting a day in the life of ordinary Americans. By all accounts 'Glimpses of the USA' was the hit of the exhibition. For all its apparent realism, however, it left the impression of a larger-than-life dream dissolving at the end into something that could not quite be grasped. The Eameses had worked magic with evanescent images."

66. Ibid., 170–71.

67. See Hélène Lipstadt, "'Natural Overlap:' Charles and Ray Eames and the Federal Government," in *The Work of Charles and Ray Eames: A Legacy of Invention*, ed. Diana Murphy (New York: Abrams, Library of Congress, and Vitra Design Museum, 1997), 161. Lipstadt adds, moreover, that unlike the popular magazines at this time such as *Life* and *Look*, which preached conformity, the Eameses' film celebrated the diverse American social landscape, showing, for example, in addition to equating "commodity capitalism with the American democracy," showing "houses of worship . . . as well as rites of all faiths, including those of white and black Protestants, Asian Americans, Native Americans, Muslims, as well as the more prominent minorities, Catholics and Jews," ibid., 164.

68. Ibid., 165.

69. Ibid., 166.

70. See Richard Wagner, *The Art-Work of the Future and Other Works*, trans. William Ashton Ellis (Lincoln: University of Nebraska Press, 1993), 88. Wagner theorizes: "The great United Art-work, which must gather up each branch of art to use it as a mean, and in some sense to undo it for the common aim of all, for the unconditioned absolute portrayal of human nature,—this great United Art-work he cannot picture as depending on the arbitrary purpose of some human unit, but can only conceive it as the instinctive and associate product of the Manhood of the Future."

71. Ibid.

72. Library of Congress, Charles and Ray Eames Papers, Charles and Ray Eames, Research/Production, Exhibits, Box 188, Folder 5, "Jehane Burns—Miscellany." See also Neuhart, Neuhart, and Eames, *Eames Design*, 177; Pat Kirkham, *Charles and Ray Eames: Designers of the Twentieth Century* (Cambridge, MA: MIT Press, 1995), 317–25; Abercrombie, *George Nelson*, 141–49. For Masey's perspective on Art X, see Masey and Morgan, *Cold War Confrontations*, 165–67.

73. George Nelson, "Design as Communication," 44.

74. Ibid.
75. See Abercrombie, *George Nelson*, 148: "The Nelson-Eames-Girard experiment was certainly precocious, coming well in advance of the surfeit of visual images now bombarding us from MTV and other sources, but it was based on an optimistic view that such bombardment, carefully planned, would convey a large amount of information." Pat Kirkham makes a reference to the "Gesamtkunstwerk" aspect of Eames's approach in the early 1950s to architecture, in *Charles and Ray Eames*, 18.
76. See Preziosi, *Brain of the Earth's Body*, 103, 133.
77. George Nelson, "Art X: The Georgia Experiment," *Industrial Design* (October 1954), 45.
78. Ibid., 46.
79. Ibid., 45.
80. Blake, *No Place Like Utopia*, 242.
81. See Eric J. Sandeen, *Picturing an Exhibition: The Family of Man and 1950s America* (Albuquerque: University of New Mexico Press, 1995); Edward Steichen, *The Family of Man* (New York: Museum of Modern Art, 1955); Roland Barthes, "The Great Family of Man," in *Mythologies* (Paris: Editions du Seuil, 1957); Carl Sandburg, *The Family of Man*, from the prologue of the exhibition catalogue, Museum of Modern Art, 1955, 2. See Sandeen, chapter 4; for its relation to MoMA, see Arndt, *First Resort of Kings*, 370–71.
82. *Circarama* had been a feature at U.S. cultural fairs abroad since the mid-1950s. It was also prominent at Brussels. See "Circarama Goes Abroad: An Outline of Walt Disney's New Camera Process and the Role It Is Playing in the Brussels Fair," in NA RG306 Records of the USIA, Office of Research and Analysis, Research Reports, 1956–1959, 1959: P-36 thru 1959: P-57, Box 7, Folder "P-47-59."
83. Cull, *The Cold War and the United States Information Agency*, 211. See also Abercrombie, *George Nelson*, 163–67; NA RG306 Records of the USIA, Records relating the *American National Exhibition*, Moscow, 1957–59, Airgrams and Cables through Radio and TV Coverage, Box 1, Folder "McClellan's Personal File" (has photographed letter to Ike). Also NA RG306 Records of the USIA, Records relating the *American National Exhibition*, Moscow, 1957–59, Airgrams and Cables through Radio and TV Coverage, Box 1, Folder "Personnel, Data and Stories files."
84. Sergei Khrushchev, from panel discussion at "Face-off to Facebook" (George Washington University, Washington, DC, July 23, 2009).
85. *Life*, August 10, 1959, 30–31.
86. As quoted by Michael L. Krenn, *Fallout Shelters for the Human Spirit: American Art and the Cold War* (Chapel Hill: University of North Carolina Press, 2005), 157.
87. Ibid., 168. See also Hilton Kramer, "The End of Modern Painting," *Reporter: The Magazine of Facts and Ideas*, July 23, 1959. In this article, Kramer claims that "the real meaning of the abstract expressionist movement in New York" at this time was "that it has promised a liberation from culture in the name of an art which, whether violent or serene, resigns from all the complexities of mind which Europe still regards as the sine qua non of artistic seriousness. It has thus brought modern painting to an end,

hastening its demise out of some compulsive curiosity to see what the future of art can be without it." Alfred H. Barr described the phenomenon of abstract expressionism as seen in the New American Painting exhibition, which had traveled to eight countries in Europe as "symbolic demonstrations of freedom in a world in which freedom connotes a political attitude." See Eva Cockcroft, "Abstract Expressionism, Weapon of the Cold War," in *Pollock and After: The Critical Debate*, ed. Francis Frascina (New York: Harper & Row, 1985), 131. For a more detailed discussion of art as public diplomacy tool at the ANEM, see Marilyn S. Kushner, "Exhibiting Art at the American National Exhibition in Moscow, 1959: Domestic Politics and Cultural Diplomacy," *Journal of Cold War Studies* 4, no. 1 (Winter 2002): 6–26. The Whitney Museum of American Art hosted the exhibition "Paintings and Sculpture from the *American National Exhibition* in Moscow" from October 28 through November 15, 1959.

88. See Frank Getlein, "Pictures at an Exhibition," *New Republic* 141, Issue 8/9 (August 24, 1959): 12.

89. For additional discussion of Greenberg's attitude toward abstract expressionism, see, for example, Louis Menand, "Unpopular Front: American Art and the Cold War," *New Yorker*, October 17, 2005.

90. Masey and Morgan, *Cold War Confrontations*, 211.

91. Ibid., 242.

92. Hixson, *Parting the Curtain*, 156–57.

93. Masey, interview, August 23, 2010.

94. For a cogent analysis of the capitalist vs. the communist zeitgeists surrounding domestic comforts, see the work originally published in 1953: Czesław Miłosz, *The Captive Mind*, trans. Jane Zielonko (London: Penguin, 1980), 33. Miłosz writes: "In the United States, something has occurred which is without analogy in the preceding centuries: a new civilization has arisen which is popular, vulgar, perhaps in some respects distasteful to more 'refined' people, but which assures its masses a share in the output of its machine production. It is true that what these masses rejoice in is frequently tawdry and superficial, and that they purchase it with hard labor. Yet a girl working in a factory, who buys cheap mass-production models of a dress worn by a movie star, rides in an old but nevertheless private automobile, looks at cowboy films, and has a refrigerator at home, lives on a certain level of civilization that she has in *common* with others. Whereas a woman on a collective farm near Leningrad cannot foresee the day when even her great-granddaughter will live on a level that approaches such an average."

95. Bennett, "The Exhibitionary Complex," 92.

96. Jane Fisk, "Mitarachi: Design as a Political Force," *Industrial Design* (February 1957): 2–3.

97. Matthew Roth, "Face Value: Objects of Industry and the Visitor Experience," *Public Historian* 22, no. 3 (Summer 2000): 45–46. Roth discusses the origins of the diorama in the taxidermic displays of Charles Willson Peale in the early nineteenth century and later by Carl Akeley at the American Museum of Natural History in their effort to create "perfect little worlds." Roth further acknowledges that the liv-

ing diorama of the nineteenth century would beget the modern-day theme park, in which, for example, "the experience of peering into a fully realized scene of a distant (or fantasy-based) time and place was central to Walt Disney's vision for his seminal theme park that opened in 1955," ibid., 46.

98. Jean Baudrillard, "The System of Collecting," in *The Cultures of Collecting*, ed. John Elsner and Roger Cardinal (London: Reaktion, 1994), 7.

99. Ibid., 18.

100. Curtis M. Hinsley, "The World as Marketplace: Commodification of the Exotic at the World's Columbian Exposition," in *Exhibiting Cultures: The Poetics and Politics of Museum Display*, ed. Ivan Karp and Steven Levine (Washington, DC: Smithsonian Institution, 1991), 356.

101. Bennett, "The Exhibitionary Complex," 96.

102. Ibid.

103. Ibid.

104. Masey, interview, August 23, 2010.

105. Haddow, *Pavilions of Plenty*, 210.

106. Don Wallace, "Shaping America's Products: Design and Craftsmanship in Large Scale Industry," *Industrial Design* (April 1956): 38–39.

107. For a compelling discussion of the "mythologies of housework," see Adrian Forty, *Objects of Desire: Design and Society Since 1750* (London: Thames & Hudson, 2000), 207–21. For theoretical discussions of the symbolism embedded in everyday domestic objects as influential of quality of life, see Ian Woodward, "Domestic Objects and the Taste Epiphany: A Resource for Consumption Methodology," *Journal of Material Culture* 6, no. 2 (2001): 115–36; Arjun Appadurai, ed., *The Social Life of Things: Commodities in Cultural Perspective* (Cambridge: Cambridge University Press, 1986).

108. See William Safire, *Safire's Political Dictionary* (Oxford: Oxford University Press, 2008), 74. See also Cristina Carbone, "Staging the Kitchen Debate: How Splitnik Got Normalized in the United States," in *Cold War Kitchen: Americanization, Technology, and European Users*, ed. Ruth Oldenziel and Karin Zachmann (Cambridge, MA: MIT Press, 2009), 59–81.

109. See Charlie Chaplin, *Modern Times*, United Artists, 1936. There had already been artistic statements via the cinematic medium toward the mechanization of society, long before Chaplin's iteration of this theme. See, for instance, Fritz Lang's *Metropolis*, released in 1924.

110. See Arthur J. Pulos, "United States: The Wizards of Standardized Aesthetics," in *History of Industrial Design: 1919–1990, The Dominion of Design*, ed. Carol Pirovano (Milan: Electa, 1991), 169.

111. William Safire, from panel discussion at "From Face-off to Facebook: From the Nixon-Khrushchev Kitchen Debate to Public Diplomacy in the 21st Century" (conference, George Washington University, Washington, DC, July 23, 2009).

112. Nina Gilden Seavey, from remarks at "From Face-off to Facebook: From the Nixon-Khrushchev Kitchen Debate to Public Diplomacy in the 21st Century" (conference, George Washington University, Washington, DC, July 23, 2009).

113. Safire, from panel discussion at "From Face-off to Facebook." West Berlin was key, according to Jack Masey, as it became a special location for the free sharing of culture in the early to mid-1950s: "We were then doing a lot of stuff in West Berlin. This place is key. We're going in there with exhibitions where East Berliners are allowed in. These were the Amerika Haus exhibitions. And those East Berliners are visiting the West. They're watching," from interview, August 23, 2010.

114. Masey, interview, August 24, 2010: "There were two major areas where Khrushchev and Nixon took each other on. One was the television studio, which recorded about eleven minutes', twelve minutes' worth. Then there was the Kitchen Debate in the house, in the home, which went on for about an hour. It wasn't recorded, because there was no equipment. Just eyewitnesses. What's beautiful is that there is no absolute record, because all the eyewitnesses gave different reports."

115. Marvin Kalb, from panel discussion at "From Face-off to Facebook: From the Nixon-Khrushchev Kitchen Debate to Public Diplomacy in the 21st Century" (conference, George Washington University, Washington, DC, July 23, 2009).

116. See "The Vice President in Russia: A Barnstorming Masterpiece," *Life*, August 10, 1959, 22–27; Richard M. Nixon, "Russia As I Saw It," *National Geographic* 116, no. 6 (December 1959), 715–50.

117. Safire, from panel discussion, "Face-off to Facebook" conference.

118. Haddow, *Pavilions of Plenty*, 210–11.

119. Tuch, conference, July 23, 2009. See also *American National Exhibition in Moscow, 1959, Official Training Book for Guides*, USIA Historical Collection, State Department, Washington, DC.

120. Masey, interview, August 23, 2010.

121. Feiffer, from panel discussion, "From Face-off to Facebook: From the Nixon-Khrushchev Kitchen Debate to Public Diplomacy in the 21st Century" (conference, George Washington University, Washington DC, July 23, 2009).

122. Gottlieb, from panel discussion, "From Face-off to Facebook: From the Nixon-Khrushchev Kitchen Debate to Public Diplomacy in the 21st Century" (conference, George Washington University, Washington DC, July 23, 2009).

123. Dwight D. Eisenhower, *Waging Peace: The White House Years* (Garden City, NY: Doubleday, 1965), 410. See John R. Thomas, "Report on Service with the American Exhibition in Moscow," Social Science Division, RAND Corporation, P-1859 (March 15, 1960), 25. Thomas's personal take on his experience and thoughts concerning the ANE prove quite valuable for a more expansive understanding of the exhibition. He discusses the American guides, in particular, who he claims "changed the black-and-white image of America, fostered by Soviet propaganda, to some shade of gray. And the American guides left the Soviet visitors with facts about the U.S. which they could use in the future to evaluate the correctness of the official view of America."

124. See Tomas Tolvaisas, "Cold War 'Bridge-Building': U.S. Exchange Exhibits and Their Reception in the Soviet Union, 1959–1967," *Journal of Cold War Studies* 12, no. 4 (Fall 2010): 3–31.

125. Tomas Tolvaisas, from panel discussion at "From Face-off to Facebook: From the Nixon-Khrushchev Kitchen Debate to Public Diplomacy in the 21st Century" (conference, George Washington University, Washington, DC, July 23, 2009).

126. Masey, interview, August 23, 2010. See also Theodore Shabad, "U.S. and Soviet Sign Expanded Cultural Exchange Pact in Moscow," *New York Times*, February 23, 1964, 1, 13. This article highlights the stipulation that exhibition exchanges would continue routinely: "On United States insistence, exchanges of exhibitions will be continued, although the Russians evidently find costs abroad a heavy drain on their foreign exchanges reserves." For a chronology of the U.S. thematic exhibitions that toured the Soviet Union from 1961 to 1991, see "Chronology: American Exhibits to the U.S.S.R.," http://www.state.gov/p/eur/ci/rs/c26473.htm.

127. Dwight D. Eisenhower, "State of the Union Address" (speech, Washington, DC, January 9, 1958).

128. Masey, interview, August 23, 2010.

129. Ivan Chermayeff, interview with author, August 23, 2010.

130. Masey, interview, August 23, 2010.

131. Beverly Payeff-Masey, interview with author, New York City, August 23, 2010. For a discussion of the small thematic exhibits that were spawned from the *American National Exhibition* in Moscow, see Tolvaisas, "Cold War 'Bridge-Building,'" 3–31.

132. See Tolvaisas, "Cold War 'Bridge-Building,'" 5–6, in which he states: "The Kennedy and Johnson administrations, like the administration of Dwight D. Eisenhower, wanted to promote gradual, peaceful change in relations with Moscow based on official agreements, reciprocity, and mutual benefit. U.S. officials reshaped cultural initiatives to reach more Soviet citizens and to communicate with them more effectively. The cultivation of cultural contacts became a core objective of John F. Kennedy's 'peaceful engagement' and Lyndon B. Johnson's 'bridge-building' policies toward the USSR and other Communist countries"; Hixson, *Parting the Curtain*, 153–54, 182. See also U.S. Department of State, *United States Treaties and Other International Agreements* (Washington, DC: U.S. Government Printing Office, 1960–1969).

CHAPTER FOUR

Of Pleasure Domes
and Moon Rocks

The United States at the Montreal and
Osaka Expos, 1965–1970

It is of great importance, gentlemen, that we participate in the Montreal
exhibition in a major way. This event will celebrate the hundredth anniversary of the Canadian Confederation, a celebration as important
to Canadians as the celebration of 1976 will be to us. The Canadian
Commissioner General expects that some 80 countries will take part.
By our participation, we can reaffirm our high regard for Canada and
the Canadians and help correct some of the misconceptions regarding
Americans which exist among our neighbors to the north and among
many of the million visitors who are expected to come to the fair from
countries other than Canada and the United States.[1]

On February 10, 1965, USIA director Carl Rowan explained the underlying
concept for the U.S. pavilion at Montreal. In a hearing to request funding
before the House Appropriations Committee, the director emphasized President Johnson's decision to accept the invitation of the Canadian government to participate in the Montreal fair, as stipulated under the authority
of the Mutual Education and Cultural Exchange Act of 1961.[2] The theme
of the U.S. pavilion would be "Creative America" and would address "such
fields as architecture, space exploration, technology, painting, and the
graphic arts" as well as a motion picture that would show "our social creativity, our commitment to the goals of the Great Society."[3] Asked by Chairman
Representative John J. Rooney of New York why the USIA required the

construction of a twenty-story building as designed by R. Buckminster Fuller, Director Rowan responded:

> This 20-story height refers not to floor levels as in an ordinary building . . . but to the height of the sphere itself, and the decision was made to do it at this height because we want something that is attractive, something that is attention-getting, something that is unusual. In building the sphere this height we think we do achieve an architectural breakthrough and something the country can be proud of.[4]

This chapter explores the U.S. pavilions at the Montreal and Osaka Expos, which would prove a strict return to Bayerian "total environment" exhibition development for U.S. cultural exhibitions abroad. Unlike the *American National Exhibition* in Moscow which, once visitors passed through the "information machine" of the Fuller dome could follow their own path through the various sections of the exhibition, the American pavilions at Montreal in 1967 and at Osaka in 1970 would, in effect, give precedence to blockbuster pavilion architecture that housed these nationalistic narratives.

Whose Dome? Bucky Fuller as Pavilion Architect or Cambridge Seven Associates as Pavilion Interior Architects?

> The Cold War, meanwhile, was in full throttle . . . and Canadian soil provided a less-than-hysterical setting for the inevitable showdown between the American and Soviet pavilions, and their competing worldviews. It is also significant that the summer months of 1967 would achieve renown both as the "summer of love" and as a time of violent racial clashes in the United States, which is to say that Expo 67 coincided with the rise of youth and counterculture movements, feminism, civil rights activism, and anti-war protests.[5]

In 1965, the USIA began in earnest its preparations for an American pavilion at the first category one world expo since Brussels in 1958.[6] For the six-month Canadian World Exhibition in Montreal, Expo 67, the agency tapped Jack Masey to coordinate and manage the creation of the American pavilion. His decision to retain Buckminster Fuller as the pavilion's architect and Cambridge Seven Associates as the architects and interior designers of the pavilion came at the conclusion of rounds of extensive interviews with prominent American architects and exhibit designers. Among those interviewed were Louis Kahn, Ludwig Mies van der Rohe, Paul Rudolph, Philip Johnson, Marcel Breuer, George Nelson, Charles and Ray Eames, R. Buckminster Fuller, and the Cambridge Seven Associates. In the end, the partnership of Fuller and Cambridge Seven would yield fascinating results.[7]

The revolutionary three-quarter dome for which Fuller took credit publicly was initially suggested by Peter Chermayeff of Cambridge Seven Associates, with the goal to house within its two hundred thousand square feet a series of levels connected by what would become the longest escalator in the world at the time. This free-floating interior structure of open-air gallery spaces without walls would also accommodate the Expo monorail, for which Cambridge Seven lobbied the expo organizers. Unlike the previous emphasis on commercialized domestic products and quaint simulacra of American kitchens and beauty salons, which were traditionally displayed at trade fairs, the nine million visitors to the U.S. pavilion at Montreal would witness instead cutting-edge architectural, graphic, and scenic design in a transparent dome housing an exhibit called *American Paintings Now*, a display of giant abstract expressionist artworks,[8] large-scale portraits of Hollywood movie stars, and other more tangible items such as American folk art, musical instruments, and even an array of Raggedy Ann and Andy dolls. Art Kane's film *A Time to Play*, its title inspired by verses from the book of Ecclesiastes, featured three 35mm projectors showing an integrated film that interpreted "universally-played children's games reflecting the highly-competitive nature of adult society."[9] But the scene stealer would be the unprecedented dome,[10] which towered above all other country pavilions at the Expo, something the Soviets would remember well when they were preparing for Expo 70 in Osaka three years later. As Masey describes this era of U.S. cultural exhibitions abroad:

> I think, essentially, a lot of these exhibitions happened because of the absence of managerial interference at USIA. There was no control! It's 1964, and we've come up with an idea: we should have a dome. We should have twenty or thirty foot high paintings. I never had to go to the Canadian desk, at USIA to get approval for this exhibit. I was never called up and asked, "What the hell are you doing? And before you go any further, we want to know what's going to be in it." The policy people? They felt uncomfortable getting into the design part, the mixing of policy with design. They felt they didn't know enough about it: "Mixing policy with design? Let's get out of that!" So there was really little of any of that with Expo 67.[11]

At the beginning of 1964, Masey was tasked with recommending which designers and architects should be commissioned to design the U.S. pavilion. Pavilion organizers enjoyed free rein to make the important decisions on the selection of architects and designers, since there was no one in the U.S. government outside this curiously specialized group who wanted to intervene in the development of the pavilion. According to Masey, the State Department's Canadian desk said, "Who cares, just do something!" With bureaucracy sidestepped, at least for the time being, Masey could establish a plan for the pavilion:

> Everything is sort of happening at the same time, with budgets and so forth. It's kind of like a chicken-or-egg situation. I already had a budget number in mind because I knew what our show in Moscow had cost. And so I went to Bucky, and said, "How much would so-and-so tall a dome cost?" "It might cost three million to put that up. It might cost four million." And I was just logging these numbers, and I could figure out, based on square footage, what the inside would cost . . . so I just put all these things together and came up with a budget. I then worked for a terrific guy who was then head of the USIA exhibits division, whose name was Bob Sivard.[12]

Masey admits that from the outset he wanted Buckminster Fuller to design the U.S. pavilion structure.[13] Cambridge Seven Associates, on the other hand, had been in business for just two years, which made this relatively new design and architecture firm a harder sell than someone more established in the field, such as Raymond Loewy, whose name was also considered. Masey reiterates that he "wanted a fresh approach. I wanted people who had never done these things. I knew that the creative potential of Cambridge Seven was considerable and that a lot would grow out of it. I knew what they were capable of doing. I didn't need to go any further. I said, 'Hey, we've got time to work this out.' I'm not about to go out and find the best-dressed industrial designer of our time."[14] Masey's entrepreneurial derring-do of choosing Cambridge Seven emphasized his point that "they knew that if they did this right, they'd be off and running. They all knew that."[15] Peter Chermayeff, brother of graphic designer Ivan Chermayeff, also a member of Cambridge Seven, was a full-fledged architect and also supported the idea of enlisting Fuller because Cambridge Seven preferred not to work with a big-name architect. Since Bucky was the visionary engineer, they forecast that his effort would be more an engineering statement than anything else. With no outright conflict between Fuller and Cambridge anticipated, planning on the pavilion proceeded, with Cambridge Seven being assigned responsibility for the design of the interior architecture and exhibit contents for the U.S. pavilion. According to Masey, "This was very important to establish this relationship."[16]

However, problems did arise at the outset when it became known that Fuller and his partner Shoji Sadao wanted to design something other than a dome. Fuller's original intent was to develop a space frame, or, in other words, an *antidome*, a prototype of the "World Game" vision Fuller held for the future survival of humanity (figure 4.1). As Masey states:

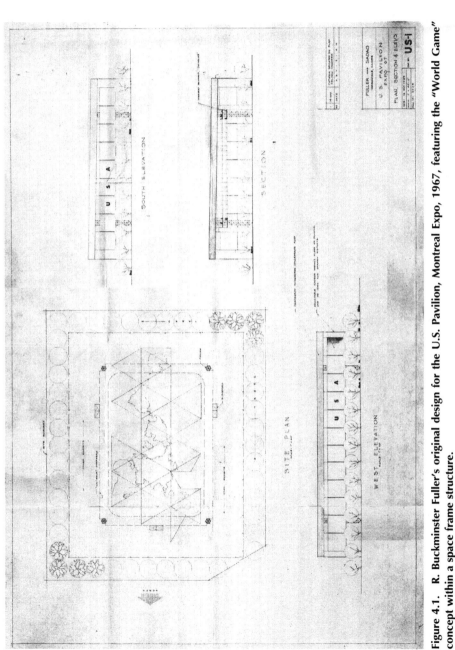

Figure 4.1. R. Buckminster Fuller's original design for the U.S. Pavilion, Montreal Expo, 1967, featuring the "World Game" concept within a space frame structure. Courtesy, Jack Masey Collection.

It's a gigantic flat roof made out of steel. It had no walls, it was just a frame, a super-cover. But this had been done before, and I was against that. We had some difficulty with people on Bucky's staff, who wanted that. So I said, "Hey, I'm sorry, I'm prejudiced for domes, and I think we should go for the 'super-dome' of all time." So anyway, we got rid of the space frame.[17]

One can point to the advocacy and vision of Masey who, though he rejected Fuller's submission of the space frame and World Game concept, was able to suggest a design for an alternative structure, an enormous geodesic dome, similar to one Masey had advocated for following the success of the Fuller dome at Kabul in 1956. The space frame was rejected on two other counts: first, its world map design addressed the problems of the world, not the realities of the United States, and second, it would not allow larger crowds. This concern of crowd management for Masey dated back to the Indian Industries Fair, where lessons were learned as to how best move people through an exhibition space.

On December 8, 1964, the USIA officially designated Fuller & Sadao as the architects of the pavilion. Cambridge Seven Associates would likewise be retained as the "Exhibit Architects and Coordinating Exhibit Designers." Peter Chermayeff, prior to the Expo 67 project, had worked in the United States with the Cambridge Seven Associates designing popular aquaria, including the New England aquarium in Boston. It would be Peter Chermayeff who suggested to Peter Floyd of Geodesics Inc., representing Fuller & Sadao, at a meeting at the Cambridge Seven offices, for Bucky to develop a three-quarter dome, rounded, "like a golf ball," since Bucky always did the so-called "hemispheric casserole cover." As Ivan Chermayeff states:

> Making the 67 dome three-quarter was our request to Bucky Fuller to work that out, which he took full credit for. He took it on as a challenge. It was quite an experience, developing the longest escalator at the time. That is another piece of engineering. But all the people that we worked with . . . nobody said no. Everybody thought, great, let's do it. Everyone took on these challenges. A lot of people jumping on board with enthusiasm. It was a great experience.[18]

The final redesign featured a proposed "five-eighths sphere" dome measuring three hundred feet in diameter. To achieve this feat, the original Fuller hemispheric dome design, patented in 1954 and which Masey had seen years earlier, was added to with stacked concentric rings with diminishing radii, the recommendation of Peter Chermayeff that Peter Floyd of Geodesics, Inc. agreed to. These tensegrity rings make each layer smaller, looking as though it is all a smooth dome. Congress would later cut funding, which would reduce the dome's size to its final diameter of 250 feet. On January 11, 1965, Masey blessed the plan and wrote in "Recommended Design and Content of USIA Participation,"

> The United States Government is tentatively planning to occupy a 200,000 square foot site in Montreal, 40% of which will be covered by a 20-story high transparent geodesic "bubble." . . . Designed by R. Buckminster Fuller . . . this pavilion will mark a significant breakthrough in the use of spherical structures. Measuring three-quarters of a sphere, the transparent bubble . . . will provide more than 7,000,000 cubic feet of enclosed volume.[19]

Whose Vision? Fuller's or Cambridge Seven's?

After Buckminster Fuller, his partner, Shoji Sadao, and the team of designers and engineers of the geodesic dome were recruited to create the dome, some tensions grew up along the way, according to Masey, because

> it was inevitable that a lot of people would fall in love with the dome. They (Fuller and his associates) felt that they didn't even need anything inside! So the people who worked on the inside were shunted aside, and Bucky almost never talked about them. Bucky was Bucky, this fantastic figure. And this was his crowning glory. And he was very pleased with what Cambridge Seven produced inside his dome, but he wasn't about to go out of his way and say, "Hey, what happened inside was brilliant." He never mentioned that, which upset the Cambridge Seven people.[20]

Fuller's dome made a particular statement since hemispheric designs at this point in time were ubiquitous, as seen in the Kabul fair prototype and the later gold-anodized dome for the *American National Exhibition* in Moscow in 1959. Though the three-quarter dome idea came from Peter Chermayeff and the Cambridge Seven Associates, Fuller would later assert that he had proposed a three-quarter dome (figure 4.2). As Masey remembers, "It was as if Bucky said, 'Hey, this is a great idea, but I already had this idea.' So we just went with the flow."[21] Peter Chermayeff would enhance Bucky's dome concept with the idea of bringing the Expo monorail through the U.S. pavilion, which the Canadians supported with enthusiasm. This provided an extra challenge to the Cambridge Seven Associates as they designed the interior exhibits. Ivan Chermayeff states: "See, this is all tricky stuff. And at what point would it leave? Because we don't want it to be in conflict with the stuff inside. We're not gonna build something the damn monorail can't get through! So all these terribly integrated, important components had to come together."[22] Referring to the development of exhibit themes in the pavilion,

Figure 4.2.   Bucky Fuller, Jack Masey, Terry Rankine of Cambridge Seven, and Peter Floyd, an architect who collaborated with Fuller's firm, Fuller & Sadao (left to right) in front of model for American Pavilion for the Montreal Expo, 1967.
United States Information Agency (USIA).

Ivan Chermayeff confirms, "The content of it came from us collectively. Not from some outside source. Or from the government itself."[23]

As a direct result of the lack of interference by the USIA policy people, the Cambridge Seven designers did not feel compelled to approach the development of the interior of the pavilion based on any political agenda from its client, the U.S. government. Ivan Chermayeff discloses:

> We didn't feel as if we had to defend ourselves politically. We did what we thought would be interesting to visitors. But, for example, not everyone will be interested in little dolls. But they are very American . . . and they're surprising. No one expected to see them there. There's something great about real stuff. When it's right there next to you, it's very different than seeing them in a photo.[24]

Masey tells a different story about the conflict between his vision of the pavilion and what the higher-ups at the USIA wanted. Whereas Masey and the Cambridge Seven Associates organized the interior of the dome and did "whatever it took to get it done,"[25] with whimsical exhibits that included, for example, a cluster of several hundred hats on hat makers' forms "to exhibit the great variety of occupations, professions and services—the police, firefighters, welders, nurses, motorcyclists—who make up this country,"[26] some USIA folk in upper management wanted what they felt the Soviets would show in their pavilion: power and technology. Though these were the very same themes the Soviets were addressing in their pavilion, Masey and the Cambridge Seven wanted "to show the other side, the tender side, the creative side, the improvisation, the experimentation. All those things that create what America really is."[27] In the end, the designers soldiered on and produced the pavilion and the exhibits that they wanted: "We got some terrible letters at the beginning from Congressmen because we didn't show our military might and heavy industry. But everyone knows the U.S. is a strong, industrial nation. We didn't have to tell people that."[28]

Fuller's Vision

> I'm sure that you don't really sense yourself to be aboard a fantastically real spaceship—our spherical Spaceship Earth. Of our little sphere you have seen only small portions. However, you have viewed more than did pre-twentieth century man, for in his entire lifetime he saw only one-millionth of the Earth's surface. You've seen a lot more.[29]

Designer Peter Blake described the creator of the geodesic dome as follows: "Bucky believed in a future so far distant that he could afford to dream about it, and no one (in his lifetime, anyway) could ever prove him wrong."[30] What is not typically understood about Fuller's concept for the Montreal dome was his vision not only for the exterior of the pavilion itself but what he may have wanted to see installed in its interior if he had had complete creative control over the pavilion.

Fuller's exercise for a utopian vision of the world, or "World Game," was tempered by his philosophy that the interconnectedness of the world's people was both the recipe for the earth's peril as well as its remedy. Echoing Marshall McLuhan's "Global Village" concept, he also viewed Spaceship Earth with cold realism, controlled on the one hand by the Soviets and on the other by the Americans. According to David Crowley, Fuller's idea for the interior of the Montreal dome was that it should be "an internationalist vision of the planet," and that "visitors on raised platforms would be presented with an accurate spherical representation of 'Spaceship Earth' depicting all the cities of the world, suspended at the heart of the spherical pavilion."[31]

For Fuller, the U.S. pavilion would have the potential to become an avatar of world civilization, a primer for all the visitors to Expo 67 of the potential for a utopian existence on earth. Fuller himself would at this time frame for humanity the choice that lay before it, "utopia or oblivion,"[32] and when asked what the message of his dome was, the visionary replied, "When we designed it we didn't think what it was going to look like, but what it was going to do."[33] While the interior of the dome would become more of a lighthearted entertainment of all things American, it is arguable that the dome's contents did indeed reflect the shift in the counterculture from a materialist viewpoint to one of ideas and concepts. Meikle cites Fuller's "totalizing vision" and "visionary optimism" which "appealed to cultural radicals who anticipated the transformation of human consciousness" with the idea of "doing more with less."[34] Fuller would take this anthem to a new conceptual level when he declared: "The unpleasant effects of climate, heat, dust, bugs, glare, etc., will be modulated by the skin to provide a Garden of Eden interior."[35] Jonathan Massey discusses the U.S. pavilion's overall message of "an internationally ascendant American culture," stating that in contrast to Masey's "intensification of the consumerism that had proved so effective at the 1959 *American National Exhibition* in Moscow," Fuller's dome implied the visionary's ideal of a "transnational deliberative forum in which world-citizens would use information technology to model a more egalitarian global distribution of resources."[36] Fuller himself would admit his vision for geodesic domes translated directly to how human beings subsist and thrive in their environment:

> It is possible, as our own human skin, all of our pores, all of the cells organize, so that some are photo-sensitive and some are sound-sensitive, and they're heat-sensitive, and it would be perfectly possible to create a geodesic of a very high frequency where each of these pores could be circular tangencies of the same size. One could be a screen, others breathing air others letting light in, and the whole thing could articulate just sensitively as a human being's skin.[37]

Though the "self-regulating shading system" designed for Bucky's dome proved faulty during the run of the Expo, Massey speculates "by selectively incorporating elements of his proposal and combining them with the Cambridge Seven exhibits, Jack Masey co-opted Fuller's idealism for triumphalist purposes."[38] This assertion reflects the dominant and in this case erroneous interpretation of a consumerist approach to world fair pavilion design. One could argue that neither Fuller nor the Cambridge Seven Associates, by virtue of compromising their respective visions for the American pavilion, were able to follow through with delivering either of their versions of "America." What this compromise of expression brings to light more directly is that neither vision—Fuller's nor Cambridge Seven's—were realistic manifestations of a real America. Both, in a sense, were unique assertions toward an idealized image of America. Just how this progressive social visionary and counterculture advocate would converge with a robust team of young, talented architects and designers would be evident in the final product that would be the U.S. pavilion at Montreal. At a point in time when the Vietnam conflict and civil strife raged, Fuller and the Cambridge Seven Associates would be forced to compromise on what the overall message of their creation would be.

Cambridge Seven's Vision

The USIA's final report on the U.S. pavilion at Montreal describes the Cambridge Seven Associates' task for "creating an overall mood or atmosphere in their exhibits" within the Fuller dome moved forward with the intention of "developing an artistic symbol rather than the conventional exhibition . . . a portrait of a nation."[39] Their exhibit, centrally positioned within the seven million cubic feet of the dome, was intended, according to Cambridge Seven, to "celebrate the space itself in the design. And one way was to create this inner landscape of terraced platforms. The whole idea of having a three-dimensional environment was to have a series of lily pads in depth provide a natural solution to that incredible volume of space. So, inevitably, things had to be big, had to be strong, had to be capable of standing on their own two feet."[40] The lily pad approach would carry visitors to the highest platform, which was fittingly dedicated to showcasing U.S. achievements in space exploration. "Destination: Moon" would be sponsored by the National Aeronautics and Space Administration, and the construction of the "Lunar Landscape" overseen by the United States Army Map Service. At this point in the U.S.-U.S.S.R. "space race," the United States was still en route to fulfilling President Kennedy's mandate that America send a man to the moon within the decade.[41] This section of the pavilion served undeniably as a propagandist message that U.S. capabilities in space exploration were reaching ever higher toward the grand prize: landing the first human being on the moon (figures 4.3–4.4). Peter Chermayeff, however, interprets the space exhibition as a legitimate example of U.S. culture for visitors: "We wanted everything to be real so that you could feel the sense of that capsule returning through the upper atmosphere, see that burning bottom of Apollo. But to sit in the astronauts' couch was a big thing for them, you know, that was contact. They were really part of it."[42] The space display included an Apollo command module, the Gemini VII pilot's compartment, astronaut John Glenn's helmet from the Mercury program, Explorer satellites, and astronaut "space couches" used during the launch, reentry, and landing phases of missions. Dangling high above the rest of the space exhibit were the Mercury parachutes with their telltale orange-and-white nylon sails. The presence of the lunar module on the lunarscape would foretell NASA's manned moon landing on July 21, 1969. As historian Michael Smith points out, the hardware of space exploration merely gave form to the rhetoric that lay behind the artifacts on display: "Missiles, astronauts, and lunar footprints simply provided a visually dramatic new iconography through which the real product could be conveyed: an image of national purpose that equated technological preeminence with military, ideological, and cultural supremacy."[43] Located at the top of the longest escalator in the world, visitors would then take the "trip downwards from platform to platform, which was really a linear sequence of exposure to very dramatic exhibits."[44] On a quest to display what could be described as "quintessentially American," Cambridge Seven showed "the pure nostalgia of Hollywood" so that visitors could "recognize their favorite old movies, and they'd melt into that" (figure 4.5). In an effort to demonstrate "how wonderful that a great big country like the United States can turn a whimsical cheek to the world," the designers "combined our space program with Raggedy Ann dolls. We had mousetraps, we had modern art. We had the American cinema in all its expression and diverse creativity of Americans."[45] Not losing sight of the method of conveyance through these various displays, the interior pathway for visitors would, curiously, according to Cambridge Seven Associates, conjure "a kind of Piranesi scene of people moving in all directions. And, to ride those escalators was a most beautiful experience because at that point you could stand still while your eye changed its position and floated vertically as well as horizontally through this changing perspective. It had a wonderful, dreamlike quality, really, to go through that space."[46]

It is questionable whether or not this "dreamlike" state of shifting perspective yielded the results so confidently put forth by the Cambridge Seven team. Piranesi's designs, after all, were intended as *carceri d'invenzione* or "imaginary prisons," which eerily inform the exhibitionary complex as this concept was activated in the U.S. pavilion. In a rounded iteration of the Crystal Palace, the Fuller dome, its interior pathways and platforms, offered what Bennett describes as the dual nature of the exhibition as controlling mechanism of all who enter: "While everyone could see, there were also vantage points from which everyone could be seen, thus combining the functions of spectacle and surveillance."[47] It is important to remember the origin of the surveillance element of the Crystal Palace, which according to Bennett was the panopticon—originally conceived by Bentham as a utilitarian method for controlling prisoners—with modern prison architecture "designed so that everyone could be seen." The Crystal Palace, in effect,

Figure 4.3. The "Destination Moon" exhibit in the U.S. Pavilion, Montreal Expo, 1967.
Courtesy, Chermayeff and Geismar.

Figure 4.4.   Space exhibit, U.S. Pavilion, Montreal Expo, 1967.
Courtesy, Chermayeff and Geismar.

perfected the panopticon for noncarceral use, as it was, moreover, "designed so that everyone could see."[48] Art historian Tom McDonough pushes the argument that the fantasy, or make-believe, nature of the U.S. pavilion, displaying in similar fashion its "utopian content"[49] as other national expo sites, such as the German pavilion, realized the "pervasive fantasy of the moment: that of the self-enclosed city."[50] McDonough stresses that the "new conditions of architectural production" were on display within the Fuller dome in "the proliferation of platforms and even more strikingly the mechanization of human movement through an almost baroque multiplication of escalators." This "portent of the future," moreover, echoed earlier experiments in "mechanized movement," particularly in the "spectacular vertical ascent of the Eiffel Tower," in which visitors face "the complete abandonment of such

Figure 4.5.   Hollywood exhibit, U.S. Pavilion, Montreal Expo, 1967.
Courtesy, Chermayeff and Geismar.

a phenomenological referent, and the substitution of a wholly artificial or man-made one in its place."[51]

Unwittingly, the united team of Fuller & Sadao and the Cambridge Seven Associates participated in what would become a conceptual reiteration of what Foucault describes as "coercive technologies of behaviour previously found in the cloister, prison, school or regiment and which, in being brought together in one place, served as a guide for the future development of carceral institutions."[52] Bennett further argues that a natural progression occurs in which these technologies of behavior would become mainstreamed for a more general representation of humanity and no longer reserved for controlling prisoners:

> The Great Exhibition of 1851 brought together an ensemble of disciplines and techniques of display that had been developed within the previous histories of museums, panoramas, Mechanics' Institute exhibitions, art galleries, and arcades. In doing so, it translated these into exhibitionary forms which, in simultaneously ordering objects for public inspection and ordering the public that inspected, were to have a profound and lasting influence on the subsequent development of museums, art galleries, expositions, and department stores.[53]

The utopian urge of Fuller's Garden of Eden vision for the grand space of the three-quarter dome itself would find its counterpoint in the Piranesi (or

Bayerian) presence of prescribed pathways of behavior throughout the visitor's experience of the U.S. pavilion.

As Bennett avers, the mentality around the creation of the panopticon as reforming tactic toward prison design and that of exhibition making is very similar. In essence, the methods of social control and "power/knowledge relations" activated at the 1851 Crystal Palace differ little from the carceral paradigm put forth by Foucault:[54]

> Nor are these entirely separate histories. At certain points they overlap, often with a transfer of meanings and effects between them. To understand their interrelations, however, it will be necessary, in borrowing from Foucault, to qualify the terms he proposes for investigating the development of power/ knowledge relations during the formation of the modern period. For the set of such relations associated with the development of the exhibitionary complex serves as a check to the generalizing conclusions Foucault derives from his examination of the carceral system.[55]

The carceral theories of Foucault and the exhibitionary complex of Bennett diverge, however. These "technologies of surveillance" as described by Foucault through his analysis of the "disciplinary mechanisms which came to suffuse society with a new—and all-pervasive—political economy of power," are transformed within the exhibitionary complex "with new forms of spectacle" that "produced a more complex and nuanced set of relations through which power was exercised and relayed to—and, in part, through and by—the populace."[56] To reiterate, it was through the emerging spectacle "of museums, art galleries, expositions, and department stores" in which the exhibitionary complex shifted carceral remedies for the problem of order by transforming

> that problem into one of culture—a question of winning hearts and minds as well as the disciplining and training of bodies. As such, its constituent institutions reversed the orientations of the disciplinary apparatuses in seeking to render the forces and principles of order visible to the populace—transformed, here, into a people, a citizenry—rather than vice versa. They sought not to map the social body in order to know the populace by rendering it visible to power. Instead, through the provision of object lessons in power—the power to command and arrange things and bodies for public display—they sought to allow the people, and en masse rather than individually, to know rather than be known, to become the subjects rather than the objects of knowledge.[57]

This warring conundrum of Fuller's Garden of Eden versus Cambridge Seven's playful interior mirrors perhaps the larger essence of what the world expo symbolized. As Peter Chermayeff recalls: "It was an exhilarating experience to arrive at the top of our largest escalator and look out through the skin, through this very transparent, diaphanous, beautiful surface at the whole of the Expo grounds all around you. You saw tens of thousands of people."[58] Roland Barthes interprets the principles behind another iconic world's fair structure, the Eiffel Tower, which, "repeated in countless subsequent expositions" rendered "the project of specular dominance feasible in affording an elevated vantage point over a micro-world which claimed to be representative of a larger totality."[59] According to Barthes, "the Tower," the "first obligatory monument," is "a Gateway, it marks the transition to a knowledge."[60] Bennett's interpretation of Barthes, as it conforms to the exhibitionary complex, is as follows: "And to the power associated with that knowledge: the power to order objects and persons into a world to be known and to lay it out before a vision capable of encompassing it as a totality."[61]

It is clear that Masey, free from the constraints of USIA policy makers who were not involved in the planning for the U.S. pavilion, did in a way intentionally commit to establishing a "specular dominance" over the rest of the Montreal Expo fairgrounds. Moreover, Masey, Fuller, and Cambridge Seven sought an attitude of inclusion. The participation of the expo audience made them feel as if this dream world—predicated on Fuller's theory of interconnectedness as well as Cambridge Seven's "visitor as spectacle"—was also available to them.[62]

LBJ and Vietnam at the Expo

On April 7, 1954, when asked to comment on the strategic importance of Indochina to the rest of the free world, Eisenhower articulated the "domino theory"[63] that Presidents John F. Kennedy and his successor Lyndon B. Johnson would use as a guide toward U.S. involvement in Vietnam. This philosophy served as the rationale for Robert McNamara—secretary of defense under both Kennedy and Johnson—to escalate the war in Vietnam in mid-1964. On February 27, 1965, the State Department released a fourteen-thousand-word report titled "Aggression from the North—The Record of North Vietnam's Campaign to Conquer South Vietnam." This argument for the expansion of war—particularly the invasion of North Vietnam—further rationalized President Johnson's resolve to increase U.S. participation in the conflict. By 1967, editorials in *Life* magazine were condemning "the dropping of anti-personnel bombs on North Vietnamese villages" as well as "senseless, inhumane American atrocities in North Vietnam"[64] while celebrating the American pavilion in later pages of the same issue. Masey recalls: "Never, ever did the word 'war' come up when we planned the U.S. pavilion at Montreal. Nobody ever said,

'Hey, we're in a war, let's do everything in our power to throw off the scent. Don't mention Vietnam.' That was never said. Having said that, it doesn't mean that Vietnam went unnoticed."[65] Despite efforts to keep the Vietnam War at arm's length, attitudes toward the conflict would infiltrate the Fuller bubble at Montreal. Masey remembers the day President Johnson, accompanied by USIA director, Leonard Marks,[66] visited the U.S. pavilion on May 25, 1967. Riding on the escalator a few feet behind the president, Masey recalls:

> I watched the president. And I remember seeing Max Frankel, a reporter with the *New York Times*, with the news delegation that followed LBJ. It was Frankel who had torn us apart at the 1959 Moscow show, and we wanted him to eat crow with this one, because he bought the Soviet line about the importance of showcasing strength and technology in Moscow. What did we give the Soviets? Consumer goods, fashion shows. And so Frankel was not very happy with us. So now here's LBJ walking through the U.S. pavilion in Montreal in 1967: he's tired, he just wants to get the hell out of the American pavilion and just call it a day, and he stops and looks at the dolls display. And I could not believe this. Frankel's review in the *New York Times* of LBJ's visit to the U.S. pavilion mentioned that what stopped President Johnson was a toy American soldier in a showcase. How Frankel concluded that LBJ was troubled by the toy soldier is baffling since the toy soldier was among many civilian dolls. In short, there is no evidence that the toy soldier doll was the one that really bothered LBJ.[67]

As Masey points out, the inclusion of a toy soldier display was not deliberately planned as a commentary on Vietnam. However, it was unavoidable that antiwar rhetoric surrounding the United States in Vietnam would find its way into the pavilion itself: shortly after Expo 67 opened, a young man entered the American pavilion, removed his jacket, and stood next to the large introductory photo of President Johnson. His shirt read "Genocide." As crowds started filing around him, Masey was summoned by one of the Bill Blass-costumed American guides who explained: "Jack, there's turmoil, you gotta come over here. There's a Vietnam protestor and he's right in the pavilion" (figures 4.6–4.7). Masey replied: "That's fine. What's wrong with that?" Masey then approached the young man, who declared: "I really resent everything you've done here." To which Masey replied, "We all have the right to speak our piece."[68] As Masey confirms: "Both Canadians and Americans were protesting in the pavilion. This very act of protest proved to be a very powerful exhibit to itself."[69]

Conclusion to Montreal

The final report published by the USIA on the American pavilion at Expo 67 emphasizes the consensus of U.S. government representatives be-

Figure 4.6. War protestors, U.S. Pavilion, Montreal Expo, 1967.
Courtesy, Chermayeff and Geismar.

Figure 4.7. American guides in Bill Blass–designed uniforms, U.S. Pavilion, Montreal Expo, 1967.
United States Information Agency (USIA).

lieving the pavilion did not follow USIA objectives. According to Beverly Payeff-Masey, the continuous subtext in the public/private partnerships of U.S. cultural exhibitions abroad, from the 1950s trade fairs, through the era of détente with the Soviet Union, "is really the story of these big exhibitions. Who designs it? Who controls it? This is the tension that's inherent in this story."[70] As the report indicates, the prevailing opinion of the American pavilion within the upper levels of USIA generally condemned "the 'frivolity'" of the U.S. effort and would have preferred instead "the traditional display of industrial and technological strength"[71] (figures 4.8–4.9). However, the final section of the report, titled "Effectiveness," elicited an overall confirmation by USIA staff in Montreal that the U.S. pavilion was a success, even expressing surprise that

> a government agency could so completely break with tradition and present a gay, lighthearted, soft sell type of pavilion. This soft sell even penetrated the thinking of Soviet Pavilion officials who commented several times to U.S. officers that they would obviously have to try a new approach themselves at the next world exposition. But the Exhibit's achievement was to put an important dent in "hate America" attitudes.[72]

Figure 4.8.   The Expo Monorail enters the U.S. Pavilion, Montreal Expo, 1967.
Courtesy, Chermayeff and Geismar.

Figure 4.9.   Pop Art artist Tom Wesselmann's painting, *Mouth #10*, for the U.S. Pavilion, Montreal Expo, 1967.
Courtesy, Chermayeff and Geismar.

Osaka

On September 22, 1966, the United States was invited by the Japanese government to participate in the Japan World Exposition, set to open in Osaka in 1970. The United States accepted on November 17 of that year, "subject to the appropriation of funds by Congress."[73] In a way, the American pavilion, which would be dubbed "the Band-Aid" or "the casserole cover" at Osaka, was the literal opposite of the Montreal dome architecturally. David Geiger's translucent inflated pavilion hid the "America" at Osaka underground. At Montreal, the U.S. pavilion—at twenty stories high—opened itself to scrutiny, while at Osaka, the United States shied from the world at three stories underground. Eyewitnesses indicate, however, there was no lack for public interest in viewing for the first time on earth the moon rock retrieved by the Apollo 11 astronauts during their moon walk the previous year. In Masey's words, "Osaka was the opposite of Montreal. Visitors had no idea what they were getting themselves into."[74] Meanwhile, the Soviets, believing that the Americans would once again dominate the Osaka fairgrounds as they did in Montreal, made a concerted effort to build higher than the American dome at Montreal. According to Masey: "So the Soviets were thinking, 'Okay, those bastards are coming to Osaka, we're going to build the tallest thing there.' So they build this forty-story monstrosity, and we, this time, are almost completely underground. Very exciting"[75] (figure 4.10). One explanation for the continual

Figure 4.10.   U.S. Pavilion, Expo 70, Osaka, Japan.
United States Information Agency (USIA).

reshaping of national identity through world's fair pavilion design comes from
Masey: "It mattered because the cultural arena was claimed equally by both
sides, and at various levels. There was an almost implicit agreement that winning militarily, winning economically, and winning politically were all important goals, but that winning culturally would also be a major victory."[76] Seen
similarly from a perspective of industrial design, which contends regularly with
the principle of obsolescence, "America" can also be seen as a product that is
unceasingly growing obsolete, an entity that requires continual re-creation and
rebirth.[77] How the United States pavilion would draw a crowd at Osaka was as
yet unknown. America first had to fit into the theme of the expo itself, which,
as Pieter von Wesemael attests, ultimately differed little from the near-utopian
vision of past world's fairs:

> The Expo had to be seen as a plaza for the world where . . . people could meet
> one another and exchange ideas. It was a festival where both Japanese and
> foreigners could see that the last few decades had produced a modern, highly
> developed society built on the foundation of age-old traditions. It was an
> impulse to cultivate a new, modern, Japanese cultural identity in which tradi-
> tional concepts were reconciled with modernisation and internationalization
> in a new global consciousness. However, Osaka '70 only gave a noncommittal
> impression of such a better future—it appeared to be more of a stimulus to-
> wards international discussion and reflection than a blueprint.[78]

By the time Expo 67 was in full swing, the Bureau International des Expositions decided to have another category one expo, this time a mere three
years after Montreal instead of the typical ten years. Osaka would become
just the fourth universal and international exhibition of this type and the
first ever to be held in Asia,[79] the previous three "first category" expositions
being Montreal in 1967, Brussels in 1958, and Paris in 1937. Osaka's central
theme, "Progress and Harmony for Mankind," was supported by subthemes
of "Toward Fuller Enjoyment of Life," "Toward Fuller Engineering of Our
Living Environment," and "Toward Better Understanding of Each Other."[80]
Other than the official USIA-sponsored pavilion, there were seven other
American pavilions, sponsored by, for instance, the State of Hawaii, IBM,
Kodak, Pepsi-Cola, and the American Park complex, which included sub-
pavilions sponsored by American Express, the City of Los Angeles, and
Kentucky Fried Chicken. According to Howard Chernoff, Commissioner
General of the U.S. pavilion, the various American venues proved

> not only confusing to the average fairgoer but in some cases, downright ir-
> ritating. For example, virtually within seconds of the opening of Expo 70, the
> lunar rock exhibit in the official U.S. government pavilion became the hit of
> Expo 70. Shortly thereafter, it was announced that the State of Washington

was also featuring lunar rock in its pavilion—a revelation which caused no end of bewilderment among the lunar rock–crazed multitudes. . . . This flogging-of-a-good-thing-into-the-ground achieved little more than placing the United States in competition with itself.[81]

With the recommendation that the United States at all future world's fairs maintain a singular presence, the official U.S. pavilion organized by Jack Masey, now deputy commissioner general for planning and design at Osaka, would yet draw the most attention from both visitors and media alike.

To select the designers of the U.S. pavilion at Osaka, Masey initiated a creative competition among designers in which six architects were designated to associate with six exhibit designers and vice versa. Ultimately, what would occur was a one-of-a-kind joint venture between a Japanese construction team and the hybrid architecture and design team from the United States. According to Masey:

> Expo 70 was important. Frightfully important. The beginning of Asia coming on the scene. The most gigantic fair ever to be mounted in Asia. Sixty million visitors expected at Osaka. The U.S. pavilion was rather extraordinary. Where the American bubble was twenty stories high at Expo 67 in Montreal, we now went three stories underground. We dropped like a pancake! We were known as the "Band-Aid." There was nothing like it. In a way, it was more advanced than Bucky Fuller's dome. It was an air-supported structure covering the size of two football fields. Fuller would judge the success of a building by its weight compared to its size, and so, by Bucky's own measure, David Geiger's "Band-Aid" at Osaka was more successful than Bucky's own geodesic dome at Montreal.[82]

Whichever design the USIA's exhibits team decided on could not mask the reality that this was the second wartime pavilion the United States would erect at what was still widely considered a critical moment in America's participation in the Vietnam conflict.

The Design Competition

Masey asserts that the method of developing a design team in Montreal, in which he "got the people he wanted by interviewing *other* people," would no longer work, particularly for planning the U.S. pavilion in Osaka.

> Now, to do Osaka I did it a little differently to Montreal, where we made use of the simple technique of interviewing prospective designers. For Osaka I set up a competition. I said, "What I'm gonna do is go to six architects and have them associate with six exhibit designers." It's like going to a Bucky Fuller and

asking him to find a Cambridge Seven. And then I'm gonna go to six exhibit designers and ask them to associate with six architects. I felt I needed to do a package. Otherwise, you have real conflicts. You have exhibit people fighting the structural people. I wanted them to be a unified package at the outset.[83]

With a total of twelve teams, Masey established the parameters of the competition. Each team was given six weeks, a thousand dollars, and the mandate to deliver "not necessarily a design of a pavilion but a design direction you'd like to take." The purpose of this exercise was to "enable the Agency to determine how a given team would go about solving design problems relating to both architecture and interior exhibits."[84] Treading cautiously, Masey gave the teams an idea of what the contents of the pavilion would be. With the understanding that time and funds were short to develop a full-scale design for the U.S. pavilion, Masey at the very least wanted a design approach. After five weeks, twelve designs were submitted to a jury of twelve people that included Masey. Star architects like Philip Johnson and his firm presented models. In selecting the competing design teams, Masey was able to pick the people he wanted to work with on the pavilion: "This was not in the bag for anybody. Of course, we had twelve people on the jury, architects. This was the way I felt we really had to do it this time. So, in essence, I asked six architects to find six exhibit designers, and six exhibit designers to find six architects."[85]

It would be Ivan Chermayeff and Tom Geismar, with the addition of Rudy de Harak, a well-known exhibits designer for the Metropolitan Museum of Art, who approached the twelve-person jury with Davis & Brody, whom they had selected as their co-architects, with a "pumpkin design," which the jury thought unattractive, although "feasible." The saving grace of the design was that it was air inflatable, which the jury liked for its temporary nature, and that it could be "constructed quickly, be around for six months, and then be demounted quickly." As Masey states, "They liked the air-inflatable quality of it, not necessarily the air-inflated pumpkin. So, in other words, it won the jury's votes."[86] The winning team—Davis, Brody, Chermayeff, Geismar, and de Harak—recruited as a consultant David Geiger, a thirty-year-old engineer who would play a major role in the design of the air-inflated pavilion at Osaka. The process was now in motion:

So, we come up with a budget, mutually, roughly, with the selected design team. This is about a year and a half before the Expo. I think we needed $15 million, and this figure would have to cover everything, including guides. It is every expense connected. You know, Osaka's 12,000 miles away. We've got to fly stuff out. So I go for $15–16 million. In the meantime, we do a redesign, because even the winners agree that we don't want the pumpkin. So they come up with something called the "four-ball scheme." It was four globes, kind of crazy, and they were going to have theaters in each of them. It's movie theaters in each of the four balls. It's a theater show. I wasn't wild about it. Luckily, the Congress cut the budget again, so we couldn't do the four balls![87]

Congress would also agree to a $10 million budget, which pushed the design and architectural team toward, as Masey remembers, "the Band-Aid. It covered two football fields, without a single column, inflated. I saw the *casserole* cover go up, I saw when they inflated it. This building went up in four hours. And it came down in two."[88] Using a material engineered during the space program, this cutting-edge building design would be compared by *Architectural Forum* to other breakthrough designs at past world's fairs:

> Earlier major structural innovations (such as the Galerie des Machines, the Eiffel Tower, Brooklyn Bridge, hyperbolic paraboloid and thin shell) have resulted in a highly visible and often startling change in physical form. This innovation is an exception. Like the sophisticated high-speed computer, its potential is not revealed by unusual physical form. It is a structural revolution barely visible to the professional and almost entirely invisible to the layman.[89]

The *superellipse* of the American pavilion featured a translucent fiberglass roof anchored by a concrete ring under which an earth berm supported the entire structure of cables and blowers that helped maintain the bubble-like appearance (figure 4.11). Furthermore, it is important to acknowledge that Fuller's domes in Kabul and Montreal were selected because they were practical to put up and easy to take down, since they were lightweight and relatively inexpensive to build. Moreover, the geodesic framework in the Kabul and Montreal domes carried 100 percent of the load of its own weight as well as the weight of the dome's surface covering. In contrast, the Osaka "Band-Aid" pavilion was considered the most radically-engineered U.S. pavilion because, unlike its Fuller-designed predecessors, the roof material was supported by the interior air pressure within the building rather than by the crisscrossed metal grid beneath the fabric roof. The metal grid stabilized the roof from side to side but did not support it, as was the case with Fuller's pavilions. The U.S. pavilion in Osaka—a typhoon-prone area—had to be able to withstand severe buffeting from extreme winds. Forced to address this fact with limited funding, the designers used a series of advanced building techniques to create a very flexible, resilient structure that could and would survive a massive typhoon. The "Band-Aid" was not only the most lightweight (pounds per square foot) and least expensive (dollars per square foot) pavilion the United

Figure 4.11. Detail of the David Geiger–designed inflatable roof, U.S. Pavilion, Expo 70, Osaka, Japan.
United States Information Agency (USIA).

States had ever built; in 1970 it was the largest clear-span structure in the world. *Progressive Architecture* magazine lauded the experimental pneumatic system and described its purpose as "not to shock with architectural pyrotechnics nor to propagandize for America, but rather to provide, simply, an economical, large space as an enclosure for exhibits."[90]

It was no mystery to Expo 70 planners that the United States had reached the moon the year before, and the fruits of this mission that brought a man on the moon for the first time—the lunar rock and space vehicles—would prove irresistible to audiences. In essence, there was no need for a hedonistic or ostentatious architectural program this time. This "America" could hoard its cultural treasures underground, seemingly free from negative judgment of its suspect social and political policies. Symbolically, it was reported the Geiger-designed structure could resist "earthquakes and typhoons."[91] The stark and calculating design of the U.S. pavilion was, according to *The Nation*, "so flat as to be almost invisible," which seemed appropriate "for a nation seeking a low political profile in the world."[92] Though subtler than in previous world's fairs, America's triumphalist message—albeit cultural— would continue to be projected to audiences at Osaka.

The competition to build the experimental U.S. pavilion structure was handed to a coterie of the top building contractors in Japan, who were ordered to bid out the project down to the last detail. The idea of selecting a Japanese contractor to build the pavilion was driven by the commissioner general of the U.S. pavilion, Howard L. Chernoff. As Masey recalls:

> So we go to Osaka. And in the room are ten of the top contractors in Japan. And I mean top. They have built most of Japan's major skyscrapers. By the way, we've sent the drawings in advance. And we tell them, through interpreters: "Gentlemen, you're in this room because you're the best. And we want the best. And we know we have no time. Regrettably, we have not been able to develop these drawings beyond preliminary stage drawings. We are asking you, to the best of your ability, to come up, each of you, with a fixed price." Some asked, "Does that mean guaranteed, because you're asking us to take a big risk here? What if, in the working drawings you will eventually make, you come up with something very elaborate and which costs twice as much as we originally quoted?" Howard replied: "That's your problem."[93]

With the decision to reconvene in ten days to receive fixed-price bids for building the U.S. pavilion at Osaka, it would be Ohbayashi-Gumi, Ltd. who came up with the idea of building the Geiger space frame at a vast magnitude. Ohbayashi-Gumi confirmed they were willing to guarantee the project with the stipulation they were allowed input. Masey and Chernoff agreed to the joint venture between the Japanese construction firm and the New York design team. As soon as the contract was signed, twenty Japanese engineers flew off to the New York office of Davis & Brody. As Masey concludes, "The goddamn arrangement worked. So, it was great. And Howard Chernoff? I needed that toughness. He said this is how we're going to do it. We're not going to do it any other way. And luckily, we found this avenue. You have to be totally sure of what you want to do. Notwithstanding the fact that everything that can go wrong will go wrong, by some miracle the Japan-New York alliance worked."[94]

Construction of the U.S. pavilion began on December 21, 1968, and would draw comparisons with Buckminster Fuller's ideal of a "city-scale enclosed environment." The "dreams go much further than that," insists architectural writer Marguerite Villecco, in that, echoing Davis & Brody, the "Band-Aid" had the potential to "encourage the virtues of small lively towns, which they feel have so conspicuously ceased to exist. Not only towns but civilizations."[95] This little corner of America in the U.S. pavilion at Osaka featured the theme of "Images of America" and would accommodate up to 90,000 visitors per day for a total attendance during the run of the Expo of 16,200,000 people.[96] Reduced to the spectacle of cutting-edge architecture, space exhibits, and avant-garde displays, the "America" of Osaka would, as in past world's fairs, supply and support an image of the United States that, though dazzling from afar, would actually permit a window into its darker social realities. Masey and Chernoff, however idealistic an image they wanted to portray of the United States through this "Small Town of the Future," agreed to enlist the help of longtime USIA collaborator, the Museum of Modern Art, which would be hired to develop the first exhibit visitors would see in their tour of the U.S. pavilion. Little did they suspect that the MoMA's photography exhibit would become a lightning rod of controversy faintly resembling America's *Unfinished Business* exhibit at the U.S. pavilion at Brussels in 1958.

The USIA Tames the Museum of Modern Art

The first exhibit one saw as you entered the United States pavilion in Osaka was a photography show. It was explosive. It was the equivalent of *Unfinished Business.* And by the way, I think this is a terrific story. And I said to Ivan Chermayeff, one of the pavilion's co-designers during the planning phase of the pavilion, "Don't you think the Japanese would like a photography show? What we need to do is a photo portrait of 1970 America. The good, the bad, and the ugly." He said, "Absolutely, Jack!"[97]

Two years before the opening of the pavilion at Osaka, Masey paid a visit to John Szarkowski, the head of photography at the Museum of Modern Art, to commission him to plan the photo show. Masey told Szarkowski of the plans for the U.S. pavilion in Japan and that he wanted to show how the best American photographers depicted the United States. Szarkowski agreed, with one caveat: he would be the one to choose all of the photos, stating, "I think what I'd like to do is pick ten photographers. Realistic photographers, landscape people, inner city people, small town people. And I'm going to have each of them submit ten photos. You'll get a total of 100 photos. And it will be a snapshot of the United States in 1970."[98] Masey agreed, and said: "It sounds great. Go!" Howard Chernoff, on the other hand, who was wary of controversy after having testified before Congress for the funding for the U.S. pavilion, wondered whether giving the MoMA carte blanche at curating the first exhibit in the pavilion was a politically prudent decision. For Masey, this was a time-tested process where USIA would commission an outstanding American museum to produce an exhibit for the American pavilion. Six months later, Masey received a call from Szarkowski, who invited him to New York to see the photos selected for the photography exhibit. The meeting took place at the MoMA, and Masey methodically reviewed the one hundred choices:

> And then we get to the tenth photographer. It's Diane Arbus, an outstanding photographer. Diane Arbus does not do Norman Rockwell-style portraits. She's the opposite. I said, "So far they all look really good to me." John Szarkowski saved for me, the tenth photographer, Diane Arbus, knowing that she was the most controversial. He never committed himself until I was in his office. He said, "You told me I was supposed to put together this show, and you'd go with all of my recommendations. No censorship, right?" So, I go through the whole pile. I go through all of Diane Arbus. The last shot in the Arbus group that he shows me is "Bomb Hanoi." It's Vietnam. I knew that was anathema. It would be dangerous. This was going to hit people. This is going to get people loving it. This is going to get people hating it. In other words, Howard Chernoff would predictably be offended by this particular photo.[99]

Masey agreed to take back to Chernoff all of Szarkowski's recommendations. As before, the Diane Arbus image was saved for the last presentation. "Chernoff did not like a lot of what I showed him," Masey recalls. "There was some very rough horrible stuff. No Mapplethorpe though. That in Chernoff's view would have been like pornography."[100] As Chernoff reached the last image, he said, "Jack, this young man's wearing a button that says 'Bomb Hanoi' and another button that says 'God Bless America.' And 'Vietnam: Support our Boys.' This cannot go in, Jack." Masey replied, "Howard, I've got a problem. I think I told you at the outset: the sole intent of the U.S. government going out to the Museum of Modern Art to produce this exhibit was that they would take responsibility for it." Chernoff replied, "I don't want to make Vietnam part of what we're showing. And that's final." Masey then returned to New York, sat down with Szarkowski, and conveyed Chernoff's decision to drop the Arbus photo. Szarkowski responded that he was not surprised by Chernoff's reaction, but added, "Jack, remember, we made a deal? There's no censorship. What do you mean it can't go in? That's changing the rules. I don't like it. What I may do is protest this and go to the press with this."[101]

Aware of the political fallout that such a news story would provoke, Masey told Szarkowski, "John, you know and I know this is political dynamite. The country is at war in Vietnam. I don't think Chernoff will accept it. It's controversial. It's a no-win." Soon after this conversation, it would be Chernoff who would threaten to pull the MoMA's photography show from the pavilion. Szarkowski ultimately chose, with much reluctance, to replace the Arbus image. As Masey recalls: "Howard knew how to play the game. Take no prisoners." Szarkowski, cornered, phoned Masey the next day to say, "Okay, I feel this is absolutely outrageous, but I've put so much into this project and I've made so many commitments to all of these photographers. So I'll replace that last Arbus shot."[102] When the U.S. pavilion opened in Osaka, Masey remembers the American response to the photography exhibit, which was the first exhibit visitors would see as they entered the pavilion:

> We had Americans coming through the pavilion who wondered why we were showing this horrible stuff? There were letters written to their Congressmen: "I came through with a tour group from America. That first exhibit . . . why is it there? It shows Harlem tenements, people living like rodents, why are we doing this? I just came from the Soviet pavilion where everyone is smiling." It was beautiful! And, luckily, who rescued us? The Japanese press saved the photography show: "The Americans did it again! They're honest and telling it like it is." We may not have made it with the Americans, but we certainly made it with the Japanese.[103]

The *Ten Photographers* exhibit told more of a story than just the righteous personal preferences of a celebrated curator from the Museum of Modern Art. In a way, the photos, whose sizes ranged from two to twenty feet, served as an artistic correlative to the real social and political landscape of America in 1970. No culture would, arguably, openly seek to air its dirty laundry at an event that upward of sixty million visitors may visit. So why was Szarkowski given such latitude in building this exhibit? The exhibition, sans Arbus's "Hanoi" photo, should be regarded as less of a creative rendering of the unsightliness of American social issues and more characteristic of the attitudes of the person ultimately responsible for the creation of the U.S. pavilion in the first place: Jack Masey. Trained as a designer and steeped in New York avant-garde artistic cachet, Masey would, arguably, if working alone, have had no problem with promoting these real images of America, as wrought by

Arbus and others. Designer Peter Blake further lauded the efforts of Masey and "the work of half a dozen New Yorkers," the design and architecture team—not the U.S. government—who turned out what would be "the smash hit of Expo 70." The U.S. pavilion building itself, Blake would claim, "represents a very big forward step in the Art of Structure."[104]

Other photographs in the *Ten Photographers* exhibit included pictures of "the farm lands of the upper Midwest by Paul Vanderbilt; images of New York City by Andre Kertesz and majestic views of the American landscape by Ansel Adams."[105] Art historian Michael Camille describes photography as "another crucial medium of twentieth-century image making . . . for which the simulacrum came as a useful, though complicated, term of reference."[106] Invoking Baudrillard's essay, "The Precession of Simulacra," Camille discusses the use of the photographic image—and its simulacral content—in real versus "camera reportage."[107] Further discussion of the simulacral or make-believe aspect of pictorial images comes from E. H. Gombrich's seminal art historical work, *Art and Illusion*. Here he discusses images, namely paintings and statues that "had no voice."[108] Gombrich adds, "Art had to be satisfied with working its wonders within its own medium and within its own isolated world." The question perhaps remains unanswered as to what it means for art to "work its wonders" on an audience. If in this case the photographic image can be treated similarly to other pictorial images in art, there exists a constant tension between what is real and what is not. Gombrich points out that "Even within this world of conscious make-believe, it was found, genuine illusion held its own."[109] Arbus herself described her human subjects as

> people who appear like metaphors somewhere further out than we do, beckoned, not driven, invented by belief, author and hero of a real dream by which our own courage and cunning are tested and tried; so that we may wonder all over again what is veritable and inevitable and possible and what it is to become whoever we may be.[110]

For good or ill, the photography exhibit in the U.S. pavilion would be seen as offensive by some, artistic by others, and real by yet other visitors. Ultimately, what was viewed was, similar to the *Unfinished Business* display at the U.S. pavilion in Brussels twelve years earlier, a representation of America, a simulated America that in hindsight seems to have elegantly run the gamut of searing sociopolitical commentary as witnessed in the Arbus photographs to the quietly infinite distances of Adams's American landscapes. The bilingual brochure handed out at the pavilion revealed this caption regarding the array of images within the photo exhibit in both English and Japanese:

"Neither individually nor cumulatively do they show the whole truth except in the sense meant by Ernest Hemingway who said, 'Any part you make will represent the whole if it is made truly.'"[111]

After viewing *Ten Photographers*, visitors turned a corner and discovered a selection of twenty-one original American works of art from the eighteenth through the twentieth centuries. Loaned exclusively by the Metropolitan Museum of Art, subject themes included colonial portraits, early nineteenth-century landscapes, and genre and figure paintings from the mid-nineteenth century, impressionist landscapes from the end of the century, and cityscapes and portraits from the twentieth century. Artists represented included Gilbert Stuart, Winslow Homer, Maurice Prendergast, Edward Hopper, and Andrew Wyeth. The USIA's "Final Report on the U.S. Pavilion" states that the paintings were chosen "for their high quality, for their realistic depiction of wide variety of subject matter popular among American artists, and as a brief but rounded survey of American painting in its most familiar aspects."[112] Masey would recall, however, "It was a bore. The Metropolitan Museum of Art, never before in its history, loaned us twenty to thirty paintings. And we had to build a special way of viewing them so that no one could touch them. They were behind plastic. There were realistic scenes, genre scenes. Ho-hum. So, in a way, that was the antithesis of the photography show. But both were having problems."[113]

Kept at arm's length from the artworks, the audience preferred the next section, which tied in directly to the Japanese national love for baseball.

> We knew baseball was it for the Japanese. Babe Ruth's locker laid them low. It was a shrine. Everybody knew who Babe Ruth was. So this was really going to the audience. We had every conceivable American sport: football, baseball, racing cars . . . but that locker, by the way, we got that from Cooperstown. Babe Ruth's locker had never before left the Hall of Fame. They said, "You know what you're doing? You're taking the key exhibit." I said, "I've gotta have it for Japan. It'll be worshipped." We had Ruth's bat and uniform [figure 4.12].[114]

The May 25, 1970, issue of *Sports Illustrated* magazine describes the visit by Prince Hiro to the U.S. pavilion, greeted by Commissioner General Chernoff, who said,

> "Your Highness, I suppose you would like to see the moon rock?" Chernoff supposed wrong. What His Highness really wanted to see was Babe Ruth's uniform. He was escorted on a tour of the sports exhibit, which includes murals depicting various American sports heroes. Finally a member of the royal party

Figure 4.12.　Babe Ruth's locker on display in the sports section of the U.S. Pavilion, Expo 70, Osaka, Japan.
Courtesy, Chermayeff and Geismar.

pointed to one of the paintings and announced "Babe Ruth!" "That is not Babe Ruth," the prince informed him coldly. "That is Lou Gehrig."[115]

The panorama of American sports also included an automobile section, featuring a Granatelli Turbocar, a dragster, an Indy 500 Championship racecar, and a handful of dune buggies.

The scene stealer that created the daily two- to five-hour-long queues to enter the U.S. pavilion was the space exhibit. Having reached the moon in 1969, America was now preeminent in space exploration. Masey describes his preparations for developing the space exhibit: "I called Houston and said, 'I want everything that's been flown, nothing fake.' There isn't a fake in that show. Everything's real. I wanted it to say all this in the captions. The Soviets, on the other hand, didn't have a single piece of real stuff."[116] The moon rock exhibit, however, in hindsight was not to Masey's expectations: "Now I'll tell you what I would've done differently. We had it here as a kind of elegant piece of jewelry. I think that was a mistake. Here's what I would've done: I would've shown it in such a way that the people could have touched it. So they could've said, 'I touched the moon.' Everybody at the fairground wanted to see it. It was the most popular exhibit at the entire Expo"[117] (figures 4.13–4.16). Organized with the cooperation of the National Aeronautics and

Figure 4.13.   The Apollo 12 space capsule on display in the U.S. Pavilion, Expo 70, Osaka, Japan.
Courtesy, Chermayeff and Geismar.

Figure 4.14. Astronaut space suit and gear on display, U.S. Pavilion, Expo 70, Osaka, Japan.
Courtesy, Chermayeff and Geismar.

Figure 4.15. A visitor tries out an astronaut seat in the U.S. Pavilion, Expo 70, Osaka, Japan.
Courtesy, Chermayeff and Geismar.

Figure 4.16. The moon rock display in the U.S. Pavilion, Expo 70, Osaka, Japan. Courtesy, Jane Helms.

Space Administration, the space exhibit showed "a full scale simulation of the Apollo 11 landing site in the Sea of Tranquility complete with an actual lunar module and the paraphernalia left on the moon by the astronauts—a TV camera, an American flag, a laser beam reflector, a 'solar wind' sheet, a special stereo camera and a sun-powered seismometer."[118]

The architecture exhibit that followed enlisted the help of longtime USIS architect, writer, and critic Peter Blake and photographer Elliott Erwitt and showed every conceivable type of American building, including skyscrapers, residences, and hospitals. The photographic transparencies were placed in illuminated light boxes, which lent a creative element to the juxtaposing of images of traditional American architecture with more avant-garde examples. Pavilion designers hoped the Native American folk art display would resonate with Japanese audiences: "handcrafted stuff, which they do exquisitely in Japan and what we used to do exquisitely in the U.S."[119] On loan from the Smithsonian Institution and the Museum of the American Indian, this exhibit showed a broad range of American folk art, from masks and pottery to weathervanes and quilts (figure 4.17).

Figure 4.17.   The Shaker Room on display in the U.S. Pavilion, Expo 70, Osaka, Japan.
Courtesy, Chermayeff and Geismar.

Pavilion designers Chermayeff and Geismar collected dozens of weather-vanes as one exhibit within the folk art display, calling this technique "the supermarket principle." C. Ray Smith describes this type of display:

> As in the supermarkets, the display of relatively unrefined package designs in mass often produces a cumulative effect far beyond the quality of the individual package. It makes an overall pattern that becomes something more than the sum of the individual parts. Even with patently undesigned or ugly things—air-conditioning outlets, crumpled car parts, worn-out gloves—the massing of them can diffuse the ugliness of the single item and create a transcendingly effective overall pattern and rhythm.[120]

"Mandatory" America: Claes Oldenburg's Giant Ice Bag

> Being essentially experimental in nature, the New Arts exhibit contained an assortment of works which had never before been attempted. As is frequently the case with such experiments, some succeed and others fail. Perhaps the most successful and amusing object in New Arts was Claes Oldenburg's mechanized giant "Ice Bag" while Tony Smith's cave of tetrahedral and octahedral cardboard units left most visitors puzzled and confused.[121]

The New Arts exhibit would finish the tour within the U.S. pavilion and would highlight the marriage of art and technology. In the late 1960s, Los Angeles County Museum of Art (LACMA) curator Maurice Tuchman had been developing a conceptual show called Art and Technology, with the understanding that technology "was beginning to become dominant in cultural life and societal experience."[122] According to Tuchman, artists were working with industry to fashion new techniques, new laser techniques, new ways of presenting art. It was arranged for Masey to speak with Maurice Tuchman, who offered parts of the show for Osaka. Masey's goal with New Arts was to show the Japanese cutting-edge aspects of American art. As Tuchman points out, "They didn't have to reorganize an entire show. They could deal with one curator and one show, lent out by the LACMA. This made things very efficient."[123] In a twist of the Bayerian and the overtly prescriptive path visitors must take through exhibitions, Tuchman recalls:

> The most significant decision from my point of view is that the American pavilion was designed mandatorily so that any visitor who entered would have to go through and see everything inside, and then emerge. That was tremendous, because I knew the American pavilion would draw millions and millions and millions of visitors and that everyone would have to walk through my show,

which was positioned, as I recall, at the very end of the pavilion. I knew that introducing artists like Andy Warhol and Claes Oldenburg and the other six artists, I knew that this would have a real impact on the development of art in Japan and maybe other unforeseen ramifications.[124]

Tuchman reiterates that when the exhibition came about in the late 1960s, there was no particular message in mind or in the minds of the artists who participated. Curator Ann Collins Goodyear, on the other hand, offers an explanation for the genealogy of the joining of art and technology both in the museum and in the Expo setting:

> The launch of Sputnik by the Soviet Union in 1957 created a climate favorable to art projects embracing new science and technology. In response to the perceived Soviet threat, American education emphasized science and technology, while influential theorists such as C. P. Snow, Reyner Banham and Marshall McLuhan stressed the need for interconnection between art, science and technology.[125]

Collins contends the demise of optimism for the union of art and technology among artists occurred in the late 1960s as a result of the Vietnam War, which, in her words, "dramatically undermined public confidence in the promise of new technology, linking it with corporate support of the war."[126] Ironically, it would be Tuchman himself, the visionary behind the *Art and Technology* exercise at the Los Angeles County Museum of Art, who would embrace "the imprimatur" of the USIA.[127] There is no evidence that the Vietnam conflict undermined the presentation of the iteration of either *Art and Technology* or the other exhibits in the U.S. pavilion at Osaka. At the Expo, this exhibit was merely one of many parts that worked together as a cohesive presentation of "America," a spectacle already dominated by a panoramic take on American life through the medium of photography, American baseball heroes, and moon rocks. Even President Nixon's April 30, 1970, announcement that the United States and South Vietnam had invaded Cambodia—in order to "sustain America's credibility with the world"—did not bring a barrage of sour press coverage to the U.S. pavilion.[128]

With the project en route to being organized into a large-scale exhibition at LACMA sometime in 1970, Tuchman jumped at the chance to show a representative sample of these works first in Osaka for its potential to bring prestige to what was then a young county fine arts museum. As typical, working with Masey, Tuchman reports that there was no pressure to choose art with a specific message and that all the artists who were asked were "happy to join in."[129] In spite of the goodwill and bonhomie among the artists and the USIA pavilion organizers, the planning for the New Arts exhibit was rushed. The contract between LACMA and USIA was signed on May 20, 1969, with the expectation that the artworks would be delivered and installed in Osaka by March 15, 1970.[130]

When asked to explain the origins of the Art and Technology concept, Tuchman responded:

> The museum for the first five or six years of its tenure seemed to be a museum of modern art. And we were riding the crest of that idea in the late sixties. And I would say that after the Art and Technology show opened in a much fuller version the following year in 1971, it was such a spectacular hit. So many artists today were then people in high school trying to find their way in the world, and this show at LACMA really opened up all kinds of possibilities for them as artists. I had asked over one hundred artists to be in the show, and I went about it based on intuition.[131]

As Masey remembers, Oldenburg "was the knockout. He's done eight-story-high baseball bats. The guy's a madman. It's all wonderful. And by the way, I met him. He came to Montreal and we had a dinner for all the artists there, and he said, 'I wanna be the waiter.' He stood up, grabbed a towel, and took orders from everyone around the table. The guy's marvelous."[132]

Howard Chernoff would report on the drawbacks of the New Arts exhibit. Masey admits Chernoff did not enjoy working with Tuchman, whom he described as an *enfant terrible* of the art world. Taking the risk of displaying this conceptual art collaborative from Los Angeles, the Japanese reportedly were delighted by the Oldenburg ice bag (figure 4.18). Masey recalls the challenges of conveying a message with artist Tony Smith's cardboard sculptures:

> There was another artist who worked out this cardboard interior. But one day, Chernoff, who never liked the Art and Technology exhibit, came to see me, and said, "We've been open for about a month, and Jack, I want to show you something in the Art and Technology exhibit." I knew I was in trouble, the way he said it. We go and the U.S. pavilion was mobbed. But this particular day, he takes me to the exhibit of the cardboard piece. Some visitor had gone to the bathroom there. And Chernoff turns to me and says, "See Jack, here's the purpose of the Art and Technology exhibit. It's a men's room!" He said, "This is what this exhibit has accomplished." He was half-serious, and he said that the incident was that visitor's commentary on the show. But people were desperate since there were no bathrooms. But anyway, that was life in the U.S. pavilion at Osaka—with visitors who sometimes waited as long as five hours to gain entry.[133]

Figure 4.18.   Claes Oldenburg's giant ice bag kinetic sculpture on display in the *New Arts* exhibit in the U.S. Pavilion, Expo 70, Osaka, Japan.
Courtesy, Chermayeff and Geismar.

Conclusion to Osaka

The U.S. pavilion at Expo 70 should be remembered as the uneasy and altogether awkward mingling of American scientific ingenuity, pop culture, and avant-garde art forms, all housed in the radically designed "Band-Aid." The folksy popularity of Babe Ruth's uniform and the spectacle of American space technology—in the shape of the moon rock—are certainly understandable and inspired tens of millions of visitors to the American pavilion (figure 4.19). The added emphasis of the elitist *Art and Technology* exhibit and the gritty realism of *Ten Photographers* revealed the colliding values of both a conservative and liberal America. As Masey suggests, "We had controversy, too, something every exhibition should have," and *Ten Photographers* showed turmoil and problems in America. Though detractors asked why portraits of grim urban families should decorate the most-visited pavilion at the Expo, after the political fallout with disgruntled U.S. congressmen and the support of an enthusiastic Japanese press, the exhibit in the end would be regarded by pavilion organizers as the highlight of the U.S. effort.[134]

Ivan Chermayeff sums up what visitors had seen at these pavilions through the 1960s:

Figure 4.19.   Visitors queue at the entrance to the U.S. Pavilion, Expo 70, Osaka, Japan.
United States Information Agency (USIA).

We designers didn't have to worry about how we were portraying America. If one had to run these things through committees and boards, these ideas wouldn't have happened. And what did America show of itself at these exhibitions? They showed that we were pretty entrepreneurial people. And I think this is why we will not disappear from the face of the earth because we can imagine and we know how to get things done with good ideas. We have the energy to make these great ideas happen. And that's what makes this country really great. There's no better place to be, no matter what, than this one.[135]

While the United States could celebrate its showing at Osaka, it continued to send thematic traveling exhibitions throughout the Soviet Union.[136] As a new period of détente lessened tensions between the United States and the U.S.S.R., the signing of the SALT I and the Helsinki Accords would coincide with the planning, now outside the auspices of the USIA, for how America would present itself to the world for its bicentennial in 1976. This looming event and the intractable bureaucracy that nearly doomed the American bicentennial would eclipse all other cultural programming for at least half a decade leading up to the event itself.

Notes

1. Carl Rowan, Director of the United States Information Agency, Second Supplemental Appropriation Bill, 1965, Hearings before Subcommittees of the Committee on Appropriations, House of Representatives, Eighty-Ninth Congress, First Session, Part 1 (Washington, DC: U.S. Government Printing Office, 1965), 168–169. For 1964–65 USIA surveys measuring Canadian attitudes toward the United States, see Papers of Leonard H. Marks, Director, United States Information Agency, 1964–67, Box 22, November 7, 1967, Folder "Montreal World Exposition" (Expo '67), Lyndon Baines Johnson Presidential Library Archives. For further understanding of the official USIA attitude toward the Montreal Expo, see this box, which also contains folders "Expo '67 Advisory Commission" and "Expo '67 Administration."

2. See MC468, Box 179, Folder #22, "Mutual Educational and Cultural Exchange Act," Bureau of Educational and Cultural Affairs Historical Collection (CU), Special Collections, University of Arkansas, Fayetteville. For excellent background to Canadian politics during the era, as understood by the USIA, see Papers of Lyndon Baines Johnson, President, 1963–1969, National Security Files, Country File, Canada, Box 166, Folder "Canada, Cables [1 of 2], Vol. V, 1/67–10/68." This folder also contains a noteworthy January 6, 1967, memo from the American Embassy in Montreal that refers to Canada as America's "querulous neighbor."

3. Rowan, Hearings before Subcommittees, 169.

Chapter Four

4. Ibid. For the play-by-play planning by the USIA for the U.S. pavilion at Montreal, see "Dates of Decisions and Actions Pertaining to U.S. Participation in Montreal Fair." USIA Historical Collection, State Department.

5. Rhona Richman Kenneally and Johanne Sloan, eds., *Expo 67: Not Just a Souvenir* (Toronto: University of Toronto Press, 2010), 6–7. See also "Day by Day," *Expo 67*, http://expo67.morenciel.com/an/day_by_day.php.

6. For a discussion of the nomenclature surrounding world fairs and expos, see Bureau International des Expositions, http://www.bie-paris.org/site/en/main.html. This resource also includes a bibliography of sources directly related to world fairs and expos from 1851 to the present.

7. Cambridge Seven Associates, a transdisciplinary design firm, was founded in Cambridge, Massachusetts, and New York City in 1962 by architect Peter Chermayeff and consisted of six other principals: architects Paul Dietrich, Terry Rankine, Louis J. Bakanowsky, and Alden Christie, and graphic designers Ivan Chermayeff and Tom Geismar. The work of this collaborative would transcend architectural and graphic design and would include urban design, exhibition design, and landscape architecture.

8. Artists and their works enlisted to show at the U.S. pavilion included Jim Dine's *Wall Painting for Sylvia Guiray*, Ellsworth Kelly's *Blue White*, Robert Indiana's *The Cardinal Numbers*, Helen Frankenthaler's appropriately titled *Painting for Expo*, Robert Motherwell's *Large Painting No. 2*, and Roy Lichtenstein's *Big Modern Painting*. For discussion of art in the U.S. pavilion, see, for instance, David Bourdon, "Expo '67," *Art International* 11, no. 7 (September 20, 1967): 21–22. For a complete listing of the artworks on display and other items on display in the U.S. pavilion, see "Report: *Expo 67: United States Pavilion*," Office of the United States Commissioner General, Montreal, Canada, April 28, 1967; USIA Historical Collection, State Department, Washington, DC.

9. Ibid.

10. See K. Michael Hays and Dana Miller, *Buckminster Fuller: Starting with the Universe* (New York: Whitney Museum of American Art; New Haven, CT: Yale University Press, 2008), 148, which addresses Fuller's attempts at a three-quarter dome back in 1951.

11. Jack Masey, interview with author, August 23, 2010.

12. Ibid.

13. Fuller himself would partner with Shoji Sadao and Geodesics, Inc. on the design and building of the dome.

14. Masey, interview, August 24, 2010.

15. Ibid.

16. Ibid.

17. Masey, interview, August 24, 2010. When Fuller accepted the job to design the pavilion at Montreal, he inscribed on a cover of the August 29, 1964, edition of the *Saturday Review* a message to Jack Masey: "To Jack Masey—whose confidence in

me has given me my most important opportunities to make myself of some use to our fellow men. In affectionate regard, Buckminster Fuller, December 8, 1964."

18. Ivan Chermayeff, interview with author, August 23, 2010.

19. See "Recommended Design and Content of USIA Participation," Masey Archives.

20. Masey, interview, August 23, 2010.

21. Ibid.

22. Ivan Chermayeff, interview, August 23, 2010.

23. Ibid. When asked whether it was fortuitous to have a designer (Jack Masey) on the government side guiding the project, Chermayeff responded: "Oh, it was invaluable. The only way you could get it done well. Without that, it would be laborious and nowhere near as good. But what we did do was pretty good."

24. Ibid.

25. Ibid.

26. C. Ray Smith, "Ivan Chermayeff and Thomas Geismar," American Institute of Graphic Arts, 1980, http://www.aiga.org/medalist-ivanchermayeffandtomgeismar/.

27. Peter Chermayeff, "Design for a Fair: The United States Pavilion at Expo '67 Montreal," YouTube video, 7:24, posted by "Pchermayeff," July 26, 2010, http://www.youtube.com/watch?v=6TnT2lSLHxo. One Montreal magazine described the pavilion as "the airiest, gentlest propaganda ever," an "ice-cream sundae" of "fun . . . and joy and freedom and youth," as quoted in Jonathan Massey, "Buckminster Fuller's Cybernetic Pastoral: The United States Pavilion at Expo 67," *Journal of Architecture* 11, no. 4 (2006): 479.

28. Masey, interview, August 23, 2010. For more discussion of official censure of the U.S. pavilion, see editorial, "Expositions: Disaster or Masterpiece?" *Time*, June 2, 1967, 47–49. Ivan Chermayeff, when asked by a journalist his feelings toward the disapproval of U.S. congressmen, replied, "If every congressman likes what we're doing, we might as well shoot ourselves," in "A Controversial 'Happening': U.S. 'Bubble' Promises to be a Ball at Expo!" *Montreal Star*, April 24, 1967, 8.

29. R. Buckminster Fuller. *Operating Manual for Spaceship Earth* (Carbondale, IL: Southern Illinois University Press, 1963).

30. Peter Blake, *No Place Like Utopia: Modern Architecture and the Company We Kept* (New York: Norton, 1993), 96.

31. See David Crowley, "Looking Down on Spaceship Earth: Cold War Landscapes," in *Cold War Modern: Design, 1945–1970*, ed. David Crowley and Jane Pavitt (London: V&A Publishing, 2008), 263. Crowley adds: "The United States Information Agency rejected the internationalist vision of 'World Game' (and in fact the ground-floor entrance to the Pavilion was dominated by a massive wall-mounted eagle fashioned in golden panels)," ibid., 293. For further discussion of Fuller's values system as evidenced in his geodesic theories, see Hays and Miller, *Buckminster Fuller*, 9–10.

32. See R. Buckminster Fuller, "Vision 65 Summary Lecture," *Perspecta* 11 (1967): 63.

33. See "A Controversial 'Happening:' U.S. 'Bubble' Promises to be a Ball at Expo!" *Montreal Star*, April 24, 1967.

34. See Jeffrey Meikle, *Design in the USA* (Oxford: Oxford University Press, 2005), 182.

35. R. Buckminster Fuller, as quoted in John Allwood, *The Great Exhibitions* (London: Studio Vista, 1977), 169.

36. Massey, "Buckminster Fuller's Cybernetic Pastoral," 463–64.

37. As quoted in Linda Sargent Wood, *A More Perfect Union: Holistic Worldviews and the Transformation of American Culture after World War II* (Oxford: Oxford University Press, 2010), 73.

38. Massey, "Buckminster Fuller's Cybernetic Pastoral," 464. Massey's analysis of the functionalist theme in the U.S. pavilion's architecture includes a discussion of Fuller's initial plan for the U.S. pavilion—a space-frame structure—that would elicit understanding to visitors the World Game project Fuller had been exploring with Fuller's desire, in Massey's words, "to globalise democracy," ibid., 476. For additional analysis of the U.S. pavilion, see John Samuel Margolies, "Building for Art: Export America in a Splendid Dome, The United States Pavilion at Expo '67," *Art Voices* 5, no. 4 (Fall 1966): 82–86; and David Bourdon, "Expo '67," 21–22.

39. Final Report, Office of Public Affairs of the United States Pavilion (IME), USIA Historical Archives, State Department, 1967. For a privately funded report on the U.S. pavilion at Expo 67, see NA RG306 Records of the USIA, Office of Research, Special Reports (S); 1953–1997, S-16-67 thru S-25-68, Box 24, Folder "S-25-67."

40. Peter Chermayeff, "Design for a Fair."

41. See LBJL, Papers of Lyndon Baines Johnson, President, 1963–1969, White House Confidential File, (Subject Reports) Agency Reports, U.S. Information Agency, Box 135 [1 of 2], Folder "United States Information Agency, 1965, 2 of 2," which contains a September 21, 1965, weekly report that demonstrates a foreign public opinion that holds the United States ahead of the Soviets in the space race. This attitude clearly was shared by the designers of the American pavilion in Montreal.

42. Peter Chermayeff, "Design for a Fair."

43. Michael L. Smith, "Selling the Moon: The U.S. Manned Space Program and the Triumph of Commodity Scientism," in *The Culture of Consumption: Critical Essays in American History, 1880–1980*, ed. Richard Wightman Fox and T. J. Jackson Lears (New York: Pantheon, 1983), 177.

44. Peter Chermayeff, "Design for a Fair."

45. Ibid.

46. Ibid.

47. Tony Bennett, "The Exhibitionary Complex," *New Formations* 4 (Spring 1988): 78.

48. Ibid. See Michel Foucault's discussion of the panopticon as it pertains to theories of surveillance in *Discipline and Punish: The Birth of the Prison* (Harmondsworth: Peregrine, 1986). For related discussion, see Peter Marks, "Imagining Surveillance:

Utopian Visions and Surveillance Studies," *Surveillance and Society* 3, nos. 2/3: 222–39. See also Stanley Cohen, *Visions of Social Control: Crime, Punishment and Classification* (Cambridge: Polity, 1985), 199. Cohen analyzes the "social control ideology" as it is witnessed in the "context of utopian and dystopian visions."

49. See Kenneally and Sloan, *Expo 67*, 12.

50. Tom McDonough, "Obsolescence as Progress and Regression: Technology, Temporality, and Architecture at Expo 67," in *Expo 67: Not Just a Souvenir*, ed. Rhona Richman Kenneally and Johanne Sloan (Toronto: University of Toronto Press, 2010), 86. See also Will Straw, "Tabloid Expo," in Kenneally and Sloan, 221–38, in which he cites Pieter von Wesemael's notion that as world's fairs "have come to be filled with media-based displays which offer their own protocols of instruction," these newer fairs, according to von Wesemael, "also reflected changing notions on popular education: from pedantic conveyance of information to a passive audience . . . to self-realisation and image creation in which the public itself plays the active role," ibid., 224–25. For original source, see Pieter von Wesemael, *Architecture of Instruction and Delight: A Socio-historical Analysis of World Exhibitions as a Didactic Phenomenon (1798-1851-1970)* (Rotterdam: 010 Publishers, 2001), 18.

51. McDonough, "Obsolescence as Progress and Regression," 86–87.

52. See Bennett, "The Exhibitionary Complex," 76.

53. Ibid.

54. See also Foucault, *Discipline and Punish*.

55. Bennett, "The Exhibitionary Complex," 74.

56. Ibid., 76.

57. Ibid.

58. Peter Chermayeff, "Design for a Fair."

59. Bennett, "The Exhibitionary Complex," 96–97.

60. Ibid., 98. In this case, the American pavilion structure itself, to borrow a term from Penelope Davies and her study of monumental architecture in ancient Rome, becomes an "imperial idiom."

61. Ibid.

62. Bennett, from a decidedly more paranoid perspective, states: "In their interrelations, then, the expositions and their fair zones constituted an order of things and of peoples which, reaching back into the depths of prehistoric time as well as encompassing all corners of the globe, rendered the whole world metonymically present, subordinated to the dominating gaze of the white, bourgeois, and . . . male eye of the metropolitan powers. But an eye of power which, through the development of the technology of vision associated with exposition towers and the positions for seeing these produced in relation to the miniature ideal cities of the expositions themselves, was democratized in being made available to all."

63. President Eisenhower's news conference, April 7, 1954, *Public Papers of the Presidents*, 1954, 382.

64. See *Life*, April 28, 1967, 30A.

65. Masey, interview, August 24, 2010.

66. See LBJL, Papers of Lyndon Baines Johnson, President, 1963–1969, NSF, Agency File, USIA, Box 74, Folder "USIA, Vol. 5 [2 of 2]," Lyndon Baines Johnson Presidential Library Archives. This folder contains the minutes from the August 31, 1965, swearing in of Leonard H. Marks as director of the USIA and includes this comment: "This Nation—and this Government—have no propaganda to peddle. We are neither advocates nor defenders of any dogma so fragile or doctrine so frightened as require it. But we are—as our forefathers were 189 years ago—respectful of the opinions of mankind."

67. Masey, interview, August 23, 2010. See also Lyndon B. Johnson, "Remarks in Montreal upon Visiting EXPO '67," May 25, 1967, at Gerhard Peters and John T. Woolley, *The American Presidency Project*, http://www.presidency.ucsb.edu /ws/?pid=28269. See also Papers of Lyndon Baines Johnson, President, 1963–1969, White House Confidential File, Subject File, EX FG 296, Box 315, Folder "4/25/67– 6/15/67." This folder contains a very positive letter from LBJ to Marks regarding the president's trip to the expo; and Papers of Lyndon Baines Johnson, President, 1963–1969, White House Confidential File, (Subject Reports) Agency Reports, U.S. Information Agency, Box 135 [2 of 2], Folder "United States Information Agency, 1967, 3 of 3," which contains an October 3, 1967, biweekly report with the following opening remarks: "The nature of USIA activity abroad does not lend itself to an exact description or a specific evaluation of results. Moreover, the most spectacular achievements are those for which we should not claim credit in public."

68. Masey, interview, August 24, 2010. Masey went on to say during the interview, "He really did have every right to hate what we were doing there. Well, here we are at an international expo. I don't think the Soviet wanted to get into any of their wars. We certainly didn't want to get into any of our wars. I don't think it was appropriate. We deliberately did not want to touch Vietnam."

69. Jack Masey, "21st-Century World's Fairs" (lecture at the National Building Museum, October 25, 2010), http://www.nbm.org/media/audio/21st-century-worlds -fairs-3.html.

70. Payeff-Masey, interview, August 24, 2010.

71. Final Report, Office of Public Affairs of the United States Pavilion (IME), USIA Historical Collection, State Department, 1967, 60.

72. Ibid., final section.

73. See "Expo 70: Estimated Attendance." USIA Historical Collection, State Department, 3.

74. Masey, interview, August 24, 2010.

75. Ibid. Art and cultural historian Elie Faure offers insight into the totalitarian architecture of the Soviet Union: "One thing only seems probable . . . that systems of government in which authority dominates—theocracy, autocracy, aristocracy— almost everywhere favor the rise of architecture and subordinate all other arts to it that is to a central and primitive edifice about which the crowds assemble and upon which all eyes are fixed." See Elie Faure, *History of Art: The Spirit of the Forms* (New York: Garden City, 1937), 442–43.

76. Jack Masey and Conway Lloyd Morgan, *Cold War Confrontations: U.S. Exhibitions and Their Role in the Cultural Cold War* (Baden, Switzerland: Lars Müller, 2008), 18.

77. For a designer's perspective on the theory of obsolescence, see George Nelson, "Obsolescence," *Perspecta* 11 (1967): 170–76. See also Jane Pavitt, "Design and the Democratic Ideal," in *Cold War Modern: Design 1945–1970*, ed. David Crowley and Jane Pavitt (London: V&A Publishing, 2008), 276. In a footnote, Pavitt states, "The practice of streamlining in design and product obsolescence also came under attack in the USA, with designers such as George Nelson protesting against 'superficial' design practices."

78. See Wesemael, *Architecture of Instruction and Delight*, 617–18.

79. "United States Pavilion, Japan World Exposition, 1970: A Report," USIA Historical Collection, State Department, 1.

80. Ibid.

81. Ibid., 3.

82. Masey, interview, August 24, 2010.

83. Ibid.

84. USIA, Japan World Exposition: A Report, 8.

85. Masey, interview, August 24, 2010. For a complete list of design and architectural teams and jury, see "United States Exhibition, Japan World Exhibition, Osaka, 1970," *USIA News Release*, No. 2, February 1, 1968, USIA Historical Collection, State Department.

86. Masey, interview, August 24, 2010. See also Masey and Morgan, *Cold War Confrontations*, 353–68.

87. Masey, interview, August 24, 2010. See also budget request of Howard Chernoff, Acting Commissioner General, Osaka World Exposition, in Second Supplemental Appropriation Bill for Fiscal Year 1968, June 12, 1968, 395, USIA Historical Collection, State Department, Washington, DC. This hearing was an effort to restore more than $4 million to the U.S. pavilion budget after Congress slashed the original request of $14,619,000 to $7,876,000.

88. Masey, interview, August 24, 2010.

89. See Marguerite Villeco, "Technology: The Infinitely Expandable Future of Air Structures," *Architectural Forum* (September 1970): 40.

90. See "U.S. Pavilion—The Ultimate Understatement." *P/A* (August 1970): 64–67. For a philosophical discussion of the genealogy of pneumatic architecture that includes reference to the U.S. pavilion at Osaka, see Marc Dessauce, *The Inflatable Moment: Pneumatics and Protest in '68* (New York: Princeton Architectural Press/ Architectural League of New York, 1999), 111–12, 145.

91. Masey and Morgan, *Cold War Confrontations*, 360. See also David Geiger, "U.S. Pavilion at Expo 70 Features Air-Supported Cable Roof," *Civil Engineering— ASCE* (March 1970): 48–50.

92. Ervin Gallantay, "Osaka Expo: Designing the Environment," *Nation*, August 31, 1970, 136.

93. Masey, interview, August 24, 2010.

94. Ibid. Fellow pavilion designer Ivan Chermayeff recalls the anticipation leading up to the opening of the pavilion: "It was an air-inflated structure. It was very innovative at that time, and very cheap too, for the square footage involved. And there were all kinds of concerns that it would deflate and land on people. And they made a test and a guy slashed it with a samurai sword, and the equipment was such that air rushing out of a giant gash, nothing happened. So then they were satisfied it would not kill a lot of Japanese tourists." Chernoff would later comment in the Final Report for Osaka: "The U.S. structure was ranked, in importance, with Paxton's Crystal Palace in London in 1851 and with Sullivan's Transportation Building at the 1893 Chicago World's Fair. It was also called the most daring structure at Expo 70 and its potential for spanning vast areas with an easily erected cover was deemed 'colossal,'" 17. For a discussion of the advent of new materials used in the construction of the Geiger space frame, see "Plastiscope 3," Modern Plastics (March 1970): 162.

95. Villeco, "Future of Air Structures," 43.

96. USIA, Japan World Exposition: A Report, 21.

97. Masey, interview, August 24, 2010.

98. As quoted by Masey, interview, August 24, 2010.

99. Ibid.

100. Ibid.

101. Ibid.

102. Ibid. Masey, in this interview, would go on to admit, "I have always had this guilt feeling that I, Masey, was the go-between for a censorship thing, which I myself didn't want to be. That black-and-white photo show turned out to be our Unfinished Business show. Why? Americans are coming and always have problems with exhibitions."

103. Ibid.

104. See Peter Blake, "Raising the Roof at Osaka," New York Magazine, April 13, 1970, 51–52.

105. USIA, Final Report, Osaka, 22. Chernoff mentions that while the Japanese visitors and press were impressed with "the straightforwardness and honesty of the Ten Photographers exhibit," the emperor of Japan himself admitted the exhibit was "not only an exhibit of photographs but that it was also art," ibid., 23.

106. See Michael Camille, "Simulacrum," in Critical Terms for Art History, 2nd ed., ed. Robert S. Nelson and Richard Shiff (Chicago: University of Chicago Press, 2003), 39.

107. Ibid., 40.

108. E. H. Gombrich, Art and Illusion: A Study in the Psychology of Pictorial Representation (London: Phaidon, 2002), 174.

109. Ibid.

110. Diane Arbus, "The Full Circle," Infinity 11, no. 2 (February 1962): 9. See also Doon Arbus and Marvin Israel, eds., Diane Arbus (New York: Aperture, 1972) and Charlotte Higgins, "V&A to Put New Focus on Work of a Camera Genius,"

Guardian, July 4, 2005, 13. Higgins quotes Arbus, who described her work as a "kind of contemporary anthropology," and V&A curator Martin Barnes, who stated, referring to *Bomb Hanoi* and other works by Arbus: "She was almost creating her own contemporary mythology and legends. The photographs are partway between bruisingly real and a kind of fiction."

111. USIA Brochure, "United States Pavilion, Japan World Exposition," Osaka 1970, USIA Historical Collection, State Department, Washington, DC, 4.

112. USIA, Final Report, Osaka, 23.

113. Masey, interview, August 24, 2010.

114. Ibid.

115. *Sports Illustrated*, May 25, 1970.

116. Masey, interview, August 24, 2010.

117. Ibid.

118. USIA, Final Report, 25.

119. Masey, interview, August, 24, 2010.

120. C. Ray Smith, "Ivan Chermayeff and Thomas Geismar."

121. USIA, Final Report, 27.

122. Maurice Tuchman, interview with author, May 14, 2011.

123. Ibid. In the interview, Tuchman mentions that his personal files relating to *Art and Technology* were destroyed in a fire at a facility that the museum had off-site. This was during the 1992 riots in Los Angeles.

124. Ibid.

125. Ann Collins Goodyear, "From Technophilia to Technophobia: The Impact of the Vietnam War on the Reception of 'Art and Technology,'" *Leonardo* 41, no. 2 (April 2008): 169.

126. Ibid.

127. Ibid., 170.

128. See Nicholas J. Cull, *The Cold War and the United States Information Agency: American Propaganda and Public Diplomacy, 1945–1989* (Cambridge: Cambridge University Press, 2008), 308–9.

129. Tuchman, interview, May 14, 2011.

130. See Maurice Tuchman, *Art and Technology: A Report on the Art and Technology Program of the Los Angeles County Museum of Art, 1967–1971* (New York: Viking, 1971), 26–29. For a richly philosophical and mechanical explanation for Oldenburg's "Giant Ice Bag," see 241–69.

131. Maurice Tuchman, interview, May 14, 2011.

132. Masey, interview, August 24, 2010.

133. Ibid.

134. Ibid. One of Japan's leading economic newspapers wrote the following about the U.S. pavilion: "The desire 'not to lie' is evident. This is true not only in the Space Exhibit but throughout all the exhibits. In the sports corner, there's Babe Ruth's locker . . . children, who had been clowning around, all stop their nonsense and seem to become hypnotized when they near the locker." As quoted in USIA,

Japan World Exposition, Report, 36. For more international press coverage of the
U.S. pavilion at the time of Expo 70, see the above report, 33–39.

135. Ivan Chermayeff, interview, August 23, 2010.

136. See letter to Macomber and Frankel from Walter J. Stoessel, MC468, Box
230, Folder #3, "Talking Paper-US-USSR Exchanges, 1967," Bureau of Educational
and Cultural Affairs Historical Collection (CU), Special Collections, University
of Arkansas, Fayetteville. In this letter, Stoessel writes: "Our exchange program is
primarily a political instrument with the long-range goal of helping to open up Soviet society." See also MC468, Box 232, Folder #41, "US-USSR Exchanges: Some
Recent Developments, by Yale Richmond," which includes an important appraisal
of agency operations of the late 1960s through the 1970s. Richmond was at the time
director of the Office of Eastern European Programs for the Bureau of Educational
and Cultural Affairs.

CHAPTER FIVE

The Unfinished Reality of Our Revolutionary Experiment

The World of Franklin and Jefferson, 1971–1977

One area in which we are sorely in need of some serious play is the planning for the 1976 Bicentennial of the United States. In this instance, we have begun to confuse celebration with synthetic gaiety or the building of bandstands. During the Depression, the W.P.A. was faced with a disastrous situation, but everyone pulled together and the result was a genuine national celebration. I think our professional societies, including the American Academy of Arts and Sciences, have a responsibility for developing celebrations in the spirit of something real but exceptional—something that is needed but can only be realized within the context of a special occasion.[1]

The planning for the bicentennial of the American Revolution began in 1966, with the establishment of the American Revolution Bicentennial Commission (ARBC), an independent government body made up of "legislators, business leaders, academics, and *ex officio* members such as the secretaries of defense and state and the librarian of Congress."[2] The USIA would partner with the ARBC in an official capacity solely around informing the commission on foreign public opinion of the United States. It would be in 1971 that the commission formally approached the USIA to assist with a bicentennial exhibition focused on Thomas Jefferson as a subject and slated for a Paris opening in 1974. As Jack Masey describes, the commission, made up of more than two hundred members, proved a blunt instrument in the long run, and "couldn't agree even on what to order for lunch. They were the essence of how not to do a bicentennial."[3]

Unlike the government exhibitions at trade fairs and world fairs in the preceding decades, the American Revolution bicentennial programming was not organized as an ideological statement planned to battle the policies of the Soviet Union.[4] As a result of nuclear parity with the Soviet Union, deterrence would become a shared binational policy of the two superpowers. As historian Angela Romano emphasizes, "A significant relaxation of tensions between East and West occurred after the mid-sixties. Between 1963 and 1968 an increasing dialogue between the superpowers started to develop. Its genesis was in the Soviet achievement, in 1964–65, of the second-strike capability on nuclear weapons, which meant the possibility of mutual assured destruction (MAD) in case of war."[5] On July 1, 1968, the United States and the U.S.S.R. signed the Nonproliferation Treaty in an effort to limit the global spread of nuclear weapons. On February 5, 1969, new U.S. president Richard M. Nixon proclaimed an "era of negotiations" that would help alleviate the strain of America's "international situation—Vietnam disaster, crisis of internal consent, financial problems, strategic parity with the U.S.S.R.—the end of the policy of containment, which had been guiding American action since 1947."[6] With a stable, albeit politically uncertain, relationship between the superpowers, Nixon and Henry Kissinger, the secretary of state, envisioned a new brand of détente whose goal was "to secure stability of the bipolar order and, fundamentally, to gain the United States new freedom of action at lower cost."[7]

The focus of the American bicentennial programming was to help push a more positive image of the United States during a time that was politically challenging to America's global image. When *The World of Franklin and Jefferson* opened at the Grand Palais in Paris in 1975, President Gerald Ford would announce, "The state of the Union is not good." The Watergate scandal and the subsequent tearing down of the "imperial" presidency was further exacerbated by the oil crisis of failed petro-politics in 1973, in addition to the already dour realities of high unemployment, inflation, and a profoundly deep recession.[8] Historian Jeffrey Kimball instructs that a legacy of this period is the "shattering of the myth of American omnipotence."[9] Just what could America show of itself to foreign audiences who had perhaps become inured to the highly publicized social, political, and economic setbacks the United States faced at this point in history? The retelling of the stories of Benjamin Franklin and Thomas Jefferson would allow the American Revolution Bicentennial Commission and the USIA, who would direct its overseas engagements, to bring America's message back to basics. As historian James Patterson illustrates, the "me decade" in the United States, coined by author

Tom Wolfe in 1976, was not completely what Christopher Lasch described as a "culture of narcissism" nor one of self-defeating cynicism:

> Jeremiads such as these left the false impression that American society and culture were suddenly falling apart. On the contrary, many features of American life in the post–World War II years persisted after 1974. As before, the United States remained one of the most stable societies in the world. Most Americans still held strongly to long-established values, including commitment to the Constitution, respect for the law, belief in the necessity of equal opportunity, and confidence in the utility of hard work.[10]

Nixon, the USIA, and the American Revolution Bicentennial Commission

Planning in earnest for the American bicentennial celebrations began under President Nixon, who, newly elected to the presidency in 1968, came with the promise to restore law and order to a country wracked by civil unrest and clashing attitudes toward Vietnam. In late 1969, the ARBC drafted its first report to Nixon, which the president conveyed to Congress in September of 1970. The report recommended a nationwide celebration "with a multitude of activities focused on the past, present and future of the United States," which would be supported by public- and private-sector interests.[11] With the Department of State already an *ex officio* member of the commission, it was decided in 1971 that the United States Information Agency would join the process to facilitate "international planning" for the festivities. This relationship, as the report indicates, would continue throughout the life span of the ARBC, which, by act of Congress in late 1973, was replaced with the American Revolution Bicentennial Administration (ARBA) in early 1974. As Cull explains, the USIA's plan for overseas audiences was to establish "a range of programs of its own . . . creating films, magazines, VOA broadcasts, and touring exhibits and even bicentennial materials for English language teaching, but above all the agency planned to boost the discipline of American studies by building library research collections around the world."[12]

Jack Masey was transferred for temporary duty from the USIA to the ARBA offices across the street from the White House at Jackson Place during the planning phase for the bicentennial programming.[13] One of his early ideas for domestic audiences—for the Bicentennial Administration was intended for domestic and overseas programming—was to establish "bicentennial parks." What became evident immediately was the question of to what degree the U.S. government should be involved—in relation to private-sector sponsorship—with the bicentennial activities planning. Masey recalls while pitching his parks idea to Nixon's representative on the commission, William Safire, who had been at the *American National Exhibition in Moscow* in 1959, that there was an institutional fear of doing something too extravagant. It was David Mahoney, then director of the commission, who told Masey following the presentation: "Safire thinks it's a sensation. But it's a little too much U.S. government, as if this were a campaign. It's not enough of *do it yourself* kind of thing. The government can't be doing these types of things. Safire thought it was wonderful but not enough private sector involvement."[14] Masey underscores: "Here we go again. I'd heard this before. It's private sector versus the U.S. government, or in other words: 'We don't want the government in our lives.' You follow me? I said, 'Well, I don't know how else we can do this.' This was about the time Eames came on." The commission dithered on plans for the American bicentennial until someone mentioned that Charles Eames might be doing something related with a grant from IBM. According to Masey:

> Now when he started on this alone, he wanted to do something on the American Revolution. IBM was his benefactor. IBM loved Eames. In 1972, Eames was thinking of something that could be displayed at IBM headquarters in 1976. So it started with IBM. And he was always very thorough in his examination of everything. He started walking around the subject, and the more he did, he realized there was no *Franklin and Jefferson*, no exhibition, and no sponsor. He stumbled upon, in the research phase, the idea that just to do Jefferson would not give it the range he thought was necessary. He was already veering toward Franklin. It really was a terrific idea that started coming together.[15]

In 1973, the USIA received word from the American embassy in Paris that a venue had become available the following year for an American bicentennial exhibition.[16] The opportunity for the commission to stage a one-off bicentennial show at the Grand Palais, the Beaux-Arts exhibition hall located at the Champs-Élysées and originally built for the Universal Exposition of 1900, inspired immediate action. But just how the commission would proceed, mired in bureaucratic goodwill to create substantial programming for the bicentennial, was the main question. According to Masey, this arrangement was a boondoggle:

> There were about two hundred members in this commission. I knew it was doomed. And I don't know how many commission meetings I went to and just sat there, wanting to die. They said they just had to do something, but they just

couldn't. So I heard about what Eames was doing. I had worked with him in the 1959 *American National Exhibition in Moscow*, and I had worked with IBM before. IBM said that if I did the exhibit with Eames, they would finance and ship the exhibit. It would be free for the U.S. government. That was the best thing about this. And Eames did not come without a big tab. So it was a happy marriage: Eames, IBM, and us.[17]

Masey held no concern that the exhibition planning by the Eames Office would clash with the stated goals of the USIA for all American bicentennial planning. As with his previous work with world-famous designers, Masey's implicit trust of the Eames Office would provide a smooth working relationship between Eames, the ARBA, and the USIA. In a November 1, 1973, memorandum from USIA director James Keogh to Anne Armstrong, counsellor to President Nixon, Keogh outlines the agency's "Bicentennial Program Review." In this memo, the USIA's director dictates the themes to be stressed through the USIA's involvement with the American bicentennial:

1. Heritage—the basic ideas and ideals which created and have sustained the world's oldest experiment in democratic government.
2. Contemporary America—the cultural diversity, political dynamism, social innovation and the scientific and technological achievements which underlie the democratic experience in present-day America.
3. Future Goals—the role of the Bicentennial in reaffirming the American commitment to the proposition that, just as independence summoned the 13 colonies of 1771, interdependence challenges the community of nations in 1976 to build peace and enhance the quality of life on this planet.

—In all of its overseas output, the Agency will emphasize the relevance of the American experience to the interests and aspirations of its overseas audiences.[18]

Future planned collateral activities for *The World of Franklin and Jefferson* were to include a smaller version of the exhibition for use by USIA posts worldwide, with the ultimate goal being to "result in greater foreign governmental and private involvement in the Bicentennial."[19] As project manager from the government side, Masey gave Eames carte blanche to follow his vision for *The World of Franklin and Jefferson*, except for one caveat, delivered in typical Masey vernacular: "Just get the goddamn thing ready in time for the Paris showing."[20] Originally planned as a smaller IBM installation on Jefferson alone, this subject matter would soon expand to incorporate the stories of both Franklin and Jefferson and "a broader sweep of eighteenth-century life,"[21] at the recommendation of Eames.

The Aura of Eames

The office's last major project, *The World of Franklin and Jefferson*, celebrated the nation's Bicentennial with a book, three films, and an exhibition that traveled internationally. Projects such as these elevated the Eameses to the status of U.S. ambassadors overseas and cultural interpreters to the meaning of America at home.[22]

Unlike USIA shows that were limited to foreign audiences alone due to stipulations within the Smith-Mundt Act, *The World of Franklin and Jefferson* could be shown in the United States because the Bicentennial Commission drove it.[23] The development of the initial partnership between the government agencies, IBM, and the Eameses also included the Metropolitan Museum of Art, which planned to host the exhibition after its run in Europe. According to Masey, "We were fortunate . . . *Franklin and Jefferson* was the one big opportunity for the Bicentennial. I've never seen such a shambles of America being unable to come up with a grand idea."[24] It would be the enthusiasm and expertise of Eames that drove the project from the very beginning. When Masey and Eames flew to Paris to negotiate the logistics of showing the exhibition at the Grand Palais, according to Masey,

> The French were freaked out over it. Again, it was Eames. The aura of Eames made it happen. Charles would walk into a room and paralysis would take place. And I was with Eames tying up all the loose details. And he didn't speak a word of French. My French was atrocious. We had two interpreters from the embassy. Eames laid them dead. He said, "We should do this . . . we will do something that you will be proud of. We were friends, we were allies. And we want the world to know it." It was beautiful.[25]

Charles and Ray Eames maintain a relatively stalwart presence throughout the trajectory of U.S. cultural exhibitions abroad, as discussed in previous chapters. In a sense, their work serves as a kind of stitching together of the image America projected to foreign audiences in the second half of the twentieth century. As Hélène Lipstadt acknowledges, the Eames Office had since the early 1950s enjoyed a working relationship—a "natural overlap," according to Charles Eames—with the U.S. government, particularly in the realm of cultural exhibitions abroad.[26]

It was the 1959 *Glimpses of the USA* film that garnered enthusiastic reactions from USIA personnel and Russian visitors alike, marking what Meikle has described as a harbinger of the cultural shift of the material to the immaterial, namely the transition from the three-dimensional object to the photograph.[27] It would be the Eameses' last significant government project that would mark

yet another conceptual shift in how the Eames Office would go about presenting subject matter in cultural exhibitions. As Joseph Giovannini engages, it
was furniture that "dominated the office's defining decades," in the 1940s and
1950s, through the *Good Design* shows at the Chicago Merchandise Mart and
the Museum of Modern Art, but it was Eames himself who "started turning his
attention to information and communication theory in the early 1950s" with
the Art X project for teaching university fine art students. This "paradigm
shift" would find yet another iteration in the early 1970s with the development
of *The World of Franklin and Jefferson* for the American bicentennial, which
"marked a change of emphasis from image to word."[28] The exhibition catalogue, also produced by the Eames Office, describes the inspiration to showcase
these two Founding Fathers from the perspective of language: "Franklin and
Jefferson, more than any others, helped transform their world by their written
words. Franklin's sociable, opportunistic good sense, and Jefferson's imaginative insistence on principle, provided the model, and the impetus, for much
that was attempted in the next 100 years of American life."[29]

Through the persistence of the Eameses' vision, which would go largely
unchallenged by Masey and the ARBA, the American bicentennial exhibition would illustrate for visitors the values on which America was founded,
through the lens of Franklin and Jefferson. The tenaciously personal treatment of the subject matter that characterized all of Charles and Ray Eames's
projects would reach its apogee in *The World of Franklin and Jefferson*. As
Kathleen McLean argues in reference to the evolution of exhibition designers—from the historically predetermined roles of "stylists" and "trades-
men"—the Eames themselves, through the project of *The World of Franklin
and Jefferson*, demonstrate how "designers replaced the curator as auteur, creating conceptual frameworks for the exhibitions and developing the content
as well as the design."[30] It should be clear from the discussion of the Eameses'
projects for the federal government, particularly at Moscow in 1959 and their
bicentennial exhibition program in the mid-1970s, that the design process
went largely unchecked by government restrictions or financial limitations.
As discussed in previous chapters, the official message of the U.S. government
would time and again fall squarely on the designers themselves. Masey, a design veteran himself, helped create this system by giving designers free rein to
develop their vision for the exhibition themselves since the government did
not have the capacity to do what the industrial designers were doing. When,
early on in the ARBA's discussions of content for a bicentennial exhibition,
the government wanted statues of Lincoln and Gilbert and Sullivan, Masey
would again become the strong advocate for designers like the Eameses to
develop their vision for the exhibition on their own. Furthermore, Lipstadt
asks, "How did the Eameses come to be responsible for conversations with

nations on behalf of the government? And why did they believe that the interests of the United States in this domain naturally overlapped with their own?"[31] It became, after all, standard practice, as a result of the government's lack both of know-how and interest in designing "America" for the outside world that indicated the primacy of industrial designers and their work during this period. A few years later, when Masey retired from the USIA, this capability on the government side was not replaced.

Further, Charles and Ray Eames had shaped the fields of industrial and exhibition design for decades. Thus, they were both a convenient and auspicious choice for staging "America" for its bicentennial celebration overseas. But it should be stressed that the Eameses arrived out of the blue to rescue the exceedingly bureaucratic ARBA, which struggled to execute any substantial programming that would portray the United States in a positive light. Charles and Ray Eames, in short, entered the picture like a *deus ex machina*, at a time when domestic and foreign issues threatened to overshadow the nation's two-hundredth birthday party.

The Eameses made a rule, as Lipstadt observes, "of collaborating only with clients whose objectives they shared," and, importantly, like the USIA, for example, "both wanted to enter into conversations with other countries."[32] While Lipstadt argues the *Franklin and Jefferson* exhibition offered the Eameses "the opportunity to create the forum to report to the people, the occasion that the Eameses had sought since 1943,"[33] it would be Eames himself who, in preparation for his 1969 *What Is Design* exhibition, stated, perhaps more diplomatically, "We have found it a very helpful strategy to restrict our work to subjects that are of genuine and immediate interest to us—and are of equal interest to the client."[34] Yet the engagement of the Eames Office for the centerpiece of the U.S. bicentennial programming remains all the more curious. According to Peter Blake, designer and longtime collaborator on U.S. government exhibitions overseas, the Eameses were "hardly in the mainstream of American Culture."[35]

Eames Dreams Up *The World of Franklin and Jefferson*

In the early 1970s, IBM approached the Eames Office—renowned experts at multimedia exhibition development—to design and install an exhibition in their offices in New York City, in honor of the American bicentennial. Pat Kirkham notes the Eames-designed exhibitions showed similarities to their "films and their multiple-image presentations in the use of 'information overload,' bombarding the consciousness with a rich superabundance of information in visually interesting ways . . . although some of their later exhibitions were criticized as too dense and too demanding."[36] Indeed, one way the Eameses developed their multilevel narrative for *The World of Franklin and Jefferson* occurred by means of creating short experimental films that would provide a clearer picture of what the finished exhibition would accomplish. As Masey recalls, "There are two films: one short film that sold the idea. It's better than the actual second film, which is much longer. When he [Eames] was presenting the idea, he did a film to explain *Franklin and Jefferson*. It's nothing short of perfect. It's staggering. Staggering. By means of models, he built a model of the exhibition. And it's totally brilliant. I've never seen anything as good in my life."[37]

Making films to explain larger exhibit and architectural projects was nothing new for Charles and Ray Eames. In 1958, when Finnish architect Eero Saarinen explored concepts for his commission to design the new Dulles Airport terminal outside of Washington, D.C., he enlisted the help of Charles Eames, a close friend from their years at the Cranbrook Academy of Art, to create a film to sell the idea to the client. Eames developed a short narrative that included an illustration of the "mobile lounges," the transports that would in the future take passengers to and from the main terminal to the planes. The film, entitled "The Expanding Airport," became one of many "explaining" movies that would become a signature aspect to many of the Eames Office's larger projects and not intended for wide distribution.[38] As Eames himself affirmed, "A film of ours comes into being because it is either a logical extension of an immediate problem we are working on or it is something we have been wanting to do for a long time and cannot put off any longer."[39]

Thus, in 1973 the Eames Office created a "study film" for its client, the USIA, so to better understand the layout, themes, and content of the *Franklin and Jefferson* exhibition concept. The thirteen-minute film, *Franklin and Jefferson: Authors of Independence and Architects of the American Experiment*, served as a "cinematic trip through the proposed exhibition" and was intended for later use by American embassies and museums to show during the bicentennial year in 1976.[40]

Later, Eames sought to produce a full-length treatment of *The World of Franklin and Jefferson*. While in Paris, working on the exhibition itself, Eames asked Masey who he thought would be suitable to narrate the film. Masey suggested the British actor Peter Ustinov. Immediately they telephoned Ustinov and invited him to the USIA headquarters on the Right Bank to watch the original short film. According to Masey, Eames asked, "Oh, you think he'll even consider it?" Masey replied: "Yes. He's a very civilized, highly intelligent guy." Ustinov shuffled his schedule and showed up at the theater where Eames and Masey were waiting. Masey describes the exchange:

I introduce Eames to Ustinov, and Charles said, "How good of you to come by." And Ustinov is very nice and very wonderful, and says, "Okay." Eames runs his introductory movie. Ustinov applauds. I'm watching Eames. And Eames himself was never predictable. Sitting there. And I'm waiting for Eames to say, "Would you be interested . . . ?" Because this is why I set this up. "Would you, Peter Ustinov, be interested in narrating a real movie?" Not a word comes out. Some awkwardness. This is the complicated Eames.[41]

After chatting, Ustinov looked at his watch and said that he must be going. Masey: "And I'm embarrassed. I've gotten Ustinov in from the outer reaches of Paris, maybe to be considered for this. And no offers are made." As Masey walked Ustinov outside to the front of the building on Rue Florentin, people instantly recognized the film star. As people crowded around, Ustinov suddenly turned to Masey and performed an imitation of Eames, saying, "Jack, I think I ought to be going," in an American accent. With the awkwardness diminished, Ustinov told Masey, "I just wanted you to know, I got the message here, don't worry." Ustinov departed. As Masey watched him disappear down the street, he recalls: "Eames could have at least said something to Ustinov. But whoever he got didn't touch Ustinov. He did get somebody else, I saw the movie. It's lacking. But Ustinov did this wonderful satire of Eames, saying, 'I understand what you're going through, Jack, goodbye.' I never saw Ustinov again. It was quite something."[42]

This second film would also be the subject for Charles Eames's talk at the American Academy of Arts and Science in November 1976. Here he preached for what he called "reducing discontinuity" in education in general and more specifically in the related storylines of *Franklin and Jefferson*, two people "finding out things piece by piece, in pursuit of their own needs, loves, and curiosities."[43] These two figures were, according to Eames, the "two early Americans who seemed to stand for the connection between European culture and American immediacy."[44] Clearly identifying with his subjects, Eames promotes in this essay the virtues of "found education," lamenting what he viewed as the decline of learning in spite of the overemphasis on teaching in schools in the 1970s.

As Charles Eames himself declared, this "vision of complexity"[45] required viewers to "negotiate the material themselves and make their own connections."[46] In a significant return to Misha Black's exhibition values of allowing, even promoting, visitors to explore the range of the exhibition on their own, *The World of Franklin and Jefferson* would certainly align with this philosophy. Yet, as Kirkham points out, the Bayerian exhibition "field of vision" tendencies would also make their way into the Eameses' exhibition design, with the use of "panels to spell out themes as well as to partition space," based on Bayer's strategy "of showing familiar material in unfamiliar ways."[47] (figure 5.1). And yet it is important to acknowledge, according to Kirkham, the genealogy of

Figure 5.1. Detail of signage panels in *The World of Franklin and Jefferson*.
© 2014 Eames Office LLC (www.eamesoffice.com).

American exhibition design. Prior to Bayer's influential work in the United States, American designers were already delivering compelling and spectacular exhibition design at the time of the arrival of the "Bauhaus-blinkered world of high culture" in the 1930s. These designers included Walter Dorwin Teague and Norman Bel Geddes, and these designers rightfully should be acknowledged as contributors to the hybrid style the Eames Office would adopt later.[48]

Taking visual cues from such earlier endeavors as the Art X curriculum design from the 1950s in their quest to communicate large amounts of information through the exhibition medium, the Eameses planned an exhibition in four parts. The first section, "Friends and Acquaintances," displayed large, four-sided monoliths featuring photographs and label copy of a legion of figures in Franklin and Jefferson's circles, including Samuel Adams, Patrick Henry, Thomas Paine, and the Comte du Buffon, while Plexiglas cases showed original artifacts, including "eighteenth-century Paul Revere silver, Wedgwood ceramics, toys, books, games, and scientific and musical instruments"[49] (figures 5.2–5.5). The second section, "Contrast and Continuity," offered biographical information on Franklin and Jefferson. The third section, "Three Documents," studied the Charters of Freedom of the United States (the Declaration of Independence, the Constitution, and the Bill of Rights), and these facsimiles of the original documents were accessible to visitors through a full-scale replica of a Georgian-style doorway (figures 5.6–5.7). The fourth and final section, "Jefferson and the West," revisited the president's obsession and acquisitive approach to all things western. As usual, the Eameses did not shy from a visually dominating, multimedia approach. It featured sensational artifacts, such as stuffed megafauna—a life-size bison on loan from the Field Museum in Chicago as well as the mastodon bones Jefferson sent to Buffon in the early nineteenth century to dissuade the French naturalist of his "degeneracy" theory of America (figures 5.8–5.9). Featuring a blown-up map of the Lewis and Clark expedition, this section also included several examples of fine art from the period, including paintings by George Catlin from the Museum of Natural History in New York and Native American arts from the Heye Foundation and the Southwest Museum.[50]

The Eameses thrived in many of their projects, moreover, in discovering the optimum method for information sharing by revealing the interconnectedness within the various subnarratives at hand. *The World of Franklin and Jefferson* as a concept proved no different, as Lipstadt argues, in that the Eameses saw the American Revolution as "a galaxy of American patriots, European and American scientists, and other cultural innovators who orbit around the twin suns of Benjamin Franklin and Thomas Jefferson."[51] The exhibition included a detailed timeline of the 120 years spanning the lives of Franklin and Jefferson, as well as "wall-mounted graphic panels with supple-

Figure 5.2.   Detail of display of Benjamin Franklin's books, *The World of Franklin and Jefferson*.
© 2014 Eames Office LLC (www.eamesoffice.com).

mentary images and information, and overhead cloth banners of quotations from the writings and speeches of the two men."[52] Kirkham describes the Eameses' signature approach of overabundant visual and textual stimulation:

> Since the intention behind most of the Eameses' exhibitions was "information overload," the charge of superabundance did not unduly worry them; they believed that viewers were sufficiently intelligent, discriminating, and skilled to take from an exhibition what they wanted. What some saw as confusing in its inclusiveness could, they thought, be approached in many different ways and negotiated by many different routes.[53]

Figure 5.3. View of *Franklin and Jefferson* with text in English.
© 2014 Eames Office LLC (www.eamesoffice.com).

Figure 5.4. View of artifacts on display, including printing press and scientific instruments, *The World of Franklin and Jefferson.*
© 2014 Eames Office LLC (www.eamesoffice.com).

Figure 5.5. Artifacts on display in *The World of Franklin and Jefferson*.
© 2014 Eames Office LLC (www.eamesoffice.com).

Figure 5.6. Charles Eames's model for the Georgian architecture and adjacent gallery spaces for *The World of Franklin and Jefferson*.
© 2014 Eames Office LLC (www.eamesoffice.com).

Figure 5.7.   The World of Franklin and Jefferson prior to grand opening in Paris, 1975.
American Revolution Bicentennial Administration (ARBA).

This laissez-faire principle of allowing visitors to engage with what Neuhart, Neuhart, and Eames describe as the "hypermedia" within the exhibition represented the Eameses' democratic approach to education through their particular style of communication. As Kirkham stresses, "The Eameses moved into exhibition design because they were passionately interested in ideas and communicating those ideas to others."[54] The ultimate appearance of these endeavors mirrored the idiosyncratic approach of the Eameses toward conveying the meaning of historical material, which would be a "mix of scholarship and festivity."[55]

The research for *The World of Franklin and Jefferson* reflected the Eames Office's typical attention to detail and transcended all previous exhibition efforts in its sheer complexity and design. For this, the Eames Office enlisted the help of Jehane Burns, who took on an array of responsibilities, from drafting label copy to finding images for display from archives in the United States, Great Britain, France, and Poland. She in turn would, early in the planning process, work with dozens of consultants from academia. I. Bernard Cohen, history of science professor at Harvard University, urged the Eameses to stress the importance of the notion that America, on the eve of the Revolution, was questioning its own identity, in the spirit of St. John de Crevecoeur, who asked: "What is this new man? This American?"

Figure 5.8. Charles Eames admiring the bison on loan from the Field Museum for the run of *The World of Franklin and Jefferson*, 1975–1977.
© 2014 Eames Office LLC (www.eamesoffice.com).

Figure 5.9. The bison from the "Jefferson and the West" section of *The World of Franklin and Jefferson*, 1975–1977.
© 2014 Eames Office LLC (www.eamesoffice.com).

Cohen further hypothesized the following in his recorded shorthand notes for Charles Eames:

> Certainly there was reason to suspect that a man living in the air of the New World, far removed from Europe with its decadence, its immorality, time worn views of nature and society, even removed from the slavery of the Old World, might have something to say in a way that would be original or forceful denied to Europeans. One must remember the concept of the Noble Savage was a real one, nourished by the concept we associate with J. J. Rousseau, and exemplified to the highest degree by Am. Indian [sic], simple of heart, great in courage, noble of aspect and mien. Franklin typified this New Man in many ways.[56]

Historian James Flexner's notes to the Eames Office grumbled about the importance of the geography on the shaping of the American character: "The effect of the land on the people who came here is terribly important. A new kind of man was created by the American land. The American Revolution was due to the land, the geography."[57] Flexner, after reading the first round of label copy on which the exhibition would be based, urged for "more careful editing." From Flexner's point of view, the Eames approach was all too often "absorbed in details" that included several subplots that would prove unnecessary to tell the main narrative of Franklin and Jefferson and the Revolutionary period. For example, Flexner, in his notes, assertively wonders at the purpose of discussing optics theory and Newton's *Principia* in relation to Franklin's scientific achievements: "Also, what the hell are the transits of Venus? This is way over people's heads."[58] A unifying theme that emerges from the various comments from the legion of consultants hired to assist the Eames Office was the consultants' concern at both the overly idealistic approach and one that was all too often bogged down in useless details that would ultimately confuse foreign audiences in Paris, Warsaw, and London.[59]

Jack Masey admits, "Eames could be multitiered. Well, he got to the bottom of it. He went deep, deep, deep."[60] In a conversation with Owen Gingerich, Harvard professor of astronomy, Charles Eames himself admitted: "It is true that we set out originally to be quite critical and hard about the main characters, but as we went on, we were so impressed by how much someone like James Madison was able to pull off time and again that we came out pretty much all admiration."[61]

Eames Reboots Jefferson: A Return to Mammoth Politics?

While the foreign media responses to the bison and the exhibition as a whole in Paris, Warsaw, and London would convey wholly positive feedback, an artifact in the exhibition which seemed to escape media attention was the addition of the mammoth bones that Jefferson had sent to the Comte du Buffon almost two hundred years earlier. As discussed in chapter 1, it is clear why Jefferson aimed to prove to European naturalists the robustness of all things American: in order to counter the jingoistic claims that America's flora, fauna, and humanity were in some sense degenerate. Perhaps the showing of the bones in *The World of Franklin and Jefferson* should be interpreted as nothing more than a poetic flourish of exhibition auteur Charles Eames. Yet this transhistorical display of mammoth bones, two instances separated by nearly two hundred years, would occur at two crucial junctures in U.S. history and merits a brief discussion. Both occasions reveal a nation whose identity was less than certain amid turbulent political climates. In his attempts to steer a fledgling America through the uncertain terrain of new nation status, Jefferson as "a gentleman scientist" held aspirations of winning over the hearts and minds and changing the age-worn and fictitious belief structure of Buffon himself and other European naturalists. What was Charles Eames's motive, then? Was it merely to reference a quaint episode from the formative years of our nation, one in which Jefferson, once dubbed "the Mammoth President," played a key role? Or did Eames go even further, incredulously, by employing the metaphor of megafauna as national symbol by adding the enormous stuffed bison for all to see? According to Masey, the bison was, curiously, Eames's favorite artifact in *The World of Franklin and Jefferson*, and it visually dominated the final section of the exhibition on Jefferson and the West. In similar sensational fashion to Jefferson's efforts to send first a moose carcass to Paris and later, with the help of Charles Willson Peale, a selection of bones from the American *incognitum*, Eames sends a bison, a hulking stuffed animal for foreign consumption. According to Eames, the fledgling American republic would emerge as a nation-state full with doubt regarding its survival as an independent sovereign nation: "In 1776 the people who pledged 'their lives, their fortunes, and their sacred honor' did not even feel that the odds were in their favor. They were resolute, but not at all secure, about their chances of surviving on their own. Jefferson, drafting a statement grounded in reason that committed them to total risk, found words that carried a more than rational authority."[62] Perhaps it would be folly to hazard the pairing of these two instances of cultural diplomacy. Both, however, were sanctioned by individuals who sought to make a statement about America. While acknowledging the historical specificity of these two events, it is nevertheless possible to find parallels that suggest a type of American respect for the grandiose and the powerful as evidenced in the mammoth and the bison—two examples of America's national heritage. Essentially, in both instances, the goal of the exhibitors was to educate foreign publics about American society. Historians Leone and Little analyze artifacts as "expressions of society and culture" and foreground the purpose of "historical knowledge, including that of things," in order "to allow for critical knowledge of our own society."[63] Certainly the inclusion of the mammoth bones by Charles Eames could be seen as little more than a reference to Jefferson's obsession with the remains of the mammoth as it fueled his illusions, albeit misguidedly, of American natural and intellectual strength. However, it should be argued that like Jefferson, Charles Eames, too, suffered a similar seduction by the idea of the West. As scholar James Ronda notes, "The most tempting illusion about the West—the one Jefferson clung to with fierce tenacity—was his faith in the West as a unique political and social environment."[64] Did Eames also share this view? There is no reason to doubt that Eames loved his country. But it would be difficult to ascertain whether he saw the bison as a playful symbol of the American West that would charm foreign audiences—specifically Europeans who most likely would not have seen a bison, living or dead, up close—or, as an aesthetically and ideologically alluring symbol of an American identity itself: untamed, uncertain, and without doubt unconventional.

Though obvious contrasts abound between the national self-identity as seen by Jefferson and Peale, and later by Eames, there exist alarmingly few formal differences between the display of the mammoth nearly two hundred years earlier and that of the bison for the American bicentennial. Leone and Little make the charge that

> because we Americans are still embedded in Peale's philosophy about how to think and behave as citizens by learning from an "accurately" and "naturally" presented past, which has inevitably to our present condition, we as "naturally free" and "independent" individuals are trapped in a social presentation of history that forecloses an ability to use history to see our own society in a different way.[65]

It would be imprudent to consider Peale's exhibitionary work through the lens of American politics at the time of the bicentennial. Likewise, to interpret Eames's curatorial choices by way of national self-image in the late eighteenth century proves equally unwise. Importantly, however, both sought to show idealized and perhaps make-believe evidence of American self-worth through the mammoth and the bison. For Peale this should be expected, for he passionately strove to produce a "world in miniature" in his Philadelphia museum. Similarly, Eames employed every display technique necessary to make his exhibitionary statement. Yet through his "inundation effect" of multimedia as the conveyance of the exhibition narrative, the inclusion of the bison should be seen as provocatively allegorical. Jefferson and

Peale were, according to Leone and Little, through their paleontological and archaeological efforts, "rationalizing past time for the natural order," which for them "were their rights, especially their liberty."[66] Eames's idealizing of American megafauna—both the bison and the mammoth bones—in the exhibition setting would serve, arguably, a similar purpose: to narrate the myth of a strong, resilient America in a time of, to borrow President Ford's thought, "extraordinary circumstances." Like Peale in his self-portrait, *The Artist in His Museum*, in which the viewer catches a partial glimpse of the American *incognitum*, Eames provides a similar, just as quizzical entrée into the American identity through the rather surprising appearance of the bison in the final section of *The World of Franklin and Jefferson*. Certainly the mastodon and the bison are real, but are they "America?"

What makes these artifacts intelligible is keeping under consideration the zeitgeist of the era—in which America's identity was in doubt—in which each showman was plying his craft. As Rigal notes, "Peale too had founded his museum in the act of distancing himself from political warfare. As a monument to Peale's dislike of social conflict, the museum constituted social control through the arts of exhibition and display,"[67] yet she claims Peale's museum was in itself "a Jeffersonian-Republican text and a monument to continental empire."[68] Perhaps, as historian Susan Stewart argues, Peale's "collections of cultural and natural objects provided in miniature a synopsis of the New World, linking recent historical events [the American Revolution] to the grand context of nature and providing evidence of a natural providence legitimizing those events."[69]

Within the setting of national museums in Europe, it is questionable whether Eames, whose clients were at the same time both the corporate giant IBM and America's cultural diplomacy instrument, the USIA, would also be able to distance himself from the profound uncertainties of the current American political landscape. Like Peale's exhibits, it is certainly probable *The World of Franklin and Jefferson* would serve for Eames as "an antidote to war's losses and as a gesture against disorder."[70] Equally important, the thematic content of the exhibition held the potential for the ARBA to reclaim the core American values as elucidated in the Declaration of Independence, the Constitution, and the Bill of Rights. Reclamation appropriately designates these values as perhaps the once great ideals that had been eclipsed by the sociopolitical zeitgeist of the early 1970s. At the same time, the exhibition recontextualized the meaning of America by virtue of its focus on the life and times of two of the nation's Founding Fathers, thereby aspiring to breathe new life into a muddled national identity.

As Lipstadt observes, "For the Eameses, the exhibition represented an opportunity to redirect America away from the narcissistic excesses of 'self-love' and its retreat from reason in the 1970s."[71] Yet, in Masey's view, one "never

knew with Eames, what was ideology, what was stuff."[72] This display of nos-
talgia for American democratic virtues, based on the unilateral decisions of
Charles Eames, would also serve as the official government celebration of
"American" heritage, when the exhibition began its two-year tour to Paris,
Warsaw, London, and Mexico City in January of 1975.

Legitimizing the Message? U.S. Cultural Exhibitions in the World of Museums

Prior to the opening of *The World of Franklin and Jefferson* at the Grand
Palais in Paris on January 10, 1975, the USIA sent a memorandum to its
posts worldwide containing descriptions of the exhibition by Charles Eames
himself. Among the information in the memo, Eames summarized the exhibition as follows: "*The World of Franklin and Jefferson* is the world's biggest
and best color tabloid."[73] As definitions for "tabloid" refer both to something
"compressed or condensed into small scope," it also indicates a news format
"featuring stories of violence, crime, or scandal presented in a sensational
manner."[74] Museologist Donald Preziosi starkly contrasts Kirkham's notion of
a "neutral museum world" with an aggressive description of museums not as
static repositories of material culture but as sites of cultural meaning making:
"The museum is one of the most brilliant and powerful genres of modern fiction, sharing with other forms of ideological practice—religion, science, entertainment, the academic disciplines—a variety of methods for the production and factualization of knowledge and its sociopolitical consequences."[75]

The imagery and materials of *The World of Franklin and Jefferson* would
engage over an estimated one million visitors by the finish of its last showing
in Mexico City in 1977, sharing its version of America with a wide variety of
audiences in a number of the most respected museums in the Western world.
Charles and Ray Eames's relatively nonexistent mandate from the exhibition
sponsors allowed the designers extraordinary latitude in how America would
be interpreted for mass consumption at these various sites for what Preziosi
calls a form of "ideological practice." It would not be until Charles Eames's
declarative statement on America returned home following the European leg
of the tour, however, that the significant criticism surrounding the exhibition would be thrown into high relief.

The Openings in Paris, Warsaw, London, and Mexico City

According to an internal USIA bulletin dated January 10, 1975, the French
press responded with gusto to the opening of the exhibition in Paris. *Le*

Figaro celebrated the Eameses, extolling their success "in bringing alive with dazzling clarity, much talent and an infinitude of taste this world of Franklin and Jefferson."[76] Ray Eames in a friendly note to an acquaintance remarked, "At the Grand Palais people were really very kind and seemed to enjoy everything."[77] Charles Eames, in a short missive to a friend, wrote: "I really wish you could have been there—after all the struggle it was very gratifying to see the French response. The people at the show and then the reaction in the Press."[78] *Time* magazine played up the historical bonhomie between the United States and France:

> Two celebrated Americans were at home abroad last week, just as they had been two centuries before. . . . "A most amiable nation to live with" was the way Franklin described the French; and Jefferson wrote that they "love us more, I think, than they do any nation on earth." While that love has cooled somewhat, the exhibition . . . is appropriate. . . . Whatever an American is, however difficult to define, the national character surely has been shaped by Franklin's broad humanism and Jefferson's clear idealism.[79]

Live footage of the opening in Paris appears in the third film the Eames Office produced on the exhibition: *The World of Franklin and Jefferson: The Opening of an Exhibition*, in 1976. This brief, seven-minute recap of the opening served to "celebrate the first opening in the three-year run of *The World of Franklin and Jefferson* exhibition and to permanently record some of its essence and the first-night excitement."[80] (The film shows the installation in progress and the Parisian audience taking in the exhibition, set to a quartet for oboe, clarinet, horn, and bassoon, by Karl Stamitz and played by members of the Berlin Philharmonic.) As the exhibition continued its two-month Paris run at the Grand Palais, generating an estimated fifty thousand visitors, Jeannine Oppewall of the Eames Office wrote urgently to Jack Masey in search of orientation to understand better how the exhibition would connect with Polish visitors at the National Museum in Warsaw, where *The World of Franklin and Jefferson* was set to open on May 17. While the Eames Office had conducted thorough research into the life and times of the exhibition's protagonists, Oppewall deliberately reached out to Masey, typically the lead person on major USIA exhibitions abroad but now a representative of the ARBA, for feedback on reaching the Polish public. She states in a letter:

> One thing which is really important for us to have, we feel, is a statement from the American Embassy in Warsaw. . . . We really need some orientation. It would help tremendously to have something clearly set down about the Polish

contribution to the American Revolution: What people were really important and what were their contributions? What is the Polish view of the American Revolution and the Polish contribution to it?[81]

This episode reveals the attention to detail the Eames Office maintained through the run of the exhibition, tailoring the show to each of its venues. In Warsaw, the Eameses added to the display a medal given to Tadeusz Kosciuszko by the Society of the Cincinnati. The Eames Office also took on the task, through translators, of translating all label copy and catalog text for the various audiences in Paris, Warsaw, London, and Mexico City.[82] Masey, who served the ARBA as special assistant to the administrator for design and exhibitions attended each of the installations and openings for the exhibition. As Masey observes in his report on the event, the opening of *The World of Franklin and Jefferson* in Warsaw included Polish foreign minister Stefan Olszowski and Central Committee Secretariat member Ryszard Frelek, among two thousand other guests who thronged the museum's entrance, forcing important guests such as former minister of culture Stanislaw Wronski to miss the proceedings altogether. The ceremony was opened by museum director Stanislaw Lorentz, U.S. ambassador Davies, and West Virginia governor Arch A. Moore, who served as President Gerald Ford's representative at the opening. Media coverage included a sixty-second nationwide newscast in color of the opening, and several newspaper reports followed the day after, since no papers at that time published on Sunday.[83] Moore's address sought to make cogent, though somewhat facile, observations of the long history of friendship between the United States and Poland:

In 1776, the United States began its long journey to independence. The same year, the Polish patriot, Thaddeus Kosciuzko, arrived to dedicate himself to the ideals of the young American Republic. Thus, at the very inception of the United States, the histories of our two countries were joined—a process which was to repeat itself with cumulative force during the next two centuries. Far apart geographically, the two nations have traditionally been united by common principles and vision.[84]

The two-month Warsaw showing of the exhibition closed on July 9, 1975, and drove an estimated audience of fifty-three thousand people, including visitors from "every Eastern European country and eight republics of the Soviet Union"[85] (figure 5.10). The U.S. embassy had for the previous seven weeks sponsored over thirty special invitational events for over 3,500 political leaders and scholars. These programs included lectures, concerts, and special showings of the films of Charles and Ray Eames in the National Museum

Figure 5.10.   Members of the general public in Warsaw visit *The World of Franklin and Jefferson*, 1975.
American Revolution Bicentennial Administration (ARBA).

theatre, which garnered much enthusiasm from artist unions, design professionals, and architecture organizations. In a cable to the State Department,
the American ambassador declared that Polish National Museum Director
Lorentz "expressed his gratitude and congratulations to the embassy for the
presentation of the exhibition in Poland," adding, "the museum's daily attendance figures for the exhibition had been nearly triple the normal daily
attendance at the museum."[86]

The World of Franklin and Jefferson enjoyed a stately opening reception in
London on September 15, 1975, in the British Museum's Duveen Gallery,
which houses the Elgin Marbles. Both BBC and commercial television and
radio stations covered Vice President Nelson Rockefeller's stroll through
the exhibition, following brief remarks by United States Ambassador Elliot
Richardson, Lord Trevelyan of the British Museum, Rockefeller, and Prime
Minister Harold Wilson. The vice president himself provided a diplomatic
rendering of the shared history of the United States and Great Britain:
"Franklin and Jefferson are representatives of that group of remarkable men
who pledged their lives, their fortunes and their sacred honor to the American cause—mindful of their English heritage and the principles of English
liberty, but determined to build a new Nation in which these principles of
freedom and justice would be guaranteed to all citizens."[87]

Media coverage included over eighty journalists who had turned out for a
Friday preview of the exhibition and question-and-answer session with Charles
Eames. John Warner, from the ARBA, was accompanied by singer and actress
Pearl Bailey, Hopi Indian chief Abbott Sekaquaptewa, USIA director James
Keogh, R. W. Hubner of IBM, and others (figures 5.11–5.12). The British press
lavished praise on the show's creators, with the *Times* declaring, "*The World
of Franklin and Jefferson* has been skillfully contrived by the designers, Charles
and Ray Eames."[88] *The Sunday Times* diagnosed immediately the public-private
partnership that has punctuated American cultural exhibitions abroad since
the beginning: "It is appropriate that the enterprise, called *The World of Franklin and Jefferson*, is that typical, attractive American mix of private and public:
The government has transported the show, but IBM has underwritten much
of the financing." Not losing sight of the Eames and their trademark obsession
with conveying vast amounts of information in the limited space of an exhibition hall, the article stated, "In the area of design, Eames himself is almost as
much a polymath as the heroes his exhibition celebrates. . . . Energy is neatly
conveyed in the intelligent clutter of the exhibition."[89] Ultimately, the *Guardian* on September 17 announced: "This show is . . . a kind of shrine to the
Enlightenment . . . built without the iron logic of Franklin, and without any
visual symbol for the simple, stirring flight of Jefferson's best prose. The prose

Figure 5.11. Jack Masey, John Warner, and guests enjoy the opening reception of *The World of Franklin and Jefferson* in London, 1975.
American Revolution Bicentennial Administration (ARBA).

Figure 5.12.   Queen Elizabeth II visits *The World of Franklin and Jefferson* at the British Museum, London, 1975.
American Revolution Bicentennial Administration (ARBA).

is there, of course, in those thousands of Eames-approved words. In hundreds of smaller panels, nestling uneasily between the little photographs."[90] In London, the final statement in the exhibition concerning Jefferson and his obsession with the exploration of the American wilderness and its by-product, Manifest Destiny, was, according to Cull, "sharpened . . . by cutting back the Jefferson and the West material," which was seen, curiously, "as extraneous to the main purpose of the show."[91] As Masey recalls:

> There was resistance from the director of the British Museum, who said to Charles and me: "I could get some criticism, 'cause, you know you guys took us on in those days." But Eames said, "Quality is what we care about. There will be no propaganda in this exhibition. Here's what happened: two Americans came together and formed a revolution, and this is what they saw, and this is what they felt. And these are the artifacts we're going to show. We're gonna show things that certainly we're going to get from British museums."[92]

Planning for the Mexico City stop for the exhibition took place at the last minute. Following its visits to New York, Chicago, and Los Angeles, Mexico City was considered as an add-on venue promoted by Deputy Assistant

Secretary of State for Inter-American Affairs Bill Luers, in cooperation with the U.S. Information Service of the American embassy and Mexico's Secreatarias de Relaciones Exteriores and Educacion Publica and the Instituto Nacional de Antropologia e Historia. After weeks of translating the label copy and catalogue from English to Spanish at the Eames Office in Venice, California, the exhibition opened on April 15, 1977, for a two-month run at the National Museum of Anthropology in Chapultepec Park. The opening featured comments from Mexican first lady Carmen Lopez Portillo and U.S. poet and author James Dickey, who served as President Jimmy Carter's representative at this event. For this final leg of the tour, a twist was added to the exhibition, based on the Eames Office recommendations, in order to reach out to Mexican audiences. Inserted into the already lengthy list of artifacts, "contemporary portraits, furniture, pottery, large silver ingots and dies of medals made in Mexico were added."[93]

Despite the evident success of the showings of *The World of Franklin and Jefferson* in Paris, Warsaw, London, and Mexico City, the exhibition was, according to Masey, "a drop in the bucket, a seven-city bicentennial" that covered the 120 years of American history from the birth of Franklin in 1706 to Jefferson's death in 1826. While the Eames Office promulgated its own evangelistic vision of what "America" meant, this endeavor revealed through stylized framing of the artifacts a brand of American entrepreneurialism, an aspirational and visionary America, and at times a make-believe America, an image provided by Charles and Ray Eames. As museum scholar Susan Pearce states, "We can analyse the making of meaning in museums. The formation of a collection is an outward extension of the inward self, a private effort to shape the world and create romantic sense of a souvenir, fetishistic or systematic kind."[94] Even without any concrete recommendations from the government, the Eames Office seemed instinctively to set out to project a redeeming image of America to foreign publics. Yet herein lies the conundrum: If the exhibition was indeed an extension of this designer's personal beliefs, then what within the exhibition is identifiable as real versus make-believe? Certainly an exhibition that celebrates the life and times of Franklin and Jefferson is acceptable theoretically for a bicentennial show. However, the derring-do of earlier attempts to show an imperfect image of America, for example, in the *Unfinished Business* section of the American pavilion at Brussels in 1958, would prove glaringly absent from *The World of Franklin and Jefferson*. No attempt to address America as an ongoing "experiment" is evident here. In a way, Eames, IBM, the USIA, and, ultimately, the ARBA played it safe by providing a stable and complimentary snapshot of an idealized and, somewhat arrogantly, a still-exceptional America. As a State Department report states,

> For three years, both the occasion and the spirit of the Bicentennial celebration have been a focal point for USIA's planning and program production. Programs dealing with the history, culture, present-day society, democratic ideals and international objectives—ideas and concepts with which we deal regularly—have been placed in the context of a now two-hundred year old evolving and involved society whose ideals still reverberate around the world.[95]

This official government statement evidences both the certainty of American values and the still-evolving nature of a distinctly American identity.

Epilogue: Opposition to Franklin and Jefferson at Home

> There is a feeling that the Eameses and the American Revolution Bicentennial Administration wanted to portray the full characters, the ironies and ambiguities of their subjects. . . . But in keeping with Bicentennial enthusiasts' generally rosy overview of the last 200 years, some things are glorified to the necessary exclusion of others. For instance, Jefferson's vision of Westward expansion occupies one-quarter of the exhibit. The wholesale massacre of the American Indian this precipitated, however, is not mentioned.[96]

The fourth showing of *The World of Franklin and Jefferson* was scheduled to run from March 5 through May 2, 1976, at the Metropolitan Museum of Art, which served as a cosponsor of the exhibition. In early negotiations with Thomas Hoving, director of the Met, Charles Eames persuasively announced: "I know we're not doing art here, but we're doing an important event."[97] Hoving agreed to host the show during the bicentennial year. The reception by some members of the American press, however, would ultimately devastate the Eameses.

Detractors in the United States, led by art critic Hilton Kramer, perceived *The World of Franklin and Jefferson* as the overstated patriotism of a design team that throughout their careers had remained staunchly apolitical, at least on the surface. Furthermore, this "neatly packaged" and "tremendously well-informed and informative exhibition" conveyed the story of westward expansion naïvely, "within a framework of the inevitability of unproblematic progress."[98] Ultimately, the nation's fraught history over slavery and ongoing catastrophic interactions with Native Americans proved embarrassingly absent from the exhibition narrative.

But *The World of Franklin and Jefferson* was first created with overseas audiences in mind. The foreign press in Paris, Warsaw, and London responded with overwhelming praise for the exhibition. Critics at home, however, would not overlook the involvement of the government agency—the USIA—which many Americans considered nothing more than the propaganda arm of the federal government overseas, when the exhibition traveled to the Metropolitan Museum of Art, the Art Institute of Chicago, and the Los Angeles County Museum of Art. The severest critiques of *Franklin and Jefferson* blasted the exhibition and its designers for presenting a whitewashed version of the history of two utterly complex figures from the American Revolution.

For a nation which had recently dealt with the Watergate scandal and the disgrace of President Nixon, the closing of the door on Vietnam, and out-of-control economic stagnation and monetary inflation, or "stagflation," as it would be called, it would be newly minted President Gerald Ford who, in his State of the Union speech on January 15, 1975, declared: "The state of the Union is not good."[99] Certainly, the dissonance between the harsh sociopolitical realities of early 1970s America and the halcyon vision portrayed in *The World of Franklin and Jefferson* raised the ire of critics who complained the exhibition was "shallow—garish and jingoist" and "a Turkish bazaar of *American Heritage*-like images and disconnected bits of information."[100] Several critics, moreover, condemned what turned out to be one of Charles Eames's favorite artifacts in the exhibition, the stuffed bison from the Field Museum in Chicago: "The bison, golden russet, vast, hairy, very dead—is a climax of the Bicentennial display, designed by Charles and Ray Eames through a grant by IBM, the computer giant, which sponsors the event on its international tour (Paris, Warsaw, London, New York, Chicago, Los Angeles, Mexico City, and then, I suppose, a Hollywood contract)."[101]

The night of the grand opening in New York, IBM put on a party at the Met, a sit-down dinner in the armory gallery. For a few brief moments, everything seemed to be moving along smoothly. As Masey describes,

> It was fabulous. Everybody spoke and Eames was glorious. It was wonderful. And the press came through because IBM invited them to dinner. But then I'm having breakfast with the Eameses the next morning in this broken-down coffee shop near the Met, saying "Wasn't last night great, the opening?" Somebody from Eames's staff arrives at the table, looking kind of shaken: "Did any of you at this table see the *New York Times* today?" We said no. "I don't know if I should show this to you or not." I had never seen Eames so shaken in my life.[102]

In the *New York Times* arts and leisure section that morning, Hilton Kramer excoriated *The World of Franklin and Jefferson* in a full-page review of the show. The title of the article, "What's This Stuff Doing at the Met?" set the tone for what followed. The photo accompanying the article featured the prized bison Eames had borrowed from the Field Museum, symbolizing Jefferson and the westward movement, the unknown territory America was claiming under the rationale of Manifest Destiny. Kramer's direct and bitter message, a questioning of why a government exhibition would be displayed in one of the leading art museums in the world, aimed directly at Hoving and Eames himself. Kramer unleashes on the appearance of the show:

> These color photographs . . . give us an anonymous, immaculate, idealized, unreal glimpse of a never-never land—a world at once cozy and glamorous, without flaws or imperfections, where the light always glows with an amber warmth and all emotions are either noble or picturesque. The effect of these photographs, which truly dominate the exhibition and determine its character, is deliberately sedative, deliberately designed to comfort and reassure. What is true of these slick photographs is true of the show as a whole—it is designed to "sell" us something. . . . We do not go to museums to be "sold" something, to be propagandized, to look at reproductions or be treated to laughable simplifications about one of the most heroic and complex periods in the history of the modern world.[103]

But the question remains: Why would foreign audiences look so favorably on *Franklin and Jefferson* while critics at home scorned its message? It is certainly worth consideration that the foreign publics who visited the exhibition in Europe and Mexico would be less attuned to the troubled contemporary political scenario in the United States at the time and thus more disposed to welcoming an exhibition featuring an objectified "America" that ultimately poses no challenge to one's identity. At home, critics desecrated what they deemed an oversimplified explanation of American identities and values as conceived by the Eames Office. Compounded by the arguably less-than-ideal choice of the Metropolitan Museum of Art as a venue, *The World of Franklin and Jefferson* provided critics the necessary incentive to lay low what they saw as little more than a propaganda exhibition on home soil.

On July 12, 1976, historian Barbara Tuchman wrote an article for *Newsweek* titled, "On Our Birthday—America as Idea." While the United States is "a nation consciously conceived," she states, the United States has "slid a long way from the original idea." And yet, citing a comment from a foreign visitor that hope is "domiciled in America as the Pope is in Rome," Tuchman reflects positively on America: "The ideal society for which mankind has been striving through the ages will remain forever beyond our grasp.

But if the great question, whether it is still possible to reconcile democracy with social order and individual liberty, is to find a positive answer, it will be here."[104] After an opportunity to hear Charles Eames himself describe the *Franklin and Jefferson* exhibition, USIA representative Al Jones offered the following: "This is an exhibit which seeks to capture the tentative, the cluttered, the unfinished reality of our Revolutionary experiment by avoiding rigid didacticism and precise definition."[105]

In a way, the domestic criticism surrounding *The World of Franklin and Jefferson* offered a corrective, however harshly, of the idea that not only did America have "unfinished business," but the nation itself was an unfinished reality, continually endeavoring to discover its elusive self. Jehane Burns, in her extensive research notes for the exhibition, declared that "the truer and more interesting story is one of gradual developments in America, snowballing her towards autonomy," of which a contributing factor was "an increasing sense of American identity."[106] Referencing the continental wilderness acquired through the Louisiana Purchase, Jones interprets the final section of the exhibition, based on the comments by Charles Eames:

> But another wilderness—the labyrinth of international involvement—also confronted the new American republic. Could the Constitution survive this challenge as well? That is the unanswered question with which *The World of Franklin and Jefferson* ends, reminding us not only of the great achievements of the two men and their generation, but also of the unfinished tasks they left to their heirs.[107]

In the end, *The World of Franklin and Jefferson* exhibition offered an aspirational take on the best ideas on which the nation was founded at a time during the mid-1970s when the United States sought a way to remake itself in the eyes of the world. Cull interprets the global reach of the bicentennial programming as gaining significantly positive results for America's self-image:

> The celebration had reintroduced the world—and especially Western Europe—to the America of its best imaginings. With the USIA's help, Europe remembered the idealistic land of Franklin and Jefferson: the land of Kennedy rather than the land of Nixon. With Watergate and Vietnam now closed books, Western Europe seemed to be ready to take a second look at America. Looking back on the period, Mike Schneider of ICS put the agency's achievement simply: "The bicentennial rehumanized the image of America."[108]

This time, the telling of "America's story to the world" brought the evolution of the American character back to square one, describing a time when Americans established their independence from Europe, attained self-government, and began to forge an identity that remains unresolved.

Notes

1. Charles Eames, "The Language of Vision: The Nuts and Bolts," *Bulletin of the American Academy of Arts and Sciences* 28, no. 1 (October 1974): 23.

2. Nicholas J. Cull, *The Cold War and the United States Information Agency: American Propaganda and Public Diplomacy, 1945–1989* (Cambridge: Cambridge University Press, 2008), 351.

3. Masey, interview with author, August 24, 2010.

4. According to Lipstadt, it was as early as 1970 that "the Paris post of the USIA . . . conceived a show on Jefferson as the 'counterpoint' to a recent Soviet Union–sponsored exhibition on Lenin." See "'Natural Overlap:' Charles and Ray Eames and the Federal Government," in *The Work of Charles and Ray Eames: A Legacy of Invention*, ed. Diana Murphy (New York: Abrams / Library of Congress / Vitra Design Museum, 1997), 168. However, unlike the smaller thematic shows sent by the USIA to the Soviet Union after the Moscow exhibition in 1959, *The World of Franklin and Jefferson* was never intended to visit the Soviet Union. Originally planned for a Paris showing only, it grew from there. As Masey states, "Of course, because we saw how really quite great it was to be the symbol of the American bicentennial, we planned extensively for it to move on to Warsaw and London, and then to the Met in 1976," from interview, August 24, 2010.

5. See Angela Romano, "Détente, Entente, or Linkage? The Helsinki Conference on Security and Cooperation in Europe in U.S. Relations with the Soviet Union," *Diplomatic History* 33, no. 4 (September 2009): 703. The United States, at this time, continued to demand an open reciprocity in cultural exchange with the Soviet Union. The 1975 Helsinki Accords looms large in this effort. For an understanding of the "third basket" of the Helsinki Accords, which advocated for the free flow of cultural exchanges between the West and the Eastern Bloc, see Cull, *The Cold War and the United States Information Agency*, 340. For a Russian perspective that promoted the same, see Andrei Sakharov, "Open Letter to the United States Congress," in *The Human Rights Reader*, rev. ed., ed. Walter Laqueur and Barry Rubin (New York: New American Library, 1979), 334–36.

6. Romano, "Détente, Entente, or Linkage?," 707.

7. Ibid., 707–8.

8. For more analysis on the issues that beset the United States and its leadership at the time, see historian James T. Patterson, *Grand Expectations: The United States, 1945–1974* (Oxford: Oxford University Press, 1996), 781: "Policy-making from 1974 through 1976 did not differ much from what it would likely have been with Nixon in command. President Ford, after pardoning his predecessor, avoided new frontiers. Instead, he struggled much of the time to deal with already existing problems: tensions over court-mandated busing and affirmative action, highly emotional debates over abortion, and above all stagnation of the economy."

9. Jeffrey P. Kimball, "Out of the Primordial Cultural Ooze: Inventing Political and Policy Legacies about the U.S. Exit from Vietnam," *Diplomatic History* 34, no. 3 (June 2010): 577.

10. Patterson, *Grand Expectations*, 787. See also Tom Wolfe, "The Me Decade and the Third Great Awakening," in *The Purple Decades: A Reader*, ed. Tom Wolfe (London: Vintage, 2005), 165–96; Christopher Lasch, *The Culture of Narcissism: American Life in an Age of Diminishing Expectations* (London: Norton, 1991).

11. See "The American Revolution Bicentennial Commemoration: International Programs, A Summary Report," in MC468 Bureau of Educational and Cultural Affairs Historical Collection (CU), Box 355, Folder "American Revolution Bicentennial Commission," University of Arkansas, Fayetteville, 2. For President Nixon's September 11, 1970, report to Congress, see also Library of Congress, Charles and Ray Eames Papers, Research/Production, Exhibits, World of Franklin and Jefferson, United States Information Agency, 1970–1971, Box 192, Folder 9.

12. Cull, *The Cold War and the United States Information Agency*, 352.

13. Masey recalls: "The commission was run by a guy named John Warner, who would later become a U.S. senator. He married Elizabeth Taylor. He brought her by Jackson Place. They didn't last long," from interview, August 24, 2010.

14. Ibid.

15. Ibid.

16. For more background on events leading to the engagement of Eames as the exhibition designer for *The World of Franklin and Jefferson*, see August 23, 1973, letter from Hugh A. Hall, Acting Director, American Revolution Bicentennial Commission (ARBC), to Anne L. Armstrong, Counsellor to the President, in which Hall invites White House personnel to view Charles Eames's introductory film on the idea for the exhibition, in NA RG452, American Revolution Bicentennial Administration, Design and Exhibit Prog. Rec. Franklin and Jefferson Exhibit, '73–'75, Box 136, E-30, Folder "EXH 5-5, The World of Franklin and Jefferson, General (Memos, letters, info)."

17. Masey, interview, August 24, 2010. See also "The American Revolution Bicentennial Commemoration: International Programs, A Summary Report," in MC468 Bureau of Educational and Cultural Affairs Historical Collection (CU), Box 355, Folder "American Revolution Bicentennial Commission," University of Arkansas, Fayetteville, 16. Under the heading "Major Problems," the ARBA cited issues that "beset the development and implementation of the international program—uncertainty as to funding, delayed decisions, lack of an effective mechanism for programming certain incoming artistic groups and exhibits, high level visits, and assistance for international visitors."

18. Memorandum, James Keogh, Director, USIA, to Anne Armstrong, Counsellor to the President, in MC468 Bureau of Educational and Cultural Affairs Historical Collection (CU), Box 355, Folder "American Revolution Bicentennial Commission," University of Arkansas, Fayetteville. As usual, the USIA's focus with cultural programming was geared to foreign audiences and the message USIA-sponsored programs would convey to these publics. President Nixon, at the same time, extended a "Bicentennial Invitation to the World" in his address of July 4, 1972. Nixon had earlier in the Bicentennial Commission's Report to the Congress in September 1970 hoped "that foreign visitors and visiting groups, including artists and performers, will travel to every corner of the Nation and participate in as many Bicentennial events

as possible." Nixon would call the period from 1972 to 1976 the "Bicentennial Era." For more on the president's aspirations for the bicentennial, see circular airgram from Department of State to all diplomatic posts, in above folder.

19. Ibid., 11.

20. Masey, interview, August 24, 2010.

21. Cull, *The Cold War and the United States Information Agency*, 352. For elucidation of government concerns of expanding the theme from Jefferson to both Franklin and Jefferson, see also February 20, 1973, letter from Charles H. Clarke, Acting Chief, Exhibits Division, United States Information Agency to Charles Eames, in Library of Congress, Charles and Ray Eames Papers, Research/Production, Exhibits, World of Franklin and Jefferson, United States Information Agency, 1973, Box 192, Folder 10. See additional letters in this folder for more from the USIA's point of view toward the Charles Eames–led shift from the original *Age of Jefferson* exhibition concept to include both Franklin and Jefferson.

22. See Donald Albrecht, "Introduction," in *The Work of Charles and Ray Eames: A Legacy of Invention*, ed. Diana Murphy (New York: Abrams / Library of Congress / Vitra Design Museum, 1997), 15.

23. For an understanding of the separation of duties among the USIA, the ARBC, and the Eames Office, see the November 8, 1974, letter from William B. Davis, Deputy Assistant Director (Exhibits), USIA, to Masey, which includes: "Agreement between the American Revolution Bicentennial Administration and the United States Information Agency for Showing 'The Age of Franklin and Jefferson' Exhibit in Paris, Warsaw, and London in 1975," in RG452, American Revolution Bicentennial Administration, Design and Exhibit Prog. Rec. Franklin and Jefferson Exhibit, '73–'75, Box 136, E-30, Folder "EXH 5-1, The World of Franklin and Jefferson, Transfer Agreement/USIA-ARBC-Eames."

24. Masey, interview, August 24, 2010.

25. Ibid.

26. See Lipstadt, "Natural Overlap," 151.

27. See Jeffrey Meikle, *Design in the USA* (Oxford: Oxford University Press, 2005), 171–72.

28. Joseph Giovannini, "The Office of Charles Eames and Ray Kaiser: The Material Trail," in *The Work of Charles and Ray Eames: A Legacy of Invention*, ed. Diana Murphy (New York: Abrams / Library of Congress / Vitra Design Museum, 1997), 66.

29. Jehane Burns, "Introduction," in *The World of Franklin and Jefferson*, ed. Jehane Burns (Los Angeles: Office of Charles and Ray Eames, 1976), 2.

30. Kathleen McLean, "Museum Exhibitions and the Dynamics of Dialogue," *Daedalus* 128, no. 3 (Summer 1999): 93.

31. Lipstadt, "Natural Overlap," 151.

32. Ibid., 154. Lipstadt makes clear that for the Eameses, their beliefs were not "identical to those of the federal government, only that the Eameses did not shrink from using the USIA commissions as an opportunity for conveying political ideas, just as the USIA did not shrink from employing the Eameses to convey its own ideas," ibid.

33. Ibid., 166.

34. See John Neuhart, Marilyn Neuhart, and Ray Eames, *Eames Design: The Work of the Office of Charles and Ray Eames* (New York: Abrams, 1989), 14.

35. Lipstadt, "Natural Overlap," 152.

36. Pat Kirkham, *Charles and Ray Eames: Designers of the Twentieth Century* (Cambridge, MA: MIT Press, 1995), 263. See also Philip C. Repp, "The Information Design Lessons: Selected Films by Charles and Ray Eames," *LOOP: AIGA Journal of Interaction Design Education*, no. 2 (April 2001): 1: "Even Alvin Toffler, who popularized the term 'information overload,' could not have imagined the scale with which our culture moves and consumes information today—the creation and management of information has become a multibillion-dollar global industry. The Eameses realized that one of the critical 'handlers' of information was the designer."

37. Masey, interview, August, 24, 2010.

38. See Neuhart, Neuhart, and Eames, *Eames Design*, 231.

39. See Charles Eames, "Language of Vision: The Nuts and Bolts," 16; and Lucia Dewey Eames, "The Eames Films Are the Eames Essays" (Los Angeles: Eames Office, 2001), www.eamesoffice.com/resources/essay.html. In this short essay, Lucia Dewey Eames comments on the rationale behind the Eameses' films: "To discover the films as essays is to uncover a rich vein. . . . This quality of films is closely tied to the notion of models. Models in the Eames view were an important way to get a handle on the world and to understand a problem. Looking at the Eames' work in overview, one sees a strong thread of model making; a sense that the best way to understand a problem was to create a model of it, and then rework it and refine it constantly."

40. See Neuhart, Neuhart, and Eames, *Eames Design*, 391.

41. Masey, interview, August 24, 2010.

42. Ibid. For the extended-length film, which ran roughly twenty-eight minutes, Eames hired Orson Welles and Nina Foch to narrate, with the soundtrack composed by Elmer Bernstein. For more on this film, see Neuhart, Neuhart, and Eames, *Eames Design*, 429.

43. See Charles Eames, "On Reducing Discontinuity," *Bulletin of the American Academy of Arts and Sciences* 30, no. 6 (March 1977): 32.

44. Ibid., 24–25.

45. See Charles Eames, "Language of Vision: The Nuts and Bolts," 67.

46. Kirkham, *Charles and Ray Eames*, 266. Kirkham adds: "The best of the exhibitions were exciting experiences; in the worst there was just too much of everything," and that "in the case of *The World of Franklin and Jefferson* (1975–1977), for example, it seemed to some that the Eameses did not know when to stop the additive process," ibid., 266, 457.

47. Ibid., 269. Repp summarizes the three main lessons of information management as evidenced in the Eameses' films. These lessons, arguably, should be considered when studying *The World of Franklin and Jefferson* exhibition, which, in a way, was conceptualized through film first. The three lessons are as follows: "1. Redundant information must have an association with the familiar. If the viewer is given too

much unique information, the result is visual noise. 2. Simultaneous display of information must be predicated on the notion of simplicity. There is a critical point at which the synchronous presentation of information crosses over to the confusion of noise. 3. The comprehension of information is not a passive experience; rather it can be an active one. The viewer has the capacity, through the design of the information, to dynamically sort among the layers of data presented," in Repp, "The Information Design Lessons," 10.

48. See Kirkham, *Charles and Ray Eames*, 272.

49. See Neuhart, Neuhart, and Eames, *Eames Design*, 417.

50. For the institutional and private lenders to the exhibition, including the list of artifacts, documents, and photographs borrowed, see Library of Congress, Charles and Ray Eames Papers, Research/Production, Exhibits, Folder: World of Franklin and Jefferson, Inventories and Lists, Box 177, Folder 5. For lender agreements, see Folder 6.

51. Lipstadt, "Natural Overlap," 153.

52. See Neuhart, Neuhart, and Eames, *Eames Design*, 418. The exhibition space also included "two panoplies of flags, weapons, and musical instruments from the Revolutionary War." And "new paintings, sculpture, costumes, and artifacts from the eighteenth century were added to each installation," ibid.

53. Kirkham, *Charles and Ray Eames*, 292.

54. Ibid., 304.

55. Ibid.

56. Library of Congress, Charles and Ray Eames Papers, Research/Production Exhibits, World of Franklin and Jefferson, Consultants, Box 174, Folder 5, "Consultants, I. Bernard Cohen," 1.

57. Library of Congress, Charles and Ray Eames Papers, Research/Production Exhibits, World of Franklin and Jefferson, Consultants, Box 174, Folder 6, "Consultants, James Flexnor," 2.

58. Ibid., 15–16.

59. For the extensive list of consultants, board members, and the advisory council attached to *The World of Franklin and Jefferson* exhibition, see Library of Congress, Charles and Ray Eames Papers, Research/Production, Exhibits, Folder: World of Franklin and Jefferson, Consultants, General, Box 174, Folder 7.

60. Masey, interview, August 24, 2010.

61. As quoted in Kirkham, *Charles and Ray Eames*, 295. See also Owen Gingerich, "A Conversation with Charles Eames," *American Scholar* 46, no. 3 (Summer 1977): 335.

62. Charles Eames, "On Reducing Discontinuity," 28. This quote comes from the narration for the film *The World of Franklin and Jefferson* that accompanied the exhibition from 1974 through 1976 to Paris, Warsaw, London, and Mexico City.

63. Mark P. Leone and Barbara J. Little, "Artifacts as Expressions of Society and Culture: Subversive Genealogy and the Value of History," in *Museum Studies: An Anthology of Contexts*, ed. Bettina Messias Carbonell (Malden, MA: Blackwell, 2004), 362.

64. James P. Ronda, "Passion and Imagination in the Exploration of the American West," in *A Companion to the American West*, ed. William Deverell (Malden, MA: Blackwell, 2004), 55.

65. Leone and Little, "Artifacts as Expressions of Society and Culture," 363.

66. Ibid., 367.

67. Rigal, 108.

68. Ibid. See also Susan Stewart, "Death and Life, in That Order, in the Works of Charles Willson Peale," in *The Cultures of Collecting*, ed. John Elsner and Roger Cardinal (London: Reaktion, 1994), 207. Stewart similarly describes Peale's museum collections as a "nationalist narrative . . . linked to Peale's own psychological history and to the religious and intellectual climate of his day."

69. Stewart, *The Cultures of Collecting*, 207.

70. Ibid., 223.

71. Lipstadt, "Natural Overlap," 170.

72. Masey, as quoted in Lipstadt, "Natural Overlap," 171.

73. See memorandum from Al Jones to all USIS Staff, January 9, 1975, Library of Congress, Charles and Ray Eames Papers, Research/Production, Exhibits, Folder: World of Franklin and Jefferson, Reviews, Publicity, Box 181, Folder 2, 1.

74. *Merriam-Webster's Collegiate Dictionary*, 11th ed., s.v. "tabloid."

75. Donald Preziosi, "Collecting/Museums," in *Critical Terms for Art History*, 2nd ed., ed. Robert S. Nelson and Richard Shiff (Chicago: University of Chicago Press, 2003), 407.

76. See Library of Congress, Charles and Ray Eames Papers, Research/Production, Exhibits, Folder: World of Franklin and Jefferson, Publicity, Box 180, Folder 10, USIA Bulletin, 3. For reviews in French newspapers, see, for instance, Jean-Marie Dunoyer, "Le Nouveau Monde au Grand Palais: Franklin et Jefferson," *Le Monde* (Paris), January 12, 1975.

77. Library of Congress, Charles and Ray Eames Papers, Research/Production, Exhibits, Folder: World of Franklin and Jefferson, Publicity, Box 180, Folder 10. Richard Arndt points out in the preface to his study of American cultural diplomacy that Franklin and Jefferson had long before charmed the French people: "Speaking French after a fashion and learning by trial and error, these men set two distinct styles for formal US diplomacy—Franklin leading from his worldwide scientific reputation, his wit, his guile, and a touch of theater, and Jefferson, from his hands-on experience of shaping democracy, impeccable diplomatic behavior, wise political counsel, intellectual curiosity, and shrewd eye for France's landholdings." Richard Arndt, "Preface," in *The First Resort of Kings: American Cultural Diplomacy in the Twentieth Century* (Washington, DC: Potomac, 2006), 11.

78. Library of Congress, Charles and Ray Eames Papers, Research/Production, Exhibits, Folder: World of Franklin and Jefferson, Publicity, Box 180, Folder 10.

79. *Time*, January 20, 1975. See also Memorandum from CU—L. Arthur Minnich to CU—Mr. John Richardson, Jr., January 7, 1975, Subject: Paris Bicentennial Exhibit (includes 1. Bicentennial Delegation for Exhibit Opening, 2. Events—January 10, 1975,

3. France and the Bicentennial, 4. Exhibit Press Releases; Memorandum from CU—L. Arthur Minnich to CU—Mr. John Richardson, Jr., March 18, 1975, Subject: Weekly Activities Report, March 12–18: "The exhibit was acclaimed for its imagination, innovation and exquisite taste. Significant for the long term is the impact of the Exhibit in reflecting the high intellectual power of American society even 200 years ago and in exposing thousands of young people to the wellsprings of our society. The Exhibit now moves to Warsaw for its May opening."

80. Neuhart, Neuhart, and Eames, *Eames Design*, 427.

81. Letter to Jack Masey from Jeannine Oppewall, January 31, 1975, in Library of Congress, Charles and Ray Eames Papers, Research/Production, Exhibits, World of Franklin and Jefferson, United States Information Agency, 1975, Box 193, Folder 2.

82. See, for example, the June 17, 1974, letter from Masey to Michael D. Schneider, Special Assistant, Office of Assistant Director (Information Centers), U.S. Information Agency, that addresses the urgency and vagaries of translating into French all label copy and catalog text of *The World of Franklin and Jefferson* prior to the Paris opening, in RG452, American Revolution Bicentennial Administration, Design and Exhibit Prog. Rec. Franklin and Jefferson Exhibit, '73–'75, Box 136, E-30, Folder "EXH 5-5, The World of Franklin and Jefferson, General (Memos, letters, info)."

83. See Masey report on Warsaw opening, in Library of Congress, Charles and Ray Eames Papers, Research/Production, Exhibits, World of Franklin and Jefferson, Venues, National Museum, Warsaw, Miscellany, Box 198, Folder 3, 1–2.

84. See entirety of Governor Moore's address in Library of Congress, Charles and Ray Eames Papers, Research/Production, Exhibits, World of Franklin and Jefferson, Venues, National Museum, Warsaw, Miscellany, Box 198, Folder 3. The address included an unsubtle comment on Soviet political tactics in Poland: "Speaking for all of us, the sons and daughters of immigrants, President Wilson said, 'We came to America, either ourselves or in the persons of our ancestors, to better the ideals of men, to make them see finer things than they had seen before, to get rid of the things that divide and to make sure of the things that unite.' It is no coincidence that President Wilson also demanded the restoration of an independent Poland. . . . In the 1970s, the message of the World of Franklin and Jefferson assumes greater significance. The world grows smaller; we are all members of an increasingly complex and interdependent global community," 1–2.

85. See cable from Ambassador Richard Davies, American Embassy, Warsaw, in Library of Congress, Charles and Ray Eames Papers, Research/Production, Exhibits, World of Franklin and Jefferson, Venues, National Museum, Warsaw, Miscellany, Box 198, Folder 3, 1. The cable further states: "Comments have been unanimously favorable, ranging from guardedly mild praise to absolute enthusiasm, for what has been, without a doubt, the most successful and impressive show the United States has ever mounted in Poland."

86. Ibid., 2.

87. For entire text of Rockefeller's opening remarks, see: RG452, American Revolution Bicentennial Adminstration, Design and Exhibit Prog. Rec. Franklin and

Jefferson Exhibit, '73–'75, Box 136, E-30, Folder "EXH 5-10, The World of Franklin and Jefferson, London."

88. See *Times* (London), September 17, 1975.

89. See *Sunday Times* (London), September 14, 1975.

90. See *Guardian*, September 17, 1975.

91. See Cull, *The Cold War and the United States Information Agency*, 355.

92. Masey, interview, August 24, 2010.

93. See Neuhart, Neuhart, and Eames, *Eames Design*, 419. For publicity surrounding the Mexico City opening, see Library of Congress, Charles and Ray Eames Papers, Research/Production, Exhibits, World of Franklin and Jefferson, Venues, National Museum of Anthropology, Publicity, Box 199, Folder 2.

94. See Susan M. Pearce, *Museums, Objects, and Collections: A Cultural Study* (Washington, DC: Smithsonian Institution, 1992), 257.

95. See "USIA and the Bicentennial Celebration Report," in MC468 Bureau of Educational and Cultural Affairs Historical Collection (CU), Box 291, Folder "USIA, [1976]," University of Arkansas Libraries Special Collections Division, ii.

96. Emily Van Ness, "A Slick Salute to Aesthete Tom and Practical Ben," *Evening Times* (Trenton, NJ), March 5, 1976, C1.

97. As quoted by Masey, interview, August 24, 2010.

98. Kirkham, *Charles and Ray Eames*, 294–95.

99. See Romano, "Détente, Entente, or Linkage?," 718. Describing the domestic zeitgeist at the time of *The World of Franklin and Jefferson*, historian Romano observes: "In early 1975, the economic crisis that had hit the industrialized countries after the oil shock in 1973 markedly affected the United States: unemployment, inflation, a growing balance deficit, and the deepest recession since the thirties. . . . He [President Ford] therefore declared that the first goal of the administration was to recover the American economy and thus postponed the building of good international relations," ibid.

100. See Larry Rosing, "Bison-tennial Show: The Bazaar World of Franklin & Jefferson," *New Age Examiner* (Summer 1976), 65.

101. See, for example, Thomas B. Hess, "From 'Bisontennial' Beasts to Cornell Boxes," *New York Magazine*, March 22, 1976, 59.

102. Masey, interview, August 24, 2010.

103. See Hilton Kramer, "What Is This Stuff Doing at the Met?" *New York Times*, March 14, 1976, 28. Masey remembers the Eameses' reaction to the review: "They were so shaken. They had their souls in this exhibit. So I said, 'Calm down. It's life. We have to endure it. If this is the worst review you ever got, boy, you're lucky.' They were hurt. They felt it would be a great experience. But you never can predict," from interview, August 24, 2010. For the Eameses' discussion of the Kramer article, see Library of Congress, Charles and Ray Eames Papers, Research/Production, Exhibits, Folder: World of Franklin and Jefferson, Publicity, Kramer, Hilton, Box 180, Folder 10.

104. See the entire article in Barbara W. Tuchman, *Practicing History: Selected Essays* (New York: Ballantine, 1982), 304–6.

105. See memorandum from Al Jones to all USIS Staff, January 9, 1975, in Library of Congress, Charles and Ray Eames Papers, Research/Production, Exhibits, Folder: World of Franklin and Jefferson, Reviews, Publicity, Box 181, Folder 2, 2.

106. See Library of Congress, Charles and Ray Eames Papers, Research/Production, Exhibits, World of Franklin and Jefferson, Burns, Jehane, Research Files (1 of 9), Box 188, Folder 6, 3.

107. See memorandum from Al Jones to all USIS Staff, January 9, 1975, in Library of Congress, Charles and Ray Eames Papers, Research/Production, Exhibits, Folder: World of Franklin and Jefferson, Reviews, Publicity, Box 181, Folder 2, 2.

108. Cull, *The Cold War and the United States Information Agency*, 358.

Conclusion

> Of all the nations in the world, the United States was built in nobody's image. It was the land of the unexpected, of unbounded hope, of ideals, of quest for an unknown perfection. It is all the more unfitting that we should offer ourselves in images. And all the more fitting that the images which we make wittingly or unwittingly to sell America to the world should come back to haunt and curse us. Perhaps, instead of announcing ourselves by our shadows and our idols, we would do better to try to share with others the quest which has been America.[1]

For 150 years before the onset of the Cold War, the United States sporadically employed cultural exhibitions—the display of a vast range of artifacts, from natural history specimens to industrial goods to fine art—in order to project American values to foreign audiences. These endeavors revealed through the stylized framing of artifacts a brand of American entrepreneurialism, a visionary and, at times, make-believe America. These images, provided by exhibition designers, would become the official government statement on "America" at these junctures, which more often than not revealed both the certainty of American values and the still-evolving nature of a distinct American identity.

The science of exhibiting U.S. culture has been a challenge since Thomas Jefferson displayed a moose carcass from Vermont in his apartment on the Champs-Élysées to prove to the Comte du Buffon that Americans and their fauna were not degenerate. From the beginning, America has battled perceptions of degeneracy against a world public opinion that doubts its motives,

257

strength, and ability to be a free nation. Back then, the United States had yet to articulate a substantial cultural diplomacy plan and with it the decision-making process of what America would show of itself to foreign audiences. Later, President Jefferson teamed with artist, curator, and lay scientist Charles Willson Peale to display the American *incognitum*—an excavated mastodon thought to be a mammoth—to prove to European skeptics at its showing in London that the nascent American nation was in fact a worthy actor on the world stage.

President Fillmore's sponsorship, though lackluster, of the American pavilion at the Great Exhibition of 1851, with enthusiastic help from the fledgling Smithsonian Institution, set the precedent for U.S. involvement in world's fairs for the following century. There, in the Crystal Palace in Hyde Park, on an enormous parcel of gallery floor space requested by the American committee, the U.S. exhibition commissioners displayed an array of products (for the emphasis of the Great Exhibition was indeed the sharing in one place of "the industries of all nations"). This time, the "America" displayed caught the attention of a skeptical British press who, in the end, embraced the Yankee efforts at innovation through, among other products, Cyrus McCormick's Virginia grain reaper, Matthew Brady's daguerreotypes, Indian rubber goods by Charles Goodyear, and Samuel Colt's revolvers. Lesser and more curious items included an "air-exhausted coffin" that could hold off a corpse's physical decay, transparent soaps meant to resemble stained glass, Cincinnati pickles, and Hiram Powers's sculpture, *Greek Slave*, which *Punch* took as a cue to mock America's position on human slavery, an issue which the Compromise of 1850 could not prevent from tearing the United States apart ten years later.

During World War II, the U.S. government joined forces with the Museum of Modern Art to sponsor intrahemispheric unity through art competitions with the aim of thwarting the advance of Nazism in America's sphere of influence. As this study asserts, these examples represent milestones in a long trajectory of national identity making. As stated at the outset, the ultimate aim of this study is to make intelligible the significance of this singular aspect of cultural diplomacy—American cultural exhibitions sent overseas to win the hearts and minds of foreign publics. This study has established four major conclusions.

The Timeframe of 1955–1975 Was the Heyday of U.S. Cultural Exhibitions Abroad

All the exhibitions started going downhill in the late seventies and early eighties. The force in USIA diminished over time. The later years are not of much consequence. And when the Berlin Wall came down, it was over. The story, however, *is* the *expertise* in the agency and the entropy of USIA's capabilities.[2]

The cultural exhibitions executed by the U.S. government from 1955 to 1975 draw out direct references to earlier American attempts at cultural production through exhibitions for national prestige. Further, all of these attempts to rationalize American values and policies to foreign publics suggest a reliance on the sensational and at times the chauvinistic. Themes of cultural jingoism in the display of animal symbols, such as the mastodon in 1803 and the looming eagle at the Great Exhibition of 1851, resonate in the cultural paternalism of the poster competition during World War II that advocated a distinct U.S. superiority over its hemispheric neighbors. This will to national power, born from national insecurity, was paralleled by a will to identity, a process that Goffman calls "self-making," through these creative exploits.

One such method for winning over audiences was through promoting a desire for the emulation of "American" domestic life, with the goal of supplanting the notion of rational utility; a condition Thorstein Veblen called "conspicuous consumption." In this scenario, the suspension of the utilitarian in addressing one's actual needs requires an embrace of the make-believe. This study has also invoked the theories of semiotician Umberto Eco, who sees trade fairs and world fair pavilions as modern day *wunderkammern* in which the visitor is subject to a "prestige function" that celebrates "a dynasty or a town as a commercial, cultural, or religious center." This "hyperreality," according to Eco, includes fairs and expos, which he deems adult Disneylands, where "concern for the Space Age is combined with nostalgia for a fairytale past."[3]

Following Eco, it can be concluded that these exhibitions as sponsored by the United States government functioned as meaning makers in which this exhibitionary blitz of fantasy houses, cars, and other products, displayed in avant-garde architectural structures, broadcast to audiences around the world an imaginary American utopia of "domestic simulacra."[4] Certainly, after World War II, cultural diplomacy practitioners discovered a clear rationale for the winning over of foreign publics to American values: the advent of the Cold War and the ideological struggle between the United States and the Soviet Union.[5] In the mid-1950s, trade fairs became the testing ground for foreign attitudes toward America. Through trial and error, the U.S. pavilions at these events would follow a balance of both Misha Black's and Herbert Bayer's display styles, moderated by the straightforward modernism of the international style that was first introduced by the Museum of Modern Art in the early 1930s. This metaphorical and aesthetic language symbolizing the American dream, enjoyed to some degree by American consumers at home, reached its apogee in the American National Exhibition in Moscow in 1959. This cultural exhibition, executed through the participation of the American government—namely Jack Masey, the USIA's "man in the trenches"—and a crack team of industrial designers, including George Nelson, R. Buckminster Fuller, Charles and Ray Eames, and Peter Blake, served as a foreign policy tool to raise awareness of America and its values among a Soviet audience. The display of "the forbidden fruits of the West" through various types of simulacra—cooking demonstrations, fashion shows, and the Eameses' *Glimpses of the USA* film—aspired to position Soviet visitors both as participants in a version of American domestic life while reminding them, most unsubtly, of the world of sacrifice they inhabited. The most important feature at the ANEM, moreover, was the presence of young, intelligent, Russian-speaking American guides, who were instructed to answer visitors' questions truthfully, including the more difficult questions about American civil liberties and civil rights. In the sixties and seventies, world expos elevated the culture war between West and East, consumer society versus sacrifice society. Montreal in 1967 featured a version of Fuller's ideal society in a dome that contained the cultural treasures of the United States. Osaka's Expo 70 was the first world's fair held in Japan. Its theme of "Progress and Harmony for Mankind" was highlighted by the United States pavilion that boasted of its recent space accomplishments with the display of a moon rock. By the mid-1970s, the Vietnam War, Watergate, economic woes, and an energy crisis pushed the U.S. bicentennial organizers to revert to basic American principles, founding values of the nation as demonstrated in the life and times of Benjamin Franklin and Thomas Jefferson. The international exhibition based on their lives, though hardly a simple statement about America's past, both demonstrated pride in the origins of the United States while it revealed how far, in a sense, America has slipped in attending to its values of life, liberty, and the pursuit of happiness. Ultimately, it is a challenge to assert a singular meaning to all of these events, given the sheer variety of styles and zeitgeists that each exhibition embodied. Further, no single design aesthetic was employed for all the examples of exhibitions this study addresses.

How, then, is it possible to come to a conclusion as to what America showed of itself at these junctures? While the United States has made attempts to juggle effectively its image through cultural exhibitions sent abroad to influence foreign publics, one constant, which this study argues, is that the image of any version of "America" was always uncertain. Expectations of how the United States would play to the audiences of the host countries were often irrationally inflated, whether these demographics already viewed America positively or immoderately. Krenn indicates the inherent uncertainty within the practice of projecting a nation's image to foreign audiences, in this particular case through fine art:

> In short, U.S. policymakers sadly overestimated their ability to use art as a weapon in the Cold War. Many seemed to believe that a painting or other work of art, much like a surface-to-air missile, could be "aimed" and "fired" with no small degree of precision: "target" audiences were identified, the United states loaded up the most appropriate "weaponry" (modern art for some, more traditional art for others), and "launched" the art exhibits.[6]

On the whole, it can be concluded that the history of cultural exhibitions sent abroad to tell "America's story to the world" has, indeed, been at times a desperate and confused search for, and marketing of, an ideal America. From trade fairs to world fair pavilions to museum exhibitions, they all share the hallmark of a federal agency (OITF, USIA, ARBA) partnering with private corporations (General Electric, IBM, etc.) and a creative designer or team of cutting-edge designers. Later, this three-way partnership would expand to include major museums, as in the participation of the Metropolitan Museum of Art as a cosponsor of *The World of Franklin and Jefferson*.

This study's nuanced approach has attempted to discover meaning in these exhibitionary examples to determine what America aspired to communicate to these audiences. The United States was selling more than just department-store-like windows onto a graspable national utopia, a guarantee of material, spiritual, and political prosperity. This form of cultural Manifest Destiny, the colonizing of other cultures through the manipulation of images of what "America" is, certainly points to one interpretation this study has put forth. Practitioners in the field hold other views on what America showed of itself. "We showed them," according to Jack Masey, that "America invented 'invention.'"[7]

As this study holds, by the late 1970s, U.S. cultural exhibitions began to deteriorate both in quality and in creative vision, as a result of mismanaged mandates for the USIA and the rise of détente with the Soviet Union. In 1977, under "Reorganization Plan No. 2," the USIA had been merged with the State Department's Bureau of Educational and Cultural Affairs. Edmund Gullion, who coined the term "public diplomacy," railed against the impending merger. He felt, as did many of the career professionals within the USIA, that the more subtle practice of cultural exchanges would end up sidelined by the overt political drive of the State Department. What emerged in 1978 was the United States International Communication Agency (USICA). Furthermore, the Carter administration's decision to require a "second mandate" to educate the American public about other nations and their cultures transcended the agency's motto of "telling America's story to the world." This mirrored the president's concern with shaping an American foreign policy (and public image) that was visibly less abrasive and more attuned to the political agendas of allies and enemies alike. As a result, the Carter administration shied away from outright ideological confrontation with America's Cold War adversary, the Soviet Union.[8] As Cull suggests: "At the same time, the advance of détente had dramatically widened the scope for Western cultural outreach to the Eastern bloc. The Helsinki Final Act of August 1975 had cleared the way for cultural exchanges and the free flow of information on an unprecedented scale."[9] And yet the major factor that contributed to the growing ineffectiveness of government-sponsored cultural exhibition programming by the mid- to late 1970s was the nearly nonexistent expertise in the fields of industrial design and architecture on the government side. As Payeff-Masey affirms:

> When Jack Masey left the government, a large force behind these exhibitions left with him. Part of the success of even the early shows was because of Jack's personality. He's a bulldozer. Peter Blake talks about this in his book, early on when he and Jack were in West Berlin: "Even though Masey didn't speak one word of German, he managed to dominate every conversation by means of decibel count and similar techniques."
>
> This is kind of the key of what it took to push things through. It's a force. And the countervailing force within USIA, which was policy driven, was not going in that direction. There needed to be something to counter that. And so today, where is that force, that *skilled use of media*? It's absent.[10]

Designers, not Policy Makers, Became the *Deus ex Machina* for Projecting a Positive Image of the United States Abroad

This crucial period of U.S. cultural exhibitions overseas was punctuated by the efforts of unique exhibition teams that included Madison Avenue advertising executives, Museum of Modern Art curators, industrial designers as noteworthy as Herbert Bayer, Charles Eames, George Nelson, Peter Blake, Buckminster Fuller, and Ivan Chermayeff, and national agencies such as the National Aeronautics and Space Administration and the Smithsonian Institution. Unnumbered individuals, some from the unlikeliest of professional domains, had succeeded in representing America at literally hundreds of shows that communicated an image of American prestige through symbolic displays. From a perspective of industrial design, which contends regularly with the principle of obsolescence, the "America" in the examples taken on in this study should also be seen as a product that is unceasingly growing obsolete, an entity that requires continual re-creation and rebirth.

Yet policy makers within the government time and again refused to become involved in the planning for these creative endeavors. Aside from basic thematic guidance, it is questionable how much the United States itself was truly an actor in the production of these events. What has become clear through the research of these exhibitions is that the designers, through Masey, were acting, not committees of "policy wonks." Thus, it is important to remember it was the designers who were tasked with the burden of putting "America" on display. And what, in particular, were these creative teams required to deliver? As veteran designer Ivan Chermayeff has stated:

> We designers didn't have to worry about how we were portraying America. If one had to run these things through committees and boards, these ideas wouldn't have happened. And what did America show of itself at these exhibitions? They showed that we were pretty entrepreneurial people. And I think this is why we will not disappear from the face of the earth because we can imagine and we know how to get things done with good ideas. We have the energy to make these great ideas happen. And that's what makes this country really great. There's no better place to be, no matter what, than this one.[11]

Reviewing this description of how these exhibitions came about, it is clear that the often ambiguous, however patriotic, message these events portrayed through modern design was based largely on the intentions not of the U.S. government, but of those designers, historians, and advertising professionals who were enlisted to propagate a type of aspiration to American cultural ascendancy, to prove at the very least to foreign publics the superior quality of life in America.

In addition, it is worth recalling the 1956 fairs that emerged from this new dynamic of designers who were driving the content of the exhibitions were often created under "breakneck conditions."[12] As Mitarachi has explained, "Bid guesswork was just the first of their problems. The preliminary surveys, averaging several days to a week, permitted consultation with embassy officials, but the pressure of the schedule—with some contracts signed 60–70 days prior to the opening dates—did not make it easy to do basic research about national attitudes and problems."[13] The hasty and at times whirlwind process through which these events became realities would set a precedent for many of the exhibitions examined in this study. As a result, what ensued, moreover, would be a severe lack of institutional control at the Office of International Trade Fairs, the United States Information Agency, and later within the American Revolution Bicentennial Administration as a result of fierce time constraints on delivering the highly complicated pavilions and their contents to points around the world. This point is, in essence, twofold: only professional designers understood how to create these imaginative exhibitions from scratch at short notice. And, equally important, as Masey states,

> Policy wonks had no interest in meddling with design questions and exhibition people did not report to those responsible for pushing policies. The less you involve the government bureaucracy, the better off you are. I think your basic assumption here is that the U.S. government was involved in a number of things. It was a series of happy accidents, a series of strange things that took place. Frequently happy accidents.[14]

While these events provide a rich understanding of architectural and industrial design evolution as well as design as a political force within a cultural diplomacy framework, scholars have underestimated how these exhibitions became the redoubt of designers and visionaries, not, as commonly assumed, the bastion of organized government propagandists. In considering the sheer theatrics of these exhibitions—for they were performances of sorts—this research has allowed this writer a behind-the-scenes tour of these spectacles where design itself proved ascendant, not the inert policies of a government agency trying to push a particular image of the United States. Could the work of these designers be construed as patriotic? Of course, these individuals truly believed in the entrepreneurial opportunities that existed in America.

As this study has made clear, the surrender of creative control for exhibition programming to designers was not a dereliction of duty on the part of the U.S. government agencies but, rather, this practice became a self-perpetuating principle. The USIA's final report on the U.S. pavilion at Montreal, for example, describes the Cambridge Seven Associates' task for "creating an overall mood or atmosphere in their exhibits" with the intention of "developing an artistic symbol rather than the conventional exhibition . . . a portrait of a nation."[15] As described earlier, this ambitious design carried visitors to the highest platform, which was fittingly dedicated to showcasing U.S. achievements in space exploration and a nation en route to fulfilling President Kennedy's mandate of America sending a man to the moon within the decade.[16]

A year prior to Montreal, in 1966 Ronald Rubin made a study of the United States Information Agency and its apparent operating assumptions. His findings were as follows:

The USIA has been prevented from implementing the various goals established for it by the Executive Branch and Congress due to internal as well as
external factors.

1. The inability of the Agency to clarify its basic operating assumptions. These
    include a determination as to whether it is to function as an information or
    propaganda instrument. . . . In addition, USIA has failed to develop a sys-
    tematic policy as concerns the population groups whose favor should be most
    pursued in promoting American objectives.
2. The failure to clearly define the role of USIA in the Executive Branch in reach-
    ing foreign policy decisions.[17]

Throughout the research for this study, it became increasingly clear that design professionals, starting with the presence of designer Jack Masey within
the government apparatus, coordinated and choreographed these exhibitionary spectacles, typically outside the supervision of policy makers. Designers,
in other words, carried the heart of these exhibitions.

These Make-Believe Efforts Illustrate an
America of Deception and Verisimilitude

Should USIA be a mirror of American life or a show window offering a
selective and admirable picture of it? The question is answered pragmati-
cally day by day as output is selected and treated. Two major attitudes
toward story treatment may be distinguished. The first is that the "full
and fair picture idea is silly," and that instead of being exhaustive, output
must be selective. It is not enough merely to inform people and count
on them to react favorably. It is necessary to promote a point of view, to
present a picture of America that is favorable, and stir other countries
to emulate U.S. accomplishments and institutions.[18]

As this study has shown, America was essentially an image and a myth, from
the sixteenth through the eighteenth centuries, before it became a concrete
reality, much less a sovereign identity. No one really knew or could agree on
what America was, and this vagueness, this sheer lack of scientific method
in gaining a conceptual foothold would ultimately serve as less of a blessed
tabula rasa upon which America could form itself than a curse wrought by
centuries of conjecture, most of which was negative.[19] At the same time, the
myth of American exceptionalism and its conceptual by-product, Manifest
Destiny, would gain traction as an ideal of a nation whose frontier should

and would be conquered. Further, American "state fantasies," of which the exceptionalist theme was primary, as historian Pease asserts, became the "dominant structure of desire out of which U.S. citizens imagined their national identity."[20]

A founding principle of the United States that has become embedded in the American identity also yielded, according to Knell, a "future-oriented reading of the nation."[21] With no glorious past to boast of, it would appear, then, that there is something special about the opportunities to portray a forward-looking "America" at venues such as world's fairs, which have been and continue to be future-oriented events. Here, U.S. participation that engaged from a future perspective proved critical to these acts of national identity making. More importantly, the makers of these American exhibitions operated within a framework, though somewhat separated from government propagandists, in which this ideology became the standard.

Admittedly, there are goals an exhibition is capable of achieving and those an exhibition cannot accomplish. Through the collection and display of culturally relevant objects in order to frame rich historical narratives for the civic and educative enrichment of culturally diverse audiences, it is, in fact, folly to say one knows exactly just what impact an exhibition with any given theme may have on any audience whatsoever. Whether the artifacts on display are natural history specimens, cleverly designed consumer products, or works of art intended to win the hearts and minds of foreign audiences, an exhibition team will go to considerable effort to perpetrate a very specific national image on the high-stakes stage of an international forum such as a world's fair. As Carol Breckenridge asserts, world's fairs as "cultural technologies" became, starting with the Great Exhibition of 1851, "imagined communities" in a "discursive space that was global, while nurturing nation-states that were culturally highly specific."[22]

While Breckenridge raises questions as to the effectiveness of international exhibitions, it should come as no surprise these events offer idealized portraits of nations or groups that blinker the true economic, political, and social realities of these participants. Marxist discourse indicts these exhibitions simply as instruments that recklessly enable the cupidity in human nature. Undeniably, on one level the materialist spirit of the nineteenth century triumphed at these world's fairs, forums in which commodities were fetishized at the expense of any real improvement of understanding between peoples of different class and culture. Greenhalgh cites this evolution of the promotion of "the principle of display" as concurrent with the progress of the Industrial Revolution: "In the first instance this was to be a device for the enhancement of trade, for the promotion of new technology, for the education of the ignorant middle classes and for the elaboration of a political stance."[23] Similarly, Byer describes the 1858 European journey of Nathaniel Hawthorne, who saw the sculpture by Hiram Powers fittingly named "America" while traveling through Florence, Italy. The author acknowledged with skepticism American attempts at a national aesthetic in the mid-nineteenth century through "the underlying project of the monumental, exposing the wishful fictiveness of its ritual building."[24]

The exploration, then, of historical episodes in the shaping years in which America reimagined itself through, to borrow the term, the "wishful fictiveness" of cultural exhibitions that were sent abroad to shape the attitudes of foreign audiences serves to locate historically the origin and evolution of a nationalist exhibitionary impulse. But along with this initial impulse, to show itself to other nations brought with it the understanding that America could perhaps never be summed up in one particular statement. Starting in the early nineteenth century the United States became, in the words of Edward Bernays, "a creator of events"[25] and deployed cultural exhibitions that often challenged verisimilitude. As columnist Lance Morrow acknowledges:

> America is—or was at one time—a continental mood ring, a subject sufficiently vast and enigmatic in its newness to accommodate the most extravagant fantasies. The republic of the questing amateur, because it had no prehistory (for white men), none of the cultural grids grooved by centuries into old lands, yielded itself to an interminable amateurism of interpretation. Americans were a race of Adams rolling west across Eden, blowing the heads off rattlesnakes with their revolvers.[26]

These exhibitions, then, or "pseudo-events," as has been noted by Boorstin, trod a fine line between reality, myth, and make-believe, often in order to counter jingoistic attitudes toward America but also to forge an as yet unachieved identity. As these exhibitions are conveyors of cultural politics and national values, again it comes as little surprise that the scenography witnessed by visitors would by turns embody both propagandist and reality-based narratives.

Moving forward to 1955–1975, these exhibitions served also to mask the very real horror of nuclear annihilation, as previously there had been no mechanism to destroy the world in its entirety. It is arguable, then, that there was little choice among designers, in addition to singing the praises of "the Friendly Atom," of repressing the impulse to create mini, temporal American utopias for foreign audiences. While these settings often supplied a rich fantasy version of America, at the same time there was little need among designers to acknowledge the fearsome potential of nuclear holocaust, against which no General Electric kitchen or Buckminster Fuller Eden-like pleasure dome could defend human life. As militarism became the responsibility of the superpowers following World War II, so, too, it can be argued, did envisioning peaceful worlds through trade fair, world fair, and museum exhibitions become a second responsibility. As Masey contends, the U.S. pavilions at these events, particularly in the 1950s, demonstrated not only a plausible reality for Americans but also a potential future for Russians.[27]

Peter Chermayeff of the Cambridge Seven Associates, however, interprets the space exhibition at Montreal, though avant-garde, as a legitimate example of U.S. culture for visitors: "We wanted everything to be real so that you could feel the sense of that capsule returning through the upper atmosphere, see that burning bottom of Apollo. But to sit in the astronauts couch was a big thing for them, you know, that was contact. They were really part of it."[28]

By opening the discussion to all of the exhibitions addressed in this study, it would be the partnering of compelling national artifacts on display within visionary architectural settings conjured by innovative designers that would create temporary American cosmologies. These dream worlds that could momentarily negate both the horror of nuclear proliferation and misdirect attention to the "inconvenient" truths of American social and political life would ultimately show not the United States itself but, as Knell proposes, "the interpretive frame of the founders,"[29] the designers themselves.

These complex ideological symbols in which concepts of national identity and global cultural influence both coincided and clashed often proclaimed a fantastically visionary and at times illusory America, forswearing verisimilitude for impact, fact for fiction, while at the same time meeting the vague ideological imperatives of the state at a given time. Finally, these examples share other important traits, which include that of national identity as constructed through the display of decontextualized objects; the requisite suspension of disbelief; and the effort to win hearts and minds among the foreign publics who witnessed these efforts to show a version of America at each turn.

These Exhibitions Can Define the Future of U.S. Cultural Exhibitions Overseas

The tragedy is that if you ever needed a USIA, it was September 11, 2001. September 12 we should have been there, with Arabic speakers. It was important. We weren't there. We should have been everywhere. It should have been activated. It was as needed as it was in 1962. That's the tragedy, for me. And once it died, it really died. Now we have this limp thing that tries to do stuff.[30]

While some believe the golden age of these events is now over, a number of governments maintain cultural institutes (for example, the British Council, the Alliance-Française, the Goethe Institute, and the Confucius Institute) to make their domestic issues known to the rest of the world, sometimes through international exhibitions. As long as nations find the need to enhance their reputations to as broad an audience as possible, it is arguable whether Internet-based, collective participation platforms can in any way replace the people-to-people exchange that is a primary goal of international exhibitions. The current trend of tens of millions of visitors who attend international exhibitions predicts longevity to the life span of these unique phenomena. As Masey avows: "Fairs, expos, and exhibits offer the place for connects, individual connects. There's nothing like it. You can have the Voice of America, you can have press attachés, you can have whatever you want. But any medium that allows people to come together is dynamite."

To gain perspective on the U.S. record for cultural diplomacy, Richard Arndt, former diplomat and director of the Bureau for Educational and Cultural Affairs, attests: "The golden years of cultural diplomacy began to fade four decades ago. . . . Meanwhile, the sharp rise in foreign non-understanding has become a national nightmare. Yet few have suggested that a crippled cultural diplomacy might have anything to do with either cause or cure. Cultural diplomacy's decline has thus passed unnoticed, leaving a nation baffled by its apparent defenselessness against the cultural onslaught of an enraged Islamic fragment."[31] Since 9/11, a wealth of studies has emerged with recommendations toward steering the United States to create a new public diplomacy agency,[32] while others have sought to redefine public diplomacy itself in the information age.[33] Others seek answers to what some have called "the clash of civilizations" through public diplomacy models.[34] Perhaps the most important lessons come from America's recent foray into international exhibitions, Shanghai 2010 in particular.

Shanghai 2010: America at Cultural Crossroads or Cultural Twilight?

The problem with Shanghai now is that they just didn't get that they needed to have people who are skilled at communicating visually if that is going to be your chosen methodology. They don't get it. Maybe they need to rethink this, get some expertise on board. It's cheaper than screwing up.[35]

Many have derogated the U.S. presence in Shanghai, as to the problems of overt corporate marketing and the miserably inadequate "greetings" from famous American sports, entertainment, and political figures on large video monitors. Of course, the model of displaying products as "the forbidden fruits of the West" worked during the Cold War when American thematic exhibitions catered strategically to the have-not Soviet masses. But who is to blame for America's no-show at Shanghai? Public policy activist Bob Jacobson declares: "Privatizing American public diplomacy was the Bush Administration's policy. Regrettably, the Obama Administration, rather than repealing this policy, has instead accelerated its application."[36] America's presence in Shanghai was organized entirely differently from the cultural exhibitions addressed in this study. What follows is a summation of what happened.

Jose Villareal, a former fund-raiser for Hillary Clinton, was named commissioner general by Secretary Clinton. He helped raise the $61 million required for the creation of the American pavilion. What is not known exactly is what he accomplished as commissioner general because the whole pavilion had been outsourced. The U.S. government, in essence, was not involved. Why? The government did not pay for it. In 2010, the State Department would give two people the authority to raise the money for the pavilion in Shanghai. However, these two could only raise a few million dollars. Hillary Clinton entered the picture and raised around $60 million. She rewarded her chief fund-raiser Villareal by appointing him commissioner general of the American pavilion at Shanghai. To reiterate, there was, ultimately, no U.S. government involvement. It had all been "Blackwatered," as Bob Jacobson chillingly describes it.[37]

During the fund-raising period for the American pavilion, these two State Department representatives approached a theme park entertainment company called BRC Imagination Arts, who were responsible for the American pavilion at the Aichi fair in 2005, which featured, among other oddities, an actor dressed as Ben Franklin riding a Segway. BRC first came into the picture in 1992, when they were hired to design the U.S. pavilion at Seville, the beginning of the complete handing over of government control of these events to the private sector. In addition, for Shanghai the American organizers quite curiously brought in Clive Grout, a Canadian architect and designer, not an American, to design the pavilion. What, in the end, does all of this planning indicate? BRC themselves would be cornered, beholden to over sixty corporations who wanted a piece of the pavilion's limelight. Thus, at this event there would be no clear American message, whether it evolved from the government side or through the design of the exhibition team.

More importantly, fairs, expos, and international exhibitions offer a unique place for connections, individual connections on a scale of great magnitude. But did the United States reach out at Shanghai? Certainly, the American pavilion had American guides who spoke Chinese, but they did not engage the Chinese audiences. An American guide, for example, could ideally say to someone in line, "Hello, what province are you from?" The Americans should not just say, "Look at me, I speak Chinese," which was tantamount to what was actually on display in the American pavilion. The guides should have been asking, "What are your feelings about the United States? What do you like about us? What do you hate about us?" This tool of public diplomacy was first instituted in the 1947 Marshall Plan exhibitions, which were small, traveling caravans that crisscrossed Europe in order to explain the U.S. objectives in a creative and up-front fashion to a shell-shocked, post–World War II Western European population. And the presence of these able young Americans has been a constant in U.S. exhibitions abroad since then. President Eisenhower, looking back on the success of the American guides in Moscow in 1959, showed his enthusiasm for the human element in international relations: "If we are going to take advantage of the assumption that all people want peace, then the problem is for people to get together and to leap governments—if necessary to evade governments—to work out not one method but thousands of methods by which people can gradually learn a little bit more of each other."[38]

It is clear that the Obama administration has found itself situated in an Augean stable of economic recession, dangerous international scenarios, and looming questions as to how to revamp and refocus the cultural element within public diplomacy. At the outset of his first term, President Obama stated he would chart a foreign policy based on a multilateral diplomacy that respects the world rule of law. This remarkable opportunity to turn things around could have included a substantial cultural diplomacy plan. The real question now, however, is will the Obama administration restart this process of introducing America, warts and all, to foreign audiences? There is an obvious need for Americans and citizens from other countries to know one another. And one can learn much from the rich history of cultural exhibitions and the talented individuals who imaginatively represented America abroad during the agency's operating years from 1953 to 1999. As McMurray and Lee attest:

Any program of cultural relations is a program of communication. A nation's culture is the sum total of its achievement; its own expression of its own personality; its way of thinking and acting. Its program of cultural relations abroad is its method of making these things known to foreigners. Such a program is in fact a self-portrait into which go all a people's creative ability and technical skill and which it wishes the rest of the world to recognize as a speaking likeness.[39]

In past years, the U.S. government effectively oversaw the successful design of an American presence at major international events, starting with the Brussels Expo in 1958, the *American National Exhibition* in Moscow the following year, Montreal in 1967, and Osaka in 1970. Yet the government was effective also for these important reasons: Congress agreed to pay for these endeavors, and these experts (including government representatives who had expertise as designers, such as Jack Masey) drove content.

It is clear today the U.S. government employs no personnel who are serious about developing successful cultural exhibition programming. The Office of Public Diplomacy, which has been limping along, has not distinguished itself. As Masey offers: "If I even remotely had a hand in this, knowing how turned on the Chinese are by basketball, if indeed you wanted to do a video or a movie presentation, I would have gotten the Harlem Globetrotters and let them do a fifteen-minute segment of what they do best. You would drive their audience over the edge. And you'd really do it right. It's easy."[40]

If America intends to conduct a repeat of Shanghai and outsource the American pavilion again for the Milan Expo in 2015, the U.S. government will have no control over the content. Other ways the U.S. could have done much more with its pavilion at Shanghai would have been to take a cue from the American pavilion at the Brussels Expo in 1958. This first world's fair of the postwar period hosted the official U.S. pavilion that featured the *Unfinished Business* exhibit. This sensitive and creative take on American social problems, mainly segregation, amid its flashier discussion of scientific progress, art, music, and other cultural pursuits, gave visitors an intimate glimpse of some of the darker realities, more or less some truths about life in America. The idea, taken loosely from Lincoln's "unfinished work" phrase in the Gettysburg Address, emphasized what the Belgian newspaper *Le Peuple* praised as America's greatest perceived strength, at least at Brussels: "Let's face it: only strong democracies are in a position to talk as well of their qualities as their faults. Our thanks to the United States for having demonstrated this at the Heysel."[41] Though this exhibit was modified by executive order after a number of Southern congressmen took issue with its racial overtones, the United States had made a statement: that American democracy is a work in progress. In like manner, at future cultural exhibitions, the United States should consider sharing with the world its national treasures as well as faults. Echoing this idea, Edward R. Murrow, once director of the USIA, stressed that public diplomacy should be "in on the take offs as well as the crash landings" of American foreign policy.

Though the USIA no longer exists as the cultural diplomacy agency of the United States, it is hoped that the State Department and its private sector allies will follow a similar course from that of fifty years ago, by letting

America show its enduring values without the pressure to be political in an unmediated, person-to-person engagement. These values, according to Linda Gottlieb, one of the guides from the ANEM, include: pop culture, knowledge base, inventiveness, and a diverse and open society.[42] Wherever the venue, a sophisticated presentation of American arts and culture can continue to make inroads against negative perceptions of the United States. Further, if foreign audiences can obtain an impression of America free of governmental filters, the influence of international wars, or domestic election cycles, they can better decide for themselves what America really is and what it represents to them.[43]

It is useful, in the end, to borrow from two sources to offer a concluding description of what the United States showed of itself at these exhibitions. First, it was USIA representative Al Jones, in paraphrasing Charles Eames's description of *The World of Franklin and Jefferson*, who said, "This is an exhibit which seeks to capture the tentative, the cluttered, the unfinished reality of our revolutionary experiment by avoiding rigid didacticism and precise definition."[44] The second source that offers a description of how America showed itself to foreign publics comes from Emily Dickinson:

> Tell all the Truth but tell it slant—
> Success in Circuit lies . . .
> The Truth must dazzle gradually
> Or every man be blind—[45]

Lastly, the history of U.S. cultural exhibitions as an apparatus of public diplomacy is thus a composite narrative, a story of the aspirations of a nation and the designers who strategized to portray time and again an "America" relentlessly seeking a remarkable prehistory, present, and future. This is an unfinished story of perpetually reimagined American identities and values.

Notes

1. Daniel Boorstin, *The Image: Or What Happened to the American Dream* (New York: Atheneum, 1961), 245–46.

2. Jack Masey, interview with author, August 24, 2010.

3. Umberto Eco, "A Theory of Expositions," in *Travels in Hyperreality: Essays*, trans. William Weaver (San Diego: Harcourt, 1986), 293.

4. See Greg Castillo, *Cold War on the Home Front: The Soft Power of Midcentury Design* (Minneapolis: University of Minnesota Press, 2010), xxiii. Here, he invokes Beatriz Colomina's term of "exhibitionist houses," which, following their brief display in exhibition spaces, would gain prominence following in "spaces of publication, memory, and fantasy."

5. Krenn writes that after World War II, "Miltary might and economic strength were not enough for America to assert and actively pursue its leadership of the 'free world.' The United States also needed to demonstrate that it was in the vanguard of cultural developments," in Michael L. Krenn, *Fallout Shelters for the Human Spirit: American Art and the Cold War* (Chapel Hill: University of North Carolina Press, 2005), 233.

6. Ibid., 236.

7. Masey, interview, August 24, 2010.

8. See Juliet Antunes Sablosky, "Reinvention, Reorganization, Retreat: American Cultural Diplomacy at Century's End, 1978–1998," *Journal of Arts Management, Law, and Society* 29, no. 1 (Spring 1999): 30–46. For further discussion of the final years of the USIA, see Nicholas J. Cull, *The Decline and Fall of the United States Information Agency: American Public Diplomacy, 1989–2001* (Basingstoke: Palgrave MacMillan, 2012).

9. Nicholas J. Cull, *The Cold War and the United States Information Agency: American Propaganda and Public Diplomacy, 1945–1989* (Cambridge: Cambridge University Press, 2008), 359.

10. Beverly Payeff-Masey, interview with author, August 24, 2010.

11. Ivan Chermayeff, interview with author, August 23, 2010.

12. Jane Fisk Mitarachi, "Design as a Political Force," *Industrial Design* (February 1957): 14.

13. Ibid.

14. Masey, interview, August 23, 2010. Masey adds, "The Federal government was irrelevant . . . at the American National Exhibition in Moscow, irrelevant in *Franklin and Jefferson*," quoted in Hélène Lipstadt, "'Natural Overlap': Charles and Ray Eames and the Federal Government," in *The Work of Charles and Ray Eames: A Legacy of Invention*, ed. Diana Murphy (New York: Abrams / Library of Congress / Vitra Design Museum, 1997), 172.

15. Final Report, Office of Public Affairs of the United States Pavilion (IME), USIA Historical Archives, State Department, 1967. For a privately funded report on the U.S. pavilion at Expo 67, see NA RG306 Records of the USIA, Office of Research, Special Reports (S); 1953–1997, S-16-67 thru S-25-68, Box 24, Folder "S-25-67."

16. See USIA Weekly Report, September 21, 1965, Papers of Lyndon Baines Johnson, President, 1963–1969, White House Confidential File, (Subject Reports) Agency Reports, U.S. Information Agency, Box 135 [1 of 2], Folder "United States Information Agency, 1965, 2 of 2."

17. Ronald I. Rubin, *The Objectives of the U.S. Information Agency, Controversies and Analysis* (New York: Praeger, 1966), 10.

18. See Leo Bogart, *Premises for Propaganda: The United States Information Agency's Operating Assumptions in the Cold War*, abridged by Agnes Bogart (New York: Free Press, 1976), 92–93.

19. Ibid., 41. See also Boorstin, *The Americans: The National Experience* (New York: Random House, 1965), 219.

20. See Donald E. Pease, *The New American Exceptionalism* (Minneapolis: University of Minnesota Press, 2009), 1.

21. Simon J. Knell, email correspondence with author, January 9, 2013.

22. Carol A. Breckenridge, "The Aesthetics and Politics of Colonial Collecting: India at World's Fairs," *Comparative Studies in Society and History*, vol. 31, no. 2 (April 1989): 196.

23. Paul Greenhalgh, *Ephemeral Vistas: The Expositions Universelles, Great Exhibitions, and World's Fairs, 1851–1939* (Manchester: Manchester University Press, 1988), 3.

24. See Robert H. Byer, "Words, Monuments, Beholders: The Visual Arts in Hawthorne's 'The Marble Faun,'" in *American Iconology: New Approaches to Nineteenth Century Art and Literature*, ed. David C. Miller (New Haven, CT: Yale University Press, 1993), 170.

25. See Boorstin, *The Image*, 9–11, and one of the classic twentieth-century studies on the shaping of public opinion, Edward L. Bernays, *Crystallizing Public Opinion* (New York: Boni and Liveright, 1923).

26. See Lance Morrow, "On Reimagining America," *Time*, March 31, 1980, http://www.time.com/time/magazine/article/0,9171,921933,00.html.

27. Masey asserts that one reason Khrushchev advocated for American exhibitions to travel to the Soviet Union was to demonstrate that America "could be their future," the future that would one day be available to the Soviet citizenry. From interview, August 23, 2010.

28. Peter Chermayeff, "Design for a Fair: The United States Pavilion at Expo '67 Montreal," YouTube video, 7:24, posted by Pchermayeff, July 26, 2010, http://www.youtube.com/watch?v=6TnT2lSLHxo..

29. See Simon J. Knell, "Museums, Fossils and the Cultural Revolution of Science: Mapping Change in the Politics of Knowledge in Early Nineteenth-Century Britain," in *Museum Revolutions: How Museums Change and Are Changed*, ed. Simon J. Knell, Suzanne MacLeod, and Sheila Watson (London: Routledge, 2007), 30.

30. Masey, interview, August 24, 2010.

31. Richard T. Arndt, *The First Resort of Kings: American Cultural Diplomacy in the Twentieth Century* (Washington, DC: Potomac, 2006), xxi.

32. See, for instance, Nancy Snow, *Information War: American Propaganda, Free Speech and Opinion Control Since 9/11* (New York: Seven Stories / Council on Foreign Relations, 2003); Cull, *The Decline and Fall of the United States Information Agency*.

33. See, for example, Eytan Gilboa, "Searching for a Theory of Public Diplomacy," *Annals of the American Academy of Political and Social Science* 616, no. 55 (2008): 55–77.

34. There are seemingly countless studies that have emerged since the abolition of the USIA and 9/11. See Advisory Committee on Cultural Diplomacy, "Cultural Diplomacy: The Linchpin of Public Diplomacy" (report) (Washington, DC: U.S. Department of State, September 2005); William A. Rugh, ed., *Engaging the Arab and Islamic Worlds through Public Diplomacy: A Report and Action Recommendations* (Washington, DC: Public Diplomacy Council, 2004); Robert Satloff,

The Battle of Ideas in the War on Terror: Essays on US Public Diplomacy in the Middle East (Washington, DC: Washington Institute for Near East Policy, 2004); and John Brown, "Changing Minds, Winning Peace: Reconsidering the Djerejian Report," *American Diplomacy*, http://www.unc.edu/depts/diplomat/archives_roll/2004_07-09/brown_djerejian/brown_djerejian.html.

35. Masey, interview, August 24, 2010.

36. See Bob Jacobson, "US Pavilion in Shanghai Fails to Do Its Job: 'San Antonio Threw a ($500,000) Party and No One Came,'" *Huffington Post*, May 31, 2010, http://www.huffingtonpost.com/bob-jacobson/us-pavilion-in-shanghai-f_b_594315.html.

37. See Bob Jacobson, "'Blackwatering' Public Diplomacy: The US Pavilion at the Shanghai World Expo," *Huffington Post*, May 3, 2010, http://www.huffington post.com/bob-jacobson/an-epic-failure-of-planni_b_561697.html. For similar, see Cynthia Schneider, "Shanghai'd, or the USA Pavilion as a Corporate Theme Park," USC Center on Public Diplomacy, June 8, 2010, http://uscpublicdiplomacy.org/index.php/newswire/cpdblog_detail/shanghaid_or_the_usa_pavilion_as_a_corporate_theme_park/.

38. Dwight D. Eisenhower, *Waging Peace: The White House Years* (Garden City, NY: Doubleday, 1965), 411.

39. Ruth Emily McMurray and Muna Lee, *The Cultural Approach: Another Way in International Relations* (Chapel Hill: North Carolina University Press, 1947), 2–3.

40. Masey, interview, August 24, 2010.

41. As quoted in Michael L. Krenn, "'Unfinished Business:' Segregation and U.S. Diplomacy at the 1958 World's Fair," in *Race and United States Foreign Policy during the Cold War: A Collection of Essays*, ed. Michael L. Krenn (New York: Garland, 1998), 250.

42. Linda Gottlieb, from panel discussion at "From Face-off to Facebook: From the Nixon-Khrushchev Kitchen Debate to Public Diplomacy in the 21st Century" (conference, George Washington University, Washington, DC, July 23, 2009).

43. See, for example, Bruce Gregory, "Public Diplomacy and Strategic Communication: Cultures, Firewalls, and Imported Norms" (lecture, American Political Science Association, Conference on International Communication and Conflict, George Washington University and Georgetown University, Washington, DC, August 31, 2005).

44. See memorandum from Al Jones to all USIS Staff, January 9, 1975, in Library of Congress, Charles and Ray Eames Papers, Research/Production, Exhibits, Folder: World of Franklin and Jefferson, Reviews, Publicity, Box 181, Folder 2, 2.

45. Brenda Hillman, ed., *The Pocket Emily Dickinson* (Boston: Shambhala, 2009), 137.

Bibliography

Archival Sources

Library of Congress
  The Papers of Charles and Ray Eames
National Archives II, College Park, Maryland
  RG40, General Records of the Department of Commerce
    Office of International Trade Fairs
    Historic Document File
    Public and Industry Relations Records
    Design Records
  RG306, United States Information Agency
    Office of Research, Special Reports
  RG452, Records of the Office of Design and Exhibits
    American Revolution Bicentennial Administration, Design and
      Exhibit Records
  RG489, Records of the International Trade Administration
    Bureau of Foreign Commerce, Office of International Trade Fairs, Correspon-
      dence and Reports, 1954–1958
University of Arkansas, Special Collections
  State Department Bureau of Educational and Cultural Relations
USIA Historical Branch, State Department Public Diplomacy Historical Collection.
  Various files
Harry S. Truman Library, Independence, Missouri
  President's Personal File (PPF)
  George Elsey Papers

Lyndon B. Johnson Library, Austin, Texas
    National Security Files (NSF), Agency File, USIA
    White House Central Files, Confidential File, USIA
    Leonard Marks Papers
Jack Masey, Personal Archives, New York City, New York

Documentary Sources

John Adams Papers, Massachusetts Historical Society.
Foreign Relations of the United States, Washington, D.C., GPO, various dates.
Public Papers of the Presidents, Washington, D.C., GPO, various dates.
The Papers of Joseph Henry, Smithsonian Institution, Washington, D.C.
United States Treaties and Other International Agreements, Washington, D.C. GPO,
    various dates.
United States Information Agency, *USIA News Release*, Washington D.C.: USIA,
    1968.

Websites

The American Presidency Project, http://www.presidency.ucsb.edu/ws/?pid=28269
The Huffington Post, http://www.huffingtonpost.com

Author's Interviews and Correspondence

Jack Masey (in person, New York City, August 23–24, 2010)
Beverly Payeff-Masey (in person, New York City, August 23–24, 2010)
Ivan Chermayeff (in person, New York City, August 23, 2010)
Peter Chermayeff (letter to author, August 28, 2010)
Mark Smith (in person, Los Angeles, November 7, 2008)
Maurice Tuchman (by telephone, May 14, 2011)

Newspapers

Adams Centinel (Gettysburg, Pennsylvania)
Evening Times (Trenton, NJ)
Guardian (London)
Hampshire Telegraph & Portsmouth Gazette (Portsmouth, England)
Le Monde
Liverpool Times
Montreal Star
Newcastle Courant (Newcastle-upon-Tyne, England)
New York Times

Springfield Republican
Times (London)
Washington Post

Books, Articles, Magazines, Unpublished Dissertations, Weblogs

Abercrombie, Stanley. *George Nelson: The Design of Modern Design.* Cambridge, MA: MIT Press, 2000.

Adams, John. *Adams Papers.* September 1, 1800. Massachusetts Historical Society. http://www.masshist.org/adams_editorial/.

Advisory Committee on Cultural Diplomacy. "Cultural Diplomacy: The Linchpin of Public Diplomacy." Report. Washington, DC: U.S. Department of State, September 2005.

Albrecht, Donald. "Introduction." In *The Work of Charles and Ray Eames: A Legacy of Invention,* edited by Diana Murphy, 13–17. New York: Abrams / Library of Congress / Vitra Design Museum, 1997.

Allen, James Sloan. *The Romance of Commerce and Culture: Capitalism, Modernism, and the Chicago-Aspen Crusade for Cultural Reform.* Chicago: University of Chicago Press, 1983.

Allwood, John. *The Great Exhibitions.* London: Studio Vista, 1977.

Altick, Richard. *The Shows of London: A Panorama History of Exhibitions, 1600–1862.* Cambridge, MA: Harvard University Press, 1978.

Altshuler, Bruce, ed. *Salon to Biennial—Exhibitions That Made Art History,* vol. 1, *1863–1959.* London: Phaidon, 2008.

Anderson, Burnett. In *Ike and the USIA: A Commemorative Symposium,* edited by Hans N. Tuch and G. Lewis Schmidt. Washington, DC: U.S. Information Alumni Association, Public Diplomacy Foundation, 1991.

Anholt, Simon, and Jeremy Hildreth. *Brand America: The Mother of All Brands.* London: Cyan, 2004.

Antonelli, Paola. "Design and Architecture: Paola Antonelli Interviewed by Bennett Simpson." In *What Makes a Great Exhibition?,* edited by Paula Marincola, 86–93. Philadelphia: Philadelphia Exhibitions Initiative, 2006.

Appadurai, Arjun, ed. *The Social Life of Things: Commodities in Cultural Perspective.* Cambridge: Cambridge University Press, 1986.

Appy, Christian G., ed. *Cold War Constructions: The Political Culture of United States Imperialism, 1945–1966.* Amherst: University of Massachusetts Press, 2000.

Arbus, Diane. "The Full Circle." *Infinity* 11, no. 2 (February 1962): 4–13, 19, 21.

Arbus, Doon, and Marvin Israel, eds. *Diane Arbus.* New York: Aperture, 1972.

Armstrong, Matt. *www.MountainRunner.us* (blog). http://mountainrunner.us.

Arndt, Richard T. "American Cultural Diplomacy: The U.S. Government Role." In *Exporting America: Essays on American Studies Abroad,* edited by Richard P. Horwitz, 3–36. New York: Garland, 1993.

———. *The First Resort of Kings: American Cultural Diplomacy in the Twentieth Century.* Washington, DC: Potomac, 2006.

Aronczyk, Melissa, and Devon Powers, eds. *Blowing Up the Brand: Critical Perspectives on Promotional Culture.* New York: Peter Lang, 2010.

Auerbach, Jeffrey, and Peter H. Hoffenberg, eds. *Britain, the Empire, and the World at the Great Exhibition of 1851.* Aldershot: Ashgate, 2008.

Aulich, James. *War Posters: Weapons of Mass Communication.* New York: Thames & Hudson, 2007.

Banham, Reyner, ed. *The Aspen Papers: Twenty Years of Design Theory from the International Design Conference in Aspen.* New York: Praeger, 1974.

Bann, Stephen. "Meaning/Interpretation." In *Critical Terms for Art History,* 2nd ed., edited by Robert S. Nelson and Richard Shiff, 128–44. Chicago: University of Chicago Press, 2003.

Barghoorn, Frederick C. *The Soviet Cultural Offensive: The Role of Cultural Diplomacy in Soviet Foreign Policy.* Princeton, NJ: Princeton University Press, 1960.

Barratt, Carrie Rebora. "Inventing American Stories, 1765–1830." In *American Stories: Paintings of Everyday Life, 1765–1915,* edited by H. Barbara Weinberg and Carrie Rebora Barratt, 2–27. New York: Metropolitan Museum of Art, 2009.

Barthes, Roland. "The Great Family of Man." In *Mythologies,* edited by Roland Barthes, 100–102. Translated by Annette Lavers. Paris: Editions du Seuil, 1957.

Baudrillard, Jean. *Consumer Society: Myths and Structures,* Thousand Oaks, CA: Sage, 1998.

———. "Simulacra and Simulations." In *Jean Baudrillard: Selected Writings,* edited by Mark Poster, 166–84. Palo Alto, CA: Stanford University Press, 1988.

———. *Simulations.* New York: Semiotext(e), 1983.

———. *Le système des objets.* Paris: Gallimard, 1968.

———. "The System of Collecting." In *The Cultures of Collecting,* edited by John Elsner and Roger Cardinal, 7–24. London: Reaktion, 1994.

Bearden, Milton. "Afghanistan, Graveyard of Empires." *Foreign Affairs* 80, no. 6 (November/December 2001): 17–30.

Bedini, Silvio A. "Jefferson and American Vertebrate Paleontology." Virginia Division of Mineral Resources Publication 61. Charlottesville: Commonwealth of Virginia, 1985.

Bel Geddes, Norman. "Toward Design." *Advertising Arts* (March 1933): 9–11.

Belmonte, Laura. *Selling the American Way: U.S. Propaganda and the Cold War.* Philadelphia: University of Pennsylvania Press, 2008.

Benjamin, Walter. *Reflections: Essays, Aphorisms, Autobiographical Writings.* Edited by Peter Jemetz. Translated by Edmund Jephcott. New York: Harcourt Brace Jovanovich, 1978.

Bennett, Tony. "The Exhibitionary Complex." *New Formations* 4 (Spring 1988): 73–102.

———. *Pasts beyond Memory: Evolution, Museums, Colonialism.* London: Routledge, 2004.

Berger, John. *Ways of Seeing*. London: Penguin, 1972.

Bergh, Albert Ellery, ed. *The Writings of Thomas Jefferson*. Vol. 9. Washington, DC: Thomas Jefferson Memorial Association, 1907.

Berlin, Isaiah. "The Silence of Russian Culture." *Foreign Affairs* 36, no. 1 (October 1957): 1–24.

Bernays, Edward L. *Crystallizing Public Opinion*. New York: Boni and Liveright, 1923.

Bird, William R., and Harry R. Rubenstein. *Design for Victory: World War II Posters on the American Home Front*. New York: Princeton Architectural Press, 1998.

Bischof, Gunter, and Saki Dockrill, eds. *Cold War Respite: The Geneva Summit of 1955*. Baton Rouge: Louisiana State University Press, 2000.

Black, Misha, ed. *Exhibition Design*. London: Architectural Press, 1950.

Blake, Avril. *Misha Black*. London: Design Council, 1984.

Blake, Nelson Manfred. *A History of American Life and Thought*. New York: McGraw-Hill, 1963.

Blake, Peter. *No Place Like Utopia: Modern Architecture and the Company We Kept*. New York: Norton, 1993.

Blazwick, Iwona. "Temple/White Cube/Laboratory." In *What Makes a Great Exhibition?*, edited by Paula Marincola, 118–33. Philadelphia: Philadelphia Exhibitions Initiative, 2006.

Bogart, Leo. *Premises for Propaganda: The United States Information Agency's Operating Assumptions in the Cold War*, abridged by Agnes Bogart. New York: Free Press, 1976.

Bonython, Elizabeth, and Anthony Burton. *The Great Exhibitor: The Life and Work of Henry Cole*. London: V&A Publications, 2003.

Boorstin, Daniel. *The Americans: The National Experience*. New York: Random House, 1965.

———. *The Image: Or What Happened to the American Dream*. New York: Atheneum, 1961.

Bourdon, David. "Expo '67." *Art International* 11, no. 7 (September 20, 1967): 21–22.

Boyle, Peter G. *American-Soviet Relations: From the Russian Revolution to the Fall of Communism*. London: Routledge, 1993.

Breckenridge, Carol A. "The Aesthetics and Politics of Colonial Collecting: India at World's Fairs." *Comparative Studies in Society and History* 31, no. 2 (April 1989): 195–216.

Breyne, John P. "A Letter from John Phil. Breyne, M.D. . . . with Observations, and a Description of some Mammoth's Bones Dug Up in Siveria, Proving Them to Have Belong to Elephants." *Philosophical Transactions* 40 (1737–38): 124–38.

Brinkley, Alan. *The Publisher: Henry Luce and His American Century*. New York: Knopf, 2010.

Brown, John. "Arts Diplomacy: The Neglected Aspect of Cultural Diplomacy." In *America's Dialogue with the World*, edited by William P. Kiehl, 71–90. Washington, DC: Public Diplomacy Council, George Washington University, 2006. http://uscpublicdiplomacy.org/pdfs/061220_brown.pdf.

———. "Changing Minds, Winning Peace: Reconsidering the Djerejian Report." *American Diplomacy*. http://www.unc.edu/depts/diplomat/archives_roll/2004_07 -09/brown_djerejian/ brown_djerejian.html.

Buffon, Georges Louis LeClerc. *Natural History: General and Particular*, vol. 5. 2nd ed. Translated by William Smellie. London: W. Strahan and T. Cadell, 1785.

Burns, Jehane, ed. *The World of Franklin and Jefferson*. Los Angeles: Office of Charles and Ray Eames, 1976.

Byer, Robert H. "Words, Monuments, Beholders: The Visual Arts in Hawthorne's 'The Marble Faun.'" In *American Iconology: New Approaches to Nineteenth Century Art and Literature*, edited by David C. Miller, 163–85. New Haven, CT: Yale University Press, 1993.

Calabresi, Stephen G."'A Shining City upon a Hill': American Exceptionalism and the Supreme Court's Practice of Relying on Foreign Law." *Boston University Law Review* 86 (2006): 1335–1416.

Camille, Michael. "Simulacrum." In *Critical Terms for Art History*, 2nd ed., edited by Robert S. Nelson and Richard Shiff, 35–48. Chicago: University of Chicago Press, 2003.

Campbell, John C. "Negotiation with the Soviets: Some Lessons of the War Period." *Foreign Affairs* 34, no. 2 (January 1956): 305–19.

Carbone, Cristina. "Building Propaganda: Architecture at the American National Exhibition in Moscow of 1959." PhD diss., University of California, Santa Barbara, 2001.

———. "Staging the Kitchen Debate: How Splitnik Got Normalized in the United States." In *Cold War Kitchen: Americanization, Technology, and European Users*, edited by Ruth Oldenziel and Karin Zachmann, 59–81. Cambridge, MA: MIT Press, 2009.

Castells, Manuel. *The Power of Identity*. Malden: Blackwell, 1997.

Castillo, Greg. *Cold War on the Home Front: The Soft Power of Midcentury Design*. Minneapolis: University of Minnesota Press, 2010.

———. "Domesticating the Cold War: Household Consumption as Propaganda in Marshall Plan Germany." *Journal of Contemporary History* 40, no. 2 (April 2005): 261–88.

———. "Marshall Plan Modernism in Divided Germany." In *Cold War Modern: Design 1945–1970*, edited by David Crowley and Jane Pavitt, 66–71. London: V&A Publishing, 2008.

Caute, David. *The Dancer Defects: The Struggle for Cultural Supremacy during the Cold War*. Oxford: Oxford University Press, 2003.

Ceglio, Clarissa. "The Wartime Work of U.S. Museums." Research report, Department of American Studies, Brown University, Providence, RI, 2010. http://www .rockarch.org/publications/resrep/ceglio.pdf.

Chanzit, Gwen F. From *Bauhaus to Aspen: Herbert Bayer and Modernist Design in America*. Boulder, CO: Johnson Books / Denver Art Museum, 2005.

Chermayeff, Peter. "Design for a Fair: The United States Pavilion at Expo '67 Montreal." YouTube video, 7:24. http://www.youtube.com/watch?v=6TnT2lSLHxo.

Cherrington, Ben M. "Cultural Ties That Bind in the Relations of the American Nations." *Modern Language Journal* 24, no. 6 (March 1940): 403–9.

Chiappelli, Fredi, with Michael J. B. Allen and Robert L. Benson, eds. *First Images of America: The Impact of the New World on the Old.* Berkeley: University of California Press, 1976.

"Cinerama in Damascus," *Life*, September 27, 1954, 22.

Cockcroft, Eva. "Abstract Expressionism, Weapon of the Cold War." In *Pollock and After: The Critical Debate*, edited by Francis Frascina, 147–54. New York: Harper & Row, 1985.

Cohen, I. Bernard. *Science and the Founding Fathers: Science in the Political Thought of Thomas Jefferson, Benjamin Franklin, John Adams and James Madison.* New York: Norton, 1995.

Cohen, Lizabeth. *A Consumers' Republic: The Politics of Mass Consumption in Postwar America.* New York: Vintage, 2004.

Cohen, Stanley. *Visions of Social Control: Crime, Punishment and Classification.* Cambridge: Polity, 1985.

Colby, Gerard, and Charlotte Bennett. *Thy Will Be Done: The Conquest of the Amazon; Nelson Rockefeller and Evangelism in the Age of Oil.* New York: HarperCollins, 1995.

Colomina, Beatriz. "Enclosed by Images: The Eameses' Multimedia Architecture." *Grey Room*, no. 2 (Winter 2001): 5–29.

Colton, F. Barrows. "Man's New Servant: The Friendly Atom." *National Geographic Magazine*, January 1954, 86–87.

Cook, Blanche Wiesen. *The Declassified Eisenhower: A Divided Legacy of Peace and Political Warfare.* New York: Penguin, 1984.

Cort, David. "Darkness under the Dome." *Nation*, March 1, 1958, 187–88.

Cowan, Geoffrey, and Amelia Arsenault. "Moving from Monologue to Dialogue to Collaboration: The Three Layers of Public Diplomacy." *Annals of the American Academy of Political and Social Science* 616, no. 55 (March 2008): 10–30.

Cowen, Tyler. *Creative Destruction: How Globalization Is Changing the World's Cultures.* Princeton, NJ: Princeton University Press, 2003.

Cramer, Gisela, and Ursula Prutsch. "Nelson A. Rockefeller's Office of Inter-American Affairs (1940–1946) and Record Group 229." *Hispanic American Historical Review* 86, no. 4 (November 2006): 785–806.

Crary, Jonathan. "Spectacle, Attention, Counter-Memory." *October* 50 (Autumn 1989): 96–107.

Creel, George. *How We Advertised America.* New York: Harper & Brothers, 1920.

Crèvecoeur, J. Hector St. John de. *Letters from an American Farmer and Sketches of 18th-Century America.* Edited by Albert E. Stone. Harmondsworth: Penguin, 1981.

Crow, Thomas. *The Intelligence of Art.* Chapel Hill: University of North Carolina Press, 1999.

Crowley, David. "Looking Down on Spaceship Earth: Cold War Landscapes." In *Cold War Modern: Design, 1945–1970*, edited by David Crowley and Jane Pavitt, 249–67. London: V&A Publishing, 2008.

Cull, Nicholas J. *The Cold War and the United States Information Agency: American Propaganda and Public Diplomacy, 1945–1989.* Cambridge: Cambridge University Press, 2008.

———. *The Decline and Fall of the United States Information Agency: American Public Diplomacy, 1989–2001.* Basingstoke: Palgrave MacMillan, 2012.

———. *USC Center on Public Diplomacy* (blog). http://uscpublicdiplomacy.org /blog/060418_public_diplomacy_before_gullion_the_evolution_of_a_phrase.

Cummings, Milton. *Cultural Diplomacy and the United States Government: A Survey.* Washington, DC: Center for Arts and Culture, 2003.

Cunliffe, Marcus. "America at the Great Exhibition of 1851." *American Quarterly* 3, no. 2 (Summer 1951): 115–26.

Curti, Merle. "America at the World's Fairs, 1851–1893." *American Historical Review* 55, no. 4 (July 1950): 833–56.

Dalzell, Robert F. *American Participation in the Great Exhibition of 1851.* Amherst, MA: Amherst College Press, 1960.

Davies, Penelope J. E. *Death and the Emperor: Roman Imperial Funerary Monuments from Augustus to Marcus Aurelius.* Austin: University of Texas Press, 2004.

Davis, John R. *The Great Exhibition.* New York: Sutton, 2000.

Deconde, Alexander. "Historians, the War of American Independence, and the Persistence of the Exceptionalist Ideal." *The International History Review* 5, no. 3 (August 1983): 399–430.

De Grazia, Victoria. *Irresistible Empire: America's Advance through 20th-Century Europe.* Cambridge, MA: Belknap, 2005.

Dessauce, Marc. *The Inflatable Moment: Pneumatics and Protest in '68.* New York: Princeton Architectural Press / Architectural League of New York, 1999.

Dick, Philip K. "How to Build a Universe That Doesn't Fall Apart Two Days Later." In *I Hope I Shall Arrive Soon.* New York: Doubleday, 1978.

Dickens, Charles. *The Life and Adventures of Martin Chuzzlewit.* London: Chapman and Hall, 1844.

Dinnie, Keith, ed. *Nation Branding: Concepts, Issues, Practice.* Oxford: Butterworth-Heinemann, 2008.

Dizard, Wilson P. *Inventing Public Diplomacy: The Story of the U.S. Information Agency.* Boulder, CO: Lynne Rienner, 2004.

Dudley, Drew. "Molding Public Opinion through Advertising." *Annals of the American Academy of Political and Social Science* 250 (March 1947): 105–12.

Dugatkin, Lee Alan. *Mr. Jefferson and the Giant Moose: Natural History in Early America.* Chicago: University of Chicago Press, 2009.

———. "Jefferson's Moose and the Case against American Degeneracy." *Scientific American* no. 2 (2011): 84–87.

Dunlap, Henry A., and Hans M. Tuch. *Atoms at Your Service.* New York: Harper and Brothers, 1957.

Duranti, Marco. "Utopia, Nostalgia and World War at the 1939–40 New York World's Fair." *Journal of Contemporary History* 41, no. 4 (October 2006): 663–83.

Eames, Charles. "The Language of Vision: The Nuts and Bolts," *Bulletin of the American Academy of Arts and Sciences* 28, no. 1 (October 1974): 13–25.

———. "On Reducing Discontinuity." *Bulletin of the American Academy of Arts and Sciences* 30, no. 6 (March 1977): 24–34.

Eames, Lucia Dewey. "The Eames Films Are the Eames Essays." Los Angeles: Eames Office, 2001. www.eamesoffice.com/resources/essay.html.

Eby, Claire Virginia. *Dreiser and Veblen: Saboteurs of the Status Quo.* Columbia: University of Missouri Press, 1998.

Eco, Umberto. "A Theory of Expositions." In *Travels in Hyperreality: Essays.* Translated by William Weaver. San Diego: Harcourt, 1986, 291–307.

———. "Two Families of Objects." In *Travels in Hyperreality: Essays,* translated by William Weaver, 183–86. San Diego: Harcourt, 1986.

Eiseley, Loren. "Myth and Mammoth in Archaeology." *American Antiquity* 11, no. 2 (October 1945): 84–87.

Eisenhower, Dwight D. "State of the Union Address." Speech delivered before Congress, Washington, DC, January 9, 1958.

———. *Waging Peace: The White House Years.* Garden City, NY: Doubleday, 1965.

———. *The White House Years: Mandate for Change, 1953–1956.* Garden City, NY: Doubleday, 1963.

Ellwood, David W., Rob Kroes, and Gian Piero Brunetta, eds. *Hollywood in Europe: Experiences of a Cultural Hegemony.* Amsterdam: VU University Press, 1994.

Elsner, John, and Roger Cardinal, eds. *The Cultures of Collecting.* Cambridge: Harvard University Press, 1994.

Espinosa, J. Manuel. *Inter-American Beginnings of U.S. Cultural Diplomacy, 1936–1948.* Washington, DC: Bureau of Educational and Cultural Affairs, U.S. Department of State, 1976.

Esposti, Piergiorgio Degli. "Hyperconsumption." In *The Wiley-Blackwell Encyclopedia of Globalization,* edited by George Ritzer. Oxford: Blackwell, 2012. doi:10.1002/9780470670590.wbeog064.

Evans, Nicholas J. "Indirect Passage from Europe: Transmigration via the UK, 1836–1914," *Journal for Maritime Research* 3, no. 1 (2001): 70–84.

Ewing, Heather. *The Lost World of James Smithson: Science, Revolution, and the Founding of the Smithsonian.* New York: Bloomsbury, 2007.

"Expositions: Disaster or Masterpiece?" *Time,* June 2, 1967, 47–49.

Fan, Ying. "Branding the Nation: Towards a Better Understanding." *Brunel Business School Research Papers.* 2009. Available at http://bura.brunel.ac.uk/handle/2438/3496.

Faure, Elie. *History of Art: The Spirit of the Forms.* New York: Garden City, 1937.

Feigenbaum, Harvey B. "Globalization and Cultural Diplomacy." Washington, DC: Center for Arts and Culture, 2001. Available at http://xa.yimg.com/kq/groups/22587837/659966199/name/global+6.pdf.

Finn, Helena K. "The Case for Cultural Diplomacy: Engaging Foreign Audiences." *Foreign Affairs* 82, no. 6 (November/December 2003): 15–20.

Forty, Adrian. *Objects of Desire: Design and Society Since 1750*. London: Thames & Hudson, 2000.

Foucault, Michel. *Discipline and Punish: The Birth of the Prison*. Harmondsworth: Peregrine, 1986.

———. "Governmentality." In *The Foucault Effect: Studies in Governmentality*, edited by Graham Burchell, Colin Gordon, and Peter Miller, 87–104. London: Harvester Wheatsheaf, 1996.

Fowler, Don D. "Uses of the Past: Archaeology in the Service of the State." *American Antiquity* 52, no. 2 (April 1987): 229–48.

Fox, Frank. *Madison Avenue Goes to War: The Strange Military Career of American Advertising, 1941–1945*. Provo, UT: Brigham Young University Press, 1975.

Franck, Peter G. "Economic Progress in an Encircled Land." *Middle East Journal* 10, no. 1 (Winter 1956): 43–59.

Freedberg, David. *The Power of Images: Studies in the History and Theory of Response*. Chicago: University of Chicago Press, 1989.

Fuller, R. Buckminster. *Critical Path*. New York: St. Martin's, 1981.

———. *Operating Manual for Spaceship Earth*. Carbondale, IL: Southern Illinois University Press, 1963.

———. *Utopia or Oblivion: The Prospects for Humanity*, edited by Jaime Snyder. Baden, Switzerland: Lars Müller, 2008.

———. "Vision 65 Summary Lecture." *Perspecta* 11 (1967): 58–63.

Galantay, Ervin. "Osaka Expo: Designing the Environment." *Nation*, August 31, 1970, 134–38.

Gann, L. H., and Peter Duignan. "World War II and the Beginning of the Cold War" (Hoover Essays No. 14). Hoover Institution on War, Revolution and Peace, Stanford University, 1996.

Geiger, David. "U.S. Pavilion at Expo 70 Features Air-Supported Cable Roof." *Civil Engineering—ASCE* (March 1970): 48–50.

Gerbi, Antonello. *The Dispute of the New World: The History of a Polemic, 1750–1900*. Translated by Jeremy Moyle. Pittsburgh: University of Pittsburgh Press, 1973.

Getlein, Frank. "Pictures at an Exhibition." *New Republic* 141, Issue 8/9 (August 24, 1959): 12.

Gienow-Hecht, Jessica C. E., and Frank Schumacher, eds. *Culture and International History*. New York: Berghahn, 2003.

Gilboa, Eytan. "Searching for a Theory of Public Diplomacy." *Annals of the American Academy of Political and Social Science* 616, no. 55 (March 2008): 55–77.

Gillespie, Charles C, ed. *Complete Dictionary of Scientific Biography*, Vol. 15. Detroit: Scribner's, 1981.

Gingerich, Owen. "A Conversation with Charles Eames." *American Scholar* 46, no. 3 (Summer 1977): 326–37.

Giovannini, Joseph. "The Office of Charles Eames and Ray Kaiser: The Material Trail." In *The Work of Charles and Ray Eames: A Legacy of Invention*, edited by Diana Murphy, 44–71. New York: Abrams / Library of Congress / Vitra Design Museum, 1997.

Godman, John D. *American Natural History*. Philadelphia: H. C. Carey & I. Lea, 1826.

Goffman, Erving. *The Presentation of Self in Everyday Life*. New York: Doubleday, 1959.

Gombrich, E. H. *Art and Illusion: A Study in the Psychology of Pictorial Representation*. London: Phaidon, 2002.

Goodyear, A. Conger. *The Museum of Modern Art: The First Ten Years*. New York: Museum of Modern Art, 1943.

Goodyear, Ann Collins. "From Technophilia to Technophobia: The Impact of the Vietnam War on the Reception of 'Art and Technology.'" *Leonardo* 41, no. 2 (April 2008): 169–73.

Grabar, Oleg. "From Dome of Heaven to Pleasure Dome." *Journal of the Society of Architectural Historians* 49, no. 1 (March 1990): 15–21.

Greeley, Horace. *Glances at Europe*. New York: Dewitt & Davenport, 1851.

Green, Fitzhugh. *American Propaganda Abroad: From Benjamin Franklin to Ronald Reagan*. New York: Hippocrene, 1988.

Greenhalgh, Paul. *Ephemeral Vistas: The Expositions Universelles, Great Exhibitions, and World's Fairs, 1851–1939*. Manchester: Manchester University Press, 1988.

Gregory, Bruce. "Public Diplomacy and Strategic Communication: Cultures, Firewalls, and Imported Norms." Lecture, American Political Science Association, Conference on International Communication and Conflict, George Washington University and Georgetown University, Washington, DC, August 31, 2005.

Griffith, Robert. "The Selling of America: The Advertising Council and American Politics, 1942–1960." *Business History Review* 57, no. 3 (Autumn 1983): 388–412.

Guilbaut, Serge. *How New York Stole the Idea of Modern Art: Abstract Expressionism, Freedom and the Cold War*. Chicago: University of Chicago Press, 1983.

Gunther, John. *Inside Russia Today*. New York: Harper, 1957.

Gurian, Elaine Heumann. "Noodling Around with Exhibition Opportunities." In *Exhibiting Cultures: The Poetics and Politics of Museum Display*, edited by Ivan Karp and Steven D. Lavine, 176–190. Washington, DC: Smithsonian Institution, 1991.

Gurney, Peter. "An Appropriated Space: The Great Exhibition, the Crystal Palace and the Working Class." In *The Great Exhibition of 1851: New Interdisciplinary Essays*, edited by Louise Purbrick, 114–45. Manchester: Manchester University Press, 2001.

Haddow, Robert H. *Pavilions of Plenty: Exhibiting American Culture Abroad in the 1950s*. Washington, DC: Smithsonian Institution, 1997.

Hall, Peter. "A Good Argument." *Metropolis Magazine*, March 2009, http://www.metropolismag.com/March-2009/A-Good-Argument/.

Hamilton, Alexander. *Federalist Paper No. 11*. 1787.

Hamm, Bernd, and Russell Smandych, eds. *Cultural Imperialism: Essays on the Political Economy of Cultural Domination*. Peterborough, ON: Broadview, 2005.

Handler, Richard. "Is 'Identity' a Useful Cross-Cultural Concept?" In *Commemorations: The Politics of National Identity*, edited by John R. Gillis, 27–40. Princeton, NJ: Princeton University Press, 1994.

Hays, K. Michael, and Dana Miller. *Buckminster Fuller: Starting with the Universe*. New York: Whitney Museum of American Art; New Haven, CT: Yale University Press, 2008.

H-Diplo. "*Total Cold War* Roundtable Review." *H-Net: Humanities & Social Sciences Online* (February 26, 2007): 21. Accessed April 4, 2010. http://h-diplo.org/round tables/PDF/TotalColdWar-complete.pdf.

Herring, George C. *From Colony to Superpower: U.S. Foreign Relations since 1776*. Oxford: Oxford University Press, 2008.

Hess, Thomas B. "From 'Bisontennial' Beasts to Cornell Boxes." *New York Magazine*, March 22, 1976, 59.

Hevner, Carol Eaton, and Lillian B. Miller. *Rembrandt Peale, 1778–1860: A Life in the Arts*. Philadelphia: Historical Society of Philadelphia, 1985.

Hillman, Brenda, ed. *The Pocket Emily Dickinson*. Boston: Shambhala, 2009.

Hinsley, Curtis M. "The World as Marketplace: Commodification of the Exotic at the World's Columbian Exposition." In *Exhibiting Cultures: The Poetics and Politics of Museum Display*, edited by Ivan Karp and Steven Levine, 344–65. Washington, DC: Smithsonian Institution, 1991.

Hixson, Walter L. *Parting the Curtain: Propaganda, Culture and the Cold War, 1945–1961*. New York: St. Martin's, 1997.

Hobhouse, Hermione. *The Crystal Palace and the Great Exhibition: Art, Science and Productive Industry: The History of the Royal Commission for the Great Exhibition of 1851*. London: Continuum, 2002.

Holden, Robert H., and Eric Zolov, *Latin America and the United States: A Documentary History*. New York: Oxford University Press, 2011.

Hunt, Michael H. *Ideology and U.S. Foreign Policy*. New Haven, CT: Yale University Press, 1987.

Inda, Jonathan Xavier. "Governmentality." In *The Wiley-Blackwell Encyclopedia of Globalization*, edited by George Ritzer. Oxford: Blackwell, 2012.

Iriye, Akira. *Cultural Internationalism and World Order*. Baltimore: Johns Hopkins University Press, 1997.

Isenberg, Andrew C. "Environment and the Nineteenth-Century West: Or, Process Encounters Place." In *A Companion to the American West*, edited by William Deverell, 77–92. Malden, MA: Blackwell, 2004.

Jacobson, Bob. "'Blackwatering' Public Diplomacy: The US Pavilion at the Shanghai World Expo." *Huffington Post*, May 3, 2010. http://www.huffingtonpost.com/bob -jacobson/an-epic-failure-of-planni_b_561697.html.

———. "US Pavilion at Shanghai Fails to Do Its Job: 'San Antonio Threw a ($500,000) Party and No One Came.'" *Huffington Post*, May 31, 2010. http://www .huffingtonpost.com/bob-jacobson/us-pavilion-in-shanghai-f_b_594315.html.

Jacoby, Russell. *Social Amnesia: A Critique of Contemporary Psychology*. Boston: Beacon, 1975.

Jefferson, Thomas. *Writings*. New York: Library Classics of the United States, 1984.

Jensen, Kenneth M., ed. *Origins of the Cold War: The Novikov, Kennan, and Roberts 'Long Telegrams' of 1946*. Washington, DC: United States Institute of Peace, 1991.

Johnson, Benjamin P. *Report on the Industrial Exhibition*. London, 1851.

Johnson, J. Stewart. *American Modern 1925–1940: Design for a New Age*. New York: Abrams, 2000.

Kaiser, Wolfram. "The Great Derby Race: Strategies of Cultural Representation at Nineteenth-Century World Exhibitions." In *Culture and International History*, edited by Jessica C. E. Gienow-Hecht and Frank Schumacher, 45–59. New York: Berghahn, 2003.

Kaneva, Nadia. "Nation Branding: Toward an Agenda for Critical Research," *International Journal of Communication* 5 (2011): 117–41.

Kaplan, Amy, and Donald Pease, eds. *Cultures of United States Imperialism*. London: Duke University Press, 1993.

Kastner, Jeffrey. "National Insecurity," *Cabinet Magazine*, no.22 (Summer 2006). http://www.cabinetmagazine.org/issues/22/kastner.php.

Kenneally, Rhona Richman, and Johanne Sloan, eds. *Expo 67: Not Just a Souvenir*. Toronto: University of Toronto Press, 2010.

Kennedy, David M. "Imagining America: The Promise and Peril of Boundlessness." In *Anti-Americanisms in World Politics*, edited by Peter J. Katzenstein and Robert O. Keohane, 39–56. Ithaca, NY: Cornell University Press, 2007.

Kennedy, John F. "A Democrat Looks at Foreign Policy." *Foreign Affairs* 36, no. 1 (October 1957): 44–59.

Kennedy, Liam. "Remembering September 11: Photography as Cultural Diplomacy," *International Affairs* 79, no. 2 (March 2003): 315–26.

Keohane, Robert O. *After Hegemony: Cooperation and Discord in the World Political Economy*. Princeton, NJ: Princeton University Press, 1984.

Keohane, Robert O., and Joseph S. Nye Jr., eds. *Power and Interdependence: World Politics in Transition*. New York: Little, Brown, 1977.

Kimball, Jeffrey P. "Out of the Primordial Cultural Ooze: Inventing Political and Policy Legacies about the U.S. Exit from Vietnam." *Diplomatic History* 34, no. 3 (June 2010): 577–87.

Kirkham, Pat. *Charles and Ray Eames: Designers of the Twentieth Century*. Cambridge, MA: MIT Press, 1995.

Kissinger, Henry A. *Diplomacy*. New York: Simon & Schuster, 1994.

———. "Reflections on American Diplomacy." *Foreign Affairs* 35, no. 1 (October 1956): 37–56.

Knell, Simon J. "Museums, Fossils and the Cultural Revolution of Science: Mapping Change in the Politics of Knowledge in Early Nineteenth-Century Britain." In *Museum Revolutions: How Museums Change and Are Changed*, edited by Simon J. Knell, Suzanne MacLeod, and Sheila Watson, 48–60. London: Routledge, 2007.

Kracauer, Siegfried. *The Mass Ornament: The Weimar Essays*. Cambridge, MA: Harvard University Press, 1995.

Kramer, Hilton. "The End of Modern Painting." *Reporter: The Magazine of Facts and Ideas*, July 23, 1959, 41–42.

Krenn, Michael L. *Fallout Shelters for the Human Spirit: American Art and the Cold War*. Chapel Hill: University of North Carolina Press, 2005.

———. "'Unfinished Business:' Segregation and U.S. Diplomacy at the 1958 World's Fair." In *Race and United States Foreign Policy during the Cold War: A Collection of Essays*, edited by Michael L. Krenn, 237–59. New York: Garland, 1998.

Kriegel, Lara. "After the Exhibitionary Complex: Museum Histories and the Future of the Victorian Past," *Victorian Studies* 48, no. 4 (2006): 681–704.

Kroes, Rob. *If You've Seen One, You've Seen the Mall: Europeans and American Mass Culture*. Urbana: University of Illinois Press, 1996.

———. "Imaginary Americas in Europe's Public Space." In *The Americanization of Europe: Culture, Diplomacy, and Anti-Americanism after 1945*, edited by Alexander Stephan, 337–59. New York: Berghahn, 2006.

Kupperman, Karen Ordahl, ed. *America in European Consciousness, 1493–1750*. Chapel Hill: University of North Carolina Press, 1995.

Kushner, Marilyn S. "Exhibiting Art at the American National Exhibition in Moscow, 1959: Domestic Politics and Cultural Diplomacy." *Journal of Cold War Studies* 4, no. 1 (Winter 2002): 6–26.

La Roche, Chester J., Arthur Price, Arthur T. Robb, Ralph Coghlan, and Leonard Dreyfuss. "Should the Government Advertise?" *Public Opinion Quarterly* 6, no. 4 (Winter 1942): 511–36.

Lasch, Christopher. *The Culture of Narcissism: American Life in an Age of Diminishing Expectations*. London: Norton, 1991.

Latham, Richard. "Communication of Values through Design." In *The Aspen Papers: Twenty Years of Design Theory from the International Design Conference in Aspen*, edited by Reyner Banham, 86–91. New York: Praeger, 1974.

Lederer, William J., and Eugene Burdick. *The Ugly American*. New York: Norton, 1958.

Leffler, Melvyn P. *A Preponderance of Power: National Security, the Truman Administration, and the Cold War*. Palo Alto, CA: Stanford University Press, 1992.

Lennox, Sara. "Constructing Femininity in the Early Cold War Era." In *German Pop Culture: How "American" Is It?*, edited by Agnes C. Mueller, 66–80. Ann Arbor: University of Michigan Press, 2007.

Leone, Mark P., and Barbara J. Little. "Artifacts as Expressions of Society and Culture: Subversive Genealogy and the Value of History." In *Museum Studies: An Anthology of Contexts*, edited by Bettina Messias Carbonell, 362–74. Malden, MA: Blackwell, 2004.

Lipovetsky, Gilles. *Hypermodern Times*. Cambridge: Polity, 2005.

Lippmann, Walter. *The Cold War*. New York: Harper, 1947.

———. *Public Opinion*. New York: Harcourt, 1922.

Lipset, Seymour Martin. *American Exceptionalism: A Double-Edged Sword*. New York: Norton, 1996.

Lipstadt, Hélène. "'Natural Overlap': Charles and Ray Eames and the Federal Government." In *The Work of Charles and Ray Eames: A Legacy of Invention*, edited by Diana Murphy, 150–77. New York: Abrams / Library of Congress / Vitra Design Museum, 1997.

Littleton, Taylor D., and Maltby Sykes. *Advancing American Art: Painting, Politics and Cultural Confrontation at Mid-Century*. 2nd ed. Tuscaloosa: University of Alabama Press, 1989.

Looby, Christopher. "The Constitution of Nature: Taxonomy as Politics in Jefferson, Peale, and Bartram." In *Museum Studies: An Anthology of Contexts*, edited by Bettina Messias Carbonell, 143–58. Malden, MA: Blackwell, 2004.

Luňák, Petr. "Khruschev and Berlin Crisis: Soviet Brinkmanship See from Inside." *Cold War History* 3, no. 2 (January 2003): 53–82.

Lynes, Russell. *Good Old Modern: The Museum of Modern Art*. New York: Atheneum, 1973.

Mackesy, Piers. *The War for America, 1775–1783*. Cambridge, MA: Harvard University Press, 1964.

Mackinder, H. J. "The Geographical Pivot of History." *Geographical Journal* 23, no. 4 (April 1904): 421–37.

Malone, Dumas. *Jefferson and the Rights of Man*. Boston: Little, Brown, 1951.

Marchand, Roland. *Advertising the American Dream: Making Way for Modernity, 1920–1940*. Berkeley: University of California Press, 1985.

Margolies, John Samuel. "Building for Art: Export America in a Splendid Dome, The United States Pavilion at Expo '67." *Art Voices* 5, no. 4 (Fall 1966): 82–86.

Marks, Peter. "Imagining Surveillance: Utopian Visions and Surveillance Studies." *Surveillance and Society* 3, no. 2/3 (2005): 222–39.

Masani, M. R. "The Mind of Asia." *Foreign Affairs* 33, no. 4 (July 1955): 548–65.

Masey, Jack. "21st-Century World's Fairs." Lecture at the National Building Museum, October 25, 2010. http://www.nbm.org/media/audio/21st-century-worlds-fairs-3.html.

Masey, Jack, and Conway Lloyd Morgan. *Cold War Confrontations: U.S. Exhibitions and Their Role in the Cultural Cold War*. Baden, Switzerland: Lars Müller, 2008.

Massey, Jonathan. "Buckminster Fuller's Cybernetic Pastoral: The United States Pavilion at Expo 67." *Journal of Architecture* 11, no. 4 (2006): 463–83.

Matusitz, Jonathan. "Cathedrals of Consumption." In *Wiley-Blackwell Encyclopedia of Globalization*, edited by George Ritzer. Oxford: Blackwell, 2012. doi:10.1002/9780470670590.wbeog064.

Mayhew, Henry. *1851: or, the Adventures of Mr. and Mrs. Sandboys and Family*. London: Mayhew, 1851.

Mayor, Adrienne. *The First Fossil Hunters: Dinosaurs, Mammoths, and Myth in Greek and Roman Times*. Princeton, NJ: Princeton University Press, 2000.

McClellan, Andrew. *Inventing the Louvre: Art, Politics, and the Origins of the Modern Museum in Eighteenth-Century Paris*. Berkeley: University of California Press, 1994.

McDonough, Tom. "Obsolescence as Progress and Regression: Technology, Temporality, and Architecture at Expo 67." In *Expo 67: Not Just a Souvenir*, edited by Rhona Richman Kenneally and Johanne Sloan, 83–92. Toronto: University of Toronto Press, 2010.

McLean, Kathleen. "Museum Exhibitions and the Dynamics of Dialogue." *Daedalus* 128, no. 3 (Summer 1999): 83–107.

McMahon, A. Philip. "Would Plato Find Artistic Beauty in Machines?" *Parnassus* 7, no. 2 (February 1935): 6–8.

McMurray, Ruth Emily, and Muna Lee. *The Cultural Approach: Another Way in International Relations*. Chapel Hill: North Carolina University Press, 1947.

Meikle, Jeffrey. *Design in the USA*. Oxford: Oxford University Press, 2005.

———. *Twentieth Century Limited: Industrial Design in America, 1925–1939*. Philadelphia: Temple University Press, 1979.

Menand, Louis. "Unpopular Front: American Art and the Cold War." *The New Yorker* 81, no. 32 (October 17, 2005): 174–179.

Message, Kylie. *New Museums and the Making of Culture*. Oxford: Berg, 2006.

Meyer, D. H. "The Uniqueness of the American Enlightenment." *American Quarterly* 28, no. 2 (Summer 1976): 165–86.

Miller, Lillian B. "C. W. Peale as History Painter: The Exhumation of the Mastodon." *American Art Journal* 13, no. 1 (Winter 1981): 47–68.

Miller, Lillian B., and David C. Ward, eds. *New Perspectives on Charles Willson Peale: A 250th Anniversary Celebration*. Pittsburgh: University of Pittsburgh Press, 1991.

Miłosz, Czesław. *The Captive Mind*. Translated by Jane Zielonko. London: Penguin, 1980.

Mitarachi, Jane Fisk. "Design as a Political Force." *Industrial Design* (February 1957): 1–16.

Mock, James Robert, and Cedric Larson. *Words That Won the War: The Story of the Committee on Public Information 1917–1919*. Princeton, NJ: Princeton University Press, 1939.

Molella, Arthur, Nathan Reingold, Marc Rothenberg, Joan F. Steiner, and Kathleen Waldenfels, eds. *A Scientist in American Life: Essays and Lectures of Joseph Henry*. Washington, DC: Smithsonian Institution, 1980.

Morrow, Lance. "On Reimagining America." *Time*, March 31, 1980, http://www.time.com/time/magazine/article/0,9171,921933,00.html.

Museum of Modern Art. *Machine Art: March 6 to April 30, 1934, Sixtieth Anniversary Edition*. New York: Abrams, 1994.

Museum of Modern Art. Press release, April 1, 1942, 42401-24. http://www.moma.org/docs/press_archives/784/releases/MOMA_1942_0026_1942-04-01_42401-24.pdf?2010.

Museum of Modern Art. Press release, October 8, 1942, 421008-64. http://www.moma.org/docs/press_archives/828/releases/MOMA_1942_0070_1942-10-08_421008-64.pdf?2010.

"The Museum and the War." *Bulletin of the Museum of Modern Art* 10, no. 1 (October/November 1942).

Nelson, George. "Art X: The Georgia Experiment." *Industrial Design* (October 1954): 44–51.

———. "Design as Communication." *Industrial Design* (April 1954): 38–42.

———. "Obsolescence." *Perspecta* 11 (1967): 170–76.

Nelson, George, ed. *Display.* New York: Whitney, 1953.

Neuhart, John, Marilyn Neuhart, and Ray Eames. *Eames Design: The Work of the Office of Charles and Ray Eames.* New York: Abrams, 1989.

Ninkovich, Frank A. "The Currents of Cultural Diplomacy: Art and the State Department, 1938–1947." *Diplomatic History* 1, no. 3 (July 1977): 215–38.

———. *The Diplomacy of Ideas: U.S. Foreign Policy and Cultural Relations, 1938–1950.* Cambridge: Cambridge University Press, 1981.

———. *Global Dawn: The Cultural Foundation of American Internationalism, 1865–1890.* Cambridge, MA: Harvard University Press, 2009.

———. *The Wilsonian Century: U.S. Foreign Policy since 1900.* Chicago: University of Chicago Press, 1999.

Nixon, Richard M. "Russia As I Saw It." *National Geographic* 116, no. 6 (December 1959), 715–50.

Nye, Joseph S., Jr. *Soft Power: The Means to Success in World Politics.* New York: Public Affairs, 2004.

Office of Inter-American Affairs. *History of the Office of the Coordinator of Inter-American Affairs: Historical Reports on War Administration.* Washington, DC: U.S. Government Printing Office, 1947.

Official Descriptive and Illustrated Catalogue of the Great Exhibition of 1851. London: Spicer, 1851–52.

Oldenziel, Ruth, and Karin Zachmann, eds. *Cold War Kitchen: Americanization, Technology, and European Users.* Cambridge, MA: MIT Press, 2009.

Orosz, Joel J. *Curators and Culture: The Museum Movement in America, 1740–1870.* Tuscaloosa: University of Alabama Press, 1990.

Osgood, Kenneth. Lecture at the Miller Center for Public Affairs. YouTube video, 5:09. Posted by MCamericanpresident, March 10, 2008. http://www.youtube.com/watch?v=0rBdjBZooas.

———. *Total Cold War: Eisenhower's Secret Propaganda Battle at Home and Abroad.* Lawrence: University of Kansas Press, 2006.

P. "Middle Ground between America and Russia: An Indian View." *Foreign Affairs,* 32, no. 2 (January 1954): 259–69.

Pang, Alex Soojung-Kim. "Dome Days: Buckminster Fuller in the Cold War." In *Cultural Babbage: Technology, Time and Invention,* edited by Francis Spufford and Jenny Uglow, 167–92. London: Faber and Faber, 1996.

Patterson, James T. *Grand Expectations: The United States, 1945–1974.* Oxford: Oxford University Press, 1996.

Pavitt, Jane. "Design and the Democratic Ideal." In *Cold War Modern: Design 1945–1970*, edited by David Crowley and Jane Pavitt, 73–93. London: V&A Publishing, 2008.

Peale, Rembrandt. *An Historical Disquisition of the Mammoth, or, Great American Incognitum.* London: C. Mercier, 1803.

———. "Rembrandt Peale to C. W. Peale, July 30, 1803." In *Rembrandt Peale, 1778–1860: A Life in the Arts*, edited by Carol Eaton Hevner and Lillian B. Miller, 40, 97. Philadelphia: Historical Society of Philadelphia, 1985.

Pearce, Susan M. *Museums, Objects and Collections: A Cultural Study.* Washington, DC: Smithsonian Institution, 1993.

Pease, Donald E. *The New American Exceptionalism.* Minneapolis: University of Minnesota Press, 2009.

Pells, Richard H. *Not Like Us: How Europeans Have Loved, Hated, and Transformed American Culture since World War II.* New York: Basic, 1997.

Peterson, Merrill D., ed. *The Political Writings of Thomas Jefferson.* Charlottesville, VA: Thomas Jefferson Foundation, 1993.

Pevsner, Nikolaus. "At Aspen in Colorado." In *The Aspen Papers: Twenty Years of Design Theory from the International Design Conference in Aspen*, edited by Reyner Banham, 15–18. New York: Praeger, 1974.

Pimlott, J. A. R. "Public Service Advertising: The Advertising Council." *Public Opinion Quarterly* 12, no. 2 (Summer 1948): 209–19.

"Plastiscope 3." *Modern Plastics* (March 1970): 162.

Pomian, Krzysztof. *Collectors and Curiosities: Paris and Venice, 1500–1800.* Translated by Elizabeth Wiles-Porter. Cambridge: Polity Press, 1990.

Preziosi, Donald. *Brain of the Earth's Body: Art, Museums, and the Phantasms of Modernity.* Minneapolis: University of Minnesota Press, 2003.

———. "Collecting/Museums." In *Critical Terms for Art History*, 2nd ed., edited by Robert S. Nelson and Richard Shiff, 407–18. Chicago: University of Chicago Press, 2003.

Pullin, Eric D. "'Noise and Flutter': American Propaganda Strategy and Operation in India during World War II." *Diplomatic History* 34, no. 2 (April 2010): 275–98.

Pulos, Arthur J. *The American Design Adventure, 1940–1975.* Cambridge, MA: MIT Press, 1988.

———. "United States: The Wizards of Standardized Aesthetics." In *History of Industrial Design: 1919–1990, The Dominion of Design*, edited by Carol Pirovano, 160–81. Milan: Electa, 1991.

Punch XX (1851): 209, 246. http://books.google.com/books/about/PUNCH_VOL _XX_1851.html?id=EOVbAAAAQAAJ.

Rabel, Roberto, ed. *The American Century? In Retrospect and Prospect.* Westport, CT: Praeger, 2002.

Raynal, Guillaume Thomas François. *Histoire Philosophique et Politique des Établissements et du Commerce des Européens dans les deux Indes.* Amsterdam, 1770.

Reid, Susan. "The Soviet Pavilion at Brussels '58: Convergence, Conversion, Critical Assimilation, or Transcultural?" Woodrow Wilson International Center for Scholars, Cold War International History Project: Working Papers Series, Working Paper 62 (December 2010).

Repp, Philip C. "The Information Design Lessons: Selected Films by Charles and Ray Eames." *LOOP: AIGA Journal of Interaction Design Education*, no. 2 (April 2001): 1–11.

Richmond, Yale. *Cultural Exchange and the Cold War: Raising the Iron Curtain.* University Park: Pennsylvania State University Press, 2003.

———. *U.S.-Soviet Cultural Exchanges, 1958–1986: Who Wins?* Boulder, CO: Westview, 1987.

Rigal, Laura. "Peale's Mammoth." In *American Iconology: New Approaches to Nineteenth Century Art and Literature*, edited by David C. Miller, 18–38. New Haven, CT: Yale University Press, 1993.

Ritzer, George. *Enchanting a Disenchanted World: Revolutionizing the Means of Consumption.* 2nd ed. Thousand Oaks, CA: Pine Forge, 2005.

———. *The McDonaldization of Society: An Investigation into the Changing Character of Contemporary Social Life.* Thousand Oaks, CA.: Pine Forge, 1993.

Rodgers, Charles T. *American Superiority at the World's Fair.* Philadelphia: John J. Hawkins, 1852.

Romano, Angela. "Détente, Entente, or Linkage? The Helsinki Conference on Security and Cooperation in Europe in U.S. Relations with the Soviet Union." *Diplomatic History* 33, no. 4 (September 2009): 703–22.

Ronda, James P. "Passion and Imagination in the Exploration of the American West." In *A Companion to the American West*, edited by William Deverell, 53–76. Malden, MA: Blackwell, 2004.

Roosevelt, Theodore. *Address of Hon. Theodore Roosevelt Before the Naval War College.* Newport, Rhode Island, June 2, 1897.

Rosenberg, Emily S. *Spreading the American Dream: American Economic and Cultural Expansion, 1890–1945.* New York: Hill and Wang, 1982.

Rosing, Larry. "Bison-tennial Show: The Bazaar World of Franklin & Jefferson." *New Age Examiner* (Summer 1976), 65.

Roth, Matthew. "Face Value: Objects of Industry and the Visitor Experience." *Public Historian* 22, no. 3 (Summer 2000): 33–48.

Rothkopf, David. "In Praise of Cultural Imperialism." *Foreign Policy* 107 (Summer 1997): 38–53.

Rotter, Andrew J. "Feeding Beggars: Class, Caste, and Status in Indo-U.S. Relations, 1947–1964." In *Cold War Constructions: The Political Culture of United States Imperialism, 1945–1966*, edited by Christian G. Appy, 67–85. Amherst: University of Massachusetts Press, 2000.

Rubin, Ronald I. *The Objectives of the U.S. Information Agency, Controversies and Analysis.* New York: Praeger, 1966.

Rudwick, Martin J. S. *Bursting the Limits of Time: The Reconstruction of Geohistory in the Age of Revolution*. Chicago: University of Chicago Press, 2005.

Rugh, William A., ed. *Engaging the Arab and Islamic Worlds through Public Diplomacy: A Report and Action Recommendations*. Washington, DC: Public Diplomacy Council, 2004.

Rydell, Robert W. *All the World's a Fair: Visions of Empire at American International Expositions, 1876–1916*. Chicago: University of Chicago Press, 1984.

Rydell, Robert W., John E. Findling, and Kimberley D. Pelle. *Fair America: World's Fairs in the United States*. Washington, DC: Smithsonian Institution, 2000.

Sablosky, Juliet Antunes. "Reinvention, Reorganization, Retreat: American Cultural Diplomacy at Century's End, 1978–1998." *Journal of Arts Management, Law, and Society* 29, no. 1 (Spring 1999): 30–46.

Sadao, Shoji. "A Brief History of Geodesic Domes." In *Buckminster Fuller: Anthology for the New Millennium*, edited by Thomas T. K. Zung, 19–28. New York: St. Martin's, 2001.

Safire, William. *Safire's Political Dictionary*. Oxford: Oxford University Press, 2008.

Sakharov, Andrei. "Open Letter to the United States Congress." In *The Human Rights Reader*, rev. ed., edited by Walter Laqueur and Barry Rubin, 334–36. New York: New American Library, 1979.

Salisbury, Philip. "Has Advertising Come of Age?" *Journal of Marketing* 8, no. 1 (July 1943): 25–32.

Sandburg, Carl. *The Family of Man*. New York: Museum of Modern Art, 1955.

Sandeen, Eric J. *Picturing an Exhibition: The Family of Man and 1950s America*. Albuquerque: University of New Mexico Press, 1995.

Satloff, Robert. *The Battle of Ideas in the War on Terror: Essays on US Public Diplomacy in the Middle East*. Washington, DC: Washington Institute for Near East Policy, 2004.

Saunders, Francis Stonor. *Who Paid the Piper: The CIA and the Cultural Cold War*. London: Granta, 1999.

Schapiro, Meyer. *Romanesque Art: Selected Papers*. New York: George Braziller, 1977.

Schlesinger, Arthur M., Jr. *The Age of Jackson*. Boston: Little, Brown, 1945.

Schneider, Cynthia P. "Culture Communicates: US Diplomacy that Works." Discussion Papers in Diplomacy 94. The Hague: Netherlands Institute of International Relations, September 2004.

———. "Diplomacy That Works: 'Best Practices' in Cultural Diplomacy." Cultural Diplomacy Research Series. Washington, DC: Center for Arts and Culture, 2003.

———. "Shanghai'd, or the USA Pavilion as a Corporate Theme Park." USC Center on Public Diplomacy, June 8, 2010. http://uscpublicdiplomacy.org/index.php/newswire/cpdblog_detail/shanghaid_or_the_usa_pavilion_as_a_corporate_theme_park/.

Schoenbrun, David. *Triumph in Paris: The Exploits of Benjamin Franklin*. New York: Harper & Row, 1976.

Schwartz, Vanessa R., and Jeannene M. Przyblyski, eds. *The Nineteenth-Century Visual Culture Reader*. New York: Routledge, 2004.

Sellers, Charles Coleman. *Mr. Peale's Museum: Charles Willson Peale and the First Popular Museum of Natural Science and Art.* New York: Norton, 1980.

———. "Rembrandt Peale, 'Instigator.'" *Pennsylvania Magazine of History and Biography* 79, no. 3 (July 1955): 331–42.

Sellers, Horace W. "Letters of Thomas Jefferson to Charles Willson Peale, 1796–1825." *Pennsylvania Magazine of History and Biography* 28, no. 2 (1904): 136–54.

Semonin, Paul. *American Monster: How the Nation's First Prehistoric Creature Became a Symbol of National Identity.* New York: New York University Press, 2000.

Smith, C. Ray. "Ivan Chermayeff and Thomas Geismar." American Institute of Graphic Arts, 1980. http://www.aiga.org/medalist-ivanchermayeffandtomgeismar/.

Smith, Michael L. "Selling the Moon: The U.S. Manned Space Program and the Triumph of Commodity Scientism." In *The Culture of Consumption: Critical Essays in American History, 1880–1980,* edited by Richard Wightman Fox and T. J. Jackson Lears, 175–209. New York: Pantheon, 1983.

Smith, Peter H. *Talons of the Eagle: Dynamics of U.S.-Latin American Relations.* 2nd ed. Oxford: Oxford University Press, 2000.

Snow, Nancy. *Information War: American Propaganda, Free Speech and Opinion Control Since 9/11.* New York: Seven Stories / Council on Foreign Relations, 2003.

Snow, Nancy, and Philip M. Taylor, eds. *Routledge Handbook of Public Diplomacy.* New York: Routledge, 2009.

Snyder, Alvin. "U.S. Foreign Affairs in the New Information Age: Charting a Course for the 21st Century." Washington, DC: Annenberg Washington Program in Communications Policy Studies of Northwestern University, 1994. http://annenberg.northwestern.edu/pubs/usfa/default.htm.

Sontag, Susan. "Against Interpretation." In *Art History and its Methods: A Critical Anthology,* edited by Eric Fernie, 214–22. London: Phaidon, 1995.

Staniszewski, Mary Anne. *The Power of Display: A History of Exhibition Installations at the Museum of Modern Art.* Cambridge, MA: MIT Press, 1998.

Steichen, Edward. *The Family of Man.* New York: Museum of Modern Art, 1955.

Stephan, Alexander. *The Americanization of Europe: Culture, Diplomacy, and Anti-Americanism after 1945.* New York: Berghahn, 2006.

Stewart, Susan. "Death and Life, in That Order, in the Works of Charles Willson Peale." In *The Cultures of Collecting,* edited by John Elsner and Roger Cardinal, 204–23. London: Reaktion, 1994.

Straw, Will. "Tabloid Expo." In *Expo 67: Not Just a Souvenir,* edited by Rhona Richman Kenneally and Johanne Sloan, 221–38. Toronto: University of Toronto Press, 2010.

Sutton, Francis X., Seymour E. Harris, Carl Kaysen, and James Tobin. *The American Business Creed.* Cambridge, MA: Harvard University Press, 1956.

Talbott, Strobe. *The Great Experiment: The Story of Ancient Empires, Modern States, and the Quest for a Global Nation.* New York: Simon & Schuster, 2008.

"The Talk of the Town: Machine Art." *New Yorker,* March 17, 1934, 18.

Taylor, Paul A. "Hyperreality." In *The Wiley-Blackwell Encyclopedia of Globalization,* edited by George Ritzer. Oxford: Blackwell, 2012.

Teague, Walter Dorwin. "Rightness Sells." *Advertising Arts* (January 1934): 25–26.

Thomas, Harold B. "The Background and Beginning of the Advertising Council." In *The Promise of Advertising*, edited by C. H. Sandage, 15–58. Homewood, IL: Irwin, 1961.

Thomas, John R. "Report on Service with the American Exhibition in Moscow." Social Science Division, RAND Corporation, P-1859, March 15, 1960.

Thomson, Keith. *The Legacy of the Mastodon: The Golden Age of Fossils in America.* New Haven, CT: Yale University Press, 2008.

Thorp, Willard L. "American Policy and the Soviet Economic Offensive." *Foreign Affairs* 35, no. 2 (January 1957): 271–82.

Tocqueville, Alexis de. *Democracy in America* (1835). In Marie-France Toinet, "French Pique and *Piques Françaises*," *Annals of the American Academy of Political and Social Science*, May 1988.

Tolvaisas, Tomas. "America On Display: U.S. Commercial and Cultural Exhibitions in the Soviet Bloc Countries, 1961–1968." PhD diss., Rutgers, The State University of New Jersey, 2007.

———. "Cold War 'Bridge-Building' U.S. Exchange Exhibits and Their Reception in the Soviet Union, 1959–1967." *Journal of Cold War Studies* 12, no. 4 (Fall 2010): 3–31.

Tomlinson, John. *Cultural Imperialism: A Critical Introduction.* Baltimore, MD: Johns Hopkins University Press, 1991.

Tota, Antonio Pedro. *The Seduction of Brazil: The Americanization of Brazil during World War II.* Translated by Lorena B. Ellis. Austin: University of Texas Press, 2009.

Trees, Andrew S. *The Founding Fathers and the Politics of Character.* Princeton, NJ: Princeton University Press, 2004.

Tuch, Hans M. *Communicating with the World: U.S. Public Diplomacy Overseas.* New York: St. Martin's, 1990.

Tuch, Hans M., and G. Lewis Schmidt, eds. *Ike and the USIA: A Commemorative Symposium.* Washington, DC: U.S. Information Alumni Association, Public Diplomacy Foundation, 1991.

Tuchman, Barbara W. *Practicing History: Selected Essays.* New York: Ballantine, 1982.

Tuchman, Maurice. *Art and Technology: A Report on the Art and Technology Program of the Los Angeles County Museum of Art, 1967–1971.* New York: Viking, 1971.

Tudda, Chris. *The Truth Is Our Weapon: The Rhetorical Diplomacy of Dwight D. Eisenhower and John Foster Dulles.* Baton Rouge: Louisiana State University Press, 2006.

Turner, Frederick Jackson. *The Frontier in American History.* New York: Holt, 1920.

U.S. Advisory Committee on Cultural Diplomacy. *Cultural Diplomacy: The Linchpin of Public Diplomacy.* Washington, DC: U.S. Department of State, September 2005.

U.S. Department of State. *The United States Information Agency: A Commemoration.* Washington, DC: USIA, 1999.

———. *United States Treaties and Other International Agreements.* Washington, DC: U.S. Government Printing Office, 1960–1969.

"U.S. Pavilion—The Ultimate Understatement." *P/A* (August 1970): 64–67.

Veblen, Thorstein. *The Theory of the Leisure Class: An Economic Study of Institutions.* New York: Macmillan, 1899.

"Vice President in Russia: A Barnstorming Masterpiece." *Life*, August 10, 1959, 22–27.

Villeco, Marguerite. "Technology: The Infinitely Expandable Future of Air Structures." *Architectural Forum* (September 1970): 40–43.

Wagner, Richard. *The Art-Work of the Future and Other Works.* Translated by William Ashton Ellis. Lincoln: University of Nebraska Press, 1993.

Wagnleitner, Reinhold. *Coca-Colonization and the Cold War: The Cultural Mission of the United States in Austria After the Second World War.* Chapel Hill: University of North Carolina Press, 1994.

Wagnleitner, Reinhold, and Elaine Tyler May, eds. *Here, There, and Everywhere: The Foreign Politics of American Popular Culture.* Hanover, NH: University Press of New England, 2000.

Wall, Wendy L. *Inventing the "American Way": The Politics of Consensus from the New Deal to the Civil Rights Movement.* Oxford: Oxford University Press, 2008.

Wallace, Don. "Shaping America's Products: Design and Craftsmanship in Large Scale Industry." *Industrial Design* (April 1956): 38–39.

Wang, Jian. "Telling the American Story to the World: The Purpose of U.S. Public Diplomacy in Historical Perspective." *Public Relations Review* 33, no. 1 (March 2007): 21–30.

Washington, George. Letter to John Augustine Washington, June 15, 1783. *The Writings of George Washington from the Original Manuscript Sources* 27. Edited by John C. Fitzpatrick. Accessed August 10, 2010. http://etext.virginia.edu/ washington /fitzpatrick/.

Wesemael, Pieter von. *Architecture of Instruction and Delight: A Socio-historical Analysis of World Exhibitions as a Didactic Phenomenon (1798-1851-1970).* Rotterdam: 010 Publishers, 2001.

Whitehead, Christopher. "Establishing the Manifesto: Art Histories in the Nineteenth-Century Museum." In *Museum Revolutions: How Museums Change and Are Changed*, edited by Simon J. Knell, Suzanne MacLeod, and Sheila Watson, 48–60. New York: Routledge, 2007.

Wilford, Hugh. *The Mighty Wurlitzer: How the CIA Played America.* Cambridge, MA: Harvard University Press, 2008.

Williams, W. Walter. "It's Fair Weather." *Rotarian*, December 1955, 17.

Winkler, A. M. *The Politics of Propaganda: The Office of War Information, 1942–1945.* New Haven, CT: Yale University Press, 1978.

Winthrop, John. "A Modell of Christian Charity." In *Settlements to Society, 1584–1763*, edited by Jack P. Greene, 66–69. New York: McGraw-Hill, 1966.

Wolfe, Tom. "The Me Decade and the Third Great Awakening." In *The Purple Decades: A Reader*, edited by Tom Wolfe, 265–96. London: Vintage, 2005.

Wood, Gordon. *The Idea of America.* New York: Penguin, 2011.

Wood, Linda Sargent. *A More Perfect Union: Holistic Worldviews and the Transformation of American Culture after World War II.* Oxford: Oxford University Press, 2010.

Woodward, Ian. "Domestic Objects and the Taste Epiphany: A Resource for Consumption Methodology." *Journal of Material Culture* 6, no. 2 (2001): 115–36.

Wornum, Ralph N. "The Exhibition as a Lesson in Taste." In *The Crystal Palace Exhibition Illustrated Catalogue, London, 1851, The Art-Journal: Special Issue*, I–XXII. New York: Dover, 1970.

Wright, Henry Clarke. "American Slavery in the World's Fair in London." *Liberator* (Boston), February 28, 1851.

Young, Paul. *Globalization and the Great Exhibition: The Victorian New World Order.* New York: Palgrave Macmillan, 2009.

Zieger, Robert. "The Paradox of Plenty: The Advertising Council and the Post-Sputnik Crisis." *Advertising & Society Review* 4, no. 1 (2003). Accessed Jul7 21, 2012. http://muse.jhu.edu/.

Index